# Fodor's
# SOUTH FLORIDA

# Welcome to South Florida

From the resorts of Palm Beach to the humblest gingerbread cottages in the Keys, South Florida has something for everyone. Whether you're spotting alligators in the Everglades, visiting a world-class art museum, snorkeling off Key Largo, or dancing the night away in Miami, there is plenty to do. Beautiful beaches beckon, so when you're not dining in a great restaurant, grab a towel and relax in the tropical warmth. As you plan your upcoming travels to South Florida, please confirm that places are still open and let us know when we need to make updates by writing to us at this address: editors@fodors.com.

## TOP REASONS TO GO

★ **Miami:** A vibrant, multicultural metropolis that buzzes both day and night.

★ **Palm Beach:** Glamorous and sophisticated, the city offers great dining and shopping.

★ **Beaches:** Sceney in South Beach, buzzing in Fort Lauderdale, quieter in the Keys.

★ **The Everglades:** The "river of grass" is home to crocodiles, manatees, and panthers.

★ **Fort Lauderdale:** A glittering and revitalized downtown fronts a gorgeous beach.

★ **Key West:** Quirky, fun, and tacky, it's both family-friendly and decidedly not.

# Contents

## Fodor's Features

## MAPS

# Chapter 1

# EXPERIENCE SOUTH FLORIDA

# 15 ULTIMATE EXPERIENCES

South Florida offers terrific experiences that should be on every traveler's list. Here are Fodor's top picks for a memorable trip.

## 1 Beaches

Florida's many stretches of sand are just as varied as the state itself. Watch the sun set over Fort Lauderdale Beach, barhop through South Beach, or snorkel in Key Largo. If a quiet, rugged coastline appeals, head to Blowing Rocks Preserve outside Jupiter. *(Ch. 3, 5, 6, 7)*

## 2 Art Deco Architecture

Miami has the largest collection of art deco buildings in the world, with 800-plus pastel beauties. Learn more at the Art Deco Museum on Ocean Drive. *(Ch. 3)*

## 3 Snorkeling in Key Largo

Swim past a shipwreck and the nation's most vibrant patches of coral reef at John Pennekamp Coral Reef State Park in Key Largo. *(Ch. 5)*

# 4 The Wynwood Walls

Graffiti artists around the globe create murals for this hip outdoor gallery, with over 80,000 square feet of colorful walls to explore. *(Ch. 3)*

# 5 Partying in Miami

Alternate between dancing and people-watching at the late-night lounges that helped earn South Beach its party-heavy rep. *(Ch. 3)*

# 6 Everglades National Park

To really experience this national park, bike nature trails or cruise the backwaters and keep your eyes peeled for gators. *(Ch. 4)*

## 7 Shopping

Miami's Design District, Fort Lauderdale's Las Olas Boulevard, and Palm Beach's Worth Avenue constitute a shopper's paradise. *(Ch. 3, 6, 7)*

## 8 Cuban Culture

Little Havana's main drag, Calle Ocho, is where to find Miami's best Cuban restaurants and bars. Don't leave without salsa dancing at Ball & Chain or trying guava ice cream at Azucar. *(Ch. 3)*

## 9 Fresh Seafood

It's practically required on your visit to Florida to eat stone crabs plus a fresh catch of the day baked, broiled, or blackened with Cajun spice. *(Ch. 3, 4, 5, 6, 7)*

## 10 Hemingway's Key West

The legendary American author's Key West home looks nearly the same as it did in the '30s—six-toed cats (descendants of his pet, Snow White) and all. *(Ch. 5)*

# 11 Sports

Cheering for the team is a huge part of Florida culture. Make like a local and catch the Miami Dolphins or Miami Heat in action. *(Ch. 3)*

# 12 Palm Beach

In this glam town, you can stay at luxe resorts like The Breakers, shop at chic boutiques, play golf at PGA National Resort, and gawk at palatial mansions. *(Ch. 7)*

## 13 Swanky Pools

Save a day to relax and people-watch at one of South Florida's legendary and luxurious hotel poolscapes, such as at 1 Hotel South Beach. *(Ch. 3)*

## 14 Sunset Sails

Whether you set sail from Fort Lauderdale, board a yacht in Miami, or take a boat tour of Key West, this is a place best viewed from the water. *(Ch. 3, 4, 5, 6, 7)*

# 15 Tropical Gardens

Need a break from the beach? Enjoy the shade and lush greenery of gardens such as Fairchild Tropical Botanic Garden in Coral Gables or Morikami in Delray Beach. *(Ch. 3, 7)*

# WHAT'S WHERE

**1 Miami and Miami Beach.** Greater Miami is hot—and we're not just talking about the weather. Art deco buildings and balmy beaches set the scene. Vacations here are as much about lifestyle as locale, so prepare for power-shopping, barhopping, and decadent dining in between sunbathing and people-watching.

**2 The Everglades.** Covering more than 1.5 million acres, the fabled "River of Grass" is the state's greatest natural treasure. Biscayne National Park (95% of which is under-water) runs a close second and is the largest marine park in the United States. Surrounding farm towns like Homestead are the place to sample South Florida's delicious tropical fruits and even pick your own produce.

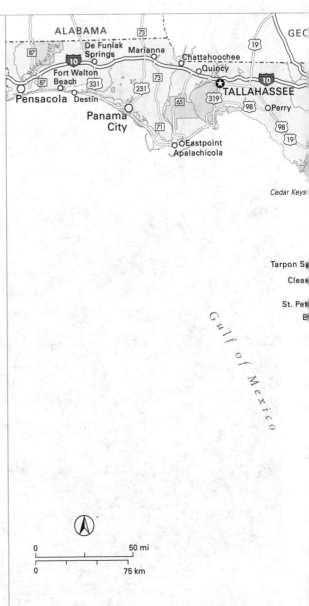

**3 The Florida Keys.** This slender necklace of landfalls from Key Largo to Key West, strung together by a 113-mile highway, marks the southern edge of the continental United States. It's nirvana for anglers, divers, literature lovers, and Jimmy Buffett wannabes.

**4 Fort Lauderdale and Broward County.** The former Spring Break Capital is all grown up. Nowadays, sparkling blue beaches are complemented by luxe lodgings, upscale entertainment options, and a decidedly more family-friendly beach atmosphere than in nearby Miami.

**5 Palm Beach and the Treasure Coast.** This area scores points for its diverse offerings. Palm Beach and its surroundings are famous for their golden sand and glitzy mansions, whereas the Treasure Coast has unspoiled natural delights in areas like Jupiter and Vero Beach.

# What to Eat and Drink in South Florida

**PASTELITOS**
Step into any Cuban bakery in Miami and you'll spot these turnover-like pastries proudly displayed (and quickly devoured). The puff pastry sweets are as critical to breakfast here as croissants are in Paris, with flavors ranging from savory ham to sweet guava and cream cheese. Order one of the flaky confections at family-run shops like La Rosa Bakery in Miami.

**STONE CRAB**
Stone crab season runs from October through May, when you'll find claws served at seafood spots throughout South Florida (one of the best is Joe's Stone Crab in Miami). Claws are presented in similar style to peel-and-eat shrimp, with crackers to help break through to the meaty flesh.

**KEY LIME PIE**
Florida's official state pie was first baked in the 1860s in Key West, where local key limes add to the dessert's characteristic tangy taste. The original recipe has three main ingredients—key lime, egg yolks, and sweetened condensed milk.

**MOJITO**
Warm weather begs for cold, summertime cocktails, so it's no surprise the classic Cuban mojito is one of Miami's unofficial drinks. The recipe is easy: a blend of white rum, fresh mint sprigs, sugar, and a splash of club soda. Head to Ball & Chain in Miami's Little Havana for something traditional or to Cafe La Trova in Little Havana for an award-winning take.

## CROQUETAS

Considered Miami's official snack, meat- and cheese-stuffed Cuban *croquetas* are sold everywhere from fine-dining restaurants to drive-through fast-food joints and even gas stations. Order the breaded, fried food rolls in classic *jamón* (ham) or a variation like goat cheese and guava jam.

Cafecito

## CUBAN SANDWICH

It's said the Cubano was invented in 1905 in Tampa's Ybor City, but the classic sandwich is also widespread (and well loved) in South Florida. The historic hoagies are made with two flaky pieces of Cuban bread topped with ham, roast pork, Swiss cheese, yellow mustard, and pickles.

## CONCH FRITTERS

Deep-fried conch fritters may have started farther south in the Bahamas, but this popular appetizer dish (typically served alongside tartar sauce) has become a favorite in Florida, especially in the Conch Republic of Key West.

## CAFECITO

Cuban coffee, or *cafecito*, is what locals in Miami drink as an afternoon pick-me-up. The strong, espresso-based drink packs a powerful punch thanks to the heavy-handed sugar whipped in. You'll find dedicated cafecito windows, or *ventanillas*, around town, especially in Little Havana.

## GATOR TAIL

Just as frog legs have become synonymous with France, alligator has become a Florida specialty. Bite-size, deep-fried pieces are served up as nugget-style snacks in the Everglades at most restaurants. Tastes like chicken.

## ROCK LOBSTER

Rock lobster (or spiny lobster) is Florida's answer to the more traditional type you'd find up in Maine. The best way to eat the tender tail meat is grilled and drizzled with rich garlic butter. Head to The Stoned Crab in Key West and order the Half Baked, served in Florida shrimp sauce.

# Best Beaches in South Florida

### SOUTH BEACH
The legend of beautiful people is very much a reality on the sands parallel to deco-drenched Ocean Drive and upscale Collins Avenue, lined with luxe boutiques. Pose for pics at the famous, brightly colored lifeguard stands or take a tour of the city's most historic buildings. *(Ch. 3)*

### FORT LAUDERDALE BEACH
The Spring Break hot spot plays host to a reinvented, more upscale beachfront; however, several of the storied (and divey) beach bars remain. Stroll and shop along Las Olas or people-watch along the beachfront promenade. *(Ch. 6)*

### JOHN PENNEKAMP CORAL REEF STATE PARK
Florida's best bet for diving and snorkeling, this state park adjacent to the Florida Keys National Marine Sanctuary encompasses 78 square miles of ecological treasures. The beaches here do attract families, but the real draw is the underwater world. *(Ch. 5)*

### HAULOVER PARK
Long known for its clothing-optional stretch of sand (between lifeguard stands 12 and 16), the beach park, which sits north of Miami Beach, also offers plenty of family-friendly attractions. Food trucks pull up to the Bill Bird Marina on Tuesday night, and the park often hosts kite-making workshops. *(Ch. 3)*

### BLOWING ROCKS PRESERVE
The beauty in Hobe Sound is in the backdrop; the rocky coastline looks like it's been transplanted from a Greek island, yet this wild strip of mangrove wetlands, turtle nesting beaches, and practically perfect dunes lies less than an hour's drive from Palm Beach. *(Ch. 7)*

### DELRAY MUNICIPAL BEACH
This super-popular stretch of sand dotted with trademark royal-blue umbrellas intersects trendy Atlantic Avenue in the alluring Village by the Sea; delicious nosh and cute boutiques are a short stroll from the waves. *(Ch. 7)*

### DRY TORTUGAS NATIONAL PARK
Forget lazily reading a book on these shores in the Florida Keys. Come here if you're looking for a beach where you can dive in—literally. Set among coral reefs, this cluster of seven islands (accessible only by boat or seaplane) offers outstanding snorkeling and diving. *(Ch. 5)*

Bahia Honda State Park

### BAHIA HONDA STATE PARK
Though the Florida Keys aren't renowned for beautiful sand beaches (most are man-made), this is an exception. The 524-acre park has three superb, white-sand beaches, including the mile-long, Atlantic-facing Sandspur Beach. *(Ch. 5)*

### HOLLYWOOD BEACH
Between Miami and Fort Lauderdale, this laid-back, family-friendly stretch of sand is the star of Broward County, where you can stroll along the 2½-mile "Broadwalk" promenade and enjoy beachfront restaurants and bars. *(Ch. 6)*

### MID-BEACH
This stretch of coastline (which starts at 24th and Collins) sits just a few blocks north of South Beach's nonstop nightlife. Miami Modern buildings sprout across the historic neighborhood, where a few famous facades, like Fontainebleau, have received billion-dollar revamps. Argentinean hotelier Alan Faena has breathed new life into the area with his flagship hotel, Faena. *(Ch. 3)*

### PALM BEACH
The shores of this tiny beach town are favored by locals and visitors alike. With Worth Avenue's clock tower nearby, the beach is central to the town's best sights and a beautiful spot to watch the sun set. *(Ch. 7)*

### BILL BAGGS CAPE FLORIDA STATE PARK
If you're looking to avoid the throngs of tourists sunbathing on South Beach, head to this park in Key Biscayne. Stroll along the shore to the beach's landmark lighthouse—the oldest standing building in the county. *(Ch. 3)*

# An Art Lover's Guide to Miami

## ART DECO AND MIMO ARCHITECTURE

In Miami, even the buildings are art. The art deco structures on Ocean Drive and Collins Avenue, with their pastels and geometric shapes, put South Beach on the map in the '30s and '40s. In North Beach, you'll see another well-known style– Miami Modern (MiMo), featuring futuristic, asymmetrical shapes.

## ART BASEL

Miami Beach's art (and social) calendars revolve around this famous art fair. Each December, more than 250 galleries from around the world showcase their work, and the city comes alive with art installations and exclusive parties.

## THE BASS MUSEUM OF ART

Housed in an art deco gem from the '30s, the museum spotlights contemporary art and its relationship to culture, design, fashion, and architecture. See whimsical contemporary pieces alongside historical works in the permanent collection.

## VIZCAYA MUSEUM & GARDENS

This European-style villa is an urban oasis where formal gardens meet the edge of Biscayne Bay. Built about 100 years ago, it has survived Miami's hurricanes, economic troubles, and redevelopment. Check out the decorative art spanning the Renaissance to rococo periods.

### PÉREZ ART MUSEUM MIAMI

Overlooking Biscayne Bay, PAMM's indoor-outdoor venue with hanging gardens, trusses, and steel frames, is a stunning home to international art of the 20th and 21st centuries. The museum is celebrated for sparking much of the city's electric arts environment.

### WYNWOOD ARTS DISTRICT

Once an unremarkable group of warehouses, this now trendy area is an international destination for edgy graffiti and galleries. Check out the Wynwood Walls, an outdoor museum of street art. Your visit will be unique: murals can disappear as quickly as they appear.

### MUSEUM OF CONTEMPORARY ART

MOCA, an intimate museum in North Miami, is home to provocative contemporary art. Its stark gallery spaces are ideal for exhibitions that require time and space to fully understand. Stop by for Jazz at MOCA on the last Friday night of each month.

### THE PATRICIA & PHILLIP FROST ART MUSEUM

Florida International University's free art museum boasts thousands of objects ranging from pre-Columbian-era artifacts and American printmaking from the '70s to contemporary works.

### LITTLE HAITI AND LITTLE RIVER GALLERIES

Several top-notch galleries—Emerson Dorsch, Nina Johnson, Mindy Solomon Gallery, Pan American Art Projects—have moved from Wynwood to the neighborhoods of Little Haiti and Little River, so it's no wonder the up-and-coming areas are being referred to as the "new Wynwood."

### DESIGN DISTRICT

The Design District is a haven for high-end fashion houses and boutiques. If you can make it past Louis Vuitton, Hermès, and Saint Laurent, you'll find several notable galleries. The Institute of Contemporary Art, Miami (ICA) is the latest addition to the city's museums; many pieces in its permanent collection and its major funders were once part of MOCA.

# South Florida Today

## NEW IN THE SPOTLIGHT

The Michelin Guide made its way to three major Florida cities in 2022: Miami, Orlando, and Tampa. With its first edition, 117 restaurants were crowned with its prestigious stars. The arrival of the guide sets a tone within the hospitality industry that Florida is indeed home to top-notch dining experiences.

## IMPROVED ACCESS

It's easier than ever to reach Florida by plane thanks to new flight routes and expanded airports. Fort Lauderdale–Hollywood International Airport (FLL) has completed a major expansion and renovation, with a new larger runway, which permits jumbo-size aircraft.

To improve access between cities, the first privately funded U.S. high-speed railway, Brightline, has opened. By the end of 2023, it will connect Miami to Orlando in three hours at speeds of up to 125 mph. Phase One, which opened in 2018, provides state-of-the-art express train service connecting Miami, Fort Lauderdale, and West Palm Beach in style and comfort. Phase Two opened in late 2022 adding Aventura and Boca Raton stops. Adding stations in Orlando and Tampa will be the third and final stage, with stops at Orlando Convention Center, near Disney World, and Downtown Tampa.

Meanwhile, getting around Florida's major destinations without a car rental has also become easier. Lyft and Uber are now available in all of Florida's major cities from Miami down to Key West. These services have made it possible to hop between nearby cities (overnight in Fort Lauderdale but dinner in Miami) for an often reasonable price.

## MORE LUXURY

From Miami's burgeoning Mid-Beach and expanding Sunny Isles Beach to the coastlines of the Keys, South Florida is embracing a luxury mantra and has plenty of new five-star properties to prove it.

Cranes and bulldozers are again dominating Miami to make way for super-high-end residential and hotel developments. Waldorf Astoria, Bentley, Aria Reserve, Aman Miami Beach, and NoMad are just a few big names to break ground recently.

Miami's Design District continues to expand with high-design retail spaces for the big brands that are moving into the neighborhood frequently.

In the northern reaches of Miami Beach, Sunny Isles Beach has witnessed a high-rise frenzy, the highlights of which are The Mansions at Acqualina (46 stories!) and The Estates at Acqualina, part of the Acqualina Resort & Residences on the Beach.

Never one to forgo the limelight, South Beach has also made waves with the half-billion-dollar collaboration between hotel and real estate titans Barry Sternlicht and Richard LeFrak: the 1 Hotel & Homes South Beach—a seductive, two-block-long, beachfront enclave, inclusive of 156 oceanfront residences—in the beach's Art Deco District.

Down in the Florida Keys, new projects have been cropping up just about everywhere. In 2019 Key Largo welcomed its first all-inclusive resort, Bungalows Key Largo, a luxury waterfront oasis. In the same year, the snazzy Isla Bella Beach Resort debuted in Marathon. In 2020 Kimpton Key West made a splash in Old Town as a collection of five reimagined boutique properties under a single brand.

# Day Trips From Miami

### THE EVERGLADES

*40 miles west of Miami.* There are five main access points into Everglades National Park, the closest of which is Shark Valley off Tamiami Trail. Here, you can hike trails, bike a 15-mile loop, and immerse yourself in raw wilderness, spotting alligators and herons. For the thrill of an airboat ride, you should go beyond the park's official boundaries. *(Ch. 4)*

### HOMESTEAD

*40 miles southwest of Miami.* Visit South Florida's agricultural heartland to enter a wonderful world of exotic fruits and experience rural Florida. Explore the 37-acre Fruit & Spice Park, home to more than 500 varieties of fruit, nuts, and spices, including 160 varieties of mango. Then, sip your way through flights of wine made from native fruits such as mango and guava at Schnebly Redland's Winery. *(Ch. 4)*

### BISCAYNE NATIONAL PARK

*40 miles southwest of Miami.* The nation's largest marine park houses diverse ecosystems both above and under the water, underscored by living coral reefs and mazes of mangroves. Book a guided tour through Biscayne National Park Institute to snorkel among the park's reefs and shipwreck or to kayak your way through mangroves. *(Ch. 4)*

### FORT LAUDERDALE

*40 miles north of Miami.* The former Spring Break capital now boasts a polished shoreline with luxury hotels and great restaurants. Come here for a memorable meal at one of the many waterfront eateries and for a delightful respite from the cacophony of Miami's beaches. Hop on the public Water Taxi and take a leisurely boat ride to understand the city's well-deserved moniker, "Venice of America." *(Ch. 6)*

### PALM BEACH

*40 miles north of Miami.* Palm Beach is to the East Coast what Beverly Hills is to the West Coast—a place to gawk at larger-than-life mansions, spot plastic surgery, and browse pricey boutiques. Start with some shopping on Worth Avenue, then admire the grounds of The Breakers resort or tour the Henry Morrison Flagler Museum, which rivals the grandeur of a European palace. *(Ch. 7)*

### KEY LARGO

*56 miles south of Miami.* Drive down to John Pennekamp Coral Reef State Park for the best diving and snorkeling in Florida. You can either DIY from the shore or take an organized tour through the park and discover a microcosm of Pennecamp's 78 nautical square miles of coral reefs and sea-grass beds. Stop for lunch at Alabama Jack's, a no-frills, oh-so-Keys waterfront restaurant, home to some epic conch fritters. *(Ch. 5)*

### ISLAMORADA

*85 miles south of Miami.* In the Middle Keys, this developed island is the self-proclaimed "Sportfishing Capital of the World," a launching pad to untouched, clear, warm waters teeming with trophy-worthy fish from sailfish to mahimahi to tarpon. More than 150 backcountry guides and 400 offshore captains are at your service. *(Ch. 7)*

### KEY WEST

*150 miles south of Miami.* Famous for its dive bars, pedestrian-friendly streets, Hemingway history, and all-welcoming community, the "Conch Republic" is the perfect place to ditch Google Maps and get lost in coastal small-town magic. Prepare for stunning views beginning at Mile Marker 113, when the Florida Keys Scenic Highway begins and then crosses 42 bridges. *(Ch. 7)*

# What to Read and Watch

### FLORIDA BY LAUREN GROFF

This collection of short stories depicts Florida with equal doses fascination and horror, dream world and harsh reality. The state is a recurring character, and the diverse settings, cast of characters, and moods give a full and complex impression of the state.

### SWAMPLANDIA! BY KAREN RUSSELL

The story of a young girl growing up in the Florida Everglades at her family's bizarre gator-wrestling entertainment park, *Swamplandia!* made Russell a finalist for a 2012 Pulitzer Prize (the year no prize was awarded). It has the right amount of fantasy to illustrate the swampy, untamed Everglades.

### THEIR EYES WERE WATCHING GOD BY ZORA NEALE HURSTON

Hurston's most-read novel journeys through Reconstruction-era rural Florida. Through the lens of African American female narrator Janie Crawford, you'll see vivid depictions of small towns, migrant worker communities, and historical events.

### THE ORCHID THIEF: A TRUE STORY OF BEAUTY AND OBSESSION BY SUSAN ORLEANS

Set largely in the Florida Everglades, this bestselling book follows an "orchid thief," a man obsessed with hunting down rare flowers and cloning them.

### TO HAVE AND HAVE NOT BY ERNEST HEMINGWAY

A desperate Key West fishing captain is forced into the illegal smuggling business during the Great Depression in Hemingway's book. It touches on the economic disparity in the Keys during that decade and the area's close but complicated relationship with Cuba.

### BAD BOYS (FRANCHISE)

Starring Will Smith and Martin Lawrence, *Bad Boys* (1995), *Bad Boys II* (2003), and *Bad Boys for Life* (2020) follow two ride-or-die Miami detectives as they protect the streets of the Magic City.

### BLOODLINE

Taking place on Islamorada in the Florida Keys, this Netflix show begins when a bad-seed brother returns home to stir up trouble. A small family inn serves as the epicenter for so much drama it could be a soap opera—full of family secrets, drug trafficking, and speedboat chases.

### MIAMI VICE

A team of undercover detectives takes on the shady drug world in South Florida in the 1980s. The television show's loud fashion and music, neon lights, palm trees, alligators, and yachts could get anyone into a South Beach mood.

### MOONLIGHT

A film in three chapters, *Moonlight* explores violence, identity, and sexuality for two young black males growing up in the Miami area. For a quiet film, it was met with loud praise—the Oscar for Best Picture. It was the first movie with an all-black cast (and first LGBTQ-theme movie) to win.

### THE BIRDCAGE

The 1996 American remake of *La Cage aux Folles* stars Robin Williams, Gene Hackman, and Nathan Lane in a gay-slanted tale of meet the parents, set in the heart of South Beach.

### THE FLORIDA PROJECT

An indie film that's both heartbreaking and joyous, *The Florida Project* follows a young, struggling mother and her hellion of a daughter through their days living in a pay-per-week motel in the shadow of Walt Disney World.

Chapter 2

# TRAVEL SMART

Updated by
Amber Love Bond

**★ STATE CAPITAL**
Tallahassee

**POPULATION**
9.3 million

**LANGUAGE**
English

**$ CURRENCY**
US dollar

**AREA CODES**
305, 561, 786, 754, 954

**⚠ EMERGENCIES**
911

**DRIVING**
On the right

**ELECTRICITY**
120–240 v/60 cycles; plugs have two or three rectangular prongs

**TIME**
Eastern Time Zone (same as New York)

**WEB RESOURCES**
www.visitflorida.com
www.miamiandbeaches.com
www.visitlauderdale.org

**AIRPORTS**
MIA, FLL, PBI, EYW

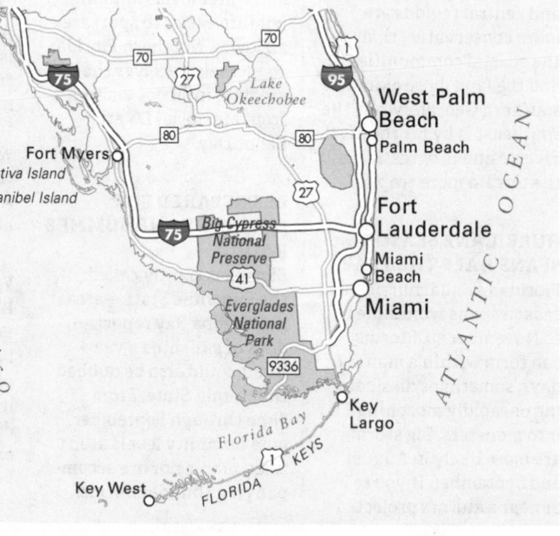

# Know Before You Go

When is the best time to visit? How do you plan around hurricane season? Do you really need a car to get around? You may have a few questions before you head out on vacation to the Sunshine State. We've got answers and a few tips to help you make the most of your trip.

**FLORIDA COULD BE SEVERAL STATES.**
If you drove from the western stretch of the Panhandle to the state's southern tip in Key West, you'd have traveled more than 800 miles. It's no wonder the state varies so widely in climate, geography, and demography. This massive peninsula's many distinct regions include the southeast, southwest, the Keys, central, northeast, and the northwest (aka the Panhandle)—and all have different vibes. Generally, the northern and central regions are more conservative than the coastal communities and the land more akin to southern Georgia, while the southeast is by far the most diverse and progressive and the terrain more tropical.

**HURRICANE SEASON SPANS HALF THE YEAR.**
Florida's annual hurricane season spans from June 1 to November 30. Storms can form within a matter of days, sometimes dissipating or rapidly morphing into monsters. Big storms are more likely in August and September. If you're in or near a storm's projected path, fly out or drive away as soon as possible, regardless of whether you're in an evacuation zone.

**WINTER IS THE BUSIEST AND MOST EXPENSIVE SEASON.**
Rates from December to April are high across the board since most visitors try to escape their own winters, avoid the risk of a hurricane, and plan around school breaks. Winter is also the time to visit the Everglades, as temperatures, mosquito activity, and water levels (making wildlife easier to spot) are all lower. Northern Florida, conversely, receives the greatest influx of visitors from Memorial Day to Labor Day.

**BE PREPARED FOR HUMIDITY AND SUMMER RAIN.**
Florida is rightly called the Sunshine State—areas like Tampa Bay report 361 days of sunshine a year! But it could also be dubbed the Humid State. From June through September, 90% humidity levels aren't uncommon, nor are accompanying thunderstorms.

In fact, more than half of the state's rain falls during these months. Be prepared for sidewalk and road flooding in Miami Beach, even during mild storms.

**RENT, OR HAIL, A CAR.**
Even Florida's urban hubs are sprawling, so a car is the preferred method of transportation. It's also the best way to string a few towns together on a road trip. If you go this route, consider purchasing a "SunPass" to cover toll roads. You can also avail yourself of Uber or Lyft, which operate in all major cities and their airports as well as the suburbs.

**TRY NEW HIGH-SPEED TRAINS.**
The new express train service called Brightline transports passengers between Miami (stations are in Downtown and Aventura), Fort Lauderdale, West Palm Beach, and Boca Raton. In 2023, the service will launch at Orlando International Airport (MCO). The train is expected to reach MCO from Miami in three hours; it'll take about two hours from West Palm Beach which is about an hour less than it would take to drive. An extension to Tampa is also in the works.

**YOU CAN GET AROUND BY WATER TAXI.**
Fort Lauderdale has long been dubbed the "Venice of America" because of its many waterways, but did you know you can explore most of them by Water Taxi? When people say that it is the "journey

not the destination that matters," this is what they mean. That said, there are lots of destinations (bars, restaurants, sights) with 15 stops on three connected routes. Get a day pass and hop on and off along the way. The trips are narrated by knowledgeable drivers who share fun and interesting information about the many mansions and mega yachts that line the waterways.

### HIT THE TRAILS.
Florida has some 5,000 miles of land-based routes (plus many more miles for paddling!). About 1,500 miles of these connect to create a continuous trail from the north to the south of the state. It's known as the Florida National Scenic Trail, or simply the Florida Trail, and it's one of only 11 National Scenic Trails in the United States.

### CHECK FOR AUTOMATIC GRATUITIES.
Before putting your payment down in South Florida, examine your itemized bill to see if a gratuity was already added. It's often automatically included as a "service fee" at restaurants, bars, and spas in South Beach and some other places in Miami, and some establishments are not as up-front about this as others. Many visitors don't know the policy and unknowingly tip twice.

### ACCOUNT FOR RESORT TAXES.
Florida has no state personal income tax, instead heavily relying on tourism revenues. The state sales tax in Florida is 6% (with the exception of most groceries and medicine); when combined with local taxes, the total sales tax rate runs as high as 8%. Hotel taxes, often called "resort taxes," vary, but include amenities like beach loungers and pool access.

Palm Beach County's resort tax is 6%, for a combined total of 12% with state sales tax (6%). In Greater Fort Lauderdale the resort tax is 5%, for a combined total of 11%. In Miami Beach visitors pay 7% sales tax, 3% Miami resort tax, plus 3% Miami Beach resort tax, for a total of 13%.

### TAKE THE SUN SERIOUSLY.
Sunburn and heat exhaustion are concerns, even in winter. So hit the beach or play outdoor sports before 10 am or after 3 pm. Even on overcast days, ultraviolet rays shine through the haze, so use a sunscreen with an SPF of at least 15, and have children wear a waterproof SPF of at least 30 or higher. Make sure your sunscreen is free of oxybenzone or octinoxate, two chemicals known to cause coral bleaching.

### PROTECT YOURSELF FROM MOSQUITOES.
Mosquitoes are most active in the wet summer months but are present year-round due to the state's climate. Even if the bugs aren't infected by diseases like West Nile or Zika, humans and pets are still susceptible to their itchy bites. Pack a repellent or lemon eucalyptus oil to ward off the pests, and wear long sleeves, pants, and socks when spending time in nature. Also, avoid the outdoors at dawn and dusk.

### CHOOSE YOUR AIRPORT WISELY.
Fort Lauderdale's airport is close enough to Miami and Palm Beach (about 45 minutes driving either way) that many people choose to fly there instead of MIA or PBI, which can have higher fares. It's worth the savings if someone is picking you up or you have your own rental car, but if you're relying on Uber/Lyft, make sure to factor in the hefty fee it takes to reach your destination city ($50–$70).

### DON'T SKIP THE EVERGLADES.
With South Florida's flashy attractions and dreamy beaches it can be easy to overlook one of the nation's most impressive national parks when planning your visit… but you shouldn't. Everglades National Park is the 3rd largest national park behind Yellowstone and Death Valley and one of the most important ecosystems in the country. It is home to 8 distinct habitats, more than 360 different species of birds, 36 endangered and threatened species (including the Florida Panther), and it is the *only place in the world* where American alligators and American crocodiles coexist in the wild. An airboat ride is one of the most popular ways to experience the park.

# Getting Here and Around

##  Air

Average flying time to South Florida's international airports is 3 hours from New York, 4 hours from Chicago, 2¾ hours from Dallas, 4½–5½ hours from Los Angeles, and 8–8½ hours from London.

### AIRPORTS

South Florida has three major airports listed from south to north: Miami International Airport (MIA), Fort Lauderdale–Hollywood International Airport (FLL), and Palm Beach International Airport (PBI). Subtropical, and often chaotic, Miami International Airport, known as the gateway to Latin America and the Caribbean, is a hub for American Airlines and the third-busiest airport for international travelers. The Miami International Airport Hotel is located within Concourse E and has 260 soundproof rooms.

Fort Lauderdale–Hollywood International Airport offers more than 700 flights a day, including nonstop flights to more than 100 U.S. and international cities. South of downtown Fort Lauderdale and north of Hollywood, it's adjacent to Port Everglades, the major cruise complex that hosts nearly 4 million passengers a year.

Palm Beach International Airport offers flights to and from about 30 destinations from many major airlines with more than 200 flights daily. PBI has parking at assorted pricing levels, including an economy lot.

In addition, Key West International Airport (EYW) is a single-runway facility on the southeast end of that island that serves carriers large and small. There are more than a dozen car rental options on arrival.

▪ TIP→ **Flying in and out of MIA requires more time and patience due to the sheer volume of travelers. Expect long lines at security, customs, and baggage claim.**

| From—To | Miles | Hours +/- |
| --- | --- | --- |
| Fort Lauderdale–Miami | 40 | 0:45 |
| Fort Lauderdale–Palm Beach | 40 | 0:55 |
| Miami–Key Largo | 67 | 1:30 |
| Miami–Palm Beach | 73 | 1:30 |
| Fort Lauderdale–Key West | 190 | 4 |

### GROUND TRANSPORTATION

Shuttle and public bus services operate from Fort Lauderdale, Miami, and West Palm Beach. There are also rental-car agencies, ride-sharing services, and taxis.

Cab fares from Florida's larger airports into town can be high. Note that in some cities, airport cab fares are a single flat rate (MIA to South Beach is $35–$40); in others, flat-rate fares vary by zone; and in others still, the fare is determined by the meter. Private car service fares are usually higher than taxi fares.

##  Car

Three major interstates lead to Florida. Interstate 95 begins in Maine, runs south through the mid-Atlantic states, and enters Florida just north of Jacksonville. It ends just south of Miami.

Interstate 75 begins in Michigan and runs south to Tampa. It follows the west coast south to Naples, then crosses the state through the northern section of the Everglades, and ends in Miami. The I-75 stretch between Naples and just west of Fort Lauderdale levies a toll each way per car.

California and most southern and southwestern states are connected to Florida by Interstate 10, which moves east from Los Angeles. It enters Florida at Pensacola and runs straight across the northern part of the state, ending in Jacksonville.

## SUNPASS

To save time and money while on the road, you may want to purchase a SunPass for your personal vehicle; many rentals come equipped with their own SunPass transponder or a process for paying through the rental car agency. SunPass provides a discount on most tolls, and it's pretty much mandatory across the state. You also can use it to pay for parking at Palm Beach, Miami, and Fort Lauderdale airports. (SunPass now interfaces with North Carolina's Quick Pass and Georgia's Peach Pass.) Transponders can be purchased online. (SunPass portable is the way to go if you want to switch cars and will run you $19.99 plus tax.)

## RENTAL CARS

In Florida, you must be 21 to rent a car and have a credit card. Rates are higher if you're under 25. Rental rates, which are loaded with taxes, fees, and other costs, sometimes can start around $55 to $110 per day.

## ROAD CONDITIONS

All major cities in Florida can get extremely congested during rush hours, usually 7–9 am and 3:30–6:30 pm or later on weekdays.

■ TIP→ **Due to construction and overdevelopment, expect delays to occur at any time of day. Plan accordingly. For real-time traffic conditions statewide, download the Florida 511 (FL511) app on your smart phone.**

## RULES OF THE ROAD

Speed limits are generally 60–65 mph on state highways, 30–35 mph within city limits and residential areas, and 70 mph on interstates and Florida's Turnpike. Supervising adults must ensure that children under age seven are positioned in federally approved child car seats.

Florida's DUI Law is one of the toughest in the United States. A blood-alcohol level of 0.08 or higher can have serious repercussions even for a first-time offender.

##  Cruise

Florida is home to two of the busiest cruise ports in the United States, the Port of Miami and Fort Lauderdale's Port Everglades, both major ports of embarkation for Caribbean itineraries. Outside Orlando, cruisers embark from Port Canaveral.

## 🚗 Ride-Sharing

Both Uber and Lyft operate at South Florida's airports and in major cities and suburbs. Download the apps and add payment methods before your trip.

## 🚆 Train

Florida's high-speed passenger train, Brightline, can help you avoid road traffic; the routes run from Miami to Fort Lauderdale to West Palm Beach—with future expansion to Orlando and Tampa. Each leg takes about 30 minutes. Brightline offers Wi-Fi, full ADA accessibility, a pet-friendly policy, and food and beverages. (⊕ *www.gobrightline.com*). Amtrak's Atlantic Coast service serves Florida from Jacksonville to Miami.

# Essentials

## 🍴 Dining

Smoking is banned statewide in most enclosed indoor workplaces, including restaurants. Exemptions are permitted for stand-alone bars where food takes a backseat to libations.

One caution: raw oysters in particular pose a potential danger for people with chronic illness of the liver, stomach, or blood and those with immune disorders. All Florida restaurants that serve raw oysters must post a notice in plain view warning of the risks associated with their consumption.

### FLORIBBEAN FOOD

A true marriage of Floridian, Caribbean, and Latin cultures yields the stylized cuisine known as "Floribbean." (Think freshly caught fish with tropical fruit salsa.) A trip to the Tampa area or South Florida, however, isn't quite complete without a taste of Cuban food. The cuisine is heavy and meat-centric and includes dishes like *lechon asado* (roasted pork) that are served in garlic-based sauces. The two most typical dishes are *arroz con frijoles* (the staple side dish of rice and black beans) and *arroz con pollo* (chicken in sticky yellow rice).

Key West is famous for its key lime pie (also served elsewhere throughout the state) and conch fritters. Stone crab claws, a South Florida delicacy, can be savored during the official season from October 15 through May 15.

### MEALS AND MEALTIMES

Unless otherwise noted, you can assume that the restaurants we recommend are open daily for lunch and dinner.

### RESERVATIONS AND DRESS

We discuss reservations only when they're essential (there's no other way you'll ever get a table) or when they're not accepted. It's always smart to make reservations when you can, particularly if your party is large or if it's high season. It's critical to do so at popular restaurants (book as far ahead as possible, often 30 days, and reconfirm before arrival).

We mention dress only when men are required to wear a jacket or a jacket and tie. Expect places with dress codes to truly adhere to them.

## ➕ Health/Safety

Sunburn and heat exhaustion are concerns, even in winter. So hit the beach or play tennis, golf, or another outdoor sport before 10 am or after 3 pm.

Even on overcast days, ultraviolet rays shine through the haze, so use a sunscreen with an SPF of at least 15 and UVA and UVB protection.

While you're frolicking on the beach, steer clear of what look like blue bubbles on the sand. These are Portuguese men-of-war, and their tentacles can cause an allergic reaction. Also be careful of other large jellyfish, some of which can sting.

As climate change accelerates and intensifies, portions of Florida's coastal areas may be dealing with harmful algae blooms (red tide) that can kill a massive amount of marine life and pose a huge threat to the respiratory health of humans and pets. For the current status, check the Florida Fish and Wildlife Conservation Commission's website (⊕ *myf-wc.com/research/redtide/statewide/*).

Mosquito-borne illnesses are also cause for concern. Standing water is prime breeding ground for these insects, and they can carry diseases like Zika, chikungunya, dengue, and encephalitis. You can stay informed by visiting the Florida Department of Health website (⊕ *www.floridahealth.gov*).

## COVID-19

Most travel restrictions, including vaccination and masking requirements, have been lifted across the United States except in healthcare facilities and nursing homes. Some travelers may still wish to wear a mask in confined spaces, including on airplanes, on public transportation, and at large indoor gatherings, but that is increasingly a personal choice. Be aware that some local mandates still exist and should be followed.

# 🛏 Lodging

In general, peak seasons are during the holidays and January through April. Holiday weekends at any point during the year are packed, so if you're considering home or condo rentals, minimum-stay requirements might be longer during these periods, too. Fall is the slowest season, with only a few exceptions (Key West is jam-packed for the 10-day Fantasy Fest at Halloween). Rates are low and availability is high, but this is also prime time for hurricanes.

Children are generally welcome throughout Florida, except for some Key West lodging; however, the buck stops at spring breakers. Although many hotels allow them—and some even cater to them—most rental agencies won't lease units to anyone under 25 without a guardian present.

Pets, although welcome at many hotels (Kimpton, The Ritz-Carlton, The W, and others), often carry an extra flat-rate fee (and must be under a certain weight). Inquire ahead if Fido is coming with you.

## APARTMENT AND HOUSE RENTALS

The state's allure for visiting snowbirds (Northerners "flocking" to Florida in winter) has always made private home and condo rentals popular, particularly for families who want to have some extra space and cooking facilities. In some destinations, home and condo rentals are more readily available than hotels. Fort Myers, for example, doesn't have many luxury hotel properties downtown. Everything aside from beach towels is provided during a stay, but some things to consider are that sizable down payments must be made at booking (15%–50%) and the full balance is often due before arrival. Check for any cleaning fees (usually not more than $150). If being on the beach is of utmost importance, carefully screen properties that tout "water views" because they might actually be of bays, canals, or lakes rather than of the Gulf of Mexico or the Atlantic Ocean.

Finding a great rental agency can help you weed out the junk. Target offices that specialize in the area you want to visit, and have a personal conversation with a representative as soon as possible. Be honest about your budget and expectations. For example, let the rental agent know if having the living room couch pull double-duty as a bed is not okay. Do research on sites like Airbnb and Vrbo to see if it makes more sense to book through them instead. Florida rental agency companies include Endless Vacation Rentals, Florida Keys Rental Store, Freewheeler Vacations, and Interhome.

## BED-AND-BREAKFASTS

Small inns and guesthouses in Florida range from modest, cozy places with home-style breakfasts and owners who treat you like family to elegantly furnished Victorian houses with four-course breakfasts and rates to match. Since most B&Bs are small, they rely on various agencies and organizations to get the word out and coordinate reservations.

# Essentials

### HOTELS AND RESORTS

Wherever you look in Florida, you'll find lots of plain, inexpensive motels and luxurious resorts, independent boutique hotels alongside national chains, and an ever-growing number of modern properties. All hotels listed have a private bath unless otherwise noted.

## ⑨ Tipping

Tip airport valets and hotel bellhops $1–$3 per bag (there typically is also a charge to check bags outside the terminal, but this isn't a tip). Housekeeping gets $1–$2 per night per guest, more at high-end resorts or if you require special services, ideally left each morning since the person servicing your room or suite could change during your stay. In-room dining servers hope to receive a 15% tip despite hefty room-service charges and service fees, which often don't go to the waiters. Check the bill to see if a gratuity is automatic before signing (it's usually included at restaurants, bars, and spas on South Beach). A door attendant or parking valet hopes to get $1–$3. Waiters generally count on 18%–20% or more, depending on your demands for special service. Bartenders get $1 or $2 per round of drinks but not if you're imbibing at a fancy cocktail bar. Those bartenders get 18%–20%. Golf caddies get 15% of the greens fee.

## 🗓 When to Go

### HIGH SEASON ($$$$)

High season in South Florida spans December to April. Snowbirds migrate down at this time to escape frosty weather back home and to avoid summer's heat and high humidity, and festivalgoers flock in because major events like Art Basel and Miami Music Week are held at this time of year.

### LOW SEASON ($)

You'll find the lowest rates in the summer months from June to September, but you'll trade savings for scorching summer temperatures and the unpredictability of hurricane season.

### VALUE SEASON ($$)

In addition to good rates, shoulder season in April and May, as well as October and November, offers some of the fairest beach conditions across the state. Most kids are still in school, so you'll miss the family crowds that head here for spring break and summer vacation.

### WEATHER

Temperatures rarely dip below 60°F in the winter season and reach the high 90s in summer. From June through September, 90% humidity levels and sudden summer storms are not uncommon. Thankfully, the weather in the Keys is more moderate than in mainland Florida. Temperatures can be 10°F cooler during the summer and up to 10°F warmer during the winter.

Booking during hurricane season (June to November) is always a gamble in Florida, which is in part why you'll find most deals during this time. Always pay heed to warnings, as many flood-prone destinations in South Florida, including Miami Beach, lie in mandatory evacuation zones. Evacuate earlier rather than later, when flights become hard to find and car traffic gets backed up.

# What to Pack for Florida

### CASUAL CLOTHING
Dress is relaxed throughout the state—sundresses, sandals, and shorts are appropriate. Even beach gear is accepted at many places, but just make sure you've got a proper outfit on (shirt, shorts, and shoes). Clothes should be breathable or, better yet, made of fabric that will drip-dry since you will be facing a hot and humid climate.

### A NICER "RESORT CHIC" OUTFIT FOR NIGHTS OUT
A very small number of restaurants request dressy attire, but most don't. Where there are dress codes, they tend to be fully adhered to. Take note that the strictest places are golf and tennis clubs. Keep in mind that some of the swankier night clubs don't allow sandals.

### A SWEATER OR LIGHT JACKET
Even in summer, ocean breezes can be cool, so it's good to have a lightweight sweater or jacket. You should be prepared for air-conditioning in overdrive anywhere you go.

### PRACTICAL SHOES
You'll need your flip-flops for the beach, but also pack a pair of comfortable walking shoes. South Florida's nonbeach destinations (think the Everglades and theme parks) are no place to go with open toes.

### SUN PROTECTION
Sunglasses, a hat, and sunscreen are essential for protecting yourself against Florida's strong sun and UV rays, even in overcast conditions. Consider waterproof sunscreens with an SPF of 15 or higher for the most protection. And to protect marine life and coral reefs, choose one without harmful chemicals such as oxybenzone and octinoxate.

### A CHANGE OF CLOTHES FOR YOUR BEACH BAG
There's nothing worse than a car ride in a wet bathing suit. Avoid it by packing underwear and a casual outfit (shorts or a sundress) that's easy to change into in your beach bag. Don't forget a plastic bag for your wet bathing suit. Note that you can generally swim year-round in peninsular Florida from about New Smyrna Beach south on the Atlantic Coast and from Tarpon Springs south on the Gulf Coast.

### RAIN GEAR
Be prepared for sudden storms all over in summer, and note that plastic raincoats are uncomfortable in the high humidity. Often, storms are quick, generally in the afternoon, and the sun comes back in no time.

### INSECT REPELLENT
Mosquitoes are always present in Florida, but especially so in the wet summer months. Pack a DEET-based bug spray for the most effective protection.

### PORTABLE SPEAKER
The perfect addition to your beach time? Music. Pack waterproof speakers that sync to your phone via Bluetooth.

### WATERPROOF PHONE CASE
Whether you want to snap photos while snorkeling or simply protect your device from kids splashing by the pool, pack a waterproof case to protect your electronics.

### HAIR PRODUCTS
South Florida's subtropical climate can wreak havoc on your hair, sending you straight to the haircare aisle of your nearest drugstore. Packing a sun hat and hair ties is the easiest way to deal with humid-hair, but if you'd like to wear your hair down you may want to pack protective serums and sprays to ward off the pouf, swell, and frizz effects of humidity.

# On the Calendar

## January

**Art Deco Weekend.** South Beach celebrates its iconic art deco with three days of events along Ocean Drive, including a jazz festival, classic car show, and street fair. ⊕ *artdecoweekend.com*

## February

**Art Wynwood.** Any time is a good time to visit Wynwood, Miami's cool, grungy neighborhood filled with street art, but come in February for its contemporary art fair. ⊕ *www.artwynwood.com*

**Coconut Grove Arts Festival.** More than 280 internationally acclaimed artists showcase their work along Biscayne Bay's waterfront streets. ⊕ *www.cgaf.com*

**South Beach Wine & Food Festival.** The Food Network & Cooking Channel gather the world's greatest chefs for five days of cooking demos and pop-up parties on South Beach. ⊕ *sobewff.org*

**South Florida Garlic Fest.** "The best stinkin' party in South Florida" is an annual community celebration of food, music, and art held in Delray Beach in early February. South Florida Garlic Fest favorites include flaming shrimp scampi, garlic crab cakes, garlic bruschetta, garlic pizza, and garlic ice cream. ⊕ *www.garlicfestfl.com*

## March

**Calle Ocho Music Festival.** With over a million visitors each year, this Miami festival (part of the larger Carnaval Miami) covers 20 blocks and has 10 stages. ⊕ *carnavalmiami.com/events/calle-ocho*

**Carnaval Miami.** This annual celebration of Latin art, music, fashion, food, and sports includes family-friendly Carnaval on the Mile, a Domino tournament, and Calle Ocho Music Festival. The festival is powered by volunteers of the Kiwanis Club of Little Havana and benefits the Kiwanis of Little Havana Foundation's youth development programs. ⊕ *carnavalmiami.com*

**Miami Music Week.** Nearly 1,000 artists perform across the city during the electronic music event that ends in Ultra Music Festival. ⊕ *miamimusicweek.com*

**Miami Open.** One of the world's largest tennis events takes place over a two-week span and features a mix of curated art and music on the tournament grounds. ⊕ *www.miamiopen.com*

## April

**Las Olas Wine & Food Festival.** Sample Fort Lauderdale's best bites and beverages at this block party on Las Olas Boulevard. ⊕ *lasolaswff.com*

**Miami Beach Pride.** Ocean Drive's popular party celebrates the LGBTQ+ community through festivals, balls, and drag-queen pageants. ⊕ *www.miamibeachpride.com*

## May

**Key West Songwriters Festival.** The largest event of its kind features five days and nights of performances on the island's beaches and boats and in bars and historic theaters. ⊕ *www.keywestsongwritersfestival.com*

**SunFest.** Florida's largest waterfront music and art festival unfolds in downtown West Palm. The festival concludes with a massive fireworks display on Sunday night. ⊕ *www.sunfest.com*

## July

**Hemingway Days.** The annual celebration salutes the Nobel Prize–winning author's writing achievements, sporting pursuits, and enjoyment of the island's easygoing lifestyle. The undisputed highlight is the Hemingway Look-Alike Contest at Sloppy Joe's Bar, a frequent hangout for the writer during his 1930s residence in Key West. Other events include a three-day marlin tournament and literary readings. ⊕ *fla-keys.com/hemingway-days*

**Lower Keys Underwater Music Festival.** Classic rock is streamed from underwater speakers in Big Pine Key to raise awareness for coral preservation. ⊕ *www.lowerkeyschamber.com/product/underwater-music-festival/*

**Miami Spa Months.** Miami's most luxurious spas offer specials on treatments for deals up to half off in summer (July and August). ⊕ *www.miamiandbeaches.com/offers/temptations/miami-spa-months*

**Miami Swim Week.** The fashion week of swimwear is a highlight of the summer, packed with runway shows and fab parties. ⊕ *miamiswimweek.net*

## August

**Miami Spa Months.** Miami's most luxurious spas offer specials on treatments for deals up to half off in summer (July and August). ⊕ *www.miamiandbeaches.com/offers/temptations/miami-spa-months*

**Miami Spice.** Your reward for visiting in the low season? Great dining deals. The city's most lauded eateries serve 3-course specials at affordable prices (August and September). ⊕ *www.miamiandbeaches.com/offers/temptations/miami-spice-months*

## September

**Miami Spice.** Your reward for visiting in the low season? Great dining deals. The city's most lauded eateries serve 3-course specials at affordable prices (August and September). ⊕ *www.miamiandbeaches.com/offers/temptations/miami-spice-months*

## October

**Fantasy Fest.** Key West takes on a Mardi Gras–like atmosphere during the 10-day, costume-filled festival. ⊕ *www.fantasyfest.com*

**Fort Lauderdale International Boat Show.** The "Yachting Capital of the World" displays 1,000+ types of boats and super-yachts. ⊕ *www.flibs.com*

## December

**Art Basel.** The hottest art fair of the year inspires satellite art fairs, public exhibits, and parties all over the city. ⊕ *www.artbasel.com/miami-beach*

# Great South Florida Itineraries

## 3 Days: Miami

### DAY 1 (FRIDAY)

Fly into Miami International Airport as early as possible on Friday morning to maximize the day at the beach or your hotel's pristine pool. If your goal is to soak up as much vitamin D as possible, opt for a hotel directly on the sand, like long-time institution Delano South Beach, or one of the eye-catching newcomers, like Faena Miami Beach. Grab lunch from the outdoor counters at La Sandwicherie on South Beach and eat on the sand a couple blocks away.

While you're in the neighborhood, go in search of art deco, Miami Modern (MiMo), and Mediterranean Revival gems on a walking tour with the Miami Design Preservation League (MDPL) through the historic architectural district. The MDPL also maintains a museum dedicated to the subject on Ocean Drive and 10th Street.

Later, dinner at buzzy Italian eatery Macchialina will fuel you for the rest of the weekend. If you're not wiped out, join in the nightlife that makes Miami so famous: start with cocktails at The Broken Shaker or Swizzle Rum Bar & Drinkery, followed by dancing at one of the glitzy nightclubs that earned Miami its party-heavy reputation. Our pick: Basement Miami or LIV. If you're looking for something more low-key, head to Sugar, a 40th-floor rooftop bar amidst the high-rises of Brickell.

### DAY 2 (SATURDAY)

Grab a late breakfast at Joe's Stone Crab (a Miami institution that's open only October–July). You can take it away for a picnic to South Pointe Park, where cruise ships and other boats go in and out of Government Cut at the confluence of the Atlantic Ocean and Biscayne Bay. Head over to the Miami Beach Marina and hitch a boat ride with one of the operators there. You'll cruise into Biscayne Bay and Biscayne National Park for a glimpse of a protected saltwater world that's home to four distinct ecosystems and 500 species of wildlife, while marveling at a cluster of wood houses from the 1930s in Stiltsville.

Then head to Coconut Grove by car to take a walk back to 1891 under the old trees of a tropical hammock overlooking the bay. Barnacle Historic State Park is a 5-acre slice of the past, and you shouldn't miss the preserved bungalow known as the oldest house in Miami-Dade County still standing in its original location. Drive to Little Havana for a late-late lunch at one of the many authentic Cuban restaurants in the Calle Ocho community. Exploring the area will result in a deeper understanding of the Cuban exile experience and its influence on Miami culture from the 1960s until now. While there are some kitschy tourist traps, you'll find legitimate tributes to the heritage at Tower Theater and Domino Park. Happy hour and live music at Ball & Chain continues the history lesson: Ball & Chain originally opened in 1935 and evolved along with the neighborhood.

To cap off the night, visit Azucar Ice Cream Company next door for artisanal ice cream and sorbet flavors inspired by Cuban-American culture.

### DAY 3 (SUNDAY)

Your last day in Miami starts with an over-the-top brunch at Zuma in the Kimpton EPIC Hotel on the Miami River. The modern Japanese *izakaya*'s brunch from 11:30 am to 2:30 pm features all the signature dishes from the kitchen, sushi bar, and robata grill in an all-you-can-eat situation known as *baikingu* in Japanese. But this isn't your typical buffet—it's super-premium and sophisticated ($98–$398 per person) and includes wasabi-infused libations worthy of the city's best craft cocktail bars.

If you'd rather go straight to lunch, Mandolin Aegean Bistro is a modernized version of a Greek taverna set in an old Florida home in the Design District. Flavors and ingredients are as fresh as you'd find in the islands, and the tucked-away, outdoor courtyard feels more Mediterranean than anything else you'll find in Miami. From here, head to the Pérez Art Museum Miami (PAMM) for modern and contemporary works of art inside an impressive building on Biscayne Bay. Its neighbor in Ferré Park (formerly Museum Park), the Phillip and Patricia Frost Museum of Science, stands as another great option if a three-story aquarium with a gigantic oculus is more your speed.

Before you venture back to the airport, take a drive through Wynwood to see the Wynwood Walls, the world's largest outdoor graffiti museum, and a swath of ephemeral murals by international street artists on literally every street.

# 2 to 3 Days: Gold Coast and Treasure Coast

The opulent mansions of Palm Beach's Ocean Boulevard give you a glimpse of how the top of the 1% lives. For exclusive boutique shopping, art gallery browsing, and glittery sightseeing, sybarites should wander down "The Avenue" (that's Worth Avenue to non–Palm Beachers). The sporty set will find dozens of places to tee it up (hardly surprising given that the PGA is based here), along with tennis courts, polo clubs, and even a croquet center. The city also appeals to

gourmands thanks to additions like the low-key, French Riviera–inspired Florie's by "World's Best" chef Mauro Colagreco, at Four Seasons Resort Palm Beach (the spa also takes on a French touch with Parisian facial remedies).

Those who'd like to see more of the Gold Coast can continue traveling south through Boca Raton to Fort Lauderdale (known as the Yachting Capital of the World). But to balance the highbrow with the low-key, turn northward for a tour of the Treasure Coast. You can also look for the sea turtles that lay their own little treasures in the sands from May through October.

# 2 to 3 Days: Florida Keys

Almost everybody equates the Florida Keys with relaxation. And they live up to their reputation, thanks to offbeat attractions and that fabled come-as-you-are, do-as-you-please vibe. Key West, alternately known as the Conch Republic, is a good place to get initiated. The Old Town has a funky, laid-back feel. So take a leisurely walk; pay your regards to "Papa" (Hemingway, that is) at iconic watering hole Sloppy Joe's; then rent a moped to tour the rest of the island, stopping for a photo op at the Southernmost Point buoy.

Clear waters and abundant marine life make underwater activities another must. After scoping out the parrotfish on a catamaran cruise off the coast, head back into town and join local "Parrotheads" in a Jimmy Buffett singalong. When retracing your route to the mainland, plan a last pit stop at Bahia Honda State Park or John Pennekamp Coral Reef State Park, which offers unparalleled snorkeling and scuba-diving opportunities.

# Contacts

##  Air

**AIRPORT INFORMATION Fort Lauderdale–Hollywood International Airport.** (*FLL*). ✉ *100 Terminal Dr., Fort Lauderdale* ☎ *866/435–9355* ⊕ *www.broward. org/airport.* **Key West International Airport.** (*EYW*). ✉ *3491 S. Roosevelt Blvd., Key West* ☎ *305/809–5200* ⊕ *eyw. com.* **Miami International Airport.** (*MIA*). ✉ *2100 NW 42nd Ave., Miami* ☎ *305/876–7000, 800/825–5642 international* ⊕ *www.iflymia.com.* **Palm Beach International Airport.** (*PBI*). ✉ *Palm Beach International Airport, 1000 Palm Beach International Airport, West Palm Beach* ☎ *561/471–7400* ⊕ *www.pbia.org.*

**SHUTTLE SERVICE Florida Shuttle Transportation.** ☎ *321/250–2820* ⊕ *www. floridashuttletransportation.com.*

##  Ferry

**Key West Express.** ✉ *100 Grinnell St., Key West* ☎ *239/463–5733* ⊕ *www. keywestexpress.net.* **Water Taxi.** ✉ *904 E. Las Olas Blvd., Fort Lauderdale* ☎ *954/467–6677* ⊕ *watertaxi.com.*

##  Bus

**Megabus.** ⊕ *www.megabus.com.* **Red Coach USA.** ⊕ *www.redcoachusa.com.*

##  Car

**Avis.** ✉ *Key West* ☎ *800/352–7900* ⊕ *www. avis.com.* **Budget.** ✉ *Key West* ☎ *800/214–6094* ⊕ *www.budget.com.* **Hertz.** ✉ *Key West* ☎ *800/654–3131* ⊕ *www.hertz.com.*

## 🚕 Taxi

**Central Cab.** ☎ *305/532–5555* ⊕ *www.facebook.com/Centralcabtaxi.* **USA Taxi.** ☎ *305/897–3333.* **Yellow Cab.** ☎ *305/444–4444* ⊕ *www.yellowtaximiami.com.*

## 🚢 Cruise

**Port Everglades.** ✉ *1850 Eller Dr., Fort Lauderdale* ☎ *954/523-3404* ⊕ *www. portevergldes.net.* **PortMiami.** ✉ *1015 North America Way, Miami* ☎ *305/347-4800* ⊕ *www. miamidade.gov/portmiami.*

## 🚆 Train

**Amtrak.** ☎ *800/872–7245* ⊕ *www.amtrak.com.* **Brightline.** ✉ *Miami Central Station, 600 NW 1st Ave., Downtown* ☎ *888/448–8491* ⊕ *www.gobrightline.com.*

##  Lodging

**Airbnb.** ⊕ *www.airbnb.com.* **Endless Vacation Rentals.** ☎ *877/782–9387* ⊕ *www.evrentals.com.* **Interhome.** ☎ *954/791–8282, 800/882–6864* ⊕ *www.interhomeusa.com.* **Vacation Rentals By Owner.** ⊕ *www.vrbo.com.*

## 📍 Visitor Information

**Discover the Palm Beaches.** ✉ *1555 Palm Beach Lakes Blvd., Suite 800, West Palm Beach* ☎ *800/554–7256* ⊕ *www. thepalmbeaches.com.* **Greater Miami Convention & Visitors Bureau.** ✉ *701 Brickell Ave., Suite 2700, Miami* ☎ *305/539–3000, 800/933–8448 in U.S.* ⊕ *www.miamiandbeaches.com.* **Visit Florida.** ✉ *Visit Florida—Corporate Office, 2540 W. Executive Center Cir., Tallahassee* ☎ *850/488–5607* ⊕ *www. visitflorida.com.* **Visit Lauderdale.** ✉ *101 N.E. 3rd Ave., Suite 100, Fort Lauderdale* ☎ *954/765–4466* ⊕ *visitlauderdale.com.*

# Chapter 3

# MIAMI AND MIAMI BEACH

Updated by
Amber Love Bond

 **Sights**
★★★★★

 **Restaurants**
★★★★★

 **Hotels**
★★★★★

 **Shopping**
★★★★★

 **Nightlife**
★★★★★

# WELCOME TO MIAMI AND MIAMI BEACH

## TOP REASONS TO GO

★ **The beach:** Miami Beach is undoubtedly one of the best beaches in the world. White sand, warm water, and a cool crowd provide just the right mix of relaxation and party.

★ **Dining delights:** The city is a museum of epicurean wonders, ranging from Cuban to Japanese–Peruvian fusion, with many New York outposts in between.

★ **Wee-hour parties:** A 24-hour liquor license means clubs stay open until 5 am, and after-parties go until noon the following day.

★ **Diverse neighborhoods:** There's more to love than just the beach. Venture to mainland Miami to explore the vibrant areas of Little Havana, Little Haiti, and Wynwood and feel as if you've visited many cities all in one trip.

★ **Art Deco District:** Famed pastels and neon lights accessorize the architecture that first put South Beach on the map in the 1930s.

**1** **South Beach.** People-watch, admire art deco, and party 'til dawn.

**2** **Fisher and Belle Islands.** Exclusive private islands.

**3** **Mid-Beach.** Blooming hotel scene beyond SoBe.

**4** **North Beach.** Peace, beach, and luxe hotels.

**5** **Aventura.** Known for high-end shopping.

**6** **Downtown.** Museums and cool hangouts.

**7** **Brickell.** Urban center full of glittering high-rises.

**8** **Wynwood.** Trendy, creative area with colorful murals.

**9** **Midtown.** Hip neighborhood between two design districts.

**10** **Design District.** Browse design rooms and haute boutiques.

**11** **Little Haiti.** Emerging arts and food scenes.

**12** **Little Havana.** The heart and soul of the Cuban community.

**13** **Coconut Grove.** Bohemian shops and lush escapes.

**14** **Coral Gables.** Dine and shop on Miracle Mile.

**15** **Key Biscayne.** Beautiful parks and beaches.

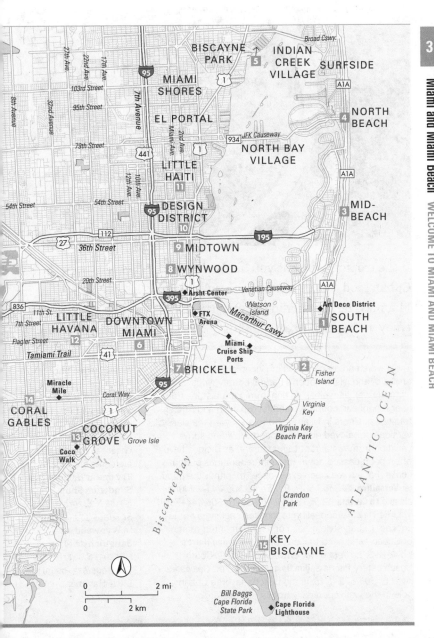

# CUBAN FOOD

Arroz con pollo

If the tropical vibe has you hankering for Cuban food, you've come to the right place. Miami is the top spot in the country to enjoy authentic Cuban cooking.

The flavors and preparations of Cuban cuisine are influenced by the island nation's natural bounty (yuca, sugarcane, guava), as well as its rich immigrant history, from near (Caribbean countries) and far (Spanish and African traditions). Chefs in Miami tend to stick with the classic versions of beloved dishes, though you'll find some variation from restaurant to restaurant, as recipes have often been passed down through generations of home cooks. For a true Cuban experience, try either the popular **Versailles** (⊠ 3555 S.W. 8th St. ☎ 305/444–0240) or classic **La Carreta** (⊠ 3632 S.W. 8th St. ☎ 305/444–7501) in Little Havana, appealing to families seeking a home-cooked, Cuban-style meal. For a modern interpretation of Cuban eats, head to Coral Gables' **Havana Harry's** (⊠ 4612 S. Le Jeune Rd. ☎ 305/661–2622). South Beach eatery **Puerto Sagua Restaurant** (⊠ 700 Collins Ave. ☎ 305/673–1115) is the beach's favorite Cuban hole-in-the-wall, open daily from 7 am to 2 am.

## THE CUBAN SANDWICH

A great Cubano requires pillowy Cuban bread layered with ham, garlic-citrus-marinated slow-roasted pork, Swiss cheese, and pickles, with butter and/or mustard. The sandwich is grilled in a press until the cheese melts and the elements are fused. Try one at **Enriqueta's Sandwich Shop** (⊠ 186 N.E. 29th St. ☎ 305/573–4681) in Wynwood, or **Sanguich de Miam** i (⊠ 2057 S.W. 8th St. ☎ 305/539–0969) in Little Havana.

# Key Cuban Dishes

### ARROZ CON POLLO
This chicken-and-rice dish is Cuban comfort food. Found throughout Latin America, the Cuban version is typically seasoned with garlic, paprika, and onions, then colored golden or reddish with saffron or achiote (a seed paste) and enlivened with a splash of beer near the end of cooking. Green peas and sliced, roasted red peppers are standard toppings.

### BISTEC DE PALOMILLA
This thinly sliced sirloin steak is marinated in lime juice and garlic and fried with onions. The steak is often served with chimichurri, an olive oil, garlic, and cilantro sauce that sometimes comes with bread. Also try *ropa vieja,* a slow-cooked, shredded flank steak in a garlic-tomato sauce.

### DESSERTS
Treat yourself to a slice of tres leches cake. The "three milks" come from the sweetened condensed milk, evaporated milk, and heavy cream that are poured over the cake until it's an irresistible gooey mess. Also, don't miss the *pastelitos,* Cuban fruit-filled turnovers. Traditional flavors include plain guava, guava with cream cheese, and cream cheese with coconut.

Cubano

Tres leches cake

### DRINKS
Sip *guarapo,* a fresh sugarcane juice that isn't really as sweet as you might think, or enjoy a *batido,* a Cuban-style milkshake made with tropical fruits like mango, *piña* (pineapple), or mamey. For a real twist, try the *batido de trigo*—a wheat shake that will remind you of sugar-glazed cereal.

### FRITAS
If you're in the mood for an inexpensive, casual Cuban meal, have a *frita*—a hamburger with Cuban flair. Made with ground beef that's mixed with chopped chorizo and spiced with pepper, paprika, and salt, it comes topped with sautéed onions and shoestring potato fries and is served on a bun slathered with a tomato-based ketchup-like sauce.

### LECHÓN ASADO
Fresh ham or an entire suckling pig marinated in mojo *criollo* (parsley, garlic, sour orange, and olive oil) is roasted until tender and served with white rice, black beans, and *tostones* (fried plantains) or yuca, a starchy tuber with a mild nut taste that's often sliced into fat sticks and deep-fried like fries.

Part island paradise, part urban metropolis, Miami is a city steeped in an intoxicating blend of old history and modern leisure, with ambitions to become the next Silicon Valley. While South Beach still attracts the scene-seekers as it continues to extend both north and west, it is no longer the only place to stand and pose in Miami. North of Downtown, the growing Wynwood and Design Districts are home to trendy stores, bustling restaurants, and an outdoor gallery of artwork by graffiti artists and muralists.

Visit Miami today and it's hard to believe that 100 years ago it was a mosquito-infested swampland with a trading post on the Miami River. Then hotel builder Henry Flagler brought his railroad to the outpost known as Fort Dallas. Other visionaries—Carl Fisher, Julia Tuttle, William Brickell, and John Sewell, to name a few—set out to develop the wilderness where the Mayaimi and Tequesta tribes had once lived for centuries. Hotels were erected, bridges were built, the port was dredged, and electricity arrived. The narrow strip of mangrove coast was transformed into Miami Beach—and the tourists started to come. They haven't stopped since.

Greater Miami is many destinations in one. At its best, it offers an unparalleled multicultural experience: melodic Latin and Caribbean tongues, international cuisines and cultural events, and an unmistakable *joie de vivre*—all against a beautiful beach backdrop. In Little Havana, the air is tantalizing with the perfume of strong Cuban coffee. In Coconut Grove, Caribbean steel drums ring out during the Miami/Bahamas Goombay Festival. Anytime in colorful Miami Beach, restless crowds wait for entry to the hottest new clubs.

Many visitors don't know that Miami and Miami Beach are really separate cities. Miami, on the mainland, is South Florida's commercial hub. Miami Beach, on 17 islands in Biscayne Bay, is sometimes considered America's Riviera, luring refugees from winter with its graceful, shady palms, warm sunshine, sandy beaches, and tireless nightlife.

The natives know well that there's more to Greater Miami than the bustle of South Beach and its art deco Historic District. In addition to well-known places such as Ocean Drive and Lincoln Road, the less-reported spots—like the burgeoning Design District in Miami, the historic buildings of Coral Gables, and the secluded beaches of Key Biscayne—are great insider destinations.

# Planning

## When to Go

Miami and Miami Beach are year-round destinations. Most people come from November through April, when the weather is close to perfect and each weekend holds a festival or event. High season kicks off in December with Art Basel, and hotel rates don't come down until the college kids have left after spring break in late March.

It's hot and steamy May through September, but nighttime temperatures are usually pleasant. Also, summer is a good time for the budget traveler. Many hotels lower their rates considerably, and many restaurants offer discounts—especially during Miami Spice in August and September, when a slew of top restaurants offers special tasting menus at a steep discount. June through November is hurricane season.

## Getting Here and Around

You'll need a car or rideshare to visit many attractions and points of interest. If possible, avoid driving during the rush hours of 7–9 am and 5–7 pm—the hour just after and right before the peak times also can be slow going. During rainy weather, be especially cautious of flooding in South Beach and Key Biscayne.

### AIR

Miami is serviced by Miami International Airport (MIA), 8 miles northwest of Downtown, and Fort Lauderdale–Hollywood International Airport (FLL), 26 miles northeast. Many discount carriers, like Spirit Airlines, Southwest Airlines, and JetBlue, fly into FLL, making it a smart bargain if you're renting a car. Otherwise, look for flights to MIA, which has undergone an extensive face-lift, improving facilities, common spaces, and the overall aesthetic of the airport.

### CAR

Interstate 95 is the major expressway connecting South Florida with points north; State Road 836 is the major east–west expressway and connects to Florida's Turnpike, State Road 826, and Interstate 95. Seven causeways link Miami and Miami Beach, with Interstate 195 and Interstate 395 offering the most convenient routes; the Rickenbacker Causeway extends to Key Biscayne from Interstate 95 and U.S. 1. The high-speed lanes on the left-hand side of Interstate 95—often separated by confusing orange poles—require a prepaid toll pass called a SunPass, available in most drug and grocery stores, or it can be ordered by mail before your trip. It is available with most rental cars (but you are billed for the tolls and associated fees later).

### PUBLIC TRANSPORTATION

Some sights are accessible via the public transportation system, run by the **Miami-Dade Transit Agency,** which maintains 800 Metrobuses on 95 routes, the 25-mile Metrorail elevated rapid-transit system, and the Metromover, an elevated light-rail system.

Those planning to use public transportation should get an EASY Ticket, available at any Metrorail station and most supermarkets, or download the EASY Pay Miami app to buy daily passes. Fares are discounted, and transfer fees are nominal. The bus stops for the **Metrobus** are marked with blue-and-green signs with a bus logo and route information. The fare is $2.25 (exact change only if paying cash). Cash-paying customers must pay for another ride if transferring. Elevated **Metrorail** trains run from Downtown Miami north to Hialeah and south along U.S. 1 to Dadeland. The system operates daily 5 am–midnight. The fare is $2.25 and accessible only by EASY Ticket or the EASY Pay app (no cash).

The free **Metromover** resembles an airport shuttle and runs on three loops around Downtown Miami, linking major hotels, office buildings, and shopping areas. The system spans about 4½ miles, including the 1-mile Omni Loop, the 1-mile Brickell Loop, and the smaller Inner Loop.

**Tri-Rail,** South Florida's commuter-train system, stops at 18 stations north of MIA along a 71-mile route. There's a Metrorail transfer station two stops north of MIA. Prices range from $2.50 to $6.90 for a one-way ticket. With all that said, most travelers prefer to rent a car or book a rideshare to cover the most ground.

**CONTACTS Miami-Dade Transit Agency.** ☎ 305/891–3131 ⊕ www.miamidade.gov/transit/. **Tri-Rail.** ☎ 800/874–7245 ⊕ www.tri-rail.com.

### TAXI

These days, most use Uber or Lyft to get around Miami, but old-school taxis still exist. Except in South Beach, it's difficult to hail a cab on the street; in most cases you'll need to call a cab company or have a hotel doorman hail one for you. Taxi drivers in Miami are notorious for bad customer service and not having credit card machines in their vehicles. If using a regular taxi, note that fares run $4.50 for the first 1/6 of a mile and $0.40 for every additional 1/6 of a mile. Waiting time is $0.40 per minute. Flat-rate fares are also available from the airport to a variety of zones (including Miami Beach) for $35. Expect a $2 surcharge on rides leaving from MIA or the Port of Miami. For those heading from MIA to Downtown, the

15-minute, 7-mile trip costs around $21. Some, but not all, cabs accept credit cards, so ask when you get in.

**TAXI COMPANIES Central Cab.** ☎ 305/532–5555 ⊕ www.centralcab.com. **Lyft.** ✉ Miami ⊕ www.lyft.com. **Uber.** ⊕ www.uber.com. **Yellow Cab.** ☎ 305/444–4444.

### TRAIN

High-speed train service Brightline connects Downtown Miami, Fort Lauderdale, and West Palm Beach. The trip from Downtown Miami to Fort Lauderdale takes about 30 minutes; it's another 30 minutes to West Palm Beach.

Amtrak provides service from 500 destinations to the Greater Miami area. The trains make several stops along the way; north–south service stops in the major Florida cities of Jacksonville, Orlando, Tampa, West Palm Beach, and Fort Lauderdale, but stations are not always conveniently located. The Auto Train (where you bring your car along) travels from Lorton, Virginia, just outside Washington, D.C., to Sanford, Florida, just outside Orlando. From there it's less than a four-hour drive to Miami. Fares vary, but expect to pay between around $275 and $350 for a basic sleeper seat and car passage each way.

■ TIP➔ **You must be traveling with an automobile to purchase a ticket on the Auto Train.**

**CONTACTS Brightline.** ✉ Miami Central Station, 600 NW 1st Ave., Downtown ☎ 888/448–8491 ⊕ www.gobrightline.com.

## Sights

If you'd arrived here 50 years ago with a guidebook in hand, chances are you'd be thumbing through listings looking for alligator wrestlers and you-pick strawberry fields or citrus groves. Things have changed. While Disney sidetracked families in Orlando, Miami was developing a unique culture and attitude that's equal parts beach town/big business, Latino/Caribbean meets European/American—all of which fuels a great art and food scene, as well as exuberant nightlife and myriad festivals.

To find your way around Greater Miami, learn how the numbering system works (or better yet, use your phone's map). Miami is laid out on a grid with four quadrants—northeast, northwest, southeast, and southwest—that meet at Miami Avenue and Flagler Street. Miami Avenue separates east from west, and Flagler Street separates north from south. Avenues and courts run north–south; streets, terraces, and ways run east–west. Roads run diagonally, northwest–southeast. But other districts—Miami Beach, Coral Gables, and Hialeah—may or may not follow this system, and along the curve of Biscayne Bay the symmetrical grid shifts diagonally. If you do get lost, make sure you're in a safe neighborhood or public place when you seek guidance.

## Restaurants

Miami's restaurant scene has exploded in the last decade, with new restaurants springing up left and right every month. The melting pot of residents and visitors has brought an array of sophisticated, tasty cuisine. Little Havana is still king for Cuban fare, and Miami Beach is swept up in a trend of fusion cuisine, which combines Asian, French, American, and Latin cooking with sumptuous—and pricey—results. Locals spend the most time in Brickell, Wynwood, and the Design District, where the city's ongoing foodie and cocktail revolution is most pronounced.

Since Miami dining is a part of the trendy nightlife scene, most dinners don't start until 8 or 9 pm and may go well into the night. To avoid a long wait among the late-night partiers at hot spots, come before 7 pm or make reservations. Attire is usually casual-chic, but patrons like to dress to impress. Prices tend to be extra inflated in tourist hot spots like Lincoln Road, but if you venture off the beaten path you can find better food for more reasonable prices.

When you get your bill, check whether a gratuity is already included; most restaurants add between 18% and 22% (ostensibly for the convenience of, and protection from, the many foreign tourists who are used to this practice in their homelands), but supplement it depending on your opinion of the service.

*Restaurant prices are the average cost of a main course at dinner or, if dinner is not served, at lunch. Restaurant reviews have been shortened. For full information, visit Fodors.com.*

| What It Costs in U.S. Dollars | | | |
| --- | --- | --- | --- |
| $ | $$ | $$$ | $$$$ |
| RESTAURANTS | | | |
| under $15 | $15–$20 | $21–$30 | over $30 |

## Hotels

Room rates in Miami tend to swing wildly. In high season, which is December through April, expect to pay at least $250 per night, even at value-oriented hotels. In fact, it's common nowadays for rates to begin around $500 at Miami's top hotels. In summer, however, prices can be as much as 50% lower than the dizzying winter rates. You can also find great deals between Easter and Memorial Day, which is actually a delightful time in Miami. Two important considerations that affect price are balcony and view. If you're willing to have a room without an ocean view, you can sometimes get a much lower price than the standard rate, even at an oceanfront hotel.

Business travelers tend to stay in Downtown Miami, and most vacationers stay on Miami Beach, as close as possible to the water. South Beach is no longer the "in" place to stay. Mid-Beach and Downtown have taken the hotel scene by storm in the past few years and become home to some of the region's most avant-garde and luxurious properties to date.

If money is no object, stay in one of the glamorous hotels lining Collins Avenue between 15th and 23rd Streets or between 29th and 44th Streets. Otherwise, stay on the quiet beaches farther north or in one of the small boutique hotels on Ocean Drive or Collins or Washington Avenues between 10th and 15th Streets.

*Hotel prices are the lowest cost of a standard double room in high season. Hotel reviews have been shortened. For full information, visit Fodors.com.*

| What It Costs in U.S. Dollars | | | |
|---|---|---|---|
| $ | $$ | $$$ | $$$$ |
| **HOTELS** | | | |
| under $200 | $200–$300 | $301–$400 | over $400 |

# Nightlife

One of Greater Miami's most popular pursuits is barhopping. Bars range from intimate enclaves to showy see-and-be-seen lounges to loud, raucous parties. There's a New York–style flair to some of the newer lounges, which are increasingly catering to the Manhattan party crowd who escape to Miami and Miami Beach for long weekends. No doubt, Miami's pulse pounds with nonstop nightlife that reflects the area's potent cultural mix. On sultry, humid nights with the huge full moon rising out of the ocean and fragrant night-blooming jasmine intoxicating the senses, who can resist Cuban salsa with some disco and hip-hop thrown in for good measure? It's no wonder many clubs are still rocking at 5 am. If you're looking for a relatively nonfrenetic evening, your best bet is one of the chic hotel bars on Collins Avenue or a lounge away from Miami Beach in Wynwood, the Design District, or Brickell.

The *Miami Herald* is a good source for information on what to do in town. Or you can pick up the *Miami New Times*, the city's largest free alternative newspaper, published each Thursday. It lists nightclubs, concerts, and special events, reviews plays and movies, and provides in-depth coverage of the local music scene. *MIAMI* and *Ocean Drive*, Miami's model-strewn, upscale fashion and lifestyle magazines squeeze club, bar, restaurant, and events listings in with fashion spreads, reviews, and personality profiles. Paparazzi photos of local party people and celebrities give you a taste of Greater Miami nightlife before you even dress up to paint the town.

The Spanish-language *El Nuevo Herald*, published by the *Miami Herald,* has extensive information on Spanish-language arts and entertainment, including dining reviews, concert previews, and nightclub highlights. *Time Out Miami* is another good resource for local happenings.

# Shopping

Beyond its fun-in-the-sun offerings, Miami has evolved into a world-class shopping destination. People fly here from all over the world just to shop. The city teems with sophisticated malls—from multistory, indoor climate-controlled temples of consumerism to sun-kissed, open-air retail enclaves—and bustling avenues and streets, lined at once with affordable chain stores, haute couture boutiques, and one-off, "only in Miami"–type shops.

Following the incredible success of the Bal Harbour Shops in the highest of the high-end market (Chanel, Alexander McQueen, ETRO), the Design District and Brickell have followed suit. Beyond fabulous designer furniture showrooms, the Design District's tenants now include Hermès, Dior Homme, Rolex, and Prada. Brickell's mega Brickell City Centre is the latest arena for high-end retail, with a number of European brands making their U.S. debuts in the chic open-air mall.

Beyond clothiers and big-name retailers, Greater Miami has all manner of merchandise to tempt even the casual browser. For consumers on a mission to find certain items—art deco antiques or cigars, for instance—the city streets burst with a rewarding collection of specialty shops.

Stroll through Spanish-speaking neighborhoods where shops sell clothing, cigars, and other goods from all over Latin America, or even head to Little Haiti for rare vinyl records.

## Activities

Sun, sand, and crystal-clear water mixed with an almost nonexistent winter and a cosmopolitan clientele make Miami and Miami Beach ideal for year-round sunbathing and outdoor activities. Whether the priority is showing off a toned body, jumping on a Jet Ski, or relaxing in a tranquil natural environment, there's a beach tailor-made to please. But tanning and water sports are only part of this sun-drenched picture. Greater Miami has championship golf courses and tennis courts, miles of bike trails along placid canals and through subtropical forests, and skater-friendly concrete paths amidst the urban jungle. And for those who like their sports of the spectator variety, the city offers up a bonanza of pro teams for every season.

# South Beach

The hub of Miami Beach is the celebrated neighborhood of South Beach (better known as SoBe), with its energetic Ocean Drive, Collins Avenue, and Washington Avenue. Here life unfolds 24 hours a day. Beautiful people pose in hotel lounges and sidewalk cafés, bronzed cyclists zoom past palm trees, and visitors flock to see the action. On Lincoln Road, café crowds spill onto the street, weekend markets draw all kinds of visitors and their dogs, and thanks to a few late-night lounges, the scene is just as alive at night. Farther north (in Mid-Beach and North Beach), the vibe is decidedly quieter and more sophisticated.

 Sights

**Art Deco Welcome Center and Museum**
**HISTORY MUSEUM** | Run by the Miami Design Preservation League, the center provides information about the buildings in the district. There's also an official Art Deco Museum within the center, as well as a gift shop that sells art deco memorabilia and posters from the 1930s through '50s, as well as books on Miami's history. Several tours also start here, including a self-guided audio tour and regular morning walking tours at 10:30 daily (excluding Tuesday and Wednesday). ⊠ *1001 Ocean Dr., South Beach* ☎ *305/672–2014, 305/531–3484 for tours* ⊕ *www.mdpl.org* ☜ *Tours from $35.*

**★ The Bass**
**ART MUSEUM** | Special exhibitions join a diverse collection of international contemporary art at this museum whose original 1930s art deco building was designed by Russell Pancoast and constructed entirely of Florida keystone (material with a coral base). A years-long, $12 million expansion by noted architects Arata Isozaki and David Gauld, completed in 2017, increased internal space nearly 50% and added four new galleries. Most

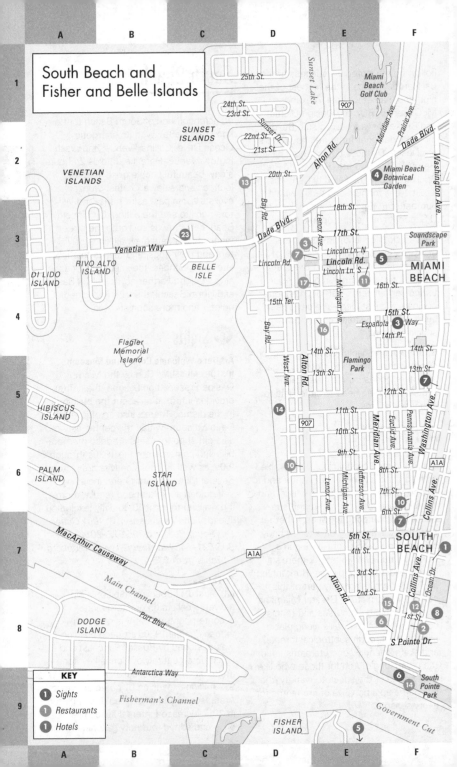

## Sights ▼

1 Art Deco Welcome
  Center and Museum ... **G6**
2 The Bass ............... **G2**
3 Española Way ........... **F4**
4 Holocaust Memorial..... **E2**
5 Lincoln Road Mall ....... **F3**
6 South Pointe Park ....... **F9**
7 Wilzig Erotic
  Art Museum (WEAM) ... **F5**

## Restaurants ▼

1 Byblos ................... **G4**
2 Carbone ................. **F8**
3 Chotto Matte ............. **E3**
4 Gianni's ................. **G5**
5 Jaya ..................... **G2**
6 Joe's Stone Crab ........ **F8**
7 Juvia ..................... **E3**
8 Katsuya
  South Beach ............ **G3**
9 LT Steak and
  Seafood................. **G4**
10 Macchialina ............ **D6**
11 MILA ................... **E3**
12 Prime 112 ................ **F8**
13 Pubbelly Sushi .......... **D2**
14 Smith & Wollensky
  Miami Beach ........... **F9**
15 Stubborn Seed ......... **F8**
16 Via Emilia 9 .............. **E4**
17 Yardbird Southern
  Table & Bar ............. **E4**

## Hotels ▼

1 The Balfour Hotel........ **F7**
2 The Betsy............... **G4**
3 Cadet Hotel ............ **G3**
4 Dream South Beach.... **G5**
5 Fisher Island Club ...... **E9**
6 Gale South Beach ...... **G3**
7 the goodtime hotel ...... **F7**
8 Hilton Bentley
  Miami/South Beach ..... **F8**
9 Hotel Victor ............. **G5**
10 Kimpton Angler's
  Hotel ..................... **F6**
11 Kimpton Surfcomber
  Miami, South Beach .... **G3**
12 Lennox Hotel ........... **G2**
13 Loews Miami
  Beach Hotel ........... **G4**
14 Mondrian
  South Beach ........... **D5**
15 National Hotel .......... **G3**
16 1 Hotel South Beach ... **G1**
17 The Ritz-Carlton,
  South Beach ........... **G3**
18 Royal Palm
  South Beach Miami .... **G4**
19 The Sagamore
  South Beach,
  the Art Hotel ........... **G3**
20 The Setai
  Miami Beach ........... **G2**
21 Shelborne
  South Beach ........... **G2**
22 SLS South Beach ...... **G4**
23 The Standard Spa,
  Miami Beach ............**C3**
24 W South Beach ........ **G2**
25 Z Ocean Hotel .......... **G3**

G   H   I

A1A

Pine Tree Dr.

23rd St.
22nd St.
Park Ave.
Collins
Park
20th St.
19th St.
18th St.

Collins Ave.

*South
Beach*

*ATLANTIC
OCEAN*

*Lummus
Park*

0        1/2 mi
0    1/2 km

G   H   I

of the exhibitions are temporary, but works on permanent display include *Chess Tables,* a sculpture by Jim Drain, and *Miami Mountain,* a sculpture by Ugo Rondinone. Visit for free the third Thursday and last Sunday of every month. ⊠ *2100 Collins Ave., South Beach* ☎ *305/673-7530* ⊕ *www.thebass.org* 🎟 *$15* ⊘ *Closed Mon. and Tues.*

### Española Way

**PEDESTRIAN MALL | FAMILY |** There's a bohemian feel to this street lined with Mediterranean-revival buildings constructed in 1925 and inspired by New York's Greenwich Village. Al Capone's gambling syndicate ran its operations upstairs at what is now The Clay Hotel, a value-conscious boutique hotel. At a nightclub here in the 1930s, future bandleader Desi Arnaz strapped on a conga drum and started beating out a rumba rhythm. Visit this quaint pedestrian-only way nowadays and find a number of personality-driven restaurants and bars. Weekly programming includes the likes of salsa dancing, flamenco dancing, and opera performances. ⊠ *Española Way, South Beach* ✛ *Between 14th and 15th sts. from Washington to Pennslyvania Ave.* ⊕ *www.visitespanolaway.com.*

### Holocaust Memorial

**MONUMENT |** A bronze sculpture depicts refugees clinging to a giant bronze arm that reaches out of the ground and 42 feet into the air. Enter the surrounding courtyard to see a memorial wall and hear the music that seems to give voice to the 6 million Jews who died at the hands of the Nazis. It's easy to understand why Kenneth Treister's dramatic memorial is in Miami Beach: the city's community of Holocaust survivors was once the second largest in the country. ⊠ *1933–1945 Meridian Ave., at Dade Blvd., South Beach* ☎ *305/538-1663* ⊕ *holocaustmemorialmiamibeach.org* 🎟 *Free.*

### ★ Lincoln Road Mall

**PEDESTRIAN MALL | FAMILY |** Lincoln Road has some of Miami's best people-watching. The eclectic interiors of myriad fabulous restaurants, colorful boutiques, art galleries, lounges, and cafés are often upstaged by the bustling outdoor scene. It's here, amid many alfresco dining enclaves, that you can pass the hours easily. Indeed, Lincoln Road is fun, lively, and friendly for everyone—old, young, gay, and straight—and their dogs. A few of the shops are owner-operated boutiques with a smart variety of clothing, furnishings, jewelry, and decorative elements, but more often you'll find typical chain stores.

Two landmarks worth checking out at the eastern end of Lincoln Road are the massive 1940s keystone building at No. 420, which has a 1945 Leo Birchansky mural in the lobby, and the 1921 mission-style Miami Beach Community Church at Drexel Avenue. The Lincoln Theatre (⊠ *541–545 Lincoln Road, at Pennsylvania Avenue*) is a classical four-story art deco gem with friezes that now houses an H&M. ⊠ *Lincoln Rd. between Washington Ave. and Alton Rd., South Beach* ⊕ *www.lincolnroadmall.com.*

### ★ South Pointe Park

**PROMENADE | FAMILY |** At the southern tip of Miami Beach is a beautifully manicured park where locals and visitors alike stroll along a palm-fringed waterfront promenade. Sunbathers lounge in hammocks, runners zoom through trails, kids enjoy a small water playground, and socialites dine al fresco at Smith & Wollensky. At the end of the promenade is access to South Beach as well as the South Pointe Park Pier, an observation deck that gives a wide angle view of the beach. ⊠ *1 Washington Ave., South Beach* ☎ *305/673-7779* ⊕ *www.miami-andbeaches.com.*

**Wilzig Erotic Art Museum (WEAM)**
**ART MUSEUM** | Late millionaire Naomi Wilzig's collection of some 4,000 erotic items is on display at this unique museum. Expect sexy art of varying quality—fertility statues from around the globe and historic Japanese *shunga* books (erotic art offered as gifts to new brides on their wedding night) share the space with some kitschy knickknacks. If this is your thing, an original phallic prop from Stanley Kubrick's *A Clockwork Orange* and an over-the-top Kama Sutra bed are worth the price of admission. Kids 17 and under are not admitted. ✉ *1205 Washington Ave., at 12th St., South Beach* ☎ *305/532–9336* 🌐 *www.weammuseum.com* 🎟 *$25.*

## Beaches

**★ South Beach**
**BEACH** | Hugging the turquoise waters along Ocean Drive from 5th to 15th Streets, this is one of the most popular beaches in America, known for its colorful lifeguard towers and social sunbathers. With the influx of luxe hotels and hot spots from 1st to 5th and 16th to 25th Streets, the stand-and-pose scene is now bigger than ever, stretching yet another dozen-plus blocks. The white sandy stretch fills up quickly on the weekends with a blend of European tourists, young hipsters, and sun-drenched locals. Separating the shore from the traffic of Ocean Drive is palm-fringed Lummus Park, with its volleyball nets and winding bike path. There are access points every few streets, including 14th Street, 12th Street, and so on. Locals hang out on the 3rd Street beach, in an area called SoFi (South of Fifth). Dogs are not allowed on the beach. **Amenities:** food and drink; lifeguards; parking (fee); showers; toilets. **Best for:** partiers; sunrise; swimming; walking. ✉ *Ocean Dr. from 5th to 15th Sts., then Collins Ave. to 25th St., South Beach* 🎟 *Free.*

## Restaurants

**★ Byblos**
**$$$ | MIDDLE EASTERN** | Dynamic and delicious flavors of the eastern Mediterranean merge over traditional and new-fashioned dishes at this photogenic local hot spot. Feast on *pides* (Turkish flat breads baked in a stone oven), Middle Eastern fried chicken (with tahini, za'atar, and house hot sauce) and *fattoush* (crunch salad) while enjoying the breezy, art deco surroundings and colorful interiors. **Known for:** creamed-spinach pide; yogurt-baked fluke; trendsetting crowd. [$] *Average main: $28* ✉ *1545 Collins Ave., South Beach* ☎ *305/508–5041* 🌐 *www.byblosmiami.com.*

**Carbone**
**$$$$ | ITALIAN** | One of the toughest tables to score on South Beach, Carbone (part of New York's Major Food Group) is an intimate and flashy Italian spot renowned for tableside salads, a famously Instagram-worthy rigatoni, and huge housemade desserts. Even those with a reservation should expect to wait upon check-in, but there's always the option to grab a drink at the bar and scope out the dimly lit dining room. **Known for:** celebrity sightings; spicy rigatoni; impeccable service. [$] *Average main: $38* ✉ *49 Collins Ave., Miami* 🌐 *www.carbonemiami.com.*

**Chotto Matte**
**$$$ | JAPANESE FUSION** | With bright graffiti walls, a buzzing bar, and an open-air roof, this trendy Japanese-Peruvian fusion restaurant has brought sophistication and edge to Lincoln Road. Order a pisco or Japanese whiskey and settle in for flavor-packed Nikkei-style cuisine and some of the best sushi in town. **Known for:** excellent sharing menu; glow-in-the-dark bathrooms; flaming Holy Water cocktail. [$] *Average main: $25* ✉ *1664 Lenox Ave., South Beach* ☎ *305/690–0743* 🌐 *chotto-matte.com/miami.*

*Continued on page 61*

# A STROLL DOWN

# DECO LANE

by Susan MacCallum Whitcomb

"It was an age of miracles, it was an age of art,
it was an age of excess, and it was an age of satire."

—F. Scott Fitzgerald, *Echoes of the Jazz Age*

The 1920s and '30s brought us flappers and gangsters, plunging stock prices and soaring skyscrapers, and plenty of headline-worthy news from the arts scene, from talking pictures and the jazz craze to fashions where pearls piled on and sequins dazzled. These decades between the two world wars also gave us an art style reflective of the changing times: art deco.

Distinguished by geometrical shapes and the use of industrial motifs that fused the decorative arts with modern technology, art deco became the architectural style of choice for train stations and big buildings across the country (think New york's Radio City Music Hall and Empire State Building).

Using a steel-and-concrete box as the foundation, architects dipped into art deco's grab bag of accessories, initially decorating facades with spheres, cylinders, and cubes. They later borrowed increasingly from industrial design, stripping elements used in ocean liners and automobiles to their streamlined essentials.

The style was also used in jewelry, furniture, textiles, and advertising. The fact that it employed inexpensive materials, such as stucco or terrazzo, helped art deco thrive during the Great Depression.

## ARCHITECTURAL HIGHLIGHTS

### FRIEZE DETAIL, CAVALIER HOTEL

The decorative stucco friezes outside the Cavalier Hotel at 1320 Ocean Drive are significant for more than aesthetic reasons. Roy France used them to add symmetry (adhering to the "Rule of Three") and accentuate the hotel's verticality by drawing the eye upward. The pattern he chose also reflected a fascination with ancient civilizations engendered by the recent rediscovery of King Tut's tomb and the Chichén Itzá temples.

Cavalier Hotel

### LOBBY FLOOR, THE WEBSTER

Terrazzo—a compound of cement and stone chips that could be poured, then polished—is a hallmark of deco design. Terrazzo floors typically had a geometric pattern, like this one in the The Webster, a 1939 building by Henry Hohauser at 1220 Collins Ave.

The Webster

### CORNER FACADE, ESSEX HOUSE HOTEL

Essex House Hotel, a 1938 gem that appears permanently anchored at 1001 Collins Avenue, is a stunning example of Maritime deco (also known as Nautical Moderne). Designed by Henry Hohauser to evoke an ocean liner, the hotel is rife with marine elements, from the rows of porthole-style windows and natty racing stripes to the towering smokestack-like sign. With a prow angled proudly into the street corner, it seems ready to steam out to sea.

Essex House Hotel

### NEON SPIRE, THE HOTEL

The name spelled vertically in eye-popping neon on the venue's iconic aluminum spire—Tiffany—bears evidence of the hotel's earlier incarnation. When the L. Murray Dixon–designed Tiffany Hotel was erected at 801 Collins Avenue in 1939, neon was still a novelty. Its use, coupled with the spire's rocket-like shape, combined to create a futuristic look influenced by the sci-fi themes then pervasive in popular culture.

The Hotel

### ENTRANCE, 1450 COLLINS AVENUE

Inspired by everything from car fenders to airplane noses, proponents of art deco's Streamline Moderne look began to soften buildings' hitherto boxy edges. But when Henry Hohauser designed Hoffman's Cafeteria in 1940 he took moderne to the max. The landmark at 1450 Collins Avenue (once Señor Frog's) has a sleek, splendidly curved facade. The restored interior echoes it through semicircular booths and rounded chair backs.

1450 Collins Avenue

# MIAMI BEACH'S ART DECO DISTRICT

With its warm beaches and tropical surroundings, Miami Beach in the early 20th century was establishing itself as America's winter playground. During the roaring '20s luxurious hostelries resembling Venetian palaces, Spanish villages, and French châteaux sprouted up. In the 1930s, middle-class tourists started coming, and more hotels had to be built. Designers like Henry Hohauser chose art deco for its affordable yet distinctive design.

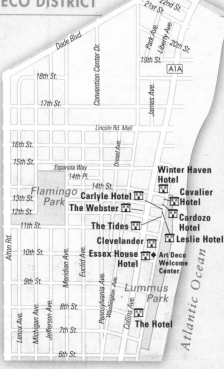

An antidote to the gloom of the Great Depression, the look was cheerful and tidy. And with the whimsical additions of portholes, colorful racing bands, and images of rolling ocean waves painted or etched on the walls, these South Beach properties created an oceanfront fantasy world for travelers.

Many of the candy-colored hotels have survived and been meticulously restored. They are among the more than 800 buildings of historical significance in South Beach's art deco district. Composing much of South Beach, the 1-square-mile district is bounded by Dade Boulevard on the north, the Atlantic Ocean on the east, 6th Street on the south, and Alton Road on the west.

Because the district as a whole was developed so rapidly and designed by like-minded architects—**Henry Hohauser, L. Murray Dixon, Albert Anis,** and their colleagues—it has amazing stylistic unity. Nevertheless, on this single street you can trace the evolution of period form from angular, vertically emphatic early deco to aerodynamically rounded Streamline Moderne. The relatively severe Cavalier and more curvaceous Cardozo are fine examples of the former and latter, respectively.

To explore the district, begin by loading up on literature in the **Art Deco Welcome Center** (✉ *1001 Ocean Dr.* ☎ *305/763–8026* ⊕ *www.mdpl.org*). If you want to view these historic properties on your own, just start walking. A four-block stroll north on Ocean Drive gets you up close to camera-ready classics: the **Clevelander** (1020), the **Tides** (1220), the **Leslie** (1244), the **Carlyle** (1250), the **Cardozo** (1300), the **Cavalier** (1320), and the **Winter Haven** (1400).

## ARCHITECTURAL TERMS

**The Rule of Three:** Early deco designers often used architectural elements in multiples of three, creating tripartite facades with triple sets of windows, eyebrows, or banding.

**Eyebrows:** Small shelf-like ledges that protruded over exterior windows were used to simultaneously provide much-needed shade and serve as a counterpoint to a building's strong vertical lines.

**Tropical Motifs:** In keeping with the setting, premises were plastered, painted, or etched with seaside images. Palm trees, sunbursts, waves, flamingoes, and the like were particularly common.

**Banding:** Enhancing the illusion that these immobile structures were rapidly speeding objects, colorful horizontal bands (also called "racing stripes") were painted on exteriors or applied with tile.

**Stripped Classic:** The most austere version of art deco (sometimes dubbed Depression Moderne) was used for buildings commissioned by the Public Works Administration.

(top) Hotel Marlin; (left) Sherbrooke Hotel; (right) U.S. Post Office in Miami Beach.

### Gianni's

**$$$$ | ITALIAN |** Set within the glitz and ostentation of Gianni Versace's former mansion, The Villa Casa Casuarina, this restaurant doles out pricey Italian-Mediterranean eats across the mansion's most prized nooks. It's more about the romantic atmosphere and eating next to Versace's storied mosaic pool than the food, which includes caviar selections, filet mignon, and black-truffle risotto. **Known for:** haute dining; wow-factor surrounds; only-in-Miami experience. $ *Average main: $52* ⊠ *The Villa Casa Casuarina, 1116 Ocean Dr., South Beach* ☎ *786/485–2200* ⊕ *vm-miamibeach.com/gianni.*

### Jaya

**$$$$ | ASIAN FUSION |** At the flagship restaurant of The Setai Miami Beach hotel, expect a pan-Asian extravaganza, representing the countries of Thailand, Vietnam, Singapore, Korea, India, China, and Japan through dishes that range from sea bass tikka to Peking duck to lobster curry. Before or after dinner, be sure to enjoy a cocktail around the harmonious courtyard reflecting pool. **Known for:** live entertainment on weekends; kimchi fried rice; dim sum. $ *Average main: $41* ⊠ *The Setai, 2001 Collins Ave., South Beach* ☎ *855/923–7899* ⊕ *www.thesetai-hotel.com/miami-beach-restaurants/jaya.*

### ★ Joe's Stone Crab

**$$$$ | SEAFOOD |** In South Beach's decidedly new-money scene, the stately Joe's Stone Crab is an old-school testament to good food and good service. Stone crabs, served with legendary mustard sauce, crispy hash browns, and creamed spinach, remain the staple at South Beach's most storied restaurant (which dates from 1913). **Known for:** best-of-the-best stone crab claws; key lime pie; no reservations (arrive very early). $ *Average main: $46* ⊠ *11 Washington Ave., South Beach* ☎ *305/673–0365, 305/673–4611 for takeout* ⊕ *www.joesstonecrab.com* ⊙ *Closed mid-May–mid-Oct. No lunch Sun. and Mon.*

### ★ Juvia

**$$$$ | JAPANESE |** High atop South Beach's design-driven 1111 Lincoln Road parking garage, rooftop Juvia commingles urban sophistication with South Beach seduction. Three renowned chefs unite to deliver an amazing eating experience that screams Japanese, Peruvian, and French all in the same breath, focusing largely on raw fish and seafood dishes. **Known for:** city and beach views; sunset cocktails on the terrace; bigeye tuna poke. $ *Average main: $35* ⊠ *1111 Lincoln Rd., South Beach* ☎ *305/763–8272* ⊕ *www.juviamiami.com* ⊙ *Closed Mon. and Tues.*

### Katsuya South Beach

**$$$ | JAPANESE |** Design impresario Philippe Starck opted to fill the smoking-hot SLS Hotel South Beach with a number of see-and-be-seen eateries, including Katsuya South Beach. At this popular Japanese restaurant, dishes come from four separate kitchens and include awesome eats like a legendary miso-marinated black cod, succulent lobster dynamite (in a creamy mushroom sauce), baked crab hand rolls, and amazing sushi rolls. **Known for:** sceney dining; spicy tuna crispy rice; high-design interiors. $ *Average main: $28* ⊠ *SLS Hotel South Beach, 1701 Collins Ave., South Beach* ⊕ *www.sbe.com/restaurants/katsuya/south-beach.*

### ★ LT Steak and Seafood

**$$$$ | STEAKHOUSE |** Miami is filled with great steak houses, but this is arguably the best. Located in the glamorous art deco open lobby of The Betsy hotel on Ocean Drive, noted chef Laurent Tourondel (of BLT Steak fame) presents a seasonally inspired menu that includes fresh seafood, sushi, the highest-quality cuts of USDA prime and certified Black Angus beef, and decadent sides (don't miss the hand-cut Parmesan truffle fries with truffle aioli). **Known for:** massive popovers; The Betsy crab cake; cocktails inspired by literary greats. $ *Average main: $38* ⊠ *The Betsy Hotel—South Beach, 1440*

*Ocean Dr., South Beach* ☎ *305/673–0044* 🌐 *www.thebetsyhotel.com/lt-restaurant.*

**★ Macchialina**
$$$ | **ITALIAN** | Framed by exposed-brick walls, decorated with daily specials on chalkboards, and packed with gregarious patrons, this local foodie hangout feels like a cozy neighborhood tavern—unless you opt to sit outside in the lush courtyard. Owner and chef Michael Pirolo nails the concept of modern Italian cuisine through a small but special selection of antipasti (try the local *burrata* and creamy polenta) and daily homemade pastas (like tagliolini *al funghi* and spaghetti *con vongole*). **Known for:** killer wine selection; melt-in-your-mouth pasta specials; devoted local following. [$] *Average main: $27* ✉ *820 Alton Rd., South Beach* ☎ *305/534–2124* 🌐 *www.macchialina.com.*

**★ MILA**
$$$$ | **ASIAN FUSION** | A swanky rooftop restaurant on Lincoln Road, MILA is a place to see and be seen while sipping well-crafted cocktails and ordering Mediterranean-Asian fusion dishes, small plates, and sushi. The stunning focal point is a Zen-like reflection pool flanked by two curtained cabanas that can be reserved for a bit of privacy while dining alfresco. **Known for:** a "dress to impress" crowd; flavorful fusion dishes like branzino tataki; top-notch cocktails. [$] *Average main: $32* ✉ *1636 Meridian Ave., South Beach* ☎ *786/706–0744* 🌐 *mila-miami.com.*

**Prime 112**
$$$$ | **STEAKHOUSE** | This wildly busy steak house is particularly prized for its highly marbleized prime beef, creamed corn with black truffles, lobster macaroni and cheese, and buzzing scene. While you stand at the bar awaiting your table—everyone has to wait, at least a little bit—you'll clamor for a drink with all facets of Miami's high society, from the city's top real estate developers and philanthropists to striking models and celebrities. **Known for:** reservations made by phone only; decadent side dishes; stellar service. [$] *Average main: $53* ✉ *112 Ocean Dr., South Beach* ☎ *305/532–8112* 🌐 *mylesrestaurantgroup.com/prime-112/.*

## Cheap Eats on South Beach 🍴

**Miami Beach is notoriously overpriced, but locals know that you don't always have to spend $30 for lunch or $45 for a dinner entrée here to have a good meal. Cheeseburger Baby (✉ *15th St. and Washington Ave.*) has been serving custom burgers, hotdogs, and shakes until 4 am since 2001. La Sandwicherie (✉ *14th St. between Collins and Washington Aves.*) is a South Beach classic that's been here since 1988, serving gourmet French sandwiches and salads.**

**★ Pubbelly Sushi**
$$ | **ASIAN FUSION** | On a residential street in SoBe's western reaches, this petite eatery attracts the who's who of beach socialites, hipsters, and the occasional tourist coming to chow down on inventive Asian-Latin small plates, sushi rolls, and grilled skewers of meat and seafood by executive chef-owner José Mendin. From bigeye tuna spicy rolls to short-rib and truffle dumplings, the menu constantly pushes the envelope on inventive cuisine, and locals simply can't get enough. **Known for:** long waits; pork belly bao buns; butter "krab" roll. [$] *Average main: $21* ✉ *1424 20th St., South Beach* ☎ *305/531–9282* 🌐 *pubbellyglobal.com.*

**Smith & Wollensky Miami Beach**
$$$$ | **STEAKHOUSE** | Enjoy one of America's premier tried-and-true steak houses in one of Miami's best locations. Situated

at the tip of South Pointe Park with fabulous views of Biscayne Bay, this waterfront outpost doles out the full range of signature cuts of 28-day, dry-aged beef and hefty sides, though the beach-conscious crowd skews toward the chilled shellfish platters and savory vegetable dishes. **Known for:** award-winning wine list; shellfish towers; 44-ounce rib eye, charred tableside. $ *Average main: $52* ✉ *1 Washington Ave., South Beach* ☎ *305/673–2800* ⊕ *www.smithandwollensky.com/our-restaurants/miami-beach.*

### Stubborn Seed

$$$$ | **AMERICAN** | Both upscale and unpretentious, this Michelin-starred contemporary American restaurant is helmed by *Top Chef* winner Jeremy Ford, who has created a small menu of exquisitely executed fresh dishes that change often. The popular prix-fixe tasting menu is known for its pâté and foie gras, as well as fresh seafood and short ribs. **Known for:** intimate setting; daily chef's tasting menu; incredible desserts. $ *Average main: $65* ✉ *101 Washington Ave., South Beach* ☎ *786/322–5211* ⊕ *stubbornseed. com.*

### Via Emilia 9

$$ | **ITALIAN** | **FAMILY** | If you're longing for a *true* taste of Italy's Emilia Romagna region and a respite from the overpriced SoBe dining scene, head to this adorable hole-in-the-wall restaurant off Alton Road. The pastas and sauces are made fresh daily, using only the best ingredients imported from the chef's homeland supplemented with local produce. **Known for:** ravioli of the day; homemade flatbreads; variety of stuffed pastas. $ *Average main: $22* ✉ *1120 15th St., South Beach* ☎ *786/216–7150* ⊕ *www.viaemilia9.com.*

### Yardbird Southern Table & Bar

$$$ | **AMERICAN** | There's a helluva lot of southern lovin' from the low country at this funky South Beach spot, where Miami's A-list puts calorie-counting aside to indulge in comfort foods and innovative drinks. The family-style menu is divided between small plates, "the bird" plates, and sides and snacks, but have no doubt that "the bird" takes center stage (or plate) here—you'll rave about Llewellyn's fine fried chicken, which requires a 27-hour marination and slow-cooking process, for weeks to come. **Known for:** smoked brisket biscuits; bourbon cocktails; chicken 'n' watermelon 'n' waffles. $ *Average main: $27* ✉ *1600 Lenox Ave., South Beach* ☎ *305/538–5220* ⊕ *www.runchickenrun. com.*

##  Hotels

If you are looking to experience the postcard image of Miami, look no farther than South Beach. Most of the hotels along Ocean Drive, Collins Avenue, and Washington Avenue are housed in history-steeped art deco buildings, each one cooler than the next. From boutique hotels to high-rise structures, all South Beach hotels are in close proximity to the beach and never far from the action. Most hotels here cost a pretty penny and for good reason. They are more of an experience than a place to crash (think designer lobbies, some of the world's best pool scenes, and unparalleled people-watching).

### The Balfour Hotel

$ | **HOTEL** | In South Beach's SoFi (South of Fifth) neighborhood, the boutique Lord Balfour hotel is a great fit for young travelers who want to get out and experience South Beach (as opposed to sitting at a resort all day) and then return to stylish digs. **Pros:** great European crowd; pleasant interior design; affordable pricing. **Cons:** small rooms and smaller bathrooms; occasional street noise from some rooms; small pool. $ *Rooms from: $175* ✉ *350 Ocean Dr., South Beach* ☎ *855/471–2739* ⊕ *www.thebalfourmiamibeach.com* ↩ *64 rooms* ⊙ *No Meals.*

**★ The Betsy**

**$$$ | HOTEL** | After a massive expansion, the original Betsy Ross Hotel (christened the "Colonial" wing) has been joined with what was the neighboring, historic Carlton Hotel to create a retro-chic, art deco treasure that delivers the full-throttle South Beach experience with style, pizzazz, and a big-time cultural bonus: year-round programs include poetry readings, live jazz, and art shows. **Pros:** unbeatable location; super-fashionable; great beach club. **Cons:** confusing hotel layout; great pet-friendly program but fee attached; pool sometimes crowded. [$] *Rooms from: $350* ✉ *1440 Ocean Dr., South Beach* ☎ *844/539–2840* 🌐 *www.thebetsyhotel.com* 🛏 *130 rooms* 🍴 *No Meals.*

**Cadet Hotel**

**$ | HOTEL** | A former home to World War II officer cadets, this gem has been reimagined as an oasis in South Beach, offering the antithesis of the sometimes maddening jet-set scene, with 34 distinctive rooms exuding understated luxury. **Pros:** excellent service; lovely garden; historical value. **Cons:** tiny swimming pool; limited appeal for the party crowd; small bathrooms. [$] *Rooms from: $169* ✉ *1701 James Ave., South Beach* ☎ *305/672–6688* 🌐 *cadethotel.com* 🛏 *34 rooms* 🍴 *No Meals.*

**Dream South Beach**

**$$ | HOTEL** | This trendy boutique hotel, which is right in the center of the South Beach action, merges two refurbished, archetypal, 1939 art deco buildings into a single project of eclectic modernism, with whimsically decorated interiors that are at once trippy and cool. **Pros:** chef Ralph Pagano's Naked Taco restaurant downstairs; heated rooftop pool; complimentary sparkling wine on arrival. **Cons:** limited natural light in some rooms; lack of bathroom privacy; not on the beach. [$] *Rooms from: $209* ✉ *1111 Collins Ave., South Beach* ☎ *305/673–4747* 🌐 *www.dreamhotels.com/south-beach* 🛏 *108 rooms* 🍴 *No Meals.*

**Gale South Beach**

**$$ | HOTEL** | Though it's not directly on the beach—it's across the street—this boutique hotel offers fabulous, style- and value-conscious accommodations in the heart of South Beach with plenty of art deco history to boot. **Pros:** Regent Cocktail Club downstairs; Pizza Room Service button on guestroom phones; crisp, clean-lined rooms. **Cons:** smaller rooms; busy pool area; crowded hallways. [$] *Rooms from: $299* ✉ *1690 Collins Ave., South Beach* ☎ *305/673–0199* 🌐 *www.galehotel.com* 🛏 *87 rooms* 🍴 *No Meals.*

**★ the goodtime hotel**

**$$ | HOTEL** | The Pharrell Williams song "Happy" is the perfect accompaniment to the 266-room hotel that he rolled out with business partner David Grutman. **Pros:** buzzy pool with daybeds; good on-site restaurant, strawberry moon; pastel decor evokes the surrounding art deco area. **Cons:** no fridges in rooms; a few avenues from the beach; rooms are on the smaller side. [$] *Rooms from: $200* ✉ *601 Washington Ave., South Beach* ☎ *786/687-0234* 🌐 *www.thegoodtimehotel.com* 🛏 *266 rooms* 🍴 *No Meals.*

**Hilton Bentley Miami/South Beach**

**$$$ | HOTEL | FAMILY** | Not to be confused with the budget Bentley Hotel down the street, the Hilton Bentley Miami is a contemporary, design-driven, and artsy boutique hotel in the emerging and trendy SoFi (South of Fifth) District, offering families just the right mix of South Beach flavor and wholesome fun while still providing couples a romantic base without any party madness. **Pros:** quiet location; rooms redeemable with points; family-friendly. **Cons:** small pool; small lobby; daily resort charge. [$] *Rooms from: $389* ✉ *101 Ocean Dr., South Beach* ☎ *305/938–4600* 🌐 *www.hilton.com* 🛏 *109 rooms* 🍴 *No Meals.*

**Hotel Victor**

$$$ | **HOTEL** | At the sleek Hotel Victor, guest rooms are equipped with Yabu Pushelberg–designed interiors invoking a modern beach cabana vibe while a sexy infinity-edge pool overlooks Ocean Drive and the beach. **Pros:** late-night pool deck; complimentary bikes; complimentary fruit and water by the pool. **Cons:** small rooms; noisy crowds at restaurants downstairs; no dedicated area on the beach. [$] *Rooms from: $329* ✉ *1144 Ocean Dr., South Beach* ☎ *305/908–1462* 🌐 *www.hotelvictorsouthbeach.com* 🛏 *91 rooms* 🍴 *No Meals.*

**★ Kimpton Angler's Hotel**

$$$$ | **HOTEL** | At this enclave of old and new South Beach, a contemporary, 85-room tower with a rooftop pool neighbors several 1930s-era villas and modern low-rise units, together capturing the feel of a sophisticated private villa community. **Pros:** gardened private retreat; pet-friendly (no fee); daily complimentary wine hour. **Cons:** no gym; not directly on beach; most units have only showers. [$] *Rooms from: $427* ✉ *660 Washington Ave., South Beach* ☎ *305/534–9600* 🌐 *www.anglershotelmiami.com* 🛏 *132 rooms* 🍴 *No Meals.*

**Kimpton Surfcomber Miami, South Beach**

$$ | **HOTEL** | As part of the hip Kimpton Hotel group, South Beach's legendary Surfcomber hotel reflects a vintage luxe aesthetic and an ocean-side freshness as well as a reasonable price point that packs the place with a young, sophisticated, yet unpretentious crowd. **Pros:** frozen spiked cappuccino at High Tide Bar; no pet fee; daily complimentary activities offered. **Cons:** small bathrooms; front desk often busy; often congested valet. [$] *Rooms from: $299* ✉ *1717 Collins Ave., South Beach* ☎ *305/532–7715* 🌐 *www.surfcomber.com* 🛏 *186 rooms* 🍴 *No Meals.*

**Lennox Hotel**

$$ | **HOTEL** | Providing understated luxury in the middle of the Collins Avenue action, this small, sophisticated hotel occupies a beautifully renovated art deco building (formerly the historic Peter Miller Hotel) and is a block from the beach. **Pros:** complimentary chairs on the beach; champagne vending machine and bar by the pool; original art deco details. **Cons:** not directly on the beach; pool is small; no beach views from rooms. [$] *Rooms from: $220* ✉ *1900 Collins Ave., South Beach* ☎ *305/531–6800* 🌐 *www.lennox-miamibeach.com* 🛏 *119 rooms* 🍴 *No Meals.*

**Loews Miami Beach Hotel**

$$$$ | **HOTEL** | **FAMILY** | This two-tower megahotel has 790 rooms with a soothing, sea-inspired motif, top-tier amenities, a massive spa, a great pool, and direct beachfront access, making it a great choice for families, businesspeople, groups, and pet lovers. **Pros:** NYC-famed Rao's Italian restaurant on site; resort atmosphere; pets welcome. **Cons:** insanely large; constantly crowded; pets desperate to go will need to wait several minutes to make it to the grass. [$] *Rooms from: $459* ✉ *1601 Collins Ave., South Beach* ☎ *305/604–1601, 855/757–2061 for reservations* 🌐 *www.loewshotels.com/miami-beach* 🛏 *790 rooms* 🍴 *No Meals.*

**Mondrian South Beach**

$$$ | **HOTEL** | Located along the beach's lesser-known western perimeter and overlooking the bay, this hotel recently underwent a multimillion-dollar transformation; the focal points are a new beach club, a spa, and a happening pool scene. **Pros:** cabana-lined pool with bay views; perfect sunsets; party vibe. **Cons:** limited dining options; a short walk from most of the action; no direct beach access. [$] *Rooms from: $350* ✉ *1100 West Ave.,*

*South Beach* ☎ *305/514–1500* 🌐 *www.sbe.com/hotels/mondrian/south-beach* 🛏 *220 rooms* 🍴 *No Meals.*

**National Hotel**

$$$ | **HOTEL** | The adults-only National Hotel is a glorious time capsule that honors its distinct art deco heritage (the building itself and wood pieces in the lobby date from 1939, and new chocolate- and gold-hue furnishings look period-appropriate) while trying to keep up with SoBe's glossy newcomers (rotating art installations complement the throwback glamour). **Pros:** cabana suites; beautiful night-lights around pool area; art deco Blues Bar. **Cons:** street noise on the weekends; gym located downstairs in back of house; no spa. [$] *Rooms from: $355* ✉ *1677 Collins Ave., South Beach* ☎ *305/532–2311* 🌐 *www.nationalhotel.com* 🛏 *152 rooms* 🍴 *No Meals.*

**★ 1 Hotel South Beach**

$$$$ | **RESORT** | This snazzy eco-minded hotel delivers a picturesque, nature-inspired aesthetic throughout the common spaces and room interiors (think heavy use of repurposed wood, living walls, preserved moss, and glassware from recycled wine bottles) and offers a choice of four swimming pools (including the best rooftop one in Florida), a luxurious beach club featuring Wave, a sea-to-table restaurant, and an excellent swath of beach. **Pros:** even basic level rooms are great; vibrant crowd; sustainability mantra. **Cons:** many rooms face street; constantly busy; balcony furniture a bit worn. [$] *Rooms from: $499* ✉ *2341 Collins Ave., South Beach* ☎ *305/604–1000* 🌐 *www.1hotels.com/south-beach* 🛏 *426 rooms* 🍴 *No Meals.*

**The Ritz-Carlton, South Beach**

$$$ | **HOTEL** | **FAMILY** | The recently renovated Ritz-Carlton is a trendy beachfront bombshell, with a dynamite staff, a snazzy Club Lounge, and a long pool deck that leads right out to the beach. **Pros:** great service; pool with VIP cabanas; unbeatable location. **Cons:** larger property; iconic but expensive; $40/night resort fee. [$] *Rooms from: $391* ✉ *1 Lincoln Rd., South Beach* ☎ *786/276–4000* 🌐 *www.ritzcarlton.com* 🛏 *376 rooms* 🍴 *No Meals.*

**Royal Palm South Beach Miami**

$$$ | **RESORT** | Royal Palm South Beach Miami, now part of Marriott's individualistic Tribute Portfolio, is a daily celebration of art deco, modernity, and design detail. **Pros:** in the heart of the action; photogenic pool areas; social lobby and excellent in-house restaurant, Byblos. **Cons:** small driveway for entering; older elevators; needs a bed refresh. [$] *Rooms from: $321* ✉ *1545 Collins Ave., South Beach* ☎ *305/604–5700, 866/716–8147 reservations* 🌐 *www.royalpalmsouthbeach.com* 🛏 *393 rooms* 🍴 *No Meals.*

**The Sagamore South Beach, the Art Hotel**

$$$$ | **HOTEL** | This supersleek, all-white, all-suites hotel in the middle of the action looks and feels like an edgy art gallery, filled with brilliant contemporary works, the perfect complement to the posh, gargantuan, 500-square-foot crash pads. **Pros:** sensational pool; great location; good rate specials. **Cons:** can be quiet on weekdays; daily resort fee; limited on-site dining. [$] *Rooms from: $429* ✉ *1671 Collins Ave., South Beach* ☎ *305/535–8088* 🌐 *www.sagamorehotel.com* 🛏 *101 suites* 🍴 *No Meals.*

**★ The Setai Miami Beach**

$$$$ | **RESORT** | This opulent, all-suites hotel feels like an Asian museum: serene and beautiful, with heavy granite furniture lifted by orange accents, warm candlelight, and the soft bubble of seemingly endless ponds complemented by three oceanfront infinity pools (heated to different temperatures) that further spill onto the beach's velvety sands. **Pros:** quiet and classy; beautiful grounds; excellent dining and spa. **Cons:** TVs are far from the beds; busy pool area; many rooms lack ocean views. [$] *Rooms from: $878* ✉ *2001 Collins Ave., South Beach* ☎ *305/520–6111, 888/625–7500*

*reservations* 🌐 *www.thesetaihotel.com* 🛏 *130 suites* 🍴 *No Meals.*

**Shelborne South Beach**

**$$ | RESORT** | The famed Morris Lapidus–designed Shelborne hotel is a retro-chic art deco treasure with stylish yet functional rooms and plenty of oh-so–South Beach amenities, including the beach's most oversized poolside cabanas (which also happen to be air-conditioned), a slick pool deck, a private beach club, and a location that offers direct access to downy sands, art deco, and superlative shopping. **Pros:** ideal location; fantastic spa; heated pool and oversize cabanas. **Cons:** entry-level rooms small; lack of balconies; some odd large spaces near lobby. [$] *Rooms from: $259* ✉ *1801 Collins Ave., South Beach* ☎ *305/704–3668* 🌐 *www.shelborne.com* 🛏 *200 rooms* 🍴 *No Meals.*

**SLS South Beach**

**$$$$ | RESORT** | Housed in a restored 1939 art deco building, SLS South Beach exudes beachfront sophistication over a commingling of Latin and Asian inspiration in its common areas, plus dining outposts The Bazaar South Beach, Katsuya South Beach, and Hyde Beach Miami—an 8,000-square-foot masterpiece of pool, beach, and cabanas attracting glitterati daily. **Pros:** great in-house restaurants; masterful design; fun pool scene. **Cons:** some small rooms; no lobby per se; $40 per day resort fee. [$] *Rooms from: $413* ✉ *1701 Collins Ave., South Beach* ☎ *305/674–1701* 🌐 *www.sbe.com/hotels/sls-hotels/south-beach* 🛏 *140 rooms* 🍴 *No Meals.*

**★ W South Beach**

**$$$$ | HOTEL** | Fun, fresh, and funky, the W South Beach flaunts some of the nicest rooms in South Beach—even the entry category evokes a wow factor—each with its own kitchen and balcony with ocean views. **Pros:** pool scene; giant Hello Kitty fountain; three in-house restaurants and bars. **Cons:** not a classic art deco building; crowded pool area; loud music at pool. [$] *Rooms from: $494* ✉ *2201 Collins Ave., South Beach* ☎ *305/938–3000* 🌐 *www.wsouthbeach.com* 🛏 *248 rooms* 🍴 *No Meals.*

**Z Ocean Hotel**

**$$ | HOTEL** | This is definitely not your grandmother's Crowne Plaza: the lauded firm of Arquitectonica designed this glossy and bold all-suites hideaway, including 27 rooftop suites endowed with terraces, each complete with Jacuzzi, plush chaise lounges, and a view of the South Beach skyline. **Pros:** across street from beach; huge rooms; green, earth-friendly hotelwide initiatives. **Cons:** tiny gym; lack of privacy on rooftop suite decks; rooms could use a refresh. [$] *Rooms from: $275* ✉ *1437 Collins Ave., South Beach* ☎ *305/672–4554* 🌐 *www.zoceanhotelsouthbeach.com* 🛏 *79 suites* 🍴 *No Meals.*

## 🍸 Nightlife

**Lost Weekend**

**BARS** | Play pinball, pool, or air hockey; chow down on bar grub; and order a few rounds from the full bar (which includes 150 different beer varieties) at this pool hall–resto–dive bar on quaint Española Way. Mingle with an eclectic crowd, from visiting yuppies to local drag queens to celebs on the down-low. It's so South Beach! ✉ *218 Española Way, South Beach* ☎ *305/672–1707* 🌐 *www.sub-culture.org/lost-weekend-miami.*

**★ Mac's Club Deuce**

**BARS** | Smoky, dark, and delightfully unpolished, this complete dive bar (cash only) is anything but what you'd expect from glitzy South Beach. Once a favorite of the late Anthony Bourdain, this spot is decorated with neon signs that were a gift when they hosted the *Miami Vice* wrap party in the '80s. Happy hour takes place from 8 am to 5 pm, and you'll always find an eclectic crowd at the bar at all hours. ✉ *222 14th St., South Beach*

Cars whiz by the Avalon hotel and other art deco architecture on Ocean Drive, South Beach.

☎ 305/531–6200 ⊕ www.macsclub-deuce.com.

### Minibar Miami

**BARS** | Aptly named, this spot is very small, but what it lacks in space it makes up for in atmosphere, enhanced by jewel-toned palm tree decor and a friendly staff. The menu changes seasonally but is always inspired by the 305: drinks are named after local chefs, neighborhoods, or commonly used Miami phrases. ⊠ *The Meridian Hotel, 418 Meridian Ave., Miami* ☎ 786/690-1858 ⊕ *www.minibarmiami. com.*

### Nikki Beach Miami Beach

**GATHERING PLACES** | Smack-dab on the beach, the full-service Nikki Beach is filled more with suburbanites and tourists than the in-crowd but promises plenty of fun nevertheless. The beach club is typically a daytime affair, opening at 10 am and closing at 6 pm (though there are often special evening events, namely on Sunday). Visitors can get their food and drink in the hammocks and beach beds (expect DJ-led tunes on weekends and rental fees all days). Sunday brunch at the club's restaurant is pretty spectacular with a true South Beach party atmosphere. ⊠ *1 Ocean Dr., South Beach* ☎ 305/538–1111 ⊕ *miami-beach. nikkibeach.com.*

### Palace

**THEMED ENTERTAINMENT** | South Beach's gay heyday continues at this fierce oceanfront bar where folks gay, straight, and everything in between—everyone's welcome—come to revel in good times, cheap cocktails, and fierce drag performances. On weekdays the bar gets busiest in the early evening, but on weekends it's all about the drag brunch. It's a true showstopper—or car-stopper, shall we say: using Ocean Drive as a stage, drag queens direct oncoming traffic with street-side splits and acrobatic tricks in heels. ⊠ *1052 Ocean Dr., South Beach* ☎ 305/531–7234 ⊕ *palacesouth-beach.com.*

### The ScapeGoat

**BARS** | At this hole-in-the-wall bar, the people-watching is just as wonderful as the drinks. The menu features classic cocktails with a large focus on whiskeys and American-made spirits. It's the kind of place you'll find yourself heading for a nightcap after a fancy South Beach dinner, but if you stop in on the earlier side, there's happy hour every day from 5 to 8 pm. ⊠ *100 Collins Ave., CU4, Miami* ☎ *786/275-6488* ⊕ *www.scapegoatsobe. com.*

### ★ Sweet Liberty
**BARS** | This tropical-chic, come-as-you-are cocktail lounge and restaurant has won all kinds of national and local awards for its incredible spirit-forward cocktails and fresh-and-funky vibe. For something extra special, reserve the Bartender's Table, which operates like a chef's table, but here you're in the thick of the bar action, tasting libations. ■**TIP**→ **Food from a full menu created by co-owner and James Beard Award winner Michelle Bernstein is served until 4 am.** ⊠ *237-B 20th St., South Beach* ☎ *305/763-8217* ⊕ *mysweetliberty.com.*

### Swizzle Rum Bar & Drinkery
**COCKTAIL LOUNGES** | Easy to miss if you don't know what you're looking for, this rum-filled drinking den is hidden just past the lobby of The Stiles Hotel. Here, bartenders in sleek outfits craft bespoke cocktails until the wee hours of the morning. If tiki-inspired drinks are what you're craving, sister bar Delirio Tiki Bar by Swizzle in the space next door has a menu full of them. ⊠ *The Stiles Hotel, 1112 Collins Ave., Miami* ⊕ *www.swizzlerumbardrinkery.com.*

### TWIST
**DANCE CLUBS** | TWIST is a gay institution in South Beach, having been the late-night go-to place for decades, filling to capacity around 2 am after the beach's fly-by-night bars and more established lounges begin to die down (though it's open daily from 1 pm to 5 am). There's never a cover here—not even on holidays or during gay-pride events—and there are a whopping seven different bars and dance

floors spread over two levels and patios. ⊠ *1057 Washington Ave., South Beach* ☎ *305/538-9478* ⊕ *www.twistsobe.com.*

### Villa Azur
**WINE BARS** | St. Tropez meets South Beach at this sceney, French resto-lounge with prolific alfresco seating in a spacious, tree-lined courtyard and personality-driven relaxation areas indoors (replete with swaying chandeliers, white tufted couches, and whimsically accessorized library shelves). Although Veuve Clicquot is a staple among patrons, the tropical-inspired cocktails and the selection from the in-house wine cellar, La Cave d'Azur, also impress. ⊠ *309 23rd St., South Beach* ☎ *305/763-8688* ⊕ *www.villaazurmiamibeach.com.*

### Watr at the Rooftop
**COCKTAIL LOUNGES** | Come 7 pm, Miami Beach's premier rooftop opens to the public as a full-service bar, restaurant, and lounge (before that it is exclusive to guests of the 1 Hotel South Beach). Up in the skies, expect tropically inspired drinks like pineapple and mint caipirinhas overlooking the twinkle of city lights, the sleek rooftop pool, and the lapping waves of the Atlantic Ocean. ⊠ *1 Hotel South Beach, 2341 Collins Ave., South Beach* ☎ *305/604-6580* ⊕ *www.1hotels. com/south-beach.*

## 🛍 Shopping

### Collins Avenue
**NEIGHBORHOODS** | Give your plastic a workout in South Beach shopping at the many high-profile tenants on this densely packed stretch of Collins between 5th and 8th Streets, with stores like FREE People, The Webster, Vans, and Armani Exchange. Sprinkled among the upscale vendors are hair salons, spas, cafés, and such familiar stores as Gap and Sephora. ⊠ *Collins Ave., South Beach* ✛ *Between 5th and 8th sts.* ⊕ *www.lincolnroadmall. com/shopping/collins-avenue.*

**Consign of the Times**

JEWELRY & WATCHES | This women's luxury resale specialist dutifully delivers on all promises. Discover a wealth of vintage and consignment items by top designers at pre-owned prices, including Chanel suits, Fendi bags, and Celine and Prada treasures. The shoes and handbag selections are particularly awesome. ⌧ *1935 West Ave., South Beach* ☎ *305/535–0811* ⊕ *www.consignofthetimes.com.*

**frankie.**

JEWELRY & WATCHES | Expect high style and eye-catching garments at this boutique. The studio-like setting matches the highly edited collection of fashionista favorites (previous brands have included Bec & Bridge, Sam&Lavi, IRO, and For Love & Lemons). Co-owner Cheryl Herger also designs her own private-label line especially for frankie. Skirts and dresses with interesting silhouettes, uniquely cut tops, and swimwear almost too good for just the pool are interspersed with easy-chic basics. ⌧ *1891 Purdy Ave., South Beach* ☎ *786/479–4898* ⊕ *www.frankiemiami.com.*

**★ Lincoln Road Mall**

NEIGHBORHOODS | The eight-block-long pedestrian mall between Alton Road and Washington Avenue is home to more than 100 shops, art galleries, restaurants, and cafés, as well as the renovated Colony Theatre. A see-and-be-seen theme is underscored by outdoor seating at every restaurant, where tourists and locals lounge and discuss the people (and pet) parade passing by. Due to high rents, you are more likely to see big corporate stores like J.Crew, H&M, and Victoria's Secret than original boutiques. Nevertheless, a few emporiums and stores with unique personalities remain, along with a number of top-notch restaurants, like Juvia and MILA. ⌧ *Lincoln Rd., South Beach* ✢ *Between Alton Rd. and Washington Ave.* ⊕ *www.lincolnroadmall.com.*

**★ Romero Britto Fine Art Gallery**

ANTIQUES & COLLECTIBLES | Though exhibited throughout galleries and museums in more than 100 countries, the vibrant, pop art creations by Brazilian artist Romero Britto have become most synonymous with Miami's playful spirit. His flagship gallery showcases original paintings and limited-edition sculptures for sale. Collectibles, fine art prints, and his signature interpretations in collaboration with some of America's most iconic characters and brands, including Disney and Coca-Cola, can be found at the Britto Concept store down the street at 532 Lincoln Road. ⌧ *1102 Lincoln Rd., South Beach* ☎ *305/531–8821* ⊕ *www.britto.com.*

**★ Showfields**

MARKET | FAMILY | Dubbing itself the "most interesting store in the world," Showfields curates everything from artwork to clothing to food to home goods created by local vendors as well as large trendy brands like Playboy, Dolce Vita, and Spanx. They make it a mission to feature women-owned, local, and/or BIPOC-owned brands, and they rotate products and interactive displays every few months, making it feel like a totally different store with each visit. ⌧ *530 Lincoln Rd., South Beach* ☎ *305/531-0672* ⊕ *www.showfields.com/pages/miami.*

**★ The Webster South Beach**

OTHER SPECIALTY STORE | Occupying an entire circa-1939 art deco building, The Webster's flagship (and original) location is a tri-level, 20,000-square-foot, one-stop shop for fashionistas. This retail sanctuary carries ready-to-wear fashions by more than 100 top designers, plus in-store exclusive shirts, candles, books, and random trendy items you might need for your South Beach experience—a kind of haute Urban Outfitters for grown-ups. ⌧ *1220 Collins Ave., South Beach* ☎ *305/674–7899* ⊕ *thewebster.com/stores/south-beach.*

## Activities

**Art Deco Walking Tour**
**WALKING TOURS | FAMILY** | Operated by the Miami Design Preservation League, a two-hour guided walking tour departs from the league's welcome center at Ocean Drive and 10th Street. It starts at 10 am and 5 pm daily. Alternatively, you can go at your own pace with the league's self-guided audio tour, which also takes roughly an hour and a half. ✉ *1001 Ocean Dr., South Beach* ☎ *305/763–8026* 🌐 *mdpl.org/tours/* 🎟 *$35 ($30 for seniors, veterans, and students) guided tour.*

★ **Miami Beach Bicycle Center**
**BIKING** | If you don't want to opt for the hassle of Citi Bike or if you want wheels with some style on South Beach, rent a bike from this shop near Ocean Drive. They have all types of two-wheelers, from e-bikes to Carbon Road and Fat Sand bikes, available by the hour, day, or week (and easily booked online). Prices are cheapest for single-speed beach cruisers at $24 per day, or $100 for the week. All bike rentals include locks, helmets, and baskets. ✉ *746 5th St., South Beach* ☎ *305/674–0150* 🌐 *www.bikemiamibeach.com.*

**Tarpoon Lagoon Diving Center**
**DIVING & SNORKELING | FAMILY** | Dedicated to all things ocean, this PADI five-star dive shop offers multiple diving and snorkeling trips weekly. For those interested in learning how to dive, they offer a range of courses depending on your current skill level. If you're already a pro, head out with them to check out Neptune Memorial Reef–a nearby underwater cemetery that divers love to explore. ✉ *300 Alton Rd., Suite 110, South Beach* ☎ *305/532–1445* 🌐 *www.tarpoonlagoon.com.*

# Fisher and Belle Islands

A private island community near the southern tip of South Beach, Fisher Island is accessible only by the island's ferry service. The island is predominantly residential, with a few hotel rooms on offer at Fisher Island Club. Belle Island is a small island connected to both the mainland and Miami Beach by road. It is a mile north of South Beach and just west over the Venetian Causeway.

## Hotels

**Fisher Island Club**
**$$$$ | RESORT** | An exclusive private island, just south of Miami Beach but accessible only by ferry, Fisher Island houses an upscale residential community that includes a small inventory of overnight accommodations, including opulent cottages, villas, and junior suites, which surround the island's original 1920s-era Vanderbilt mansion. **Pros:** great private beaches; never crowded; varied on-island dining choices. **Cons:** not the warmest fellow guests; limited rooms; only accessible by ferry. [$] *Rooms from: $1300* ✉ *1 Fisher Island Dr., Fisher Island* ☎ *305/535–6000* 🌐 *www.fisherislandclub.com* 🛏 *60 rooms* 🍴 *No Meals.*

**The Standard Spa, Miami Beach**
**$$$ | RESORT** | An extension of André Balazs's trendy and hip—yet budget-conscious—brand, this shabby-chic boutique hotel is a mile from South Beach on an island just over the Venetian Causeway and has among South Florida's most renowned spas, trendiest bars, and hottest pool scenes. **Pros:** free bike rentals; swank pool scene; great spa. **Cons:** slight trek to South Beach; small rooms with no views; nonguests visiting property spa and restaurants. [$] *Rooms from: $324* ✉ *40 Island Ave., Belle Isle* ☎ *305/673–1717* 🌐 *www.standardhotels.com/miami/properties/miami-beach* 🛏 *105 rooms* 🍴 *No Meals.*

## 🍸 Nightlife

**Lido Bayside Grill**

**GATHERING PLACES** | By day, the colorful and chic waterfront alfresco restaurant is an idyllic place to kick back, sip cocktails, and watch bay-side boats and poolside hotties go by. In the evening, lights braided into the surrounding trees illuminate the terrace, sparking a seductive atmosphere. On weekdays from 4 to 7, the bar offers a locals-frequented happy hour. ✉ *The Standard Spa, Miami Beach, 40 Island Ave., Belle Isle* ☎ *786/245–0880* 🌐 *www.lidobayside.com.*

**Monterrey Bar**

**COCKTAIL LOUNGES** | Dimly lit and romantic, this cocktail lounge located on the ground floor of The Standard transports its guests to another era with retro decor and velvet interiors. Its name pays homage to the hotel's roots as it was once The Monterrey Motel. The menu features twists on celebrated classics, like the G&T made with Suntory Roku botanical gin, elderflower tonic, citrus elixir, and sage aromatics. Bites like truffled tater tots and grilled swordfish belly will make your taste buds dance. ✉ *The Standard, 40 Island Ave., Miami* ☎ *305/673–1717* 🌐 *www.standardhotels.com/miami/features/monterrey-bar.*

# Mid-Beach

Where does South Beach end and Mid-Beach begin? North of 23rd Street, Collins Avenue curves its way to 44th Street, where it takes a sharp left turn after running into Soho House Miami and then the Fontainebleau resort. The area between these two points—and up until 63rd Street—is officially Mid-Beach.

The area has been experiencing a renaissance thanks to major revival projects. Most recently, Argentinean developer Alan Faena completed the neighborhood's latest $1 billion-plus mission: to restore the historic buildings along Collins Avenue from 32nd to 36th Streets, creating new hotels, condos, and cultural institutions to collectively become the Miami Beach Faena District. And the results have been nothing short of amazing.

## 🍴 Restaurants

**Cecconi's Miami Beach**

**$$$$** | **ITALIAN** | The wait for a table at this outpost of the legendary Italian restaurant is just as long as for its counterparts in West Hollywood and London. Expect heavy portions of atmosphere: it's a real scene of who's who and who's eating what, cast in a seductive, vintage-chic setting across the courtyard of Soho Beach House. **Known for:** light and succulent fish carpaccios; truffle pizza; beautiful lighting. [$] *Average main: $35* ✉ *Soho Beach House Miami, 4385 Collins Ave., Mid-Beach* ☎ *786/507–7902* 🌐 *www.cecconismiamibeach.com.*

★ **Hakkasan Miami**

**$$$$** | **CANTONESE** | This stateside sibling of the Michelin-star London restaurant brings the haute-Chinese-food movement to South Florida, adding pan-Asian flair to even quite simple and authentic Cantonese recipes and producing an entire menu that can be classified as blow-your-mind delicious. Superb eats notwithstanding, another reason to experience Hakkasan is that it's arguably the sexiest, best-looking restaurant on Miami Beach. **Known for:** dim sum perfected; roasted silver cod with champagne and honey; high-design interiors, including teak walls. [$] *Average main: $52* ✉ *Fontainebleau Miami Beach, 4441 Collins Ave., 4th fl., Mid-Beach* ☎ *786/276–1388 after 4 pm, 877/326–7412 before 4 pm* 🌐 *hakkasan.com/miami/* 🕒 *No lunch weekdays.*

**Matador Room**

**$$$** | **SPANISH** | In one of Miami's most captivating and seductive settings, this headline restaurant by celebrity-chef Jean-Georges Vongerichten fuses Spanish, Caribbean, and Latin American gastronomy while focusing on local products, resulting in a diverse collection of small and large plates. Indulge in tropically inspired plates like avocado pizza, Florida Keys shrimp in "Agua Diablo," and grilled Florida black-grouper tacos. **Known for:** "Light & Bright" beach-conscious options; seasonal craft cocktails; stunning terrace for outdoor dining. $ *Average main: $29* ✉ *The Miami Beach EDITION, 2901 Collins Ave., Mid-Beach* ☎ *786/257–4600* ⊕ *www.matadorroom. com.*

## 🛏 Hotels

The stretch of Miami Beach called Mid-Beach is undergoing a renaissance, as formerly run-down hotels are renovated and new hotels and condos are built. Most locals—and visitors—even prefer it to South Beach nowadays.

### Circa 39
**$$ | HOTEL |** Located in the heart of Mid-Beach, this stylish yet affordable boutique hotel has tropical-inspired rooms, as well as a pool and sun deck complete with cabanas and umbrella-shaded chaises that invite all-day lounging. **Pros:** lounge areas in the WunderGarden; beach chairs provided; art deco fireplace. **Cons:** not on the beach side of Collins Avenue; bathrooms have showers only; no spa. $ *Rooms from: $299* ✉ *3900 Collins Ave., Mid-Beach* ☎ *305/538–4900* ⊕ *www.circa39.com* ⤴ *97 rooms* ❍ *No Meals.*

### ★ The Confidante
**$$$ | RESORT |** Part of Hyatt's Unbound Collection, this hotel in Miami's burgeoning Mid-Beach district is a beachfront classic art deco building reinvented by Martin Brudnizki to channel a colorful, modern incarnation of 1950s Florida glamour, packed with all the trappings one would covet in a Miami beachfront experience.

**Pros:** highly photogenic pool area; alfresco spa and complimentary fitness classes; Hyatt points accepted for stays. **Cons:** day passes sometimes sold to nonguests; entry-level rooms are on the small side; dark hallways. $ *Rooms from: $349* ✉ *4041 Collins Ave., Mid-Beach* ☎ *304/424–1234* ⊕ *www.theconfidante-hotel.com* ⤴ *363 rooms* ❍ *No Meals.*

### Eden Roc Miami Beach
**$$$ | RESORT |** This grand 1950s hotel designed by Morris Lapidus is a lesson in old-school glamour meets modern-day swagger after hundreds of millions in renovations and expansions over the past decade (including the addition of the hotel-within-a-hotel concept Nobu Hotel Miami Beach). **Pros:** on-site Nobu and Ocean Social restaurants; great pools; revival of Golden Age glamour. **Cons:** expensive parking; $35 charge for mini-refrigerator; some small bathrooms. $ *Rooms from: $330* ✉ *4525 Collins Ave., Mid-Beach* ☎ *786/801–6886* ⊕ *www.edenrochotelmiami.com* ⤴ *345 rooms* ❍ *No Meals.*

### ★ Faena Hotel Miami Beach
**$$$$ | RESORT |** The gem of hotelier Alan Faena's Faena Arts District, this jaw-dropping beachfront hotel is as luxurious as it gets, with top-notch dining, a pampering spa, and art that includes larger-than-life murals and a gilded mammoth by Damien Hirst. **Pros:** glamorous design; excellent service; spectacular beach club. **Cons:** pricey; construction in neighborhood; dark hallways. $ *Rooms from: $900* ✉ *3201 Collins Ave., Mid-Beach* ☎ *305/535–4697* ⊕ *www.faena.com/miami-beach* ⤴ *169 rooms* ❍ *No Meals.*

### ★ Fontainebleau Miami Beach
**$$$$ | RESORT | FAMILY |** Vegas meets art deco at Miami's largest hotel, which has more than 1,500 rooms (in four separate towers, almost half of which are suites), 12 renowned restaurants and lounges, LIV nightclub, several pools with cabana islands, a state-of-the-art fitness center, and a 40,000-square-foot spa.

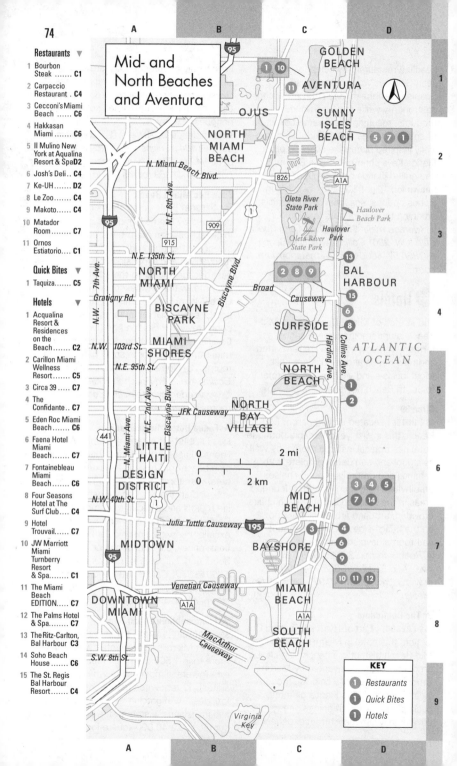

Mid- and North Beaches and Aventura

**Pros:** expansive pool and beach areas; historic allure; great nightlife. **Cons:** lots of nonguests visiting grounds; massive size; loud, weekend parties outside. [$] *Rooms from: $549* ✉ *4441 Collins Ave., Mid-Beach* ☎ *305/535–3283, 800/548–8886* 🌐 *www.fontainebleau.com* 🛏 *1504 rooms* 🍴 *No Meals.*

**Hotel Trouvail**

$ | **HOTEL** | Tucked away on Indian Creek Drive inside a restored art deco building (once the Greenbrier Hotel) is this boho-chic boutique hotel with oversize rooms and suites, each impeccably decorated with retro Mediterranean flair. **Pros:** located on a quiet street; pool feels like a private tropical oasis; house bicycles. **Cons:** $25 per night self-parking; not directly on the beach; never-ending construction in surrounding area. [$] *Rooms from: $110* ✉ *3101 Indian Creek Dr., Mid-Beach* ☎ *305/763–8006* 🌐 *www.hoteltrouvailmiamibeach.com* 🛏 *71 rooms* 🍴 *No Meals.*

**★ The Miami Beach EDITION**

$$$$ | **RESORT** | At this reinvention of the 1955 landmark Seville Hotel by hospitality duo Ian Schrager and Marriott, historic glamour parallels modern relaxation from the palm-fringed marble lobby to the beachy guest rooms. **Pros:** excellent spa; hanging gardens in the alfresco area; great beachfront service. **Cons:** a bit pretentious; open bathroom setup in select rooms offers little privacy; near a particularly rocky part of Miami Beach. [$] *Rooms from: $559* ✉ *2901 Collins Ave., Mid-Beach* ☎ *786/257–4500* 🌐 *www.editionhotels.com/miami-beach* 🛏 *294 rooms* 🍴 *No Meals.*

**The Palms Hotel & Spa**

$$ | **HOTEL** | If you're seeking a relaxed property away from the noise but close to both Mid-Beach and South Beach nightlife, you'll find an exceptional beach, an easy pace, and beautiful gardens with soaring palm trees and inviting hammocks here, with rooms as fabulous as the grounds. **Pros:** thatched chickee huts; direct beach access; beach yoga. **Cons:** standard rooms do not have balconies (but suites do); room decor a bit tired; not as "cool" as neighboring hotels. [$] *Rooms from: $250* ✉ *3025 Collins Ave., Mid-Beach* ☎ *305/534–0505, 800/550–0505* 🌐 *www.thepalmshotel.com* 🛏 *251 rooms* 🍴 *No Meals.*

**Soho Beach House**

$$$$ | **HOTEL** | Soho Beach House is a throwback to swanky vibes of bygone decades, with a maritime setting bedazzled in faded color palates and circa-1930s avant-garde furnishings, luring both somebodies and wannabes to indulge in the amenity-rich, retro-chic rooms as long as they follow stringent house rules (no photos, no mobile phones, no suits, and one guest only). **Pros:** two pools; fabulous restaurant; full spa. **Cons:** members have priority for rooms; lots of pretentious patrons; house rules are a bit much. [$] *Rooms from: $570* ✉ *4385 Collins Ave., Mid-Beach* ☎ *786/507–7900* 🌐 *www.sohohouse.com/en-us/houses/soho-beach-house* 🛏 *49 rooms* 🍴 *No Meals.*

## 🍸 Nightlife

**★ Basement Miami**

**GATHERING PLACES** | This DJ-fueled, underground adult playground, below The Miami Beach EDITION hotel, features a micro version of famed Studio 54, a four-lane bowling alley, and a very small ice skating rink. The 2,000-square-foot rink might be too tiny for Olympic-quality skaters, but it's a priceless visit if only for the memory of how you skated on your Miami Beach vacation. ✉ *The Miami Beach EDITION, 2901 Collins Ave., Mid-Beach* ☎ *786/257–4600* 🌐 *basementmiami.com.*

**★ The Broken Shaker**

**BARS** | Popular with the cool crowd, this indoor-outdoor craft cocktail joint lures in droves to revel in creative mixology and fabulous people-watching. Everything at the vintage-chic hot spot is perfectly

Instagrammable, from the daring and beautifully presented drinks to the twinkle lights over the pool. It's no wonder the venue has been awarded national titles such as America's Best Bar. ✉ *Freehand Miami, 2727 Indian Creek Dr., Mid-Beach* ☎ *305/531–2727* 🌐 *freehandhotels.com/miami/broken-shaker.*

**★ LIV**

**DANCE CLUBS** | It's not hard to see why LIV often makes lists of the world's best clubs—if you can get in, that is (LIV is notorious for lengthy lines, so don't arrive fashionably late). Past the velvet ropes, the dance palladium impresses with its lavish decor, well-dressed international crowd, sensational light-and-sound system, and seductive bi-level club experience. ■ **TIP→ Men beware: groups of guys entering LIV are often coerced into insanely priced bottle service.** ✉ *Fontainebleau Miami Beach, 4441 Collins Ave., Mid-Beach* ☎ *305/674–4680 for table reservations* 🌐 *www.livnightclub.com.*

# North Beach

Though often referred to collectively as North Beach, there are several neighborhoods above Mid-Beach before reaching the Dade/Broward border. In Miami Beach proper, nearing the 63rd Street mark on Collins Avenue, Mid-Beach gives way to what is officially North Beach (until 87th Street), followed by Surfside (up until 95th Street).

## Coffee and Quick Bites

**Taquiza**

**$ | MEXICAN** | Who doesn't love beachside tacos? These street-style ones are especially adored thanks to fresh, hand-ground blue masa tortillas and fillings, from the classic *al pastor* (grilled pork topped with pineapple) to *chapulines* (grasshopper). **Known for:** totopos chips and blue masa tortillas; quick service; squash-blossom quesadillas. $ *Average main: $5* ✉ *7450 Ocean Terr., North Beach* ☎ *786/588–4755* 🌐 *www.taquizatacos.com.*

## Hotels

**★ Carillon Miami Wellness Resort**

**$$$$ | RESORT** | This 150-all-suites beachfront hotel is defined by a 70,000-square-foot wellness spa, including a rock-climbing wall, 54 treatment rooms, and 30 exercise classes daily. **Pros:** directly on the beach; spacious suites (minimum 720 square feet); incredible spa treatments. **Cons:** far from nightlife; rooms could be a bit more stylish; day visitors at spa and gym. $ *Rooms from: $495* ✉ *6801 Collins Ave., North Beach* ☎ *866/800–3858* 🌐 *www.carillonhotel.com* 🛏 *150 suites* 🍴 *No Meals.*

# Bal Harbour

At 96th Street, the town of Bal Harbour takes over Collins Avenue from Miami Beach. Bal Harbour is famous for its outdoor high-end shops, and if you take your shopping seriously, you may want to spend considerable time in this area. The town runs a mere 10 blocks to the north before the bridge to another barrier island. After crossing the bridge, you'll first come to Haulover Park, which is still technically in the village of Bal Harbour.

## Beaches

**★ Haulover Park**

**BEACH** | The popular clothing-optional beach at this county park is embraced by naturists of all ages, shapes, and sizes; there are even sections primarily frequented by families, singles, and gays. Nevertheless, Haulover's beachfront has more claims to fame than its casual attitude toward swimwear—it's also the best beach in the area for bodyboarding and surfing as it gets what passes for impressive swells in these parts. Once you park in the North Lot, you'll walk through a short tunnel covered with trees and natural habitat until you emerge on the unpretentious beach, where nudity is rarely met by gawkers. There are volleyball nets and plenty of beach chair and umbrella rentals to protect your birthday suit from too much exposure—to the sun, that is. The sections of beach requiring swimwear are popular, too, given the park's ample parking and relaxed atmosphere. Lifeguards stand watch. More active types might want to check out the kite rentals or charter-fishing excursions. **Amenities:** food and drink; lifeguards; parking (fee); showers; toilets. **Best for:** nudists; surfing; swimming; walking. ✉ *10800 Collins Ave., North Beach* ✣ *North of Bal Harbour* ☎ *305/947–3525* 🌐 *www.miamidade.gov/parks/haulover.asp* 🎫 *Parking $5 per vehicle weekdays, $7 weekends and holidays.*

## 🍴 Restaurants

### Carpaccio Restaurant

$$$$ | **ITALIAN** | As expected for its ritzy location, this upscale restaurant matches its high-fashion neighbors: waiters don bow ties and coattails, even for lunch hours, yet are approachable in their knowledge and attentiveness. Practically everything on the menu jumps out, though the handmade mozzarella antipasti, clam linguine, and namesake beef carpaccio are signature dishes. **Known for:** myriad carpaccios; ladies who lunch; well-heeled crowd. [$] *Average main: $40* ✉ *Bal Harbour Shops, 9700 Collins Ave., Bal Harbour* ☎ *305/867–7777* 🌐 *carpaccioatbalharbour.com.*

### Josh's Deli

$ | **SANDWICHES** | An unconventional Jewish deli that's not exactly kosher, Josh's serves impressive creations like the "Jewbanize," a deli-style take on a Cubano, in addition to more traditional classics like corned beef Reubens and latkes. The menu here changes often and can be found on Instagram. **Known for:** an ever-changing menu; Josh's quirky character; great corned beef. [$] *Average main: $12* ✉ *9517 Harding Ave., Surfside* ☎ *305/397–8494* 🌐 *www.instagram.com/joshsdeli* ⏲ *Closed Tues; no dinner.*

### Le Zoo

$$$$ | **FRENCH** | Restaurateur Stephen Starr imports a bona fide Parisian brasserie to the swanky Bal Harbour shops—inclusive of vintage decorations, furnishings, and an entire bar, all of which were shipped directly from France. Expect classics perfected, such as onion soup gratiné, steak frites and moules frites, and seafood *plateaux* (towers); a few delicious deviations like the escargots in hazelnut butter (rather than garlic butter); and plenty of excellent people-watching. **Known for:** Parisian flair; seafood towers; outdoor seating. [$] *Average main: $42* ✉ *Bal Harbour Shops, 9700 Collins Ave., No. 135, North Beach* ☎ *305/602–9663* 🌐 *lezoo.com.*

### ★ Makoto

$$$$ | **JAPANESE** | Stephen Starr's Japanese headliner, executed by celebrity-chef and master of Edomae-style sushi Makoto Okuwa, now sits in a new, much larger space and offers two menus: one devoted solely to sushi, sashimi, and *maki*, the other to Japanese cold and hot dishes. Look forward to hyperfresh raw dishes, tempuras, meats, and vegetables grilled over Japanese charcoal (*robata*), rice and noodle dishes, and a variety of steaks and fish inspired by the Land of the Rising Sun. **Known for:** superfresh sushi; artistic presentation; well-dressed crowd. [$] *Average main: $34* ✉ *Bal Harbour Shops, 9700 Collins Ave., Bal Harbour* ☎ *305/864–8600* 🌐 *makoto-restaurant.com.*

## 🛏 Hotels

### ★ Four Seasons Hotel at The Surf Club

$$$$ | **HOTEL** | Built in the 1930s as a members-only club called The Surf Club, this sophisticated 9-acre oceanfront property has always been a spot for people with

good taste to have good times. **Pros:** unparalleled service; world-class spa; five-star dining. **Cons:** lots of local visitors at the bar; far from nightlife; not much in walking distance. [$] *Rooms from: $950* ✉ *9011 Collins Ave., Surfside* ☎ *305/381–3333* 🌐 *www.fourseasons.com/surfside* 🛏 *77 rooms* 🍴 *No Meals.*

**The Ritz-Carlton, Bal Harbour**

$$$$ | **RESORT** | **FAMILY** | In one of South Florida's poshest neighborhoods, this property exudes contemporary beachfront luxury design with decadent mahogany-floor guest rooms featuring large terraces with panoramic views of the water and city and over-the-top bathrooms with 10-foot floor-to-ceiling windows and LCD TVs built into the mirrors. **Pros:** proximity to Bal Harbour Shops; bathroom's soaking tubs have ocean views; great contemporary-art collection. **Cons:** narrow beach is a bit disappointing; quiet area; small lobby. [$] *Rooms from: $700* ✉ *10295 Collins Ave., Bal Harbour* ☎ *305/455–5400* 🌐 *www.ritzcarlton.com/en/hotels/miami/bal-harbour* 🛏 *187 rooms* 🍴 *No Meals.*

★ **The St. Regis Bal Harbour Resort**

$$$$ | **RESORT** | This posh resort (which cost over $1 billion to build) embodies the next level of ultraglamour and haute living along Miami's North Beach. **Pros:** beachfront setting; Sunday rosé brunch; large apartment-size rooms. **Cons:** limited lounge space around main pool; little privacy on balconies; high price tag. [$] *Rooms from: $1029* ✉ *9703 Collins Ave., Bal Harbour* ☎ *305/993–3300* 🌐 *www.stregisbalharbour.com* 🛏 *216 rooms* 🍴 *No Meals.*

## Shopping

★ **Bal Harbour Shops**

**SHOPPING CENTER** | Beverly Hills meets the South Florida sun at this swank collection of 100 high-end shops, boutiques, and department stores, which currently holds the title as the country's greatest revenue-earner per square foot. The open-air enclave includes Florida's largest Saks Fifth Avenue; an 8,100-square-foot, two-story flagship Salvatore Ferragamo store; and stores by Alexander McQueen, Valentino, and local juggernaut The Webster. Restaurants and cafés, in tropical garden settings, overflow with style-conscious diners. A $400 million expansion is currently under way to add 340,387 square feet of retail. ✉ *9700 Collins Ave., Bal Harbour* ☎ *305/866–0311* 🌐 *www.balharbourshops.com.*

# Sunny Isles Beach

Beyond Haulover Park (and on the same barrier island) is the town of Sunny Isles Beach. Once over the bridge, Collins Avenue bypasses several dozen street numbers, picking up again in the 150s; that's when you know you've arrived in Sunny Isles—an appealing, calm, and predominantly upscale choice for families looking for a beautiful beach, and where Russian may be heard as often as English. There's no nightlife to speak of, and yet the half-dozen mega-luxurious skyscraper hotels that have sprung up here in the past decade have created a niche resort town from the demolished ashes of much older, affordable hotels.

## Restaurants

**Il Mulino New York at Aqualina Resort & Spa**

$$$$ | **ITALIAN** | For decades Il Mulino New York has ranked among the top Italian restaurants in Gotham, so it's no surprise that this Miami outpost is similarly good. Start your food coma with the complimentary starters—fresh cuts of Parmesan cheese, four types of fresh bread, garlicky bruschetta, and spicy, fried zucchini whet the palate—and then move on to antipasti like calamari fritti followed by ever-changing risottos and other classic Italian dishes perfected. **Known for:** seafood risotto; excellent service;

intimate setting. $ *Average main: $45* ✉ *Acqualina Resort & Spa on the Beach, 17875 Collins Ave., Sunny Isles Beach* ☎ *305/466–9191* ⊕ *www.acqualinaresort. com/dining/il-mulino-new-york.*

##  Hotels

### ★ Acqualina Resort & Residences on the Beach

**$$$$ | RESORT | FAMILY |** The grand dame of Sunny Isles Beach continues to raise the bar for Miami beachfront luxury, delivering a fantasy of modern Mediterranean opulence, with sumptuously appointed, striking gray- and silver-accented interiors and expansive facilities. **Pros:** excellent beach; in-room check-in; huge spa. **Cons:** no nightlife near hotel; hotel's towering height shades the beach by early afternoon; hefty fee for pets. $ *Rooms from: $950* ✉ *17875 Collins Ave., Sunny Isles Beach* ☎ *305/918–8000* ⊕ *www.acqualinaresort.com* ➥ *98 rooms* ⦿ *No Meals.*

## North Miami Beach

Don't let the name fool you. North Miami Beach actually isn't on the beach, but its southeastern end does abut Biscayne Bay. Beyond the popular Oleta River State Park on the bay, the city offers little in terms of touristic appeal.

##  Beaches

### Oleta River State Park

**BEACH | FAMILY |** Tucked away in North Miami Beach, this urban park is a ready-made family getaway. Nature lovers will find it easy to embrace the 1,128 acres of subtropical beauty along Biscayne Bay. Swim in the calm bay waters and bicycle, canoe, kayak, and bask among egrets, manatees, bald eagles, and fiddler crabs. Dozens of picnic tables, along with 10 covered pavilions, dot the stunning natural habitat, which was restored with red mangroves to revitalize the ecosystem and draw endangered

birds, like the roseate spoonbill. There's a playground for tots, a mangrove island accessible only by boat, 15 miles of mountain-bike trails, a half-mile exercise track, concessions, and outdoor showers. **Amenities:** food and drink; parking (fee); showers; toilets; water sports. **Best for:** solitude; sunrise; sunset; walking. ✉ *3400 N.E. 163rd St., North Miami Beach* ☎ *305/919–1844* ⊕ *www.floridastateparks.org/park/Oleta-River* ➥ *$6 per vehicle; $2 per pedestrian.*

# Aventura

West of Sunny Isles Beach and on the mainland are the high-rises of Aventura. This city is the heart and soul of South Florida's Jewish community as well as Miami's growing Russian community (along with Sunny Isles Beach). It is known for its high-end shopping opportunities, from the mega Aventura Mall to smaller boutiques in eclectic strip malls.

## 🍴 Restaurants

### Bourbon Steak

**$$$$ | STEAKHOUSE |** Michael Mina's long-standing South Florida steak house is renowned for its seductive design, sophisticated clientele, outstanding wine list, phenomenal service, and, of course, exceptional food. Dinner begins with a skillet of fresh potato focaccia and flavor-dusted french fries as preludes to entrées like the Maine lobster potpie (with truffle cream) and any of the dozen varieties of butter-poached, wood-grilled steaks (from hormone-free prime cuts to American Wagyu). **Known for:** duck-fat fries with dipping sauces; perfectly cooked steaks; floor-to-ceiling glass wine cellar. $ *Average main: $65* ✉ *JW Marriott Miami Turnberry Resort & Spa, 19999 W. Country Club Dr., Aventura* ☎ *786/279–6600* ⊕ *www.michaelmina. net/restaurants/bourbon-steak/miami/.*

### Ornos Estiatorio

$$$$ | GREEK | FAMILY | Take a trip to the Greek Isles at Michael Mina's Mediterranean restaurant featuring bright, light fare and fish that's delivered overnight straight from the Aegean Sea. In addition to a raw bar, menu items include dishes inspired by the chef's travels, including classic Greek spreads, grilled octopus, lamb shoulder, and more. **Known for:** South Florida's only fish sommelier; a large selection of Greek spirits and wines; stylish indoor and outdoor seating. $ *Average main: $42 ✉ Aventura Mall, 19565 Biscayne Blvd., Suite 946, Miami ☎ 786/697–1681 ⊕ www.michaelmina.net/restaurants/ornos-estiatorio/estiatorio-ornos-miami/.*

##  Hotels

### JW Marriott Miami Turnberry Resort & Spa

$$$ | RESORT | FAMILY | Golfers and families flock to this 300-acre tropical resort flaunting jumbo-size suites and world-class amenities, including 36 holes of championship golf, prolific tennis courts, an on-site waterpark, the three-story âme Spa & Wellness Collective, and two renowned restaurants—Michael Mina's Bourbon Steak and Corsair kitchen & bar. **Pros:** great spa, restaurants, and activities; free shuttle to Aventura Mall; situated between Miami and Fort Lauderdale. **Cons:** not on the beach; in residential area; $37 per day resort fee. $ *Rooms from: $399 ✉ 19999 W. Country Club Dr., Aventura ☎ 305/932–6200 ⊕ www.jwturnberry.com ⊅ 625 rooms ◯ No Meals.*

##  Shopping

### ★ Aventura Mall

MALL | This three-story megamall offers the ultimate in South Florida retail therapy and houses many global top performers, including the most lucrative outposts of several U.S. chain stores, a supersize Nordstrom and Bloomingdale's, and 300 other shops, like a two-story flagship Louis Vuitton, Hermès, and Fendi, which together create one of the largest shopping malls in the United States. Recent additions include a Nike store (where you can customize your Nike gear), the massive Treats Food Hall, and the 93-foot Aventura Slide Tower, a huge spiraling landmark that's also a functioning, nine-story slide open to the public Monday through Saturday 11 am to 9 pm and Sunday 11 am to 8 pm. Consider it a one-stop, shop-'til-you-drop retail mecca for locals, out-of-towners, and—frequently—celebrities. ✉ *19501 Biscayne Blvd. ☎ 305/935–1110 ⊕ aventuramall.com.*

##  Activities

### Miami Dolphins

FOOTBALL | The Miami Dolphins have one of the largest average attendance figures in the National Football League. Come see the team that completed the NFL's only perfect season (circa 1972), ending in a victory in Super Bowl VII. They also then won Super Bowl VIII. Home games are September through January at Hard Rock Stadium. ✉ *Hard Rock Stadium, 2269 N.W. 199 St., Miami Gardens ☎ 888/346–7849 ⊕ www.miamidolphins.com.*

### Tidal Cove Waterpark

SWIMMING | FAMILY | There are plenty of ways to keep cool in the Florida sunshine at this family-friendly water park, which has seven slides, a lazy river, a Flowrider surf experience, and 25 luxe cabanas. Tickets start at $75 and function as a day pass to JW Marriott Turnberry, allowing access to other areas of the resort, like the âme Spa & Wellness Collective. ■TIP→ **Book a room at the resort and your stay includes four-day passes to the water park.** ✉ *JW Marriott Miami Turnberry Resort & Spa, 19999 W. Country Club Dr., Aventura ☎ 786/279–6152 ⊕ www.tidalcovemiami.com.*

# Downtown

Downtown Miami dazzles from a distance. America's fifth-largest skyline is fluid thanks to the sheer number of sparkling glass high-rises between Biscayne Boulevard and the Miami River. Business is the key to Downtown Miami's daytime bustle. Nevertheless, the influx of massive, modern, and once-affordable condos has lured a young and trendy demographic to the areas in and around Downtown, giving Miami much more of a "city" feel come nightfall. Because of that, Downtown has become a trendy nightlife area, inciting a cultural revolution that has fostered burgeoning areas north in Wynwood, Midtown, and the Design District, and south along Brickell Avenue. The pedestrian streets here tend to be very restaurant-centric, complemented by lounges and nightclubs, with more being developed.

The free, 4½-mile, elevated commuter system known as the Metromover runs inner and outer loops through Downtown and to nearby neighborhoods south and north. Many attractions are conveniently located within a few blocks of a station.

## ◉ Sights

### Adrienne Arsht Center for the Performing Arts of Miami-Dade County

**PERFORMANCE VENUE | FAMILY** | Culture vultures and other artsy types are drawn to this stunning performing arts center, which includes the 2,400-seat Ziff Ballet Opera House, the 2,200-seat John S. and James L. Knight Concert Hall, the black-box Carnival Studio Theater, and the outdoor Parker and Vann Thomson Plaza for the Arts. Throughout the year, you'll find top-notch performances by local and national touring groups, including Broadway hits like *Wicked* and *Hamilton,* intimate music concerts, and showstopping ballet. Think of it as a sliver of savoir faire to temper Miami's often-over-the-top vibe. The massive development was designed by architect César Pelli. Complimentary one-hour tours of the Arsht Center, highlighting the architecture and its public art, are offered every Saturday and Monday at noon. Arrive early for your performance to dine at BRAVA, where a prix-fixe menu allows you to enjoy three courses with plenty of time to make it to your seats for the show. ⊠ *1300 Biscayne Blvd., at N.E. 13th St., Downtown* ☎ *305/949–6722 box office* ⊕ *www.arshtcenter.org.*

### Fredric Snitzer Gallery

**ART GALLERY** | The gallery of this longtime figure in the Miami arts scene highlights emerging and mid-career artists, providing them that tipping point needed for national and international exposure and recognition. It maintains its warehouse roots, letting the art speak for itself amid the raw walls and ample natural light. Though a commercial gallery, the selection is highly curated. Rotating monthly exhibitions are usually thematic, with works by one of its represented artists, including Hernan Bas, Alice Aycock, Enrique Martínez Celaya, and Jon Pylypchuk. For the art novice, the team, including Snitzer himself, is readily available and willing to share their knowledge. ⊠ *1540 N.E. Miami Ct., Downtown* ☎ *305/448–8976* ⊕ *www.snitzer.com* ☉ *Closed Sun. and Mon.*

### ★ HistoryMiami Museum

**HISTORY MUSEUM | FAMILY** | Discover a treasure trove of colorful stories about the region's history. Exhibits celebrate the city's multicultural heritage, including an old Miami streetcar and unique items chronicling the migration of Cubans to Miami. Truth be told, the museum is not wildly popular with tourists; however, the museum's tours certainly are. You can take a wide range of walking, boat, coach, bike, gallery, and eco-history tours with varying prices, including culture walks through Little Haiti, informative and exciting Little Havana Arts and

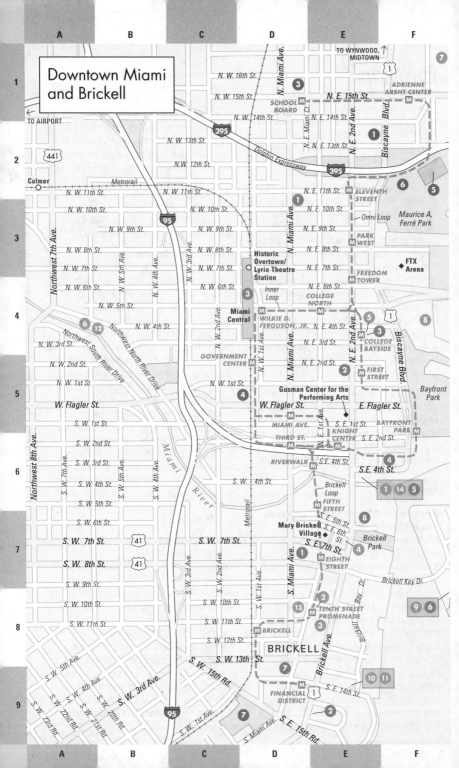

# Downtown Miami and Brickell

TO AIRPORT

TO WYNWOOD, MIDTOWN

ADRIENNE ARSHT CENTER

SCHOOL BOARD

N. E. 15th St.

N. W. 16th St.
N. W. 15th St.
N. W. 14th St.
Dolphin Expressway
N. W. 13th St.
N. W. 12th St.

N. E. 14th St.
N. E. 13th St.

Culmer

Metrorail

N. W. 11th St.
N. W. 10th St.
N. W. 9th St.
N. W. 8th St.
N. W. 7th St.
N. W. 6th St.
N. W. 5th St.
N. W. 4th St.

N. E. 11th St.
N. E. 10th St.
N. E. 9th St.
N. E. 8th St.
N. E. 7th St.
N. E. 6th St.

ELEVENTH STREET

Omni Loop

Maurice A, Ferré Park

PARK WEST

FREEDOM TOWER

FTX Arena

Historic Overtown/ Lyric Theatre Station

Inner Loop

Miami Central

WILKIE D. FERGUSON, JR.

COLLEGE NORTH

N. E. 4th St.
N. E. 3rd St.
N. E. 2nd St.

COLLEGE BAYSIDE

GOVERNMENT CENTER

FIRST STREET

Gusman Center for the Performing Arts

W. Flagler St.

E. Flagler St.

Bayfront Park

MIAMI AVE.
THIRD ST.

KNIGHT CENTER

BAYFRONT PARK

S. E. 2nd St.

RIVERWALK

S. E. 4th St.

S.E. 4th St.

Brickell Loop

FIFTH STREET

S. E. 5th St.
S. E. 6th St.

Brickell Park

Mary Brickell Village

S. E. 7th St.

EIGHTH STREET

Brickell Key Dr.

TENTH STREET PROMENADE

BRICKELL

BRICKELL

FINANCIAL DISTRICT

Northwest South River Drive
Northwest North River Drive

Miami River

Metrorail

Brickell Ave.

Brickell Bay Dr.

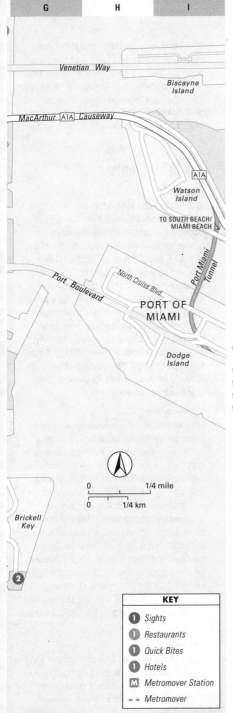

## Sights ▼

1 Adrienne Arsht Center for the Performing Arts of Miami-Dade County.............. **E2**
2 Brickell Key Park ....... **G8**
3 Fredric Snitzer Gallery ................... **D1**
4 HistoryMiami Museum ................ **D5**
5 Pérez Art Museum Miami ..................... **F2**
6 Phillip and Patricia Frost Museum of Science..... **F2**
7 Simpson Park ........... **D9**

## Restaurants ▼

1 Area 31..................... **E6**
2 DC Pie Co. ................. **E8**
3 Dirty French Steakhouse............... **E8**
4 Hutong Miami ............ **E7**
5 Jaguar Sun ............... **E4**
6 Kiki on the River......... **A4**
7 Klaw...................... **F1**
8 La Cañita.................. **F4**
9 La Mar by Gastón Acurio........... **F8**
10 LPM Restaurant & Bar..................... **E9**
11 Osaka ..................... **E9**
12 Seaspice................. **B4**
13 Sexy Fish................. **D8**
14 Zuma ..................... **E6**

## Quick Bites ▼

1 All Day ................... **D3**
2 Chicken Kitchen ......... **E5**
3 Citizens MiamiCentral............ **D4**

## Hotels ▼

1 EAST Miami ............. **D7**
2 Four Seasons Hotel Miami ............. **E9**
3 The Guild Downtown.... **E4**
4 JW Marriott Marquis Miami........... **F6**
5 Kimpton EPIC Miami..... **E6**
6 Mandarin Oriental, Miami........... **F8**
7 SLS Brickell Hotel & Residences.............. **D9**
8 W Miami.................. **E7**

### KEY

1 *Sights*
1 *Restaurants*
1 *Quick Bites*
1 *Hotels*
M *Metromover Station*
-- *Metromover*

Culture Walks, and an evening of storytelling during the Moon Over Miami tour led by HistoryMiami historian Dr. Paul George, where you'll float through Downtown on the Miami River, learning all about Miami's early history circa the Tequesta tribe's days. ✉ *101 W. Flagler St., Downtown* ✣ *Between N.W. 1st and 2nd Aves.* ☎ *305/375–1492* 🌐 *www.historymiami.org* 🎟 *$10; tour costs vary* 🕐 *Closed Mon. and Tues.*

★ **Pérez Art Museum Miami** (*PAMM*)
**ART MUSEUM** | **FAMILY** | This uber-high-design architectural masterpiece on Biscayne Bay is a sight to behold. Double-story, cylindrical hanging gardens sway from high atop the museum, anchored to stylish wooden trusses that help create this gotta-see-it-to-believe-it indoor-outdoor museum. Large sculptures, Asian-inspired gardens, sexy white benches, and steel frames surround the property. Inside, the 120,000-square-foot space houses multicultural art from the 20th and 21st centuries. Most of the interior space is devoted to temporary exhibitions, which have included the likes of *Ai Weiwei: According to What?* and *Grids: A Selection of Paintings by Lynne Golob Gelfman*. Even if you aren't a "museum type," come check out this magnum opus over lunch at Verde, the museum's sensational waterfront restaurant and bar. ✉ *1103 Biscayne Blvd., Downtown* ☎ *305/375–3000* 🌐 *www.pamm.org* 🎟 *$16* 🕐 *Closed Tues. and Wed.*

★ **Phillip and Patricia Frost Museum of Science**
**SCIENCE MUSEUM** | **FAMILY** | Equal parts style and science, this hypermodern, $300 million–plus museum along Biscayne Bay is totally worth forgoing time at the beach. The high-design museum transitions the indoors and outdoors over multiple levels and an impressive 250,000 square feet, crowned by a see-through, shark-filled, 500,000-gallon aquarium. Beyond exhibitions dedicated to oceans, engineering, and the Everglades, look forward to one of the most sophisticated planetariums in the country, which uses 16-million-color 8K projection. ✉ *1101 Biscayne Blvd., Downtown* ☎ *305/434–9600* 🌐 *www.frostscience.org* 🎟 *Mon. to Thurs. $29.95; Fri. to Sun. $32.95.*

## 🍴 Restaurants

**Area 31**
**$$$$** | **SEAFOOD** | High atop the 16th floor of Downtown Miami's Kimpton EPIC Hotel, memorable and sustainable ocean-to-table cuisine is prepared in the bustling, beautiful open kitchen. Look forward to a seafood-centric menu with innovative flavors and a hefty portion of ethos—all fruits of the sea here are certified by the Monterey Bay Aquarium Seafood Watch. **Known for:** great raw bar; excellent bay-side views; artisanal cocktails. [$] *Average main: $35* ✉ *Kimpton Epic Hotel, 270 Biscayne Blvd. Way, 16th fl., Downtown* ☎ *305/424–5234* 🌐 *area31restaurant.com.*

★ **Jaguar Sun**
**$$$** | **AMERICAN** | An intimate restaurant that's perfect for any occasion, from a birthday dinner to a pre-concert bite to a first date or a much needed martini with friends, Jaguar Sun serves funky cocktails as well as fresh pasta and crudos in a tropical-chic setting. The backbar is cleverly curated with lesser known small-batch brands and a cocktail menu to match, while the kitchen cranks out some of the best food in Miami. **Known for:** Parker House rolls; crab agnolotti; knowledgable bartenders. [$] *Average main: $22* ✉ *398 NE 5th St., Downtown* 🌐 *jaguarsunmia.com* 🕐 *Closed Sun. and Mon.*

**Kiki on the River**
**$$$$** | **GREEK FUSION** | In a contemporary waterfront garden setting along the Miami River, Kiki is a daily celebration of fabulous Greek food (hello, olive

oil–braised octopus), steamy and sceney Miami nights, and an overall Greece-meets-the-tropics joie de vivre. Expect to people-watch, eat a lot, drink even more, and dance (especially if coming for the weekly Sunday Funday party). **Known for:** lobster pasta; tomato salad; great happy hour. [$] *Average main: $38* ✉ *450 N.W. North River Dr., Downtown* ☎ *786/502–3243* 🌐 *kikiontheriver.com.*

★ **Klaw**

$$$$ | **STEAKHOUSE** | Located inside the historic Miami Women's Club, this surf 'n' turf restaurant boasts top quality dry-aged steaks and Norwegian king crab claws (flown in weekly) that can be seen in a large tank at the entrance of the stunning restaurant. Start on the fifth-floor rooftop with a cocktail and panoramic views of Biscayne Bay and the marina below. **Known for:** expertly sourced ingredients; exceptional service; tableside king crab legs. [$] *Average main: $70* ✉ *1737 N Bayshore Dr., Downtown* ☎ *305/239–2523* 🌐 *www.klawrestaurant.com* 🕒 *Closed Mon. and Tues.*

**La Cañita**

$$$ | **CUBAN** | **FAMILY** | A casual spot serving authentic Cuban food by James Beard Award winner Michelle Bernstein, this restaurant is located on the second floor of Bayside Marketplace overlooking the marina and the bay. With a full bar and live music, it's a lively spot with both indoor and outdoor seating where you can order a lunch of tostones, *ropa vieja,* and *churrasco.* **Known for:** plantain-crusted shrimp; braised oxtail; mojitos. [$] *Average main: $24* ✉ *Bayside Marketplace, 401 Biscayne Blvd., 2nd fl., Downtown* ☎ *305/392–0811* 🌐 *www.lacanitamiami.com.*

**Seaspice**

$$$$ | **CONTEMPORARY** | Half the fun of dining at this sophisticated brasserie on the Miami River is watching stylish patrons arrive by yacht. Reserve a table outdoors on the patio for the best views of Downtown, and rest assured that a knowledgeable server will guide you through an eclectic menu highlighting fresh seafood, wood-fired casseroles, and refreshing cocktails. **Known for:** waterfront dining; impeccable service; octopus a la plancha. [$] *Average main: $35* ✉ *422 N.W. North River Dr., Downtown* ☎ *305/440–4200* 🌐 *www.seaspicemiami.com.*

**Zuma**

$$$$ | **JAPANESE FUSION** | This *izakaya*-style restaurant is known the world over for its sleek design, lounge atmosphere, and contemporary Japanese cuisine. On the ground floor of the Kimpton EPIC hotel, the Miami location promises excellent bay-side views, Zuma's signature menu items, such as roasted lobster with *shiso*-ponzu butter and a 24-ounce rib eye covered in freshly shaved truffles. **Known for:** incredible Sunday brunch; own line of sake; excellent sashimi. [$] *Average main: $47* ✉ *Kimpton EPIC Hotel, 270 Biscayne Blvd. Way, Downtown* ☎ *305/577–0277* 🌐 *zumarestaurant.com/locations/miami/.*

## ☕ Coffee and Quick Bites

**All Day**

$ | **AMERICAN** | Under the glow of a green neon light in a hip industrial space, this locally loved, independent coffee shop offers quick service and a curated list of rotating coffee blends, pastries, and sandwiches for breakfast and lunch. Coffee connoisseurs will delight in the several preparations of nitro cold brew, pour over, and carefully crafted lattes. **Known for:** awesome coffee blends; knowledgeable baristas; locally made pastries. [$] *Average main: $6* ✉ *1035 N. Miami Ave., Downtown* ☎ *305/699–3447* 🌐 *www.alldaymia.com.*

**Chicken Kitchen**

$ | **AMERICAN** | **FAMILY** | This fast, casual restaurant is loved by locals for its quick and delicious chicken and rice bowls (called Chop-Chops because of how the chicken is chopped up right in front of you). Build your own using a variety of fresh toppings or opt for one of the tried-and-true menu offerings like the Deluxe Chop-Chop (rice, chicken breast, lettuce, and tomato) or the Mexican Chop-Chop (the same thing, plus cheddar cheese, guac, and sour cream). **Known for:** Cuban Chop-Chop; curry mustard sauce; locations all over Miami. $ *Average main: $9* ⊠ *146 NE 2nd Ave., Downtown* ☎ *786/580–3141* ⊕ *www.chickenkitchen. com.*

### Citizens MiamiCentral

**$$ | ECLECTIC | FAMILY |** Even if you don't have plans to take a Brightline train, the food hall inside the station is a handy stop if you're hungry and running around Downtown. It's home to 16 fast casual concepts (and two restaurants), from burgers at Umami Burger to cookies from Cindy Lou Cookies to sushi at Krispy Rice and vegan bites at Plant Nation. **Known for:** locally loved vendors; quick service; large variety of options. $ *Average main: $18* ⊠ *Brightline Miami, 600 NE 1st Ave., 2nd fl., Downtown* ⊕ *www. instagram.com/citizens_miamicentral.*

 ## Hotels

Miami's skyline continues to grow by leaps and bounds. With Downtown experiencing a renaissance of sorts, the hotel scene here isn't just for business anymore. In fact, hotels that once relied solely on their Monday–Thursday traffic are now bustling on weekends, with a larger focus on cocktails around the rooftop pool and less on the business center. These hotels offer proximate access to Downtown's burgeoning food and cocktail scene and historic sights and are a short Uber ride away from Miami's beaches.

### The Guild Downtown

**$$$ | HOTEL |** This business-friendly hotel features apartment-style suites for every guest and a sprawling level of amenities, including conference rooms, free Wi-Fi, a cutting-edge gym, and an incredible rooftop pool. **Pros:** centrally located; on-site coworking space; full kitchens in every room. **Cons:** no pets; noise control after 10 pm; expensive parking. $ *Rooms from: $329* ⊠ *230 N.E. 4th St., Downtown* ☎ *512/623–7480* ⊕ *theguild. co/property/the-guild-downtown-x-miami/* ⇱ *84 suites* |O| *No Meals.*

### JW Marriott Marquis Miami

**$$$$ | HOTEL |** The Miami marriage of Marriott's JW and Marquis brands creates a truly high-tech, contemporary, and stylish business-minded hotel—from the three-story crystal chandelier in the entry to the smart and symmetric guest rooms, rife with electronic gadgets. **Pros:** entertainment and fitness amenities; amazing technology; pristine rooms. **Cons:** swimming pool receives limited sunshine; lots of conventioneers on weekdays; congestion at street entrance. $ *Rooms from: $499* ⊠ *255 Biscayne Blvd. Way, Downtown* ☎ *305/421–8600* ⊕ *www.marriott.com* ⇱ *313 rooms* |O| *No Meals.*

### ★ Kimpton EPIC Miami

**$$$ | HOTEL |** In the heart of Downtown, Kimpton's pet-friendly, artful EPIC Hotel has 411 guest rooms with spacious balconies (many of them overlook Biscayne Bay) and fabulous modern amenities to match the sophistication of the common areas, which include a supersexy rooftop pool. **Pros:** sprawling rooftop pool deck; balcony in every room; complimentary wine hour, coffee, and Wi-Fi. **Cons:** some rooms have inferior views; congested valet area; sometimes windy around pool area. $ *Rooms from: $375* ⊠ *270 Biscayne Blvd. Way, Downtown* ☎ *305/424–5226* ⊕ *www.epichotel.com* ⇱ *411 rooms* |O| *No Meals.*

# ⓨ Nightlife

## E11EVEN Miami
**DANCE CLUBS** | An ultraclub with LED video walls, intelligent lighting, and a powerful sound system that pulses sports by day and beats by night, E11EVEN provides partygoers the 24/7 action they crave. Hospitality and VIP experiences are ample throughout the private lounges and second-level champagne room; however, the real action is in The Pit, featuring burlesque performances and intermittent Cirque du Soleil–style shows from a hydraulic-elevating stage. The fusion of theatrics and technology attracts an A-list clientele. Head up to the roof to find an intimate restaurant that serves tapas, as well as a live music lounge. ⊠ 29 N.E. 11th St., Downtown ☎ 305/829–2911 ⊕ www.11miami.com.

## Lost Boy
**BARS** | What was once a vintage denim store called Lost Boy Dry Goods is now a popular hangout with the same name. The convivial, unpretentious vibe draws imbibers for classic cocktails (half-price during the 4 to 8 pm weekday happy hour) and a long list of draft beers and wines. Those looking to soak up their cocktails can create their own charcuterie boards or enjoy homemade sandwiches and snacks. ⊠ 157 Flagler St., Downtown ☎ 305/372–7303 ⊕ www.lostboydrygoods.com.

## ★ Mama Tried
**BARS** | This edgy bar has a retro vibe most evident by its bright-red carpeting, "No Regerts" mural, and twinkling ceiling. The party lasts until 5 am seven nights a week with a menu full of bold cocktails like the popular pornstar martini and sparkling Tommy's margarita. Late nights a DJ sets the vibe, and on the last Sunday of every month, there's an emo night that draws a massive crowd. ⊠ 207 N.E. 1st St., Downtown ☎ 786/803–8087 ⊕ www.mamatriedmia.com.

## Over Under
**BARS** | Embracing all things Florida, this quirky and hip bar is known for its tropical drinks and hearty bar food, served under the light of a neon mosquito drinking a martini. Sometimes slammed and vibrant and sometimes blessedly uncrowded, it's never a bad time to order a beer and a shot. The menu is filled with bar food like smoked fish dip, alligator bites, and one of the best veggie burgers in Miami. ⊠ 151 E Flagler St., Downtown ☎ 786/247–9851 ⊕ overundermiami.com.

#  Activities

## HistoryMiami City Tours
**WALKING TOURS** | Cultural institution HistoryMiami Museum runs some fabulous walking tours of Little Havana (spiked with plenty of Cuban coffees and cigars, of course), Little Haiti, the Design District, and Wynwood. Most tours run one hour to 90 minutes and are led by HistoryMiami historian Dr. Paul George, the authority on all things Miami. ⊠ 101 W. Flagler St., Downtown ☎ 305/375–1492 ⊕ historymiami.org/city-tours/ 🎫 $30.

## Island Queen Cruises
**SAILING** | **FAMILY** | Experiences on the very touristy Island Queen Cruises run the gamut—sunset cruises, dance cruises, fishing cruises, speedboat rides, and their signature tours of Millionaires' Row, Miami's waterfront homes of the rich and famous. The Island Queen, Island Lady, and Miami Lady are three double-decker, 140-passenger tour boats docked at Bayside Marketplace that set sail daily for 90-minute narrated tours of the Port of Miami and Millionaires' Row. ⊠ 401 Biscayne Blvd., Downtown ☎ 844/295–8034 ⊕ islandqueencruises.com 🎫 From $30.

## Miami Heat
**BASKETBALL** | **FAMILY** | The 2006, 2012, and 2013 NBA champs play at the 19,600-seat, waterfront FTX Arena (formerly American Airlines Arena). The downtown venue features restaurants, a wide patio

overlooking Biscayne Bay, and a silver sun-shape special-effects scoreboard with rays holding wide-screen TVs. Home games are held November through April. ⊠ *FTX Arena, 601 Biscayne Blvd., Downtown* 🕾 *800/745–3000 ticket hotline, 786/777–1000 arena* ⊕ *www.nba.com/heat/tickets/miami-heat-tickets* 🎟 *From $11.*

# Brickell

Neighboring Downtown Miami, this metropolis with soaring high-rises is one of the hottest spots in Miami, catering to those who crave a big city feel in the tropics. Dozens of new buildings have gone up over the past decade, completely changing not only Miami's skyline but also local demographics and livability. Now, Brickell attracts young professionals with a walkable city center, where residents and visitors alike have everything they need within reach. From a massive shopping mall, Brickell City Centre, to restaurants and bars on every corner, there's always something to do in this bustling neighborhood.

The free, 4½-mile, elevated commuter system known as the Metromover runs inner and outer loops and connects Brickell to Downtown for easy travel between the two locations. It's great for traveling quickly in the area.

## ⊙ Sights

### ★ Brickell Key Park

**CITY PARK** | On the southern tip of the mostly residential Brickell Key (a tiny man-made island), this little slice of heaven is home to some of the most breathtaking views in Miami. The quaint park, which has a few benches and a small playground, faces Key Biscayne with jaw-dropping views of Brickell's skyline and the glistening Biscayne Bay.

▉ TIP→ **Take a stroll on the walking path around the island. It's exactly 1 mile, making for a short and sweet excursion with memorable views.** ⊠ *Brickell Key, Claughton Island Dr., Brickell Key* ⊕ *Behind Mandarin Oriental Hotel* 🕾 *305/416–1361.*

### Simpson Park

**CITY PARK** | **FAMILY** | This 8-acre nature preserve on the edge of Miami's busiest urban neighborhood is one of the last remnants of Brickell's natural tropical hardwood hammock. It conserves 162 plant species, most of which are native to the area, such as the strangler fig and gumbo-limbo tree. The park features lovely bike and walking trails, as well as a recreation center and plenty of intriguing historical plaques along the way. ⊠ *5 S.W. 17th Rd., Brickell Village* 🕾 *305/859–2867* ⊕ *www.miamigov.com.*

##  Restaurants

### DC Pie Co.

**$$** | **PIZZA** | From the same team behind Brooklyn's famous Lucali restaurant comes a fast casual New York–style pizzeria specializing in thin crust brick-oven pies and hearty Italian comfort dishes. Menu highlights include massive meatballs, chicken Parmesan, pepperoni chips, and salads. **Known for:** brick-oven pizza; solid cocktails; slice & spritz brunch deals. Ⓢ *Average main: $16* ⊠ *1010 Brickell Ave., Suite 200, Brickell Village* 🕾 *786/453–6888* ⊕ *www.dcpieco.com.*

### ★ Dirty French Steakhouse

**$$$$** | **STEAKHOUSE** | Step inside an unassuming office building into Dirty French and you're transported into an ultrasexy steakhouse awash in jungle decor and animal prints. The menu is simple and to the point, full of all the steak house favorites: shrimp cocktail, oysters, beef carpaccio, creamed spinach, *pommes* puree—and, of course, several cuts of dry-aged beef. **Known for:** classic steak house menu; immaculate service; solid martinis. $ *Average main: $42* ✉ *1200 Brickell Ave., Brickell Village* ☎ *305/990–8707* ⊕ *www.dirtyfrench.com/location/dirty-french-steakhouse/* ⊘ *Closed Sun. and Mon.*

### Hutong Miami
**$$$$** | **CHINESE** | This trendy, dimly lit Hong Kong outpost has brought splurge-worthy northern Chinese food to Brickell. The Miami location has unique menu items, including king scallops and a chili-infused chocolate mousse, plus a mesmerizing "Great Wall," where choreographed lights dance throughout your meal. **Known for:** Peking duck carved tableside; dim sum and cocktails; chic setting. $ *Average main: $60* ✉ *600 Brickell Ave., Brickell Village* ☎ *786/388–0805* ⊕ *www.hutong-miami.com.*

### ★ La Mar by Gastón Acurio
**$$$$** | **PERUVIAN** | **FAMILY** | Peruvian celebrity-chef Gastón Acurio dazzles with a sublime menu and an atmospheric, bay-side setting to match. Tour the far corners of Peru through La Mar's signature *cebiches* (ceviche) and *tiraditos* (similar to crudo), freshly grilled skewers of street-style *anticuchos, causa* dishes (mashed potato topped with meat and vegetable toppings), and national libations, like the pisco sour. **Known for:** edgy interior design; alfresco dining with skyline views; desserts served in dollhouses. $ *Average main: $35* ✉ *Mandarin Oriental, Miami, 500 Brickell Key Dr., Brickell Key* ⊕ *www.mandarinoriental.com/miami.*

### LPM Restaurant & Bar
**$$$$** | **FRENCH** | Located on the ground floor of a Brickell high-rise, this upscale French Mediterranean restaurant serves classic fare like escargot and ratatouille el feta. During the day, most diners are local businesspeople, but at night the bar is busy with yuppies who are looking to treat themselves with exceptional seafood, pastas, and meat dishes. **Known for:** buttery escargot; cozy banquette tables; octopus carpaccio. $ *Average main: $42*

✉ *Brickell House, 1300 Brickell Bay Dr., Brickell Village* ☎ *305/403–9133* ⊕ *www.lpmrestaurants.com/miami.*

### Osaka
**$$$$** | **JAPANESE FUSION** | Fusing Japanese and Peruvian flavors, this sultry Nikkei restaurant is known for its multisensory menu, including many *nigiri* dishes that are torched tableside, such as the *hotate* truffle with scallop, truffle butter, and lime. The menu features an array of ceviches, *tiraditos,* and seafood dishes, but there's also a 24-ounce bone-in rib eye with truffle. Japanese whiskey lovers will enjoy the 24-plus varieties on hand behind the gorgeous bar. **Known for:** expansive pisco and Japanese whiskey menu; fresh seafood; fine dining. $ *Average main: $45* ✉ *1300 Brickell Bay Dr., Brickell Village* ☎ *786/627–4800* ⊕ *www.osakanikkei.com/en/local/miami.*

### Sexy Fish
**$$$$** | **SUSHI** | Diners are greeted with a velvet rope upon entering Sexy Fish, one of the hottest tickets in Miami. Be warned that your eyes may need a few minutes to adjust to the $30 million worth of extravagant decor, from sculptures of fish hanging from the ceiling to life-size mermaids and a Daniel Craig as James Bond statue in the bathroom. **Known for:** fashion-forward crowd; live late-night entertainment; several Insta-worthy photo ops. $ *Average main: $35* ✉ *1001 South Miami Ave., Brickell Village* ☎ *305/889–7888* ⊕ *sexyfishmiami.com.*

##  Hotels

### ★ EAST Miami
**$$$$** | **HOTEL** | **FAMILY** | A lush paradise in the heart of Brickell's city center, this tropical, trendy hotel has impeccable art and design elements plus rooms with floor-to-ceiling windows and views of the twinkling city—even from the bathtubs. **Pros:** large suites available for long stays;

attached to Brickell City Centre shopping; rooftop bar, Sugar, has great sunset views. **Cons:** limited privacy on balconies; expensive valet; pool lacks sunlight by mid-afternoon. [$] *Rooms from: $550* ✉ *788 Brickell Plaza, Brickell Village* ☎ *305/712–7000* 🌐 *www.easthotels.com/en/miami* 🛏 *352 rooms* 🍴 *No Meals.*

**Four Seasons Hotel Miami**

**$$$$** | **HOTEL** | A favorite of business travelers visiting Downtown's bustling Brickell Avenue, this plush sanctuary offers a respite from the nine-to-five mayhem—a soothing water wall greets you, the understated rooms impress you, and the seventh-floor, 2-acre-pool terrace relaxes you. **Pros:** sensational service; window-side daybeds; amazing gym and pool deck. **Cons:** no balconies; not near the beach; mostly a business crowd. [$] *Rooms from: $550* ✉ *1435 Brickell Ave., Brickell Village* ☎ *305/358–3535* 🌐 *www.fourseasons.com/miami* 🛏 *221 rooms* 🍴 *No Meals.*

★ **Mandarin Oriental, Miami**

**$$$$** | **HOTEL** | At the tip of prestigious Brickell Key in Biscayne Bay, the Mandarin Oriental feels as exclusive as it does glamorous, with luxurious rooms, exalted restaurants, and the city's top spa, all of which marry the brand's signature Asian style with Miami's bold tropical elegance. **Pros:** impressive lobby; intimate vibe; top-notch spa. **Cons:** man-made beach; small infinity pool; traffic getting on/off Brickell Key. [$] *Rooms from: $579* ✉ *500 Brickell Key Dr., Downtown* ☎ *305/913–8288, 866/888–6780* 🌐 *www.mandarinoriental.com/en/miami/brickell-key* 🛏 *357 rooms* 🍴 *No Meals.*

**SLS Brickell Hotel & Residences**

**$$** | **HOTEL** | The modern rooms inside this Philippe Starck–designed, *Alice in Wonderland* reminiscent luxury escape may feature mirrors over the bed, but the real jawdropper is the rooftop pool deck with lovely city views and cabanas. **Pros:** walking distance to Brickell nightlife; Ciel Spa products; balconies for every room. **Cons:** pool loses sun in early afternoon; residents also use amenities; no bathtubs. [$] *Rooms from: $236* ✉ *1300 S. Miami Ave., Brickell Village* ☎ *305/239–1300* 🌐 *www.sbe.com/hotels/sls-hotels/brickell* 🛏 *124 rooms* 🍴 *No Meals.*

**W Miami**

**$$$$** | **HOTEL** | Formerly the Viceroy, Miami's second W hotel cultivates a brash, supersophisticated Miami attitude, likely stemming from its whimsically decorated guest rooms, floor-to-ceiling marble bathrooms, and the Philippe Starck–designed 28,000-square-foot Iconbrickell Spa. Rooms are available in a host of categories, ranging from 440-square-foot "Wonderful" rooms to a 1,550-square-foot "Wow" suite that has a living room, dining room, and sweeping views of Biscayne Bay. Each room, though, is furnished with a private balcony, a W Signature bed with down comforter and pillows, a safe, Wi-Fi, and a TV. **Pros:** smart design elements; exceptional spa; great gym. **Cons:** serious traffic getting in and out of hotel entrance; the amazing 15th floor pool is for residents, not hotel guests; many rooms allow only two persons maximum. [$] *Rooms from: $659* ✉ *485 Brickell Ave., Brickell Village* ☎ *305/503–4400* 🌐 *www.wmiamihotel.com* 🛏 *168 rooms* 🍴 *No Meals.*

## 🍸 Nightlife

**Baby Jane**

**CAFÉS** | A cozy bar with neon signs and kitschy bathroom decor serves late-night noodles and Asian bites along with craft cocktails, all to a great soundtrack. Open until the wee hours of the morning, this hot spot is known to have an impressive crowd of regulars. Reservations can be made for those who want to be sure of booth seating. ✉ *500 Brickell Ave., Suite 105e, Brickell Village* ☎ *786/623–3555* 🌐 *www.babyjanemiami.com.*

**Blackbird Ordinary**

BARS | With a vibe that's a bit speakeasy, a bit dive bar, a bit hipster hangout, and a bit Miami sophisticate, this local watering hole is hands down one of the coolest places in the city and appeals to a wide demographic. Mixology is a huge part of the Blackbird experience—be prepared for some awesome artisanal cocktails. ⊠ *729 S.W. 1st Ave., Brickell Village* ☎ *305/671–3307* ⊕ *www.blackbirdordinary.com.*

**Komodo**

CAFÉS | This swank, triple-story indoor/outdoor resto-lounge is the apex of the Downtown Miami scene, whether standing and posing at one of the three bars, dining in the floating birds nests of the 300-seat restaurant, or partying alongside celebs to DJ-led tunes inside the top-floor Komodo Lounge. The brains behind this hedonistic treehouse complex is David Grutman, the impresario behind Miami Beach's legendary LIV nightclub. ⊠ *801 Brickell Ave., Brickell Village* ☎ *305/534–2211* ⊕ *komodomiami.com.*

★ **Sugar**

BARS | This skyscraping rooftop bar, hands down the best in the city, is the essence of Brickell: futuristic, worldly, and beyond sleek. Draped in tropical flora, it crowns the 40th floor of EAST Miami, the luxury hotel tucked inside Brickell City Centre shopping complex. The sunsets here are spectacular, as are the Southeast Asian bites and cocktails. Pop into the Tea Room on the same floor for late-night brunch with bottomless drinks. ⊠ *788 Brickell Plaza, Brickell Village* ☎ *305/805–4655* ⊕ *www.easthotels.com.*

**Sweet Caroline Karaoke Bar**

LIVE MUSIC | Miami's only boutique karaoke-only bar is small but mighty. A corner stage and a narrow bar set the scene for enthusiastic singers who don props and sing their hearts out until 4 am, fueled by craft cocktails. ⊠ *1111 S.W. 1st Ave, Suite 107, Brickell Village* ☎ *786/673–2522* ⊕ *www.sweetcarolinebar.com.*

##  Shopping

★ **Acqua di Parma**

PERFUME | Brickell City Centre houses the one and only stand-alone store of this Italian fragrance and skin-care brand in the United States. But there's so much more than scents and fragrances for sample and sale in the 1,000-square-foot, marble-clad boutique; consumers can also purchase the brand's line of leather bags, travel accessories, and candles. Additionally, an in-store barbershop offers razor shaves with Acqua di Parma's coveted men's grooming products, the Collezione Barbiere. ⊠ *Brickell City Centre, Level 1, 701 S. Miami Ave., Brickell Village* ☎ *786/220–8840* ⊕ *www.acquadiparma.com/default/en/.*

★ **Brickell City Centre**

MALL | A billion dollars in the making, this sleek, three-city-block, mixed-use complex in the heart of Brickell is rife with multiple levels of designer stores, restaurants, food halls, hotel rooms, and residences. The high-end retail rivals that in Bal Harbour and the Design District, solidifying Miami's status as a true shopping destination. The center is a grand fusion of indoor and outdoor space and futuristic architectural design, underscored by the striking, glass-and-steel Climate Ribbon, which controls the enclave's microclimate. ⊠ *701 S. Miami Ave., Brickell Village* ☎ *786/704–0223* ⊕ *www.brickellcitycentre.com.*

# Wynwood

North of Downtown, between Interstate 95 and Northeast 1st Avenue from 29th to 22nd Streets, is the colorful, grungy, artistic neighborhood of Wynwood. With an impressive mix of one-of-a-kind shops and art galleries, public art displays, see-and-be-seen bars, slick restaurants, and plenty of eye-popping graffiti, it's one of the coolest areas in Miami. Almost every street is colored with funky spray-paint art, making the neighborhood a photographer's dream. Wynwood's trendiness has proven infectious, also taking root in proximate neighborhoods. The downside: you'll need a vehicle to get here, and though in close proximity to one another, you'll also need a vehicle to get to nearby Midtown and the Design District.

# Sights

### The Margulies Collection at the Warehouse
**ART GALLERY** | Make sure a visit to Wynwood includes a stop at The Margulies Collection at the Warehouse. Martin Margulies's collection of vintage and contemporary photography, videos, and installation art in a 45,000-square-foot space makes for eye-popping viewing. Admission proceeds go to Lotus Village, a local facility for unhoused individuals and families. ⊠ 591 N.W. 27th St., Wynwood ✛ Between N.W. 5th and 6th aves. ☎ 305/576–1051 ⊕ www.margulieswarehouse.com ⊑ $10 ⊗ Closed Mon.

### ★ Rubell Museum
**ART MUSEUM** | Fans of edgy art will appreciate the Rubell Museum (formerly the Rubell Family Collection). Mera and Don Rubell have accumulated work by artists from the 1970s to the present, including Jeff Koons, Cindy Sherman, Damien Hirst, and Keith Haring. New thematic and topical exhibitions debut annually, during Art Basel in December. (For example, a previous exhibition, *Still Human*, delved into the impact of the digital revolution on the human condition.) Admission always includes a complimentary audio tour; however, true art lovers should opt for a complimentary guided tour of the collection, offered Wednesday through Saturday at 3 pm. Stop in for lunch at the on-site restaurant, Leku, serving Basque cuisine that's just as beautiful as the museum's art. ⊠ 1100 N.W. 23rd St., Wynwood ☎ 305/573–6090 ⊕ rubellmuseum.org ⊑ $10.

### ★ Wynwood Walls
**PUBLIC ART** | Between Northeast 25th and 26th Streets on Northwest 2nd Avenue, the Wynwood Walls are a cutting-edge enclave of modern urban murals, reflecting diversity in graffiti and street art. More than 50 well-known and lesser-known artists have transformed 80,000 square feet of warehouse walls into an outdoor museum of sorts (bring your camera). The popularity of the walls spawned the neighboring Wynwood Doors and Garden, an industrial space replete with metal roll-down gates also used as blank canvases, complemented by a garden with singular pieces of art and an eye-popping indoor gallery. ⊠ 2520 N.W. 2nd Ave., Wynwood ⊕ museum.thewynwoodwalls.com/main ⊑ $12.

#  Restaurants

### Kush
**$$ | BURGER** | At this cozy burger joint on the edge of Wynwood, locally sourced ingredients and stellar craft beer star on a Florida-inspired menu. Order a Frita burger topped with Gruyère and guava jelly or a Key West conch salad while you sip one of 18 brews. **Known for:** Johnny Utah burger; Florida alligator bites; neon-lit bar next door while you wait. $ Average main: $18 ⊠ 2003 N. Miami Ave., Wynwood ☎ 305/576–4500 ⊕ kushhospitality.com/locations/kush-wynwood/.

### ★ KYU
**$$$$ | ECLECTIC** | Foodies and locavores love this eco-minded restaurant in the heart of Wynwood, which plants five trees for every tree burned in its Japanese wood-fired grill. The Asian-inspired, small-plates menu wows through creative dishes such as the epic roasted cauliflower with goat cheese and *shishito*-herb vinaigrette and sizzling Thai fried-rice stone pot with king crab. **Known for:** living walls; apex of Wynwood atmosphere; flavor-rich small plates. $ Average

Wynwood is famous for its murals from famous contemporary artists, including these by Shepard Fairey.

main: $32 ✉ 251 N.W. 25th St., Wyn-
wood ☎ 786/577–0150 ⊕ www.kyures-
taurants.com/location/kyu-miami-1/.

### 1-800-Lucky

**$ | ASIAN | FAMILY |** A restaurant, a bar,
and an entertainment venue with live
DJs wrapped into one space, this hip,
10,000-square-foot Asian food hall
has seven restaurants and a full bar to
choose from. Take a trip through Asia's
many cuisines with everything from
dumplings and pho to poke to sushi, and
even Peking duck. **Known for:** hidden res-
ervation-only karaoke room; ladies night
every Thursday; photo-worthy red-bean
ice cream. $ *Average main: $12* ✉ 143
N.W. 23rd St., Wynwood ☎ 305/768–
9826 ⊕ www.1800lucky.com.

### ★ Uchi

**$$$ | SUSHI |** Austin transplant and James
Beard Award–winning chef Tyson Cole
creates fresh takes on classic sushi
at Uchi. Indulge in rolls of thinly sliced
flounder atop candied quinoa or bigeye
tuna topped with *aji amarillo*, tangerine,
and pumpkin seed granola, or have all the
decisions made for you by opting for the
omakase menu featuring a selection of
dishes by the chef. **Known for:** delicious
bluefin tuna options; lively sushi bar seating; great happy-hour deals. $ *Average
main: $22* ✉ 252 NW 25 St., Wynwood
☎ 305/995–0915 ⊕ www.uchimiami.com.

## ☕ Coffee and Quick Bites

### Coyo Taco

**$ | MEXICAN |** Quick and easy tacos,
quesadillas, and burritos can be found
in this Wynwood gem. The local staple
has several locations that serve tasty
Mexican fare in a fast, casual setting and
a menu that's sure to keep the entire
group happy. **Known for:** massive taco
salad; fresh guacamole; frozen margaritas. $ *Average main: $7* ✉ 2300 NW
2nd Ave., Wynwood ☎ 786/773–3337
⊕ www.coyo-taco.com/restaurants/
wynwood.

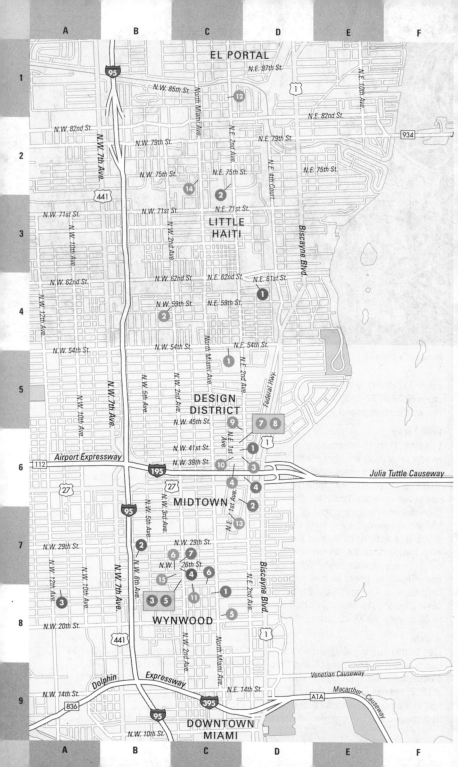

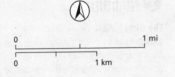

# Wynwood, Midtown, Design District and Little Haiti

JFK Causeway

**NORTH BAY VILLAGE**

0 ———————————— 1 mi
0 ———————————— 1 km

195

**KEY**

1 *Sights*
1 *Restaurants*
1 *Quick Bites*
1 *Hotels*

Venetian Causeway

### ★ Panther Coffee

$ | **CAFÉ** | The original location of the Miami-based specialty coffee roaster is smack in the center of Wynwood (it has now expanded into Miami Beach and other South Florida neighborhoods), attracting a who's who of hipsters, artists, and even suburbanites to indulge in small-batch cups of joe and super-moist muffins and fresh-baked pastries. Baristas gingerly prepare every order, so expect to wait a little for your macchiato. **Known for:** cool clientele; strong coffee; fabulous people-watching. $ *Average main: $5* ⊠ *2390 N.W. 2nd Ave., Wynwood* ☎ *305/677–3952* ⊕ *www. panthercoffee.com.*

### ★ The Salty Donut

$ | **AMERICAN** | **FAMILY** | Oversize baked doughnuts piled high with creative toppings plus fun coffee offerings like Cinnamon Toast Crunch lattes are the reasons for the sometimes long lines at this doughnut shop. Even if the national doughnut craze has subsided elsewhere, The Salty continues to live up to the hype with a rotating menu of popular pick-me-ups like the white chocolate tres leches and guava + cream cheese, made with 24-hour brioche. **Known for:** hyped-up Instagram flavor drops; baked doughnuts that are worth the wait; seasonal flavors with a Miami twist. $ *Average main: $5* ⊠ *50 N.W. 23 St., Suite 112, Wynwood* ☎ *305/639–8501* ⊕ *www.saltydonut.com.*

### Smorgasburg Miami

$ | **ECLECTIC** | **FAMILY** | Just like the one in Brooklyn, Smorgasburg Miami is an open-air food market that features local vendors every Saturday, here in a huge lot across the street from the Wynwood Walls. From noon to 7 pm, 60+ stalls serve full menus of burgers, barbecue, Japanese *sandos*, doughnuts, tacos, oysters, cheesesteaks, bubble tea, and more. **Known for:** plenty of umbrella-covered seating; weekly discounts when using Apple Pay; rotating local vendors. $ *Average main: $12* ⊠ *2600 NE 2nd Ave., Wynwood* ⊕ *www.smorgasburgmiami.com* ⊗ *Closed except Sat.*

##  Hotels

### Arlo Wynwood

$$ | **HOTEL** | Keeping with the neighborhood's vibe, the new and trendy Arlo features an industrial-meets-modern style and more than 250 works of art, its location putting visitors in the middle of Wynwood's artsy action. **Pros:** top-tier dining; only fully functioning hotel in Wynwood; rooftop pool. **Cons:** many spaces are open to the public; congested area; not every room has a balcony. $ *Rooms from: $275* ⊠ *2217 NW Miami Ct., Wynwood* ☎ *786/522-6600* ⊕ *arlohotels.com/ wynwood/* ⇄ *217 rooms* ꤶ *No Meals.*

##  Nightlife

### The Dirty Rabbit

**DANCE CLUBS** | With a neon sign that asks "Are You Dirty Enough?," this is a lively scene where 20-somethings dance until they drop. DJs play Top 40, reggaeton, and Latin pop music all night long. There's plenty of craft cocktails, beer, and hookahs, plus bottle service. ⊠ *151 NW 24 St., #107, Wynwood* ☎ *305/812–3308* ⊕ *www.thedirtyrabbitwynwood.com.*

### Grails

**CAFÉS** | A quintessential sports bar with a sneakerhead theme, this spot displays some of the world's most coveted kicks, including the rare "Back to the Future" limited edition Nikes—a sneaker collector's dream. The outdoor area is home to rotating murals (often painted live), keeping the Wynwood art vibe alive. The menu consists of classic sports bar bites with an Asian twist—think cheeseburger dumplings and poke nachos. Those looking for a slightly more refined experience can check out its sister concept next door, Spanglish, where cocktails are the main focus and the vibe is more romantic. ⊠ *2800 N. Miami Ave., Wynwood*

☎ *786/870–4313* ⊕ *www.grailsmiami. com.*

## Gramps

**BARS** | At this come-as-you-are bar that prides itself on welcoming everyone, there's a decent beer list and even better cocktails. Nightly activities like drag bingo, trivia, and karaoke keep regulars coming back for more. Those looking for late-night munchies can order from the counter at Pizza Tropical, home to some of the best pizza in Wynwood. ⊠ *176 N.W. 24 St., Wynwood* ☎ *305/699–2669* ⊕ *www.gramps.com.*

## J. Wakefield Brewing

**BREWPUBS** | Decked out in *Star Wars*–theme murals, J. Wakefield was one of the first breweries to kick off Miami's booming beer scene. The taproom boasts 15 rotating taps of beer with the most popular being Miami Madness (a Florida Weisse) and El Jefe (a coconut-infused Hefeweizen). Food trucks and local pop-ups are often found outside, giving imbibers something to munch on as they sip their way through the long list of beers. ⊠ *120 N.W. 24th St., Wynwood* ☎ *786/254–7779* ⊕ *www.jwakefieldbrewing.com.*

## ★ Veza Sur Brewing Co.

**BREWPUBS** | A newer Wynwood brewery with lively party vibes, Veza Sur serves 18 Miami-inspired brews ranging from ales to lagers and even beer cocktails. There's both indoor and outdoor seating, as well as an on-site food truck. ⊠ *55 N.W. 25th St., Wynwood* ☎ *786/362–6300* ⊕ *www. vezasur.com.*

## Wynwood Brewing Company

**BREWPUBS** | This family-owned craft brewery is hidden among Wynwood's towering walls of graffiti arts. Communal tables and ever-changing pop-up galleries by neighborhood artists make the taproom cozy; however, a peek through the window behind the bar reveals there is much more to the establishment: 15 pristine silver vats are constantly brewing variations

of blond ale, IPA, barrel-aged strong ales, seasonal offerings, and national Gold Medalist the robust Pop's Porter. All staff members are designated "Beer Servers" under the Cicerone Certification Program, ensuring knowledgeable descriptions and recommendations to your liking. ⊠ *565 N.W. 24 St., Wynwood* ☎ *305/982–8732* ⊕ *www.wynwoodbrewing.com.*

# 🛍 Shopping

## Base

**MIXED CLOTHING** | This is the quintessential fun-and-funky Miami boutique experience. Stop here for men's eclectic clothing, shoes, jewelry, and accessories that mix Japanese design with Caribbean-inspired materials. Constantly evolving, this shop features an intriguing magazine section, a record section, groovy home accessories, and the latest in men's swimwear and sunglasses. The often-present house-label designer may help select your wardrobe's newest addition. ⊠ *2215 N.W. 2nd Ave., Wynwood* ☎ *305/531–4982* ⊕ *www.baseworld.com.*

## Frangipani

**MIXED CLOTHING** | Colorful, bold prints befitting Miami feature heavily in the men's and women's clothing at this bright, independently owned boutique. Books, stationery, and locally made art and accessories also serve as perfect mementos of Florida. ⊠ *2239 N.W. 2nd Ave., Wynwood* ☎ *305/573–1480* ⊕ *www.frangipanimiami.com.*

# Midtown

Northeast of Wynwood, Midtown lies between Northeast 29th and 36th Streets, from North Miami Avenue to Northeast 2nd Avenue. This subcity is anchored by a multitower residential complex with prolific retail space, housing great dining and trusted shopping brands.

##  Restaurants

### ★ Society BBQ

$ | **BARBECUE** | Texas-inspired barbecue is all the rage at Society BBQ, where meats reign supreme and everything is smoked. The carved-to-order smoked meats and made-from-scratch sides are finger-licking good. **Known for:** burnt ends; creamy queso mac and cheese; mouthwatering brisket. $ *Average main: $13* ⊠ *3450 Buena Vista Ave., Suite 125, Midtown* ☎ *305/576–8096* ⊕ *halessocietybbq.com.*

### Sugarcane Raw Bar Grill

$$$$ | **JAPANESE** | The vibrant, supersexy, high-design restaurant perfectly captures Miami's Latin vibe while serving eclectic Latin American tapas and modern Japanese delights from three separate kitchens (*robata* grill, raw bar, and hot kitchen). Begin the Sugarcane experience in the alfresco lounge, engaging in a fabulous mix of standing, posing, flirting, and delicious-cocktail sipping, and then move on to a few of the some 60 small bites in the equally chic dining room. **Known for:** duck and waffles; crispy pig ear; great weekday happy hour. $ *Average main: $36* ⊠ *3252 N.E. 1st Ave., Midtown* ☎ *786/369–0353* ⊕ *www. sugarcanerawbargrill.com.*

## 🛏 Hotels

### Hyde Midtown Miami

$$ | **HOTEL** | Right next to The Shops at Midtown, this sbe collection hotel welcomes guests with an art-filled lobby and crisp white rooms. **Pros:** plenty of amenities; access to major highways; cabana-lined pool. **Cons:** limited street parking and expensive valet; car needed to explore outside Midtown; shared amenities with residents. $ *Rooms from: $245* ⊠ *101 N.E. 34th St., Midtown* ☎ *786/899–5300* ⊕ *www.sbe.com/ hotels/hyde/midtown-miami* ⤴ *60 rooms* ⦿ *No Meals.*

## 🍸 Nightlife

### Lagniappe

**GATHERING PLACES** | Live musicians croon from the corner, with different bands each evening. Shelves house a selection of boutique-label wines with no corkage fee. Artisanal cheeses and meats are also available for the plucking and can be arranged into tapas-board displays. Once your selection is complete, take it back into the "living room" of worn sofas, antique lamps, and old-fashioned wall photos. Additional socializing can be found out in the "backyard" of mismatched seating and strung lighting. ⊠ *3425 N.E. 2nd Ave., Midtown* ☎ *305/576–0108* ⊕ *www.lagniappehouse. com.*

# Design District

North of Midtown, from about Northeast 38th to Northeast 42nd Streets and across Interstate 195, the ultraluxurious Design District is yet another 18 blocks of clothiers, antiques shops, design stores, and bars and eateries. The real draws here are the interior design and furniture galleries as well as uber-high-end shopping that's oh-so Rodeo Drive (and rivals Bal Harbour).

##  Restaurants

### ★ Cote

$$$$ | **STEAKHOUSE** | A New York transplant, Cote is a Korean Steakhouse (not to be confused with Korean barbecue) where servers expertly cook meat and vegetables at a grill in the center of your cozy booth, cutting them into bite-size pieces with fancy scissors before serving. If you can't decide, opt for the Butcher's Feast featuring four cuts of meat and several side dishes, including a soup, veggies, rice, egg soufflé, salad, and dessert. **Known for:** wines by the glass served from magnum bottles; trendy

atmosphere; exceptional service. $ *Average main: $44* ⊠ *3900 NE 2nd Ave., Design District* ☎ *305/434-4668* ⊕ *www.cotemiami.com.*

### ★ Itamae

**$$ | JAPANESE FUSION |** Home to some of Miami's best sushi rolls, fish bowls, and ceviches, this family-run Nikkei concept (owned by James Beard–nominated brother and sister duo Nando and Valerie Chang and their father Fernando) is a hot spot amid the designer stores of the Design District. Dishes are prepared tenderly with fresh seasonal ingredients and high-quality seafood and served in a casual outdoor setting in the center of Palm Court. **Known for:** oversized ceviche bowls; Lost in Translation roll; totoro roll. $ *Average main: $18* ⊠ *140 N.E. 39th St., Suite #136, Design District* ☎ *305/631–2664* ⊕ *www.itamaemiami.com.*

### ★ L'Atelier de Joël Robuchon

**$$$$ | FRENCH |** A concept created by the legendary chef Joël Robuchon, this ultradecadent restaurant draws you in with a sexy, red-backlit bar and sleek tables. Each bite is rich in flavor and plated perfectly with immaculate French technique. **Known for:** incredible foie gras and pomme puree; gorgeous ambience; only restaurant with two Michelin stars in Florida. $ *Average main: $52* ⊠ *151 N.E. 41st St., Suite 235, Design District* ☎ *305/402–9070* ⊕ *www.latelier-miami.com.*

### Le Jardinier

**$$$ | FRENCH |** This stunning indoor-outdoor restaurant serves a vegetable-forward menu that imparts classic French techniques (no surprise, since it's the brainchild of world-renowned chef Joël Robuchon). Ingredients are sustainable and local with star dishes including heirloom beets, Heritage chicken, and chicory salad. **Known for:** lush outdoor seating; fresh seasonal offerings; perfectly plated dishes. $ *Average main: $28* ⊠ *151 N.E. 41st St., Suite 135, Design District* ☎ *305/402–9060* ⊕ *www.lejardinier-miami.com* ☉ *Closed Mon.*

### ★ Mandolin Aegean Bistro

**$$$ | GREEK |** A step inside this 1940s house-turned-bistro transports you to *ya-ya*'s home along the Aegean Sea. The Greek and Turkish cuisine is fresh and the service warm, matching its charming dining garden enlivened by an awning of trees, a rustic wooden canopy, and traditional village furnishings. **Known for:** signature Greek salad; bucolic courtyard; spectacular meze. $ *Average main: $29* ⊠ *4312 N.E. 2nd Ave., Design District* ☎ *305/576–6066* ⊕ *www.mandolinmiami.com.*

### ★ Michael's Genuine Food & Drink

**$$$ | ECLECTIC |** Michael's is often cited as one of Miami's top tried-and-true restaurants, and it's not hard to see why: this indoor-outdoor bistro in Miami's Design District is an evergreen oasis for Miami dining sophisticates. Owner and chef Michael Schwartz aims for sophisticated eclectic cuisine with an emphasis on local and organic ingredients, and he gets it right (think crispy, sweet-and-spicy pork belly with kimchi and steamed mussels in coconut milk). **Known for:** house-smoked bacon cheddar burger; sceney alfresco dining area; Sunday brunch. $ *Average main: $27* ⊠ *130 N.E. 40th St., Design District* ☎ *305/573–5550* ⊕ *www.michaelsgenuine.com.*

## ☕ Coffee and Quick Bites

### Aubi & Ramsa

**$ | AMERICAN |** At first glance, Aubi & Ramsa may seem like a sleek bar, but it's actually a 21-plus ice cream shop featuring small-batch pints infused with a bevy of spirits and wines. Imagine flavors like The Highland Truffle, made with Belgian chocolate, Macallan 12-Year scotch, and chocolate chunks; or Strawberries Rosé, a strawberry sorbet with Veuve Cliquot Rosé and St. Germain. **Known for:** boozy ice creams that cool on hot days of shopping; high-end spirits; champagne sorbet. $ *Average main: $12* ⊠ *172 N.E. 41 St., Suite 3516, Design District* ☎ *305/946–9072* ⊕ *www.aubiramsa.com.*

### Old Greg's

$$$ | PIZZA | It's easy to miss this small spot on the edge of the Design District serving pizzas (both round and square), salads, and hoagies. Old Greg's started in the home of owner Greg Tetzner during the pandemic, when he began experimenting with pizzas that went viral on social media, soon leading to a brick-and-mortar location. **Known for:** chicken parm hoagie; by the slice or the pie; OG roni pizza. $ *Average main: $25* ⊠ *3620 NE 2nd Ave., Design District* ☎ *866/653-4734* ⊕ *www.oldgregspizza.com* ⊗ *Closed Mon. - Wed.*

 ## Shopping

Miami is synonymous with good design, and this ever-expanding visitor-friendly shopping district—officially from Northeast 38th to Northeast 42nd Streets, between North Miami Avenue and Northeast 2nd Avenue (though unofficially beyond)—is a melding of public space and the exclusive world of design. High-design buildings don the creativity of architects like Aranda\Lasch, Sou Fujimoto, and the Leong Leong firm. Throughout the district, there are more than 100 home-design showrooms and galleries, including bulthaup, Ann Sacks, Poliform, and Luminaire Lab. Upscale retail outposts also grace the district. Cartier, Dolce&Gabbana, Fendi, Valentino, Veronica Beard, Alice + Olivia, Giorgio Armani, Louis Vuitton, Prada, and Rolex sit next to design showrooms. Unlike most showrooms, which are typically the beat of decorators alone, the Miami Design District's showrooms are open to the public and occupy windowed, street-level spaces. The area also has its own website: ⊕ *www.miamidesigndistrict.net.*

### En Avance x Maison Francis Kurkdjian

MIXED CLOTHING | This Forall Studio–designed space commingles the Design District's first multibrand boutique and a French-fragrance luxury house. En Avance offers a feminine compilation of on-the-cusp designers like Protagonist and Anjuna. The owner's close connection with decorative artist Fornasetti brings to the store an extensive and exclusive selection of fashion-inspired furniture and accessories for the home. Style and beauty enthusiasts will also enjoy the table displays of lotions and potions by the iconic Maison Francis Kurkdjian. ⊠ *151 N.E. 41st St., Suite 129, Design District* ☎ *305/576–0056* ⊕ *enavance.com.*

### Gelareh Mizrahi

HANDBAGS | Shop for the most stylish handbags by designer Gelareh Mizrahi at her only brick-and-mortar boutique in the world. Browse through Mizrahi's namesake collection of quirky python clutches, shoulder bags, and wallets, sometimes even running into the designer herself. ⊠ *Miami Design District, 151 N.E. 41st St., Suite 119, Design District* ☎ *301/787–5209* ⊕ *www.gelarehmizrahi.com* ⊗ *Closed Sun.*

# Little Haiti

Once a small farming community, Little Haiti is the heart and soul of Haitian society in the United States. In fact, Miami's Little Haiti is home to the largest Haitian community outside Haiti itself. Creole is commonly spoken, although some people—especially younger folks—also speak English. Its northern and southern boundaries are 85th Street and 42nd Street, respectively, with Interstate 95 to the west and Biscayne Boulevard to the east in its southern reaches, then Northeast 4th Court to the east (two blocks west of Biscayne Boulevard).

Right outside Little Haiti's boundaries, running from 50th to 77th Streets along Biscayne Boulevard, is the MiMo Biscayne Boulevard Historic District, known in short as the MiMo District. This strip is noted for its Miami Modern architecture and houses a number of boutiques and design galleries within this district and in the neighborhoods to the east—collectively known as Miami's Upper East Side. This area has been evolving over the past few years and is becoming home to trendy new restaurants and shops.

## ◉ Sights

### BaseCamp Miami
**ARTS CENTER | FAMILY |** Think of this immersive art park as the grounds of a family-friendly music festival that never ends. Local bands and DJs take the stage while visitors dance as they please before moseying over to food trucks, several lounge areas, a playground, and rotating works of art that have seen the likes of Art Basel and Burning Man. During the day you'll find pop-up shops and food vendors, and in the evening BaseCamp becomes a relaxed hangout with a full liquor bar that specializes in tequila flights. ⊠ *300 N.E. 61st St., Little Haiti.*

## 🍽 Restaurants

### Chez Le Bebe
**$$ | CARIBBEAN |** Chez Le Bebe offers a short menu of Haitian home cooking—it's been going strong for over 30 years and has been featured on shows like the Travel Channel's *Bizarre Foods with Andrew Zimmern* and *The Layover with Anthony Bourdain.* Try the stewed goat (the specialty) or the tender and flavorful chicken, fish, oxtail, or fried pork; each plate comes with rice, beans, plantains, and salad, for around $15. **Known for:** authentic Haitian eats; no-frills atmosphere; hefty portions. $ *Average main: $15 ⊠ 114 N.E. 54th St., Little Haiti* ☎ *305/751–7639.*

### ★ Clive's Cafe
**$ | JAMAICAN |** Some of the best bites come from the smallest spots, and that's especially true at Clive's Cafe. This local gem serves hearty plates of some of the best Jamaican food in Miami. **Known for:** braised oxtail; jerk chicken wings; curried goat. $ *Average main: $7 ⊠ 5890 N.W. 2nd Ave., Little Haiti* ☎ *305/757–6512* ⊕ *www.clivescafe.com* ⊗ *Closed Sun.*

### ★ Sunny's Steakhouse
**$$$$ | STEAKHOUSE |** What started as a pandemic pop-up has now become one of the city's most popular restaurants. An indoor-outdoor steak house built around a massive tree strung with pretty lights, this oasis sits in a strange warehouse area that feels like a place you shouldn't be after dark (though it's completely safe). **Known for:** seasonal oyster mignonettes; Duroc pork chops; martinis. $ *Average main: $36 ⊠ Lot 6, 7357 NW Miami Ct., Little Haiti.*

## ☕ Coffee and Quick Bites

### ★ Cindy Lou's Cookies
**$ | AMERICAN |** There's more to love than just cookies at this adorable off-the-radar bakeshop. Each day more than a dozen types of treats are baked fresh with care, including Rocky Road and Nutella swirl cookies, banana bread, carrot cake, and more. **Known for:** massive cookies; wonderful service; incredible coconut cake. $ *Average main: $4 ⊠ 7320 N.E. 2nd Ave., Little Haiti* ☎ *305/456–8585* ⊕ *cindylouscookies.com* ⊗ *Closed Mon.*

## 👜 Shopping

There's no shopping "scene" in Little Haiti—unless *botanicas* and voodoo supply shops are your thing. Nevertheless, farther east in Miami's Upper East Side lie several eclectic boutiques.

### Fly Boutique
**ANTIQUES & COLLECTIBLES |** After 13 years on South Beach, this hip vintage clothing

store moved to the up-and-coming MiMo District in Miami's Upper East Side. This resale boutique is where Miami hipsters flock for the latest arrival of used clothing. Glam designer pieces from the 1980s fly out at a premium price, but vintage camisoles and Levi's corduroys are still a resale deal. You'll find supercool art, furniture, luggage, and collectibles throughout the boutique. And be sure to look up—the eclectic lanterns are also for sale. ⊠ *7235 Biscayne Blvd., Upper East Side* ☎ *305/604–8508* ⊕ *www.instagram. com/flyboutique* ⊗ *Closed Sat.*

### Rebel

**MIXED CLOTHING** | Half new, half vintage consignment, the goods offered here make you feel as if you are raiding your stylish friend's closet. Racks are packed with all different types of styles and designers—from Lauren Moshi to Indah—requiring a little patience when sifting through. The store has a particularly strong collection of jeans, funky tees, and maxi dresses. ⊠ *7648 Biscayne Blvd., Upper East Side* ☎ *786/803–8828* ⊕ *www.instagram.com/rebelmiami.*

### Sweat Records

**MUSIC** | For a timeless version of an old-fashioned favorite, visit Sweat Records, one of Miami's last remaining record stores. Sweat sells a wide range of music—rock, pop, punk, electronic, hip-hop, and Latino—as well as turntables and vinyl accessories; there's also Miami's only vegan, organic coffee shop on the premises. ⊠ *5505 N.E. 2nd Ave., Little Haiti* ☎ *786/693–9309* ⊕ *sweatrecordsmiami.com.*

# Little Havana

First settled en masse by Cubans in the early 1960s, after Cuba's Communist revolution, Little Havana is a predominantly working-class area and the core of Miami's Hispanic community. Spanish is the principal language, but don't be surprised if the cadence is less Cuban and more Salvadoran or Nicaraguan: the neighborhood is now home to people from all Latin American countries.

If you come to Little Havana expecting the Latin version of the French Quarter in New Orleans, you're apt to be disappointed—it's not about the architecture here. Rather, it's a place to soak in the atmosphere. Little Havana is more about great, inexpensive food (not just Cuban; there's Vietnamese, Mexican, and Argentinean here as well), distinctive affordable Cuban-American art, cigars, and great coffee. It's not a prefab tourist destination—this is real life in Spanish-speaking Miami.

Little Havana's semiofficial boundaries are 27th Avenue to 4th Avenue on the west, the Miami River to the north, and Southwest 13th Street to the south. Much of the neighborhood is residential; however, you'll quickly discover the area's flavor, both literally and figuratively, along Calle Ocho (Southwest 8th Street), between Southwest 11th and 17th Avenues, which is lined with cigar factories, cafés selling guava pastries and rose-petal flan, *botanicas* brimming with candles, and Cuban clothing and crafts stores. Your "Welcome to Little Havana" photo op shines on 27th Avenue and 8th Street. Giant hand-painted roosters are found scattered throughout the entire neighborhood, an artistic nod to their real-life counterparts that roam the streets here.

You'll need to drive into Little Havana, since public transportation here is limited; but once on Calle Ocho, it's best to experience the neighborhood on foot.

 **Sights**

### Cuban Memorial Boulevard

**MONUMENT** | Four blocks in the heart of Little Havana are filled with monuments to Cuba's freedom fighters. South of Calle Ocho (8th Street), Southwest 13th Avenue becomes a ceiba tree–lined parkway known as Cuban Memorial Boulevard, divided at the center by a narrow grassy mall with a walking path through the various memorials. Among them is the *Eternal Torch of the Brigade 2506,* blazing with an endless flame and commemorating those who were killed in the failed Bay of Pigs invasion of 1961. Another is a bas-relief map of Cuba depicting each of its *municipios.* There's also a bronze statue in honor of Nestor (Tony) Izquierdo, who participated in the Bay of Pigs invasion and served in Nicaragua's Somozan forces. ✉ *S.W. 13th Ave. between S.W. 8th and S.W. 12th sts., Little Havana.*

**★ Domino Park**

**CITY PARK** | Watch a slice of Old Havana come to life in Miami's Little Havana. At Domino Park, officially known as Máximo Gómez Park, guayabera-clad seniors bask in the sun and play dominoes while onlookers share neighborhood gossip and political opinions. **TIP→ There is a little office at the park with a window where you can get information on Little Havana; the office also stores the dominoes for the older gents who play regularly, but it's BYOD (bring your own dominoes) for everyone else.** ✉ *801 S.W. 15th Ave., Little Havana* ☎ *305/859–2717 park office.*

## 🍴 Restaurants

**★ Cafe La Trova**

**$$$** | **CUBAN** | There's always a festive vibe at this Cuban hot spot from James Beard–winning chef Michelle Bernstein and famed Cantinero bartender Julio Cabrera. Old-school cocktails like the daiquiri, Hemingway fizz, and mojito are made slowly with showmanship straight from 1950s Cuba, while menu highlights include roast calabaza empanadas, *arroz con pollo,* and skirt steak *ropa vieja.* **Known for:** classic Cuban bartending; large portions; Miami Vice–theme '80s backbar. [$] *Average main: $25* ✉ *971 S.W. 8th St., Little Havana* ☎ *786/615–4379* 🌐 *www.cafelatrova.com.*

**★ Versailles**

**$$** | **CUBAN** | **FAMILY** | Miami visitors looking for that "Cuban food on Calle Ocho" experience, look no further: this storied eatery, where old émigrés opine daily about all things Cuban, is a stop on every political candidate's campaign trail, and it should be a stop for you as well. Order a heaping platter of *lechón asado* (roasted pork loin), *ropa vieja* (shredded beef), or *picadillo* (spicy ground beef), all served with rice, beans, and fried plantains. **Known for:** gossipy locals at takeout window; old-school Little Havana setting; guava-filled pastelitos. [$] *Average main: $16* ✉ *3555 S.W. 8th St., Little Havana* ☎ *305/444–0240* 🌐 *www.versaillesrestaurant.com.*

## ☕ Coffee and Quick Bites

**★ Azucar Ice Cream Company**

**$** | **CAFÉ** | **FAMILY** | More crafty than churning, flavors at this Cuban ice cream shop are inspired by and derived from ingredients at nearby fruit stands, international grocery shops, and farmers' markets. The menu features creations that nod to the culturally rich Little Havana location (*café con leche,* flan, and the signature Abuela Maria—made with Maria cookies, cream cheese, and guava) as well as seasonal specialties (like sweet creamed corn and egg nog). **Known for:** Abuela Maria ice cream; flan ice cream; one-of-a-kind frozen indulgences. [$] *Average main: $6* ✉ *1503 S.W. 8th St., Little Havana* ☎ *305/381–0369* 🌐 *www.azucaricecream.com.*

**Sanguich de Miami**

**$** | **CUBAN** | No visit to Miami is complete without a Cubano. At Sanguich de Miami every ingredient down to the mustard and pickles is made in-house, resulting in perhaps the most perfect version of the beloved sandwich. **Known for:** friendly staff; quick service; homemade Cuban classics. [$] *Average main: $12* ✉ *2057 SW 8 St., Little Havana* ☎ *305/539–0969* 🌐 *sanguich.com* ⏲ *Closed Wed.*

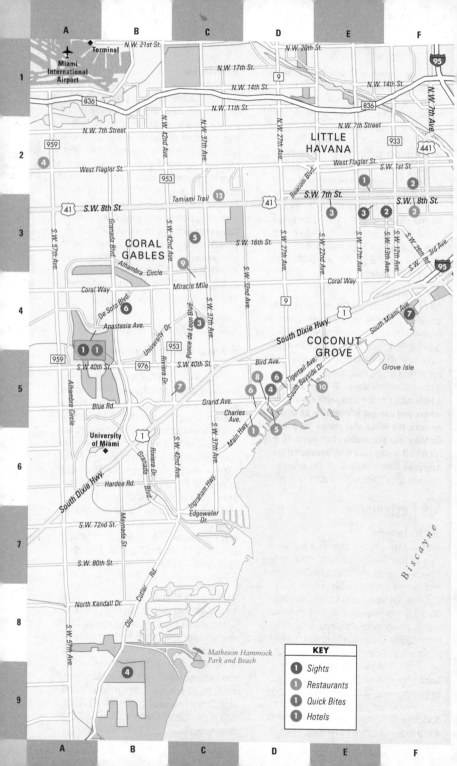

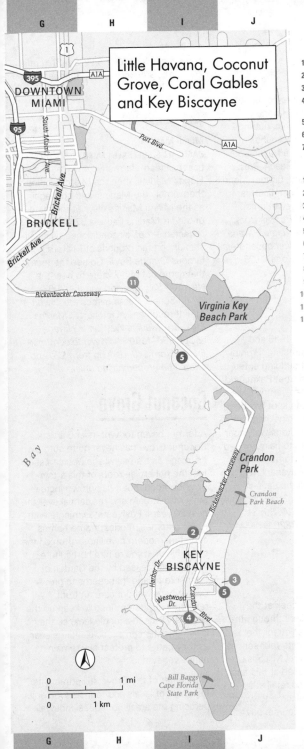

# Little Havana, Coconut Grove, Coral Gables and Key Biscayne

### Sights ▼
1 The Biltmore........................ **A4**
2 Cuban Memorial Boulevard....... **F3**
3 Domino Park........................ **E3**
4 Fairchild Tropical Botanic Garden.................... **B9**
5 Miami Seaquarium................. **I5**
6 Venetian Pool ..................... **B4**
7 Vizcaya Museum & Gardens...... **F4**

### Restaurants ▼
1 Ariete.............................. **D5**
2 Cafe La Trova...................... **F2**
3 Cantina Beach ..................... **I8**
4 El Palacio de los Jugos ........... **A2**
5 Glass & Vine....................... **D5**
6 GreenStreet Cafe ................. **D5**
7 Havana Harry's.....................**C5**
8 The Key Club ...................... **D5**
9 Luca Osteria.........................**C4**
10 Monty's Raw Bar .................. **D5**
11 Rusty Pelican...................... **H4**
12 Versailles ...........................**C2**

### Quick Bites ▼
1 Azucar Ice Cream Company....... **E2**
2 Flour and Weirdoughs ............. **I7**
3 Sanguich de Miami................. **E3**
4 Sir Pizza............................ **I8**
5 Tinta y Cafe.........................**C3**

### Hotels ▼
1 The Biltmore........................ **A4**
2 Life House, Little Havana .......... **F2**
3 Loews Coral Gables Hotel .........**C4**
4 Mr. C Miami Coconut Grove ...... **D5**
5 The Ritz-Carlton Key Biscayne, Miami............... **I8**
6 The Ritz-Carlton Coconut Grove, Miami ............ **D5**

## Hotels

**Life House, Little Havana**

**$ | HOTEL** | This tropical, retro boutique hotel in the heart of Little Havana is both budget-friendly and chic, putting you close to the sights and sounds of Miami's Cuban culture for a fraction of what you'd pay on Miami Beach. **Pros:** lush rooftop and courtyard; budget-friendly; on-site restaurant and bar. **Cons:** far from the beach; no pool; fewer amenities than large resorts. [$] *Rooms from: $150* ✉ *528 S.W. 9th Ave., Little Havana* ☎ *866/466–7534* 🌐 *www.lifehousehotels.com/hotels/miami/little-havana* 🛏 *33 rooms* 🍴 *No Meals.*

## Nightlife

★ **Ball & Chain**

**LIVE MUSIC** | Established in 1935 and steeped in legends of gambling, Prohibition protests, the rise of budding entertainers Billie Holiday and Chet Baker, and the development of Cuban-centric Calle Ocho, this storied nightlife spot has been reestablished under its original name. The high-vaulted ceilings, floral wallpaper, black-and-white photos, and palm-fringed outdoor lounge nod to its torrid history and the glamour of Old Havana. Live music flows freely, as do the Latin-inspired libations and tapas of traditional Cuban favorites. ✉ *1513 S.W. 8th St., Little Havana* ☎ *305/643–7820* 🌐 *ballandchainmiami.com.*

## Shopping

**El Titan De Bronze**

**OTHER SPECIALTY STORE** | A peek at the intently focused cigar rollers through the windows doesn't prepare you for the rich, pungent scent that jolts your senses as you step inside the store. Millions of stogies are deftly hand-rolled at this family-owned cigar factory and retail store each year. Visitors are welcome to watch the rolling action (and, of course, buy some cigars). ✉ *1071 S.W. 8th St., Little Havana* ☎ *305/860–1412* 🌐 *titandebronze.com* 🕒 *Closed Sun.*

## Activities

**Miami Marlins**

**BASEBALL & SOFTBALL** | **FAMILY** | Miami's baseball team, formerly known as the Florida Marlins, then the Miami Marlins, then simply the Marlins, and now again as the Miami Marlins plays at the state-of-the-art Marlins Park—a 37,442-seat retractable-roof, air-conditioned baseball stadium on the grounds of Miami's famous Orange Bowl. Go see the team that came out of nowhere to beat the New York Yankees and win the 2003 World Series. Home games are played April through early October. ✉ *Marlins Park, 501 Marlins Way, Little Havana* ☎ *305/480–1300* 🌐 *www.mlb.com/marlins* 🎟 *From $10; parking from $20 and should be prepurchased online.*

# Coconut Grove

A former haven for writers and artists, Coconut Grove has never quite outgrown its image as a small village. You can still feel the bohemian roots of this artsy neighborhood, but it has grown increasingly mainstream and residential over the past 20 years. Posh estates mingle with rustic cottages, modest frame homes, and stark modern dwellings, often on the same block. If you're into horticulture, you'll be impressed by the Garden of Eden–like foliage that seems to grow everywhere without care. In truth, residents are determined to keep up the Grove's village-in-a-jungle look, so they lavish attention on exotic plantings even as they battle to protect any remaining native vegetation.

The center of the Grove still attracts its fair share of locals and tourists who enjoy perusing the small boutiques, sidewalk

Vizcaya Museum and Gardens features more than 10 acres of formal gardens overlooking Biscayne Bay.

cafés, and cute galleries that remind us of the old Grove. Activities here are family-friendly with easy access to bay-side parks, museums, and gardens.

## Sights

**★ Vizcaya Museum & Gardens**
**HISTORIC HOME** | **FAMILY** | Of the 10,000 people living in Miami between 1912 and 1916, about 1,000 of them were gainfully employed by Chicago industrialist James Deering to build this European-inspired residence that resembles a tropical version of Versailles. Once comprising 180 acres, this National Historic Landmark now occupies a 30-acre tract that includes a rockland hammock (native forest) and more than 10 acres of formal gardens with fountains overlooking Biscayne Bay. The house, open to the public, contains 70 rooms, 34 of which are filled with paintings, sculpture, antique furniture, and other fine and decorative arts. The collection spans 2,000 years and represents the Renaissance, baroque, rococo, and neoclassical periods. The 90-minute self-guided Discover Vizcaya Audio Tour is available in multiple languages for an additional $5. Moonlight tours, offered on evenings that are nearest the full moon, provide a magical look at the gardens; call for reservations. ✉ *3251 S. Miami Ave., Coconut Grove* ☎ *305/250–9133* 🌐 *www.vizcaya.org* 🎟 *$25* 🕒 *Closed Tues.*

## Restaurants

**★ Ariete**
**$$$$** | **AMERICAN** | Popular with the brunch crowd, this cozy indoor-outdoor restaurant serves elegant American dishes with a Miami twist. The menu changes seasonally with offerings from pastrami-style short rib to bone marrow–topped, wood-grilled oysters. **Known for:** great cocktails; lively brunch; the Chug burger. [$] *Average main: $34* ✉ *3540 Main Hwy., Coconut Grove* ☎ *305/640–5862* 🌐 *www.arietecoconutgrove.com.*

## Glass & Vine

**$$$$ | MODERN AMERICAN | FAMILY** | With a design that fuses the indoors and out-doors in the middle of Coconut Grove's residential Peacock Park, this charming, family-friendly restaurant is as pictur-esque as it is unexpected. Parents can sit back and enjoy some incredible gour-met-style sharing plates (featuring local catch and produce) and the sensational wine selection while the little ones are thoroughly entertained outside (there's even a playground). **Known for:** local fish tiradito; plenty of veggie options; beauti-fully plated dishes. $ *Average main: $34* ✉ *2820 McFarlane Rd., Coconut Grove* ☎ *305/200–5268* ⊕ *www.glassandvine. com.*

## GreenStreet Cafe

**$ | MEDITERRANEAN** | A tried-and-true locals' hangout since it was founded in the early 1990s—with regulars including athletes, politicians, entrepreneurs, art-ists, and other prominent area names—this cozy café serves simple French-Med-iterranean delights. Despite the restaurant's see-and-be-seen reputation, diners are encouraged to sit back and simply enjoy the experience with relaxed decor, good food, and friendly service. **Known for:** fruity cocktails; Nutella French toast; late-night lounging and noshing. $ *Average main: $19* ✉ *3468 Main Hwy., Coconut Grove* ☎ *305/444–0244* ⊕ *www. greenstreetcafe.net.*

## The Key Club

**$$$$ | AMERICAN** | Located on the first floor of CocoWalk, The Key Club serves mod-ern-American dishes in a super-trendy setting. One of the newest ventures from Groot Hospitality (known for their flashy clubstaurants), this spot is signif-icantly more low-key than their other restaurants, and the food is the main focus (though there's often a DJ during late-night dinner). **Known for:** cedar plank salmon; massive twice-baked potato; chips and caviar with French onion dip. $ *Average main: $32* ✉ *CocoWalk, 3015*

*Grand Ave., Coconut Grove* ☎ *305/521–4969* ⊕ *www.thekeyclub.com.*

## Monty's Raw Bar

**$$$ | SEAFOOD | FAMILY** | Monty's has a Caribbean flair, thanks especially to live calypso and island music on the outdoor terrace. Consider it a fun, tropical-style, kid-friendly place where Mom and Dad can kick back in the early evening and enjoy a beer and the raw bar while the kids eat conch fritters and dance to the beats. **Known for:** palapa-topped outdoor seating; tropical cocktails; waterfront views. $ *Average main: $23* ✉ *Bay-shore Landing, 2550 S. Bayshore Dr., at Aviation Ave., Coconut Grove* ☎ *305/856–3992* ⊕ *www.montysrawbar.com.*

 # Hotels

Although this area certainly can't replace the draw of Miami Beach or the business convenience of Downtown, about 20 minutes away, it's an exciting bohemi-an-chic neighborhood with a gorgeous waterfront.

## ★ Mr. C Miami Coconut Grove

**$$$ | HOTEL** | An oasis in the middle of Coconut Grove, this hotel operated by the Cipriani family delivers stunning views of Biscayne Bay and the nearby skyline. **Pros:** rooftop pool; private spa suites; stellar service. **Cons:** car needed for beach visits; located at busy inter-section; sometimes windy pool area. $ *Rooms from: $320* ✉ *2988 McFarlane Rd., Coconut Grove* ☎ *305/800–6672* ⊕ *www.mrchotels.com/mrccoconutgrove* ⤢ *98 rooms* ◎ *No Meals.*

## ★ The Ritz-Carlton Coconut Grove, Miami

**$$$$ | HOTEL** | In the heart of Coconut Grove, this business-oriented hotel is an elegant and modern design master-piece that rivals top leisure properties in Miami Beach and Downtown. **Pros:** elevated pool deck; fresh from renova-tion; in an easily walkable area. **Cons:** near residential area; not on beach; lots of conventioneers. $ *Rooms from: $577*

✉ *3300 S.W. 27th Ave., Coconut Grove*
☎ *305/644–4680* ⊕ *www.ritzcarlton.com/coconutgrove* ⇥ *115 rooms* ⏣ *No Meals.*

##  Nightlife

### Sandbar Sports Grill
**PUBS** | You may recognize this divey sports bar from the show *Bar Rescue*. Typically home to a lively college crowd, it's a great place to pop in for an ice cold beer (there are 40+ beers on tap) and classic bar foods. With more than 30 TVs, there's no chance you'll miss a game. ✉ *3064 Grand Ave., Coconut Grove* ☎ *786/359–4510* ⊕ *www.sandbargrove.com.*

### The Taurus
**BARS** | Miami's oldest drinking establishment is a staple in Coconut Grove, known for its expansive whiskey collection. The atmosphere is relaxed and friendly, and the bartenders are knowledgeable in their craft. The menu features a solid mix of classic cocktails and others inspired by Coconut Grove's lush surroundings. It's also often home to weekend pop-ups from other local vendors. ✉ *3540 Main Hwy., Suite c103, Coconut Grove* ☎ *305/529–6523* ⊕ *thetauruscoconutgrove.com.*

##  Shopping

### CocoWalk
**MALL** | **FAMILY** | This three-story, indoor-outdoor mall anchors the Grove's shopping scene, and a recent renovation has given it new life. Once filled with cheesy, touristy kiosks and chain restaurants, it's now home to many local shops and some quality restaurants, like Mister 01 Extraordinary Pizza, PLANTA Queen, and Sushi Garage. On the top floor sits Cinépolis Luxury Cinemas, a multiscreen, state-of-the-art movie theater with a wine bar and lounge and in-seat food service. Overall, the space mixes the bustle of a mall with the breathability of an open-air market. ✉ *3015 Grand Ave., Coconut Grove* ☎ *305/444–0777* ⊕ *cocowalk.com.*

### Unika
**MIXED CLOTHING** | A longtime fashion resident of Coconut Grove (circa 1989), Unika takes shoppers from day to night, and all affairs in between, with a wide range of inventory for men and women. The contemporary boutique has an it-girl vibe, but the cool, relaxed one you'd actually want to be friends with. High–low pricing appeases all budgets; expect to uncover up-and-coming designer gems tucked within the racks of well-known brands. Bonus: the staff is great with styling for a head-to-toe look. ✉ *3432 Main Hwy., Coconut Grove* ☎ *305/445–4752* ⊕ *coconutgrove.com/business/unika.*

# Coral Gables

You can easily spot Coral Gables from the window of a Miami-bound jetliner—just look for the massive orange tower of The Biltmore hotel rising from a lush green carpet of trees concealing the city's gracious homes. The canopy is as much a part of this planned city as its distinctive architecture, all attributed to the vision of George E. Merrick more than a century ago.

The story of this city began in 1911, when Merrick inherited 1,600 acres of citrus and avocado groves from his father. Through judicious investment he nearly doubled the tract to 3,000 acres by 1921. Merrick dreamed of building an American Venice here, complete with canals and homes. Working from this vision, he began designing a city based on centuries-old prototypes from Mediterranean countries. Unfortunately for Merrick, the devastating no-name hurricane of 1926, followed by the Great Depression, prevented him from fulfilling many of his plans. He died at 54, an employee of the post office.

Today Coral Gables has a population of about 50,000. In its bustling downtown, more than 150 multinational companies maintain headquarters or regional offices, and the University of Miami campus in the southern part of the Gables brings a youthful vibrancy to the area. A southern branch of the city extends down the shore of Biscayne Bay through neighborhoods threaded with canals.

## ◉ Sights

### The Biltmore

**HOTEL** | Bouncing back stunningly from its dark days as an army hospital, this hotel has become the jewel of Coral Gables—a dazzling architectural gem with a colorful past. First opened in 1926, it was a hot spot for the rich and glamorous of the Jazz Age until it was converted to an army–air force regional hospital in 1942. Following World War II, the Veterans Administration continued to operate the hospital until 1968. The Biltmore then lay vacant for nearly 20 years before it underwent extensive renovations and reopened as a luxury hotel in 1987. Its 16-story tower, like the Freedom Tower in Downtown Miami, is a replica of Seville's Giralda tower. The magnificent pool is reportedly the largest hotel pool in the continental United States. ■**TIP**→ **Because it functions as a full-service hotel, your ticket in—if you aren't staying here—is to patronize one of the hotel's several restaurants or bars. Try to get a courtyard table for the Sunday champagne brunch, a local legend.** ✉ *1200 Anastasia Ave., Coral Gables* ✛ *Near De Soto Blvd.* ☎ *855/311–6903* ⊕ *www.biltmorehotel.com.*

### Fairchild Tropical Botanic Garden

**GARDEN** | **FAMILY** | With 83 acres of lakes, sunken gardens, a 560-foot vine pergola, orchids, bellflowers, coral trees, bougainvillea, rare palms, and flowering trees, Fairchild is the largest tropical botanical garden in the continental United States. The tram tour highlights the best of South Florida and exotic flora; then

you can set off exploring on your own. The 2-acre Simons Rainforest, which is complete with a waterfall and a stream, showcases tropical plants from around the world. The conservatory contains rare tropical plants, including the Burmese *Amherstia nobilis,* flowering annually with orchidlike pink flowers. The Keys Coastal Habitat, created in a marsh and mangrove area in 1995 with assistance from the Tropical Audubon Society, provides food and shelter to resident and migratory birds. ✉ *10901 Old Cutler Rd., Coral Gables* ☎ *305/667–1651* ⊕ *www.fairchildgarden.org* ✈ *$25.*

### Venetian Pool

**POOL** | **FAMILY** | Sculpted from a rock quarry in 1923 and fed by artesian wells, this 820,000-gallon municipal pool remains quite popular because of its themed architecture—a fantasy version of a waterfront Italian village—created by Denman Fink. The pool has earned a place on the National Register of Historic Places and showcases a nice collection of vintage photos depicting 1920s beauty pageants and swank soirées held long ago. Paul Whiteman played here. Johnny Weissmuller and Esther Williams swam here, and you should, too (note: children must be at least 3 years old and 38 inches tall). A snack bar, lockers, and showers make these historic splash grounds user friendly as well, and there's free parking across De Soto Boulevard. Call before visiting to confirm that renovations (which closed the pool in late 2022 through early 2023) are complete. ✉ *2701 De Soto Blvd., at Toledo St., Coral Gables* ☎ *305/460–5306* ⊕ *www.coralgables.com/venetian-pool* ✈ *$21.*

## ⊕ Beaches

### Matheson Hammock Park

**BEACH** | **FAMILY** | Kids love the gentle waves and warm (albeit often murky) waters of this beach in Coral Gables suburbia, near the Fairchild Tropical Botanic Garden. But the beach is only part of the draw—the park includes a boardwalk trail, a playground, and a golf course. Plus, the park is a prime spot for kiteboarding. The man-made lagoon, or "atoll pool," is perfect for inexperienced swimmers, and it's one of the best places in mainland Miami for a picnic. Most tourists don't make the trek here; this park caters more to locals who don't want to travel all the way to Miami Beach. The park also offers a full-service marina. **Amenities:** parking (fee); toilets. **Best for:** swimming. ✉ *9610 Old Cutler Rd., Coral Gables* ☎ *305/665–5475* 🌐 *www.miamidade.gov/parks/matheson-hammock.asp* 🎟 *$5 per vehicle weekdays, $7 weekends.*

## 🍴 Restaurants

**El Palacio de los Jugos**

$ | **CUBAN** | **FAMILY** | To the northwest of Coral Gables proper, this small but boisterous indoor-outdoor market is one of the easiest and truest ways to see Miami's local Latin life in action. Besides the rows of fresh, tropical fruits and vegetables—and the shakes you can get with any of them—Miami's original food hall has numerous counters where you can order a wide variety of Latin American food, from *pan con lechón* (roast pork on Cuban bread) to fried pork rinds. **Known for:** fresh, cold coconut water in the shell; no-frills feel; picnic-style tables. [$] *Average main: $8* ✉ *5721 W. Flagler St., Flagami, Coral Gables* ☎ *305/264–1503* 🌐 *elpalaciodelosjugos.com.*

**Havana Harry's**

$$ | **CUBAN** | **FAMILY** | When Cuban families want an affordable home-cooked meal with a twist but don't want to cook it themselves, they come to this big, unassuming restaurant. The fare is traditional Cuban: long, thin, panfried steaks known as *bistec palomilla,* roast chicken with citrus marinade, and fried pork chunks. **Known for:** mariquitas (plantain chips) with mojo; acclaimed flan; "tres leches overdose" dessert. [$] *Average main: $17* ✉ *4612 Le Jeune Rd., Coral Gables* ☎ *305/661–2622* 🌐 *www.havanaharrys.com.*

★ **Luca Osteria**

$$$ | **ITALIAN** | *Chopped* winner Giorgio Rapicavoli hones in on his Italian heritage with a menu full of dishes inspired by his childhood. Located in the center of pedestrian-friendly Giralda Avenue, it's an ideal spot for dinner with a group or an intimate bite with a friend. **Known for:** extensive wine list; housemade pastas; patate fritte with fresh truffles. [$] *Average main: $29* ✉ *116 Giralda Ave., Coral Gables* ☎ *305/381–5097* 🌐 *www.lucamiami.com* 🕒 *Closed Mon.*

## ☕ Coffee and Quick Bites

**Tinta y Cafe**

$ | **CUBAN** | A small Cuban café that's always busy and smells of fresh *cafecito,* this is the spot to visit for a quick breakfast, sandwich, or afternoon snack and coffee jolt. The small space has just a few tables and a counter that fits no more than six people. **Known for:** no-nonsense staff; strong coffee; filling Cuban breakfast. [$] *Average main: $6* ✉ *1315 Ponce De Leon, Coral Gables* ☎ *305/285–0101* 🌐 *www.tintaycafe.co.*

## 🛏 Hotels

Beautiful Coral Gables is set around its beacon, national landmark The Biltmore hotel. The University of Miami is nearby.

**The Biltmore**

$$$$ | **HOTEL** | Built in 1926, this landmark hotel has had several incarnations over the years—including a stint as a hospital during World War II—but through it all, this grande dame has remained an opulent reminder of yesteryear, with its palatial lobby and grounds, enormous pool (largest in the Lower 48), and distinctive 315-foot tower, which rises above the canopy of trees shading Coral Gables. **Pros:** breathtaking history-steeped

lobby; gorgeous pool; great golf. **Cons:** in the suburbs; a car is necessary to get around; daily $23 resort fee. ⓢ *Rooms from: $499* ✉ *1200 Anastasia Ave., Coral Gables* ☏ *855/311–6903* ⊕ *www.biltmorehotel.com* ⤳ *312 rooms* Ⓞ *No Meals.*

### ★ Loews Coral Gables Hotel
**$$$ | HOTEL |** Just four blocks off Miracle Mile, the Loews Coral Gables opened in 2022 and is an ideal hotel for those who want to be away from the South Beach party scene. **Pros:** rooftop pool with city views; brand new hotel; on-site spa and salon. **Cons:** can be full of conference-go-ers; car is needed to get around; pricy per night pet fee. ⓢ *Rooms from: $349* ✉ *2950 Coconut Grove Dr., Coral Gables* ☏ *786/772–7600* ⊕ *loewshotels.com/coral-gables* ⤳ *242 rooms* Ⓞ *No Meals.*

##  Nightlife

### The Bar
**BARS |** One of the oldest bars in South Florida (est. 1946), the old Hofbräu has been reincarnated a few times and now goes by the name "The Bar." A massive American flag hangs on the wall of this locals' hangout, arguably the only cool nightlife in suburban Coral Gables. The Bar delivers DJ-led tunes Wednesday through Saturday nights and karaoke on Tuesday night. Oh, and they have pretty awesome, farm-fresh bar food, too. ✉ *172 Giralda Ave., at Ponce de León Blvd., Coral Gables* ☏ *305/442–2730* ⊕ *www.gablesthebar.com.*

### Cebada Rooftop
**BARS |** Miami loves a rooftop bar, and Cebada is the only one in Coral Gables. Serving up tropical drinks and bites in a lush setting, this is the place to go for a happy hour meetup (there's a discounted menu from 5 to 7 pm) or after-dinner drinks. The cocktails have cheeky names and are often garnished with flamingos or pineapples, making them especially

photo-worthy. ✉ *124 Giralda Ave., Coral Gables* ☏ *786/409–2287* ⊕ *www.cebada-rooftop.com* ⊘ *Closed Sun. and Mon.*

### ★ El Carajo
**WINE BARS |** The back of a gas station is perhaps the most unexpected location for a wine bar, yet for 30 years a passion for good food and drink has kept this family-run business among Miami's best-kept secrets—although they've added a sign outside. Tables are in the Old World–style wine cellar, stocked with bottles representing all parts of the globe (and at excellent prices). A waiter takes your order from the menu of exquisite cheeses and charcuterie, hot and cold tapas, paellas, and, of course, wine. ✉ *2465 S.W. 17th Ave., Coral Gables* ☏ *305/856–2424* ⊕ *el-carajo.com.*

##  Shopping

### ★ Books & Books
**BOOKS | FAMILY |** Greater Miami's only independent English-language bookshop specializes in contemporary and classical literature as well as books on the arts, architecture, Florida, and Cuba. The Coral

Gables store is the largest of several South Florida locations. Here, you can sip and read in the courtyard lounge or dine at the old-fashioned in-store café while browsing the photography gallery. Multiple rooms are filled with myriad genres; plus there's an entire area dedicated to kids. There are book signings, literary events, poetry, and other readings, too. ✉ *265 Aragon Ave., Coral Gables* ☎ *305/442–4408* ⊕ *www.booksand-books.com.*

### Miracle Mile

**NEIGHBORHOODS** | The centerpiece of the downtown Coral Gables shopping district, lined with trees and busy with strolling shoppers, is home to a host of exclusive couturiers and bridal shops as well as some men's and women's boutiques, jewelry, and home-furnishings stores. The half-mile "mile" runs from Douglas Road to LeJeune Road and Aragon Avenue to Andalusia Avenue, but many of the Gables's best nonbridal shops are found on side streets, off the actual Mile. In addition, the street itself teems with restaurants—more than two dozen—facilitating a fabulous afternoon of shopping and eating. ■**TIP➔ If debating Miracle Mile versus Bal Harbour or the Design District, check out the others first.** ✉ *Miracle Mile (Coral Way), Coral Gables* ✛ *Douglas Rd. to LeJeune Rd., and Aragon Ave. to Andalusia Ave.*

### Silvia Tcherassi

**WOMEN'S CLOTHING** | The famed, Miami-based Colombian designer's signature boutique features ready-to-wear, feminine, and frilly dresses and separates accented with chiffon, toile, and sequins. You'll see plenty of Tcherassi's designs on Miami's Latin power players at events and A-list parties. A neighboring atelier showcases the designer's bridal collection. ✉ *207 San Lorenzo Ave., Coral Gables* ☎ *305/461–0009* ⊕ *www.silviatcherassi.com* ☾ *Closed Sun.*

##  Activities

### ★ Biltmore Golf Course

**GOLF** | On the grounds of the historic Biltmore hotel, the championship Biltmore Golf Course was designed in 1925 by Scotsman Donald Ross, the "it" golf designer of the Roaring '20s. Today, the lush course looks better than ever and is easily accessible thanks to its advanced online booking system. There's a pro shop on site, and golf instruction is available through the Biltmore Golf Academy or the more extensive on-site Golf Channel Academy. ✉ *The Biltmore, 1210 Anastasia Ave., Coral Gables* ☎ *305/460–5364* ⊕ *www.biltmorehotel.com/golf* 🖫 *From $69 for 9 holes, $118 for 18 holes* 🏌 *18 holes, 7800 yards, par 71.*

# Key Biscayne

Once upon a time, the two barrier islands that make up the village of Key Biscayne (Key Biscayne itself and Virginia Key) were outposts for fishermen and sailors, pirates and salvagers, soldiers and settlers. The 95-foot Cape Florida Light lighthouse stood tall during Seminole tribe battles and hurricanes. Coconut plantations covered two-thirds of Key Biscayne, and there were plans as far back as the 1800s to develop the picturesque island as a resort for the wealthy. Fortunately, the state and county governments set much of the land aside for parks, and both keys are now home to top-ranked beaches and golf, tennis, softball, and picnicking facilities.

The long and winding bike paths that run through the islands are favorites for in-line skaters and cyclists. Incorporated in 1991, the village of Key Biscayne is a hospitable community of about 15,300, even though Virginia Key remains undeveloped at the moment. These two playground islands are especially family-friendly.

Sights

### Miami Seaquarium

**AQUARIUM | FAMILY |** This classic family attraction promotes environmental education and raises conservation awareness yet stages shows with sea lions, dolphins, and other marine animals (including killer whales). Discovery Bay, an endangered-mangrove habitat, is home to sea turtles, alligators, herons, egrets, and ibis. You can also visit a shark pool, a tropical reef aquarium, and West Indian and Florida manatees. A popular interactive attraction is the Stingray Touch Tank, where you can touch and feed cownose rays and southern stingrays. Another big draw is the Dolphin Interaction program, including the quite intensive Dolphin Odyssey ($219) experience and the lighter shallow-water Dolphin Encounter ($159). ✉ *4400 Rickenbacker Causeway, Virginia Key* ☎ *305/361–5705* ⊕ *www.miamiseaquarium.com* ✈ *$29.99, parking $10 (cash only).*

 Beaches

### ★ Bill Baggs Cape Florida State Park

**BEACH | FAMILY |** Thanks to inviting beaches, sunsets, and a tranquil lighthouse, this park at Key Biscayne's southern tip is worth the drive. In fact, the 1-mile stretch of pure beachfront has been named several times in Dr. Beach's revered America's Top 10 Beaches list. It has 18 picnic pavilions available as daily rentals, two cafés that serve light lunches (including several Cuban specialties), and plenty of space to plant the umbrellas and chairs that you can rent. The walking and bicycle paths provide wonderful views of Miami's dramatic skyline. From the southern end of the park you can see a handful of houses rising over the bay on wooden stilts, the remnants of Stiltsville, built in the 1940s and now protected by the Stiltsville Trust. The nonprofit group was established in 2003 to preserve the structures, which showcase the park's rich history. Bill Baggs also has bicycle rentals, a playground, fishing piers, and guided tours of the Cape Florida Lighthouse, South Florida's oldest structure. The lighthouse was erected in 1845 to replace an earlier one damaged in an 1836 battle with the Seminole tribe. Free tours are offered at the restored cottage and lighthouse Thursday to Monday at 10 am and 1 pm. Be there a half hour beforehand. **Amenities:** food and drink; lifeguards; parking (no fee); showers; toilets. **Best for:** solitude; sunset; walking. ✉ *1200 S. Crandon Blvd., Key Biscayne* ☎ *305/361–5811* ⊕ *www.floridastateparks.org/park/Cape-Florida* ✈ *$8 per vehicle, $2 per pedestrian.*

### Crandon Park

**BEACH | FAMILY |** This relaxing oasis in northern Key Biscayne offers renowned tennis facilities, a great golf course, a family amusement center, and 2 miles of beach dotted with palm trees. The park is divided by Key Biscayne's main road, with tennis and golf on the bay side, the beaches on the ocean side. Families really enjoy the beaches here—the sand is soft, there are no riptides, there's a great view of the Atlantic, and parking is both inexpensive and plentiful. Nevertheless, on weekends be prepared for a long hike from your car to the beach. There are bathrooms, outdoor showers, plenty of picnic tables, and concession stands. Kiteboard rentals and lessons are offered from the northern-end water-sports concessions, as are kayak rentals. Ecotours and nature trails showcase the myriad ecosystems of Key Biscayne, including mangroves, coastal hammock, and seagrass beds. Bird-watching is great at the southern end of the park. **Amenities:** food and drink; lifeguards; parking (fee); showers; toilets; water sports. **Best for:** swimming; walking. ✉ *6747 Crandon Blvd., Key Biscayne* ☎ *305/361–5421* ⊕ *www.miamidade.gov/Parks/crandon.asp* ✈ *$5 per vehicle weekdays, $7 weekends.*

## 🍴 Restaurants

**Cantina Beach**
**$$$ | MEXICAN** | Discover a small, sumptuous piece of coastal Mexico at this feet-in-the-sand Mexican restaurant at The Ritz-Carlton Key Biscayne, Miami. (Note: non–hotel guests are welcome.) Order the guacamole, prepared tableside, a few tequila-infused cocktails (like the sour black cherry Black Diamond margarita), and then move onto heartier plates of fajitas and enchiladas. **Known for:** top-shelf margaritas; ceviche; family-friendly setting. $ *Average main: $25* ✉ *The Ritz-Carlton Key Biscayne, Miami, 455 Grand Bay Dr., Key Biscayne* ☎ *305/365–4500* 🌐 *www.ritzcarlton.com/keybiscayne.*

**Rusty Pelican**
**$$$$ | AMERICAN** | Vistas of the bay and Miami skyline are sensational—whether you admire them through the floor-to-ceiling windows or from the expansive outdoor seating area, lined with alluring firepits. The menu is split between tropically inspired small plates, ideal for sharing, and heartier entrées from land and sea. **Known for:** sunset views; crispy fried, whole local red snapper; protein-rich Rusty Pelican Board for Two. $ *Average main: $35* ✉ *3201 Rickenbacker Causeway, Key Biscayne* ☎ *305/361–3818* 🌐 *www.therustypelican.com.*

## ☕ Coffee and Quick Bites

★ **Flour and Weirdoughs**
**$ | BAKERY** | The oversize pastries at this bakery have quickly gained a cult following. The cheeky menu features items like the Chocolate Sloth (a chocolate croissant), the Basic AF (their words, not ours) croissant, and the It's Brisket B*tch, a large croissant filled with smoked brisket, provolone cheese, and grain mustard. **Known for:** fresh baked loaves of bread; cinnamon rolls; brisket-filled croissants. $ *Average main: $4* ✉ *19 Harbor Dr., Key Biscayne* ☎ *305/361–9000* 🌐 *www.flourandweirdoughs.com* 🕒 *Closed Mon.*

★ **Sir Pizza**
**$ | PIZZA | FAMILY** | A local favorite for a quick bite while hanging out on The Key, Sir Pizza keeps it simple with square-cut thin-crust pizzas, sandwiches, and hefty deli salads. Using fresh ingredients, special marinara sauce, and tiny cubes of pepperoni, these pies are ones you'll likely think about for awhile. **Known for:** loyal regulars; pepperoni pizza; deli-style salads. $ *Average main: $13* ✉ *712 Crandon Blvd., Key Biscayne* ☎ *305/361–5701* 🌐 *www.sirpizzakeybiscayne.com.*

## 🛏 Hotels

There's probably no other place in Miami where slowness is lifted to a fine art. On Key Biscayne there are no pressures, there's no nightlife outside of The Ritz-Carlton's great live Latin music weekends, and the dining choices are essentially limited to the hotel (which has five dining options, including the languorous, Havana-style RUMBAR).

★ **The Ritz-Carlton Key Biscayne, Miami**
**$$$$ | RESORT | FAMILY** | In an ultra-laid-back setting on serene Key Biscayne, it's only natural to appreciate the Ritz hallmarks of pampering with luxurious rooms, attentive service, five on-property dining options, and ample recreational activities for the whole family. **Pros:** a world away from city life; feet-in-the-sand restaurants; an adults-only pool. **Cons:** outside noise may permeate thin sliding-glass doors; beach sometimes seaweed-strewn; limited nearby dining options off property. $ *Rooms from: $599* ✉ *455 Grand Bay Dr., Key Biscayne* ☎ *305/365–4500* 🌐 *www.ritzcarlton.com/keybiscayne* 🛏 *402 rooms* 🍴 *No Meals.*

#  Activities

Perfect weather and flat terrain make Miami–Dade County a popular place for cyclists; however, biking here can also be quite dangerous. Be very vigilant when biking on Miami Beach, or better yet, steer clear and bike the beautiful paths of Key Biscayne instead.

### Crandon Golf at Key Biscayne

GOLF | On the serene island of Key Biscayne, overlooking Biscayne Bay, this top-rated, championship municipal golf course is considered one of the state's most challenging par-72 courses. Enveloped by tropical foliage, mangroves, saltwater lakes, and bay-side waters, the course also happens to be the only one in North America with a subtropical lagoon. The Devlin/Von Hagge–designed course has a USGA rating of 75.4 and a slope rating of 129, and has received national awards from both *Golfweek* and *Golf Digest*. The course is located on the south side of Crandon Park. ⊠ *Crandon Park, 6700 Crandon Blvd., Key Biscayne* ☎ *855/465–3305 for tee times* ⊕ *www. golfcrandon.com* ⊒ *Starting at $95* ⚐ *18 holes, 7400 yards, par 72.*

### Divers Paradise of Key Biscayne

SCUBA DIVING | This complete dive shop and diving-charter service, next to the Crandon Park Marina, includes equipment rental and scuba instruction with PADI and NAUI affiliation. Half-day (four-hour) dive trips and snorkel trips are offered Tuesday through Sunday. ⊠ *Crandon Park Marina, 4000 Crandon Blvd., Key Biscayne* ☎ *305/361–3483* ⊕ *keydivers.com* ⊒ *Classes start at $299.*

### Key Cycling

BIKING | On an island where biking is a way of life, this Key Biscayne bike shop carries a wide range of amazing bikes in its showroom, as well as any kind of bike accessory imaginable. Out-of-towners can rent mountain or hybrid bikes for $20 for two hours, $25 for the day, and $100 for the week. ⊠ *Galleria Shopping Center, 328 Crandon Blvd., Suite 121, Key Biscayne* ☎ *305/361–0061* ⊕ *www. keycyclingkb.com/.*

# Chapter 4

# THE EVERGLADES

4

Updated by
Amber Love Bond

⊙ Sights    ⑪ Restaurants    🍽 Hotels    💼 Shopping    ⍟ Nightlife

★★★★★      ★★☆☆☆      ★★☆☆☆      ★☆☆☆☆      ★☆☆☆☆

# WELCOME TO THE EVERGLADES

## TOP REASONS TO GO

★ **Gator spotting:** This is ground zero for alligator viewing in the United States, and odds are you'll leave having spotted your quota.

★ **Cool kayaking:** Do a half-day trip in Big Cypress National Preserve or Biscayne National Park, or grab a paddle for the ultimate 99-mile Wilderness Waterway.

★ **Backwater boating:** Tour the swampy Everglades backwaters with a guide, and you'll learn firsthand about Florida ecology.

★ **Abundant birdlife:** Check hundreds of birds off your list, including—if you're lucky—the rare Everglade snail kite.

★ **Swamp cuisine:** Want to chow down on alligator tail or frogs' legs? Or how about swamp cabbage, made from hearts of palm? Better yet, try stone crabs fresh from the traps.

★ **Tropical flavors:** The farmland surrounding the Everglades is rich in fruits like mangoes and strawberries. Stop in Homestead to pick your own or try a smoothie.

**1** **Everglades National Park.** Alligators, Florida panthers, black bears, manatees, dolphins, bald eagles, and roseate spoonbills call this vast swamp habitat home. Hike the trails, canoe, or take a boat tour.

**2** **Big Cypress National Preserve.** An outdoor lover's paradise and great spot for camping, kayaking, and stargazing.

**3** **Biscayne National Park.** The string of coral reefs and islands that form the Florida Keys starts at this mostly underwater park, where boating, snorkeling, and kayaking through mangroves are top activities.

**4** **Everglades City.** In this small swamp town, the Ten Thousand Islands and fresh seafood await.

**5** **Florida City.** This last suburb of Miami before reaching the Florida Keys is the gateway to Everglades National Park.

**6** **Homestead.** A historic district is surrounded by a mix of modern living and farmland, including an exotic-fruit winery.

**7** **Tamiami Trail.** This 100-year-old road is the path to Old Florida's wildest areas and where you'll access most airboating tours.

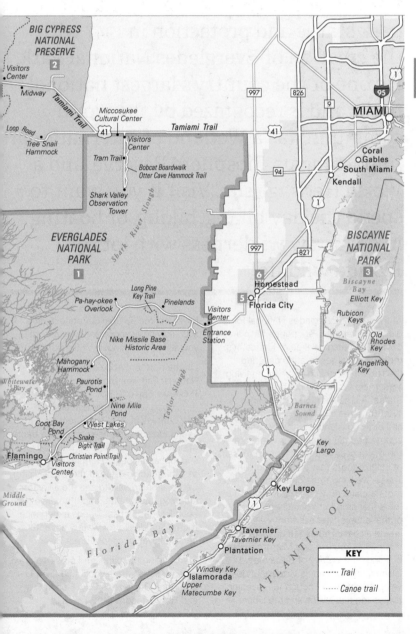

More than 1.5 million acres of South Florida's 4.3 million acres of subtropical, watery wilderness were given national park status and protection in 1947 with the creation of Everglades National Park. It's one of the country's largest national parks and is recognized by the world community as a Wetland of International Importance, a Biosphere Reserve, and a World Heritage site. Visit if you want to spend the day biking, hiking, or boating in deep, raw wilderness with lots of Florida wildlife.

To the east of Everglades National Park, Biscayne National Park brings forth a pristine and magical side of Florida. It's the nation's largest marine park and the largest national park boasting living coral reefs within the continental United States. A small portion of the park's 172,000 acres includes mainland coast and outlying islands, but 95% remains submerged. Of particular interest are the mangroves and their tangled masses of stiltlike roots that thicken shorelines. These "walking trees" have curved prop roots arching down from trunks and aerial roots that drop from branches. The roots of these trees filter salt from water and create a coastal nursery that sustains marine life. You can see Miami's high-rise buildings from many of Biscayne's 44 islands, but the park is virtually undeveloped and large enough for escaping everything that Miami and the Upper Keys have become. To truly disconnect, grab scuba-diving or snorkeling gear and lose yourself in the wonders of the coral reefs.

On the northern edge of Everglades National Park lies Big Cypress National Preserve, one of South Florida's least developed watersheds. Established by Congress in 1974 to protect the Everglades, it comprises extensive tracts of prairie, marsh, pineland, forested swamp, and slough. Hunting is allowed, as is off-roading. Stop at the Oasis Visitor Center's boardwalk to see the alligators lounging underneath, and then drive Loop Road for a backwoods experience. If time and desire for watery adventure permit, kayak or canoe Turner River.

Surrounding the parks and preserve are communities where you'll find useful outfitters: Everglades City, Florida City, and Homestead.

# Planning

## When to Go

Winter is the best, and busiest, time to visit the Everglades. From November to March, temperatures and mosquito activity are more tolerable, while low water levels concentrate the resident wildlife and migratory birds settle in for the season. Ranger-led programs are widely available this time of year. Around April the weather turns hot and rainy, and tours and facilities are less crowded. Migratory birds depart, and you must look harder to see wildlife. Summer brings intense sun and afternoon rainstorms. Water levels rise and mosquitoes abound, making outdoor activity virtually unbearable. (Insect repellent is a necessity any time of year.)

## Getting Here and Around

### AIR

Miami International Airport (MIA) is 34 miles from Homestead and 47 miles from the eastern access to Everglades National Park. ⇨ *For MIA airline information, see Travel Smart.* Shuttles run between MIA and Homestead. Southwest Florida International Airport (RSW), in Fort Myers, a little more than an hour's drive from Everglades City, is the closest major airport to the Everglades' western entrance.

### CAR

Since there is no public transportation to the Everglades, you should arrange to arrive by car. Although rideshare services like Lyft and Uber do operate in the major cities of South Florida, riders will find it hard to secure a return trip from this remote area. Rental cars, scheduled shuttles, and taxis are safer bets.

## Hotels

Accommodations near the parks range from inexpensive to moderate and offer off-season rates in summer, when rampant mosquito populations discourage spending time outdoors, especially at dusk. If you're devoting several days to exploring the east side of the Everglades, stay in park campgrounds, reasonably priced chain motels and RV parks about 11 miles away in Homestead and Florida City, in the Florida Keys, or in the Greater Miami–Fort Lauderdale area. Lodging and campgrounds are plentiful on the Gulf Coast (in Everglades City, Marco Island, and Naples; the latter features upscale accommodations).

# Everglades National Park

*45 miles southwest of Miami International Airport.*

Established in 1947 to protect the snaking sawgrass marshes, mangroves, hardwood hammocks, and many animals that call this wilderness home, the Everglades hold boundless opportunities to learn about Florida ecology, hike, kayak, and spot many a gator and heron.

If you're heading across the southern portion of Florida on U.S. 41, from Miami to Naples, you'll breeze right through the Everglades. This mostly two-lane road, also known as the Tamiami Trail, skirts the edge of Everglades National Park and cuts across Big Cypress National Preserve. You'll also be near the park if you're en route from Miami to the Florida Keys on U.S. 1, which cuts through Homestead and Florida City—communities east of the main park entrance. Basically, if you're in South Florida, you can't escape at least fringes of the Everglades.

*Continued on page 131*

# THE FLORIDA
# EVERGLADES

by Lynne Helm

Alternately described as elixir of life or swampland muck, the Florida Everglades is one of a kind—a 50-mi-wide "river of grass" that spreads across hundreds of thousands of acres. It moves at varying speeds depending on rainfall and other variables, sloping south from the Kissimmee River and Lake Okeechobee to estuaries of Biscayne Bay, Florida Bay, and the Ten Thousand Islands.

Today, apart from sheltering some 70 species on America's endangered list, the Everglades also embraces more than 7 million residents, 50 million annual tourists, 400,000 acres of sugarcane, and the world's largest concentration of golf courses.

Demands on the land threaten the Everglades' finely balanced ecosystem. Irrigation canals for agriculture and roadways disrupt natural water flow. Drainage for development leaves wildlife scurrying for new territory. Water runoff, laced with fertilizers, promotes unnatural growth of swamp vegetation. What remains is a miracle of sorts, given decades of these destructive forces.

Creation of the Everglades required unique conditions. South Florida's geology, linked with its warm, wet subtropical climate, is the perfect mix for a marshland ecosystem. Layers of porous, permeable limestone create water-bearing rock, soil, and aquifers, which in turn affects climate, weather, and hydrology.

This rock beneath the Everglades reflects Florida's geologic history—its crust was once part of the African region. Some scientists theorize that continental shifting merged North America with Africa, and then continental rifting later pulled North America away from the African continent but took part of northwest Africa with it—the part that is today's Florida. The Earth's tectonic plates continued to migrate, eventually placing Florida at its current location as a land mass jutting out into the ocean, with the Everglades at its tip.

# EXPERIENCING THE ECOSYSTEMS

Eight distinct habitats exist within Everglades National Park, Big Cypress National Preserve, and Biscayne National Park.

Carnestown   Ochopee

Gulf Coast Visitor Center   Everglades City

Chokoloskee

TEN THOUSAND ISLANDS

| ECOSYSTEMS | EASY WAY | MORE ACTIVE WAY |
|---|---|---|
| **COASTAL PRAIRIE:** An arid region of salt-tolerant vegetation lies between the tidal mud flats of Florida Bay and dry land. **Best place to see it: The Coastal Prairie Trail** | Take a guided boat tour of Florida Bay, leaving from Flamingo Marina. | Hike the Coastal Prairie Trail from Eco Pond to Clubhouse Beach. |
| **CYPRESS:** Capable of surviving in standing water, cypress trees often form dense clusters called "cypress domes" in natural water-filled depressions. **Best place to see it: Big Cypress National Preserve** | Drive U.S. 41 (also known as Tamiami Trail—pronounced Tammy-Amee), which cuts across Southern Florida, from Naples to Miami. | Hike (or drive) the scenic Loop Road, which begins off Tamiami Trail, running from the Loop Road Education Center to Monroe Station. |
| **FRESH WATER MARL PRAIRIE:** Bordering deeper sloughs are large prairies with marl (clay and calcium carbonate) sediments on limestone. Gators like to use their toothy snouts to dig holes in prairie mud. **Best place to see it: Pahayokee Overlook** | Drive there from the Ernest F. Coe Visitor Center. | Take a guided tour, either through the park service or from permitted, licensed guides. You also can set up camp at Long Pine Key. |
| **FRESH WATER SLOUGH AND HARDWOOD HAMMOCK:** Shark River Slough and Taylor Slough are the Everglades' two sloughs, or marshy rivers. Due to slight elevation amid sloughs, dense stands of hardwood trees appear as teardrop-shaped islands. **Best place to see it: The Observation Tower** | Take a two-hour guided tram tour from the Shark Valley Visitor Center to the tower and back. | Walk or bike (rentals available) the route to the tower via the tram road and (walkers only) Bobcat Boardwalk trail and Otter Cave Hammock Trail. |
| **MANGROVE:** Spread over South Florida's coastal channels and waterways, mangrove thrives where Everglades fresh water mixes with salt water. **Best place to see it: The Wilderness Waterway** | Picnic at the area near Long Pine Key, which is surrounded by mangrove, or take a water tour at Biscayne National Park. | Boat your way along the 99-mi Wilderness Waterway. It's six hours by motorized boat, seven days by canoe. |
| **MARINE AND ESTUARINE:** Corals, sponges, mollusks, seagrass, and algae thrive in the Florida Bay, where the fresh waters of the Everglades meet the salty seas. **Best place to see it: Florida Bay** | Take a boat tour from the Flamingo Visitor Center marina. | Canoe or kayak on White Water Bay along the Wilderness Waterway Canoe Trail. |
| **PINELAND:** A dominant plant in dry, rugged terrain, the Everglades' diverse pinelands consist of slash pine forest, saw palmettos, and more than 200 tropical plant varieties. **Best place to see it: Long Pine Key trails** | Drive to Long Pine Key, about 6 mi off the main road from Ernest F. Coe Visitor Center. | Hike or bike the 28 mi of Long Pine Key trails. |

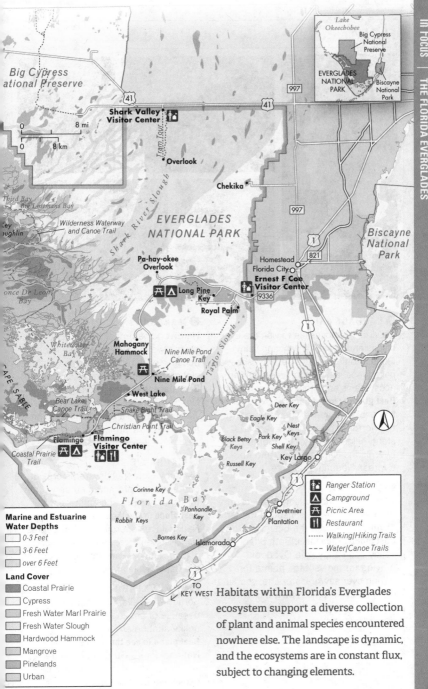

Big Cypress National Preserve

Shark Valley Visitor Center

Tram Tour

Overlook

Chekika

EVERGLADES NATIONAL PARK

Third Bay
Big Lostmans Bay

Wilderness Waterway and Canoe Trail

Key oughlin

Shark River Slough

Pa-hay-okee Overlook

Homestead
Florida City

Ernest F. Coe Visitor Center

9336

Ponce De Leon Bay

Long Pine Key

Royal Palm

Biscayne National Park

Whitewater Bay

Mahogany Hammock

Nine Mile Pond Canoe Trail

Taylor Slough

Nine Mile Pond

West Lake

Bear Lake Canoe Trail

Snake Bight Trail

Christian Point Trail

CAPE SABLE

Flamingo
Coastal Prairie Trail

Flamingo Visitor Center

Deer Key

Eagle Key

Nest Keys

Black Betsy Keys

Park Key

Shell Key

Russell Key

Key Largo

Corinne Key

Florida Bay

Rabbit Keys

Panhandle Key

Tavernier
Plantation

Barnes Key

Islamorada

1

TO KEY WEST

Lake Okeechobee

Big Cypress National Preserve

EVERGLADES NATIONAL PARK

Biscayne National Park

41

997

41

997

1

821

1

1

**Marine and Estuarine Water Depths**
- 0-3 Feet
- 3-6 Feet
- over 6 Feet

**Land Cover**
- Coastal Prairie
- Cypress
- Fresh Water Marl Prairie
- Fresh Water Slough
- Hardwood Hammock
- Mangrove
- Pinelands
- Urban

- Ranger Station
- Campground
- Picnic Area
- Restaurant
- Walking/Hiking Trails
- Water/Canoe Trails

0    8 mi
0    8 km

Habitats within Florida's Everglades ecosystem support a diverse collection of plant and animal species encountered nowhere else. The landscape is dynamic, and the ecosystems are in constant flux, subject to changing elements.

# FLORA

### ❶ CABBAGE PALM

It's virtually impossible to visit the Everglades and not see a cabbage palm, Florida's official state tree. The cabbage palm (or sabal palm), graces assorted ecosystems and grows well in swamps.
**Best place to see them:** At Loxahatchee National Wildlife Refuge (embracing the northern part of the Everglades, along Alligator Alley), throughout Everglades National Park, and at Big Cypress National Preserve.

### ❷ SAWGRASS

With spiny, serrated leaf blades resembling saws, sawgrass inspired the term "river of grass" for the Everglades.
**Best place to see them:** Both Shark Valley and Pahayokee Overlook provide terrific vantage points for gazing over sawgrass prairie; you also can get an eyeful of sawgrass when crossing Alligator Alley, even when doing so at top speeds.

### ❸ MAHOGANY

Hardwood hammocks of the Everglades live in areas that rarely flood because of the slight elevation of the sloughs, where they're typically found.
**Best place to see them:** Everglades National Park's Mahogany Hammock Trail (which has a boardwalk leading to the nation's largest living mahogany tree).

### ❹ MANGROVE

Mangrove forest ecosystems provide both food and protected nursery areas for fish, shellfish, and crustaceans.
**Best place to see them:** Along Biscayne National Park shoreline, at Big Cypress National Preserve, and within Everglades National Park, especially around the Caple Sable area.

### ❺ GUMBO LIMBO

Sometimes called "tourist trees" because of peeling reddish bark (not unlike sunburns).
**Best place to see them:** Everglades National Park's Gumbo Limbo Trail and assorted spots throughout the expansive Everglades.

# FAUNA

## ❶ AMERICAN ALLIGATOR

In all likelihood, on your visit to the Everglades you'll see at least a gator or two. These carnivorous creatures can be found throughout the Everglades swampy wetlands.

**Best place to see them:** Loxahatchee National Wildlife Refuge (also sheltering the endangered Everglades snail kite) and within Everglades National Park at Shark Valley or Anhinga Trail. Sometimes (logically enough) gators hang out along Alligator Alley, basking in early morning or late-afternoon sun along four-lane I–75.

## ❷ AMERICAN CROCODILE

Crocs gravitate to fresh or brackish water, subsisting on birds, fish, snails, frogs, and small mammals.

**Best place to see them:** Within Everglades National Park, Big Cypress National Preserve, and protected grounds in or around Billie Swamp Safari.

## ❸ EASTERN CORAL SNAKE

This venomous snake burrows in underbrush, preying on lizards, frogs, and smaller snakes.

**Best place to see them:** Snakes typically shy away from people, but try Snake Bight or Eco Pond near Flamingo, where birds are also prevalent.

## ❹ FLORIDA PANTHER

Struggling for survival amid loss of habitat, these shy, tan-colored cats now number around 100, up from lows of near 30.

**Best place to see them:** Protected grounds of Billie Swamp Safari sometimes provide sightings during tours. Signage on roadway linking Tamiami Trail and Alligator Alley warns of panther crossings, but sightings are rare.

## ❺ GREEN TREE FROG

Typically bright green with white or yellow stripes, these nocturnal creatures thrive in swamps and brackish water.

**Best place to see them:** Within Everglades National Park, especially in or near water.

● =Extremely Common ● =Very Common ● =Somewhat Common ● =Rare

## BIRDS

### ❶ ANHINGA

The lack of oil glands for waterproofing feathers helps this bird to dive as well as chase and spear fish with its pointed beak. The Anhinga is also often called a "water turkey" because of its long tail, or a "snake bird" because of its long neck.

**Best place to see them:** The Anhinga Trail, which also is known for attracting other wildlife to drink during especially dry winters.

### ❷ BLUE-WINGED TEAL

Although it's predominantly brown and gray, this bird's powder-blue wing patch becomes visible in flight. Next to the mallard, the blue-winged teal is North America's second most abundant duck, and thrives particularly well in the Everglades.

**Best place to see them:** Near ponds and marshy areas of Everglades National Park or Big Cypress National Preserve.

### ❸ GREAT BLUE HERON

This bird has a varied palate and enjoys feasting on everything from frogs, snakes, and mice to shrimp, aquatic insects, and sometimes even other birds! The all-white version, which at one time was considered a separate species, is quite common to the Everglades.

**Best place to see them:** Loxahatchee National Wildlife Refuge or Shark Valley in Everglades National Park.

### ❹ GREAT EGRET

Once decimated by plume hunters, these monogamous, long-legged white birds with S-shaped necks feed in wetlands, nest in trees, and hang out in colonies that often include heron or other egret species.

**Best place to see them:** Throughout Everglades National Park, along Alligator Alley, and sometimes even on the fringes of Greater Fort Lauderdale.

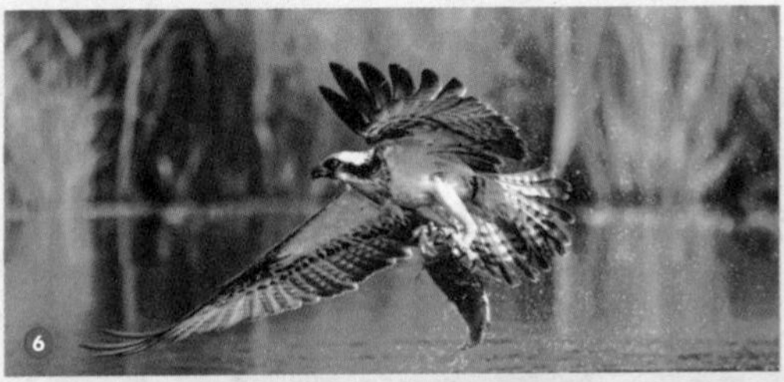


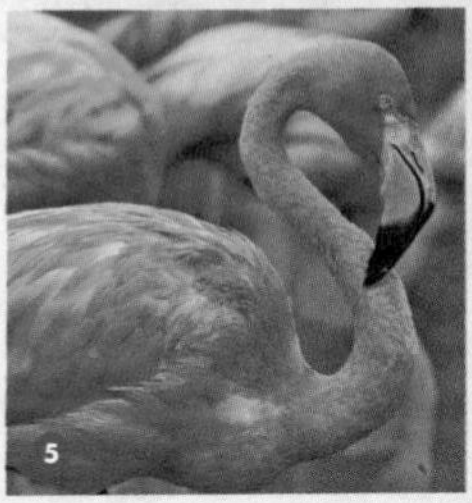


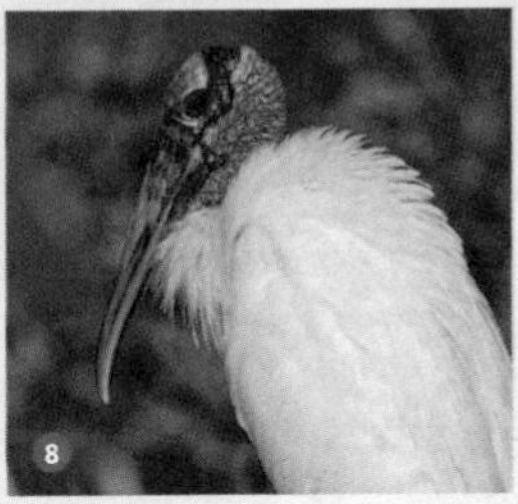


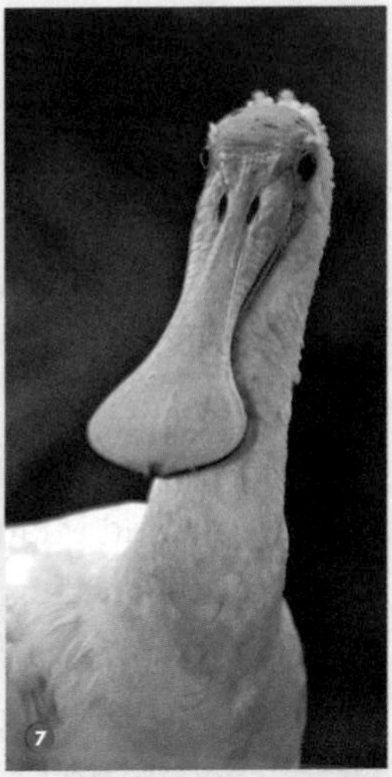


### 5 GREATER FLAMINGO

Flocking together and using long legs and webbed feet to stir shallow waters and mud flats, color comes a couple of years after hatching from ingesting shrimplike crustaceans along with fish, fly larvae, and plankton.
**Best place to see them:** Try Snake Bight or Eco Pond, near Flamingo Marina.

### 6 OSPREY

Making a big comeback from chemical pollutant endangerment, ospreys (sometimes confused with bald eagles) are distinguished by black eyestripes down their faces. Gripping pads on feet with curved claws help them pluck fish from water.
**Best place to see them:** Look near water, where they're fishing for lunch in the shallow areas. Try the coasts, bays, and ponds of Everglades National Park. They also gravitate to trees You can usually spot them from the Gulf Coast Visitor Center, or you can observe them via boating in the Ten Thousand Islands.

### 7 ROSEATE SPOONBILL

These gregarious pink-and-white birds gravitate toward mangroves, feeding on fish, insects, amphibians, and some plants. They have long, spoon-like bills, and their feathers can have a touch of red and yellow. These birds appear in the Everglades year-round.
**Best place to see them:** Sandy Key, southwest of Flamingo, is a spoonbill nocturnal roosting spot, but at sunrise these colorful birds head out over Eco Pond to favored day hangouts throughout Everglades National Park.

### 8 WOOD STORK

Recognizable by featherless heads and prominent bills, these birds submerge in water to scoop up hapless fish. They are most common in the early spring and often easiest to spot in the morning.
**Best place to see them:** Amid the Ten Thousand Island areas, Nine Mile Pond, Mrazek Pond, and in the mangroves at Paurotis Pond.

● =Extremely Common ● =Very Common ● =Somewhat Common ● =Rare

# THE STORY OF THE EVERGLADES

Dreams of draining southern Florida took hold in the early 1800s, expanding in the early 1900s to convert large tracts from wetlands to agricultural acreage. By the 1920s, towns like Fort Lauderdale and Miami boomed, and the sugar industry—which came to be known as "Big Sugar"—established its first sugar mills. In 1947 Everglades National Park opened as a refuge for wildlife.

**KEY**
*Extent of the Everglades*
1900
1999

Meanwhile, the sugar industry grew. In its infancy, about 175,000 tons of raw sugar per year was produced from fields totaling about 50,000 acres. But once the U.S. embargo stopped sugar imports from Cuba in 1960 and laws restricting acreage were lifted, Big Sugar took off. Less than five years later, the industry produced 572,000 tons of sugar and occupied nearly a quarter of a million acres.

Fast-forward to 2008, to what was hailed as the biggest conservation deal in U.S. history since the creation of the national parks. A trailblazing restoration strategy hinged on creating a water flow-way between Lake Okeechobee and the Everglades by buying up and flooding 187,000 acres of land. The country's largest producers of cane sugar agreed to sell the necessary 187,000 acres to the state of Florida for $1.75 billion. Environmentalists cheered.

But within months, news broke of a scaled-back land acquisition plan: $1.34 billion to buy 180,000 acres. By spring 2009, the restoration plan had shrunk to $536,000 to buy 73,000 acres. With the purchase still in limbo, critics claim the state might overpay for acreage appraised at pre-recession values and proponents fear dwindling revenues may derail the plan altogether.

Fortunately, due to the Everglades Forever Act that passed in 1994, long-term water quality objectives for the area are a large focus via Everglades Restoration, the area's largest ecosystem restoration project. Of 68 projects on the docket, the organization completed 24 before 2022 with plans underway for nine more.

# War on Pythons

The non-native Burmese python is an invasive species that has flourished in the Everglades for a couple of decades, likely since Hurricane Andrew wiped out homes where they were kept as pets. Studies show that the tens of thousands of pythons that inhabit the area are dramatically reducing prey for native predators, contributing to the decline of this delicate habitat— and literally squeezing the life out of the Everglades.

Because the constrictors are decimating the biodiversity here, the Florida Fish and Wildlife Conservation Commission encourages the public to remove Burmese pythons in Miami–Dade, Broward, Collier, and Palm Beach Counties (⊕ myfwc.com/ wildlifehabitats/nonnatives/python/).) In other words, you can hunt the apex predators without a permit or training, as long as the snakes are killed humanely and all laws are obeyed. The FWC has even hosted a "Python Bowl," awarding a prize to the python hunter who removed the most constrictors, all in the name of giving the native species a fighting chance.

The state's war on destructive and invasive species also includes a scout tracking program where male pythons are surgically implanted with inch-long radio transmitters to lead biologists to females. Capturing females is paramount to avoid them adding another 30 to 60 hatchlings every breeding period. The program has some MVPs—Most Valuable Pythons—including Elvis, who was tagged in 2013 and is the world's longest surviving tagged male python. The research-based removal of pythons has proven increasingly successful as technologies used to track them provide insights into python behavior.

With tourist strongholds like Miami, Naples, and the Florida Keys so close, travelers from all over the world typically make day trips to the park.

Everglades National Park has three main entry points: the park headquarters at Ernest F. Coe Visitor Center, southwest of Homestead and Florida City; the Shark Valley area, accessed by the Tamiami Trail (U.S. 41); and the Gulf Coast Visitor Center, south of Everglades City to the west and closest to Naples.

Explore on your own or participate in ranger-led hikes, bicycle or bird-watching tours, and canoe trips. The variety of these excursions is greatest from mid-December through April, and some adventures (canoe trips, for instance) typically aren't offered in the sweltering summer months. Among the more popular activities are ranger-led walks departing from the Royal Palm Visitor Center and Flamingo Visitor Center. Check with the respective visitor centers for details.

■ TIP→ **Other than campgrounds, there are no lodging options within the national park.**

## PARK ESSENTIALS

**Admission Fees.** The fee is $30 per vehicle, $25 per motorcycle, and $15 per pedestrian or cyclist. Payable online or at the gates, admission is good for seven consecutive days at all park entrances. Annual passes are $55.

**Admission Hours.** The park is open daily, year-round. Both the main entrance near Florida City and Homestead and the Gulf Coast entrance are open 24/7. The Shark Valley entrance is open 8:30 am to 6 pm.

# Ernest F. Coe Visitor Center to Flamingo Visitor Center

*About 50 miles southwest of Miami.*

The most utilized entrance to Everglades National Park is southwest of Homestead and Florida City. If you're traveling from Miami, take State Road 836/Dolphin Expressway West to State Road 826/Palmetto Expressway South to the Homestead Extension of Florida's Turnpike, U.S. 1, and Krome Avenue (State Road 997). Once you're in Homestead, go right (west) from U.S. 1 or Krome Avenue onto Palm Drive (State Road 9336) and follow signs to the entrance.

This road runs 38 miles from the Ernest F. Coe Visitor Center to Florida Bay at Flamingo, the southernmost headquarters of Everglades National Park. On the way it crosses a section of the park's eight distinct ecosystems: hardwood hammock, freshwater prairie, pinelands, freshwater slough, cypress, coastal prairie, mangrove, and marine-estuarine. Highlights include a dwarf cypress forest, the transition zone between sawgrass and mangrove forest, and a wealth of wading birds.

##  Sights

To explore this section of the park, follow Palm Drive (State Road 9336) from the main park entrance to the Flamingo Visitor Center; you'll find plenty of opportunities to stop along the way and assorted activities to pursue in the Flamingo area. Despite its name, flamingo sightings are extremely rare. Mrazek and Coot Bay Ponds are the best spots to observe wading birds like herons feeding early in the morning or later in the afternoon.

### SCENIC SPOTS

**Nine Mile Pond**

**BODY OF WATER** | Located just off the park's main road 11 miles north of Flamingo, this marked kayak trail leads through freshwater marsh and mangrove tunnels that make it a favorite spot for paddlers. You can rent a kayak or canoe at the Flamingo Marina or go on a ranger-led tour from the Flamingo Visitor Center. Don't be shocked if you see an alligator or two swimming nearby. In fact, be surprised if you don't. ⊠ *Flamingo Visitor Center, 1 Flamingo Lodge Hwy., Everglades National Park* ☎ *239/695–2945* ⊕ *nps.gov/ever.*

**Pa-hay-okee Lookout Tower**

**VIEWPOINT** | For expansive views of the River of Grass and a chance to glimpse Everglades wildlife, walk the short Pa-hay-okee Overlook Trail, which ends at a covered observation tower. Take your time here, look around, and tune into the silence of this immense landscape. It's really something. ⊠ *Everglades National Park* ⊹ *13 miles from Ernest F. Coe Visitor Center* ☎ *305/242–7700* ⊕ *www.nps.gov/ever/planyourvisit/pahayokee-overlook.htm.*

### TRAILS

Several short trails in the area each take about 30 minutes to walk. They include the junglelike yet also wheelchair-accessible Gumbo Limbo Trail; the Pineland Trail, where you can see the park's limestone bedrock; and the Snake Bight Trail.

### ★ Anhinga Trail

**TRAIL** | One of the most popular trails in the Everglades, Anhinga is known for its ample wildlife viewing opportunities. The 0.8-mile, wheelchair-accessible trail cuts through sawgrass marsh and allows you to see alligators, egrets, and herons, and, of course, the trail's namesake waterbirds: anhingas. It also provides close encounters (sometimes too close) with alligators that find it pleasing to sun themselves just feet from the walkways. *Easy.* ⊠ *Royal Palm Information Center, Everglades National Park* ⊹ *Trailhead: 4 miles from main park entrance at Ernest F. Coe Visitor Center* ☎ *305/242–7700* ⊕ *www.nps.gov/ever/planyourvisit/anhinga-trail.htm.*

### Mahogany Hammock Trail

**TRAIL** | **FAMILY** | This half-mile boardwalk trail, accessible for those with disabilities, takes you through a hardwood hammock where the lush vegetation includes gumbo-limbo trees and air plants. This thick canopy forest is typical of South Florida and also happens to be home to America's largest mahogany tree. Along the way, listen for the calls of birds that are hidden within the thick forest. *Easy. ⊠ Royal Palm Information Center, Everglades National Park ✛ Trailhead: 20 miles from main park entrance at Ernest F. Coe Visitor Center ☎ 305/242–7700 ⊕ www.nps.gov/ever/planyourvisit/mahogany-hammock-trail.htm.*

## VISITOR CENTERS

### Ernest F. Coe Visitor Center

**VISITOR CENTER** | **FAMILY** | The park's main visitor center is named after the Connecticut landscape designer, Ernest F. Coe, who moved to Miami at the age of 60 where he was at first intrigued by, and then fell in love with, the Everglades. It was Coe who became the leading proponent to turn this region into a national park; he raised funds, generated support, and worked out ways visitors could see the Everglades with minimal impact on the environment. This is a convenient first stop to pick up a map, watch an introductory film providing an overview of the Everglades, and view exhibits that reveal the nature of the park.

■**TIP→** The visitor center is outside park gates, so you can stop in without paying park admission (and use the restrooms). Also, due to the remoteness of this location, visitors arriving via ride-sharing services (Uber, Lyft) should plan for return transportation before starting their adventure. There's no public transportation to this site. *⊠ 40001 State Rd. 9336, Homestead ☎ 305/242–7700 ⊕ www.nps.gov/ever/planyourvisit/coedirections.htm ⛭ Free.*

## Picnic Spots

Worthwhile spots to pull over for a picnic are **Paurotis Pond**, 24 miles from the main park entrance near Homestead (the actual pond is closed during nesting season) and **Nine Mile Pond**, less than 30 miles from the main visitor center.

### Flamingo Marina Store—Everglades National Park Boat Tours 2

**VISITOR CENTER** | Next to the Flamingo Visitor Center, the only general store within Everglades National Park stocks limited groceries, snacks, souvenirs, bait, tackle, firewood, and camping supplies, as well as fuel for boats and vehicles. It's a sister operation to Everglades National Park Boat Tours in Everglades City. *⊠ 1 Flamingo Lodge Hwy., Everglades National Park ☎ 855/708–2207 ⊕ flamingoeverglades.com/flamingo-marina.*

### Flamingo Visitor Center

**VISITOR CENTER** | **FAMILY** | Flamingo features a visitor center where you can consult with rangers and join walking tours, and it's also where you'll find a well-stocked marina store with beverages, snacks, camping provisions, and a gift shop. There are also boat rentals, guided boat tours, walking trails, an RV and tent campground, and a collection of "eco-tents" on the shores of Florida Bay that lean toward "glamping." The winter season is traditionally the busiest, so be sure to arrive with reservations in hand, while during the hot and rainy summer season, portions of the campground may be closed due to flooding. *⊠ 1 Flamingo Lodge Hwy. ☎ 239/695–2945 ⊕ www.nps.gov/ever/planyourvisit/flamdirections.htm.*

### Royal Palm Information Station and Bookstore

**VISITOR CENTER | FAMILY |** Just a few miles past the park entrance, this is an ideal stop if you have limited time to visit the Everglades. When you arrive, note the medallion attached to the building's wall, which pays tribute to members of the Florida Federation of Women's Clubs who donated the 4,000 surrounding acres in 1916. At the small bookstore, you'll find nature guidebooks along with a limited inventory of souvenirs and snack items, while just outside in a covered pavilion, rangers present talks on the park's history and wildlife. The park's Pine Island Trails (Anhinga Trail, Gumbo Limbo Trail, Lone Pine Key Trails, Pineland Trail, Pahay-okee Overlook, and Mahogany Hammock Trail) are also around the visitor center. As always, arm yourself with insect repellent. ⊠ *Everglades National Park ✢ A little over a mile away from Ernest F. Coe Visitor Center* ☎ *305/242–7237* ⊕ *www.nps. gov/ever/planyourvisit/royal-palm.htm.*

##  Activities

### BIRD-WATCHING

Some of the region's best birding is in Everglades National Park, especially the Flamingo area.

#### Tropical Audubon Society

**SPECIAL-INTEREST TOURS |** Tropical Audubon Society is where South Florida's most enthusiastic birders flock together to conserve local ecosystems while ensuring birds and their habitats are safe. This chapter of the National Audubon Society is extremely active year-round, and its birding field trips are fun and educational. Visit the website for a calendar of events and other valuable birding resources. ⊠ *5530 Sunset Dr., Miami* ☎ *305/667–7337* ⊕ *tropicalaudubon.org.*

### BOATING

#### Everglades Back Country Boat Tour

**GUIDED TOURS | FAMILY |** Everglades National Park's official concessionaire,

## Airboat Tours

Airboat tours, though popular, have been curbed in Everglades National Park due to environmental concerns. The National Park Service authorizes just three tour companies inside park boundaries: Coopertown (⊕ *coopertownairboats.com*), Everglades Safari Park (⊕ *www.evergladessafaripark. com*), and Gator Park (⊕ *gatorpark. com*). The rest operate outside the park, even if they may advertise "Everglades." If you're concerned about your footprint, why not rent a kayak or hike the trails instead?

generically known as Guest Services, Inc., operates two similar but separate operations, with Flamingo Adventures based in Flamingo on Florida Bay, and Everglades Adventures based in Everglades City on the Gulf Coast. The marina in Flamingo runs boat tours in addition to renting canoes, kayaks, and bikes. A 90-minute backcountry cruise up Buttonwood Canal through Coot Bay and Tarpon Creek into Whitewater Bay winds under a heavy canopy of mangroves to reveal abundant wildlife—from alligators, crocodiles, and turtles to herons, hawks, and egrets. Tickets can be purchased at the marina or online. ⊠ *1 Flamingo Lodge Hwy., on Buttonwood Canal, Flamingo* ☎ *855/708–2207* ⊕ *flamingoeverglades. com/boat-tours* ⊠ *$40.*

### CAMPING

**Flamingo Campground.** Visitors can pitch tents or bring RVs to one of Flamingo Campground's 235 drive-up sites, where amenities include solar-heated showers and electricity for RV sites. Be sure to make a reservation during winter, and note that during the summer wet season, portions of the campground are closed due to flooding. At the far end of

Much skill is required to navigate boats through the shallow, muddy waters of the Everglades.

the main road to the Flamingo community along Florida Bay, you'll find a marina (with beverages, snacks, and a gift shop). Houseboats and cushy eco-tents with electricity, fans, and lamps can be booked with **Flamingo Adventures** starting at $50. Call ☎ 855/708–2207 for reservations in winter. ⊕ *flamingoeverglades. com/camping/*

**Long Pine Key Campground.** Like Flamingo Campground, this camping area is accessible from the Homestead entrance to the park and has spaces for tents and RVs. It's near popular trails, including the Long Pine Key Trail, and just a few miles from the Anhinga Trail at the Royal Palm Center. Amenities include fresh water, cold showers, and restrooms. Rates start at $27 per night. Reserve at ☎ 855/708–2207. ⊕ *flamingoeverglades.com/ camping/*

## CANOEING AND KAYAKING
The 99-mile inland **Wilderness Waterway** between Flamingo and Everglades City is open to motorboats as well as canoes,

although, depending on water levels, powerboats may have trouble navigating above Whitewater Bay. Flat-water canoeing and kayaking are best in winter, when temperatures are moderate, rainfall diminishes, and mosquitoes back off—a little, anyway. This activity is for the experienced and adventurous; most paddlers take eight days to complete the trail. But you can also do a day trip. The Flamingo area has well-marked water trails, but be sure to tell someone where you're going and when you expect to return.

### Flamingo Everglades
**KAYAKING** | At Flamingo, the community located on the southernmost point of the Florida mainland, Flamingo Everglades handles the campground, canoeing, kayaking, and houseboat rentals, the marina store, and guided tour operations. It will soon be home to a new hotel and restaurant—a first in the area's history. ✉ *1 Flamingo Lodge Hwy., Everglades National Park* ☎ *855/708–2207* ⊕ *flamingoeverglades.com.*

# Gulf Coast Visitor Center Entrance

*About 86 miles west of Miami and 37 miles southeast of Naples.*

The park's western gateway is the most convenient entrance for travelers coming from southwest Florida. From Naples, take U.S./Highway 41 east for 37 miles, and turn right onto State Road 29. To reach the Gulf Coast entrance from Miami, take U.S./Highway 41 (Tamiami Trail) west for about 90 miles, turn left (south) onto State Road 29, and travel another 3 miles through Everglades City to the Gulf Coast Ranger Station.

##  Sights

### SCENIC SPOTS

**Ten Thousand Islands**

**WILDLIFE REFUGE** | A surreal landscape by any measure, the Ten Thousand Islands are a 35,000-acre chain of islands and smaller mangrove islets south of Marco Island. The Ten Thousand Islands National Wildlife Refuge is a magnet for kayakers, naturalists, birdwatchers, and photographers thanks to the refuge's proliferation of fish, birds, and other wildlife. Finding your way through the islands can be confusing, so the National Park Service recommends that visitors consult NOAA Charts #11430 and #11432. While the northern islands lie in the national refuge, the lower islands lie within Everglades National Park and are best accessed by boat tours leaving from the Gulf Coast Visitor Center. If you're driving from Naples, you can also park at the Marsh Trail, the best spot for accessing trails. Kayaking and hiking are popular activities for day visitors, who may spot endangered species such as Florida manatees, peregrine falcons, and Atlantic loggerheads. ⊠ *815 Oyster Bar La., Everglades City* ☎ *239/657–8001* ⊕ *www.fws.gov/refuge/ten-thousand-islands.*

## VISITOR CENTERS

**Gulf Coast Visitor Center**

**VISITOR CENTER | FAMILY** | The best place to start exploring Everglades National Park's watery western side is at this visitor center just south of Everglades City (5 miles south of U.S./Highway 41/Tamiami Trail), where rangers can give you the park lowdown and provide you with informational brochures and backcountry permits. The Gulf Coast Visitor Center serves as the gateway for exploring the Ten Thousand Islands, a maze of mangrove islands and waterways that extends to Flamingo and Florida Bay and are accessible only by boat in this region. Naturalist-led boat trips are handled by Everglades Florida Adventures of Guest Services, Inc., the concessioner that also rents canoes and kayaks. ⊠ *815 Oyster Bar La., Everglades City* ☎ *239/695–3311* ⊕ *www.nps.gov/ever/planyourvisit/gcdirections.htm.*

##  Activities

### BOATING

**Everglades Florida Adventures Boat Tours**

**BOAT TOURS | FAMILY** | The same concessionaire that operates boat tours and watercraft rentals in Flamingo also sets sail on excursions into Ten Thousand Islands National Wildlife Refuge. Adventure seekers often see dolphins, manatees, bald eagles, and roseate spoonbills in the saltwater portion of the Everglades. Mangrove wilderness tours on smaller boats (up to six passengers) embark on shorter trips through the swampy, brackish areas. This is the best option to see alligators, bobcats, mangrove fox squirrels, and birds, including the mangrove cuckoo. ⊠ *Gulf Coast Visitor Center, 815 Oyster Bar La., Everglades City* ☎ *855/793–5542* ⊕ *evergladesfloridaadventures.com* 🚢 *Tours from $40.*

## KAYAKING
### ★ Everglades Florida Adventures
**KAYAKING** | Everglades Florida Adventures can arrange canoe and kayak rentals as well as guided 90-minute tours of the Ten Thousand Islands. Highlights include bird and gator sightings, mangrove forests, and spectacular sunsets, depending on the time of your tour. ✉ 815 Oyster Bay La., Everglades City ☎ 855/793–5542 ⊕ evergladesfloridaadventures.com ✍ Canoe rentals from $40; kayak rentals from $30.

# Shark Valley Visitor Center

*23½ miles west of Florida's Turnpike, off the Tamiami Trail. About an hour west of Miami.*

You won't see sharks at Shark Valley. The name originates from the Shark River, also known as the River of Grass that flows through the area. Several species of shark swim up this river from the coast (about 45 miles south of Shark Valley) to give birth, though not at this particular spot.

The Shark Valley entrance to Everglades National Park is on U.S./Highway 41 (Tamiami Trail), 25 miles west of Florida's Turnpike or 39 miles east of State Rd. 29.

##  Sights

To cover the most ground, hop aboard a two-hour tram tour with a naturalist guide. It stops halfway for a trip to the top of the 45-foot-tall Shark Valley Observation Tower via a sloping ramp.

Prefer to do the trail on foot? It takes nerve to walk the 15-mile loop in Shark Valley because in the winter months alligators sunbathe along the road. Most, however, do move out of the way when they see you coming.

You can also ride a bicycle (the folks who operate the tram tours rent well-used bikes daily from 8:30 am to 4 pm for $22

---

## Good Reads

■ *The Everglades: River of Grass.* This 1947 classic by conservationist Marjory Stoneman Douglas is a must-read.

■ *Everglades.* Jean Craighead George illustrates the park's natural history in a children's book.

■ *Everglades: The Park Story.* Wildlife biologist William B. Robertson Jr. presents the park's flora, fauna, and history.

■ *Swamplandia!* Karen Russell's story of a family's gator-wrestling theme park near Everglades City brings readers into the swamp.

---

per bike, with helmets available). Near the bike-rental area, a short boardwalk trail meanders through sawgrass, and another courses through a tropical hardwood hammock.

### SCENIC SPOTS
#### Shark Valley Observation Tower
**VIEWPOINT | FAMILY** | At the halfway point of the Shark Valley loop or tram tour, you'll see (and likely be persuaded to scale) the observation tower, which, at 50 feet, is the highest accessible point in Everglades National Park. From the summit you'll be able to see roughly 20 miles in any direction; do the math and that's 1,600 square miles of Everglades goodness. As you take in the River of Grass in all its subtle glory, observe waterbirds as well as alligators and maybe even river otters crossing the road. The tower has a wheelchair-accessible ramp to the top. If you don't want to take the tram from the Shark Valley Visitor Center, you can either hike or bike in, but private cars are not allowed. ✉ *Shark Valley Tram Tours, 36000 S.W. 8th St., Miami ⊕ www.nps. gov/places/shark-valley-observation-tower.htm.*

## VISITOR CENTER
### Shark Valley Visitor Center

VISITOR CENTER | FAMILY | If Flamingo feels too far away, Shark Valley can provide an idea of the Everglades through educational displays, a park video, and informational brochures. Books and other goods, such as hats, sunscreen, insect repellent, and postcards are available, along with restrooms. Park rangers are also available, ready for your questions. Provided the valley isn't flooded, this is where you'll find the two-hour tram tour and Observation Tower. ⊠ *36000 S.W. 8th St., Miami* ⊹ *23½ miles west of Florida's Turnpike, off Tamiami Trail* ☎ *305/221–8776* ⊕ *www.nps.gov/ever/ planyourvisit/svdirections.htm.*

 **Activities**

## BIKING
### Shark Valley Bicycle Rentals

BIKING | FAMILY | The single-speed bikes come with baskets and helmets, along with child seats for kids under 35 pounds. The fleet also includes a few 20-inch junior models. You'll need a driver's license or other ID for a deposit. ⊠ *Shark Valley Visitor Center, 36000 S.W. 8th St., Shark Valley* ☎ *305/221–8455* ⊕ *www.sharkvalleytramtours.com/ever-glades-bicycle-tours* ⊴ *$22 per bike.*

## TOURS
### Shark Valley Tram Tours

GUIDED TOURS | FAMILY | Provided Shark Valley isn't closed due to flooding (call in advance), these popular two-hour, narrated tours aboard B99 biodiesel trams (they basically run on a type of vegetable oil) depart from the Shark Valley Visitor Center on a 15-mile loop into the interior, stopping at the wheelchair-accessible observation tower along the way to give all guests access to a panoramic look at the vastness of the Everglades. Reservations are recommended December through April, and you'll want to bring your own water. ⊠ *Shark Valley Visitor Center, 36000 S.W. 8th St., Miami*

☎ *305/221–8455* ⊕ *www.sharkval-leytramtours.com* ⊴ *$28.*

# Big Cypress National Preserve

*About 60 miles west of Miami.*

Through the early 1960s, the world's largest cypress-logging operation prospered in Big Cypress Swamp until nearly all the trees were cut down. With the downfall of the industry, government entities began buying parcels of land, and now more than 729,000 acres of the swamp are included in this national preserve. *Big* refers to the swamp, which juts into the north edge of Everglades National Park like a puzzle piece. Its size and location make Big Cypress an important link in the region's hydrological system, where rainwater flows through the preserve, then south into the park, and eventually into Florida Bay.

The swamp's pattern of wet prairies, ponds, marshes, sloughs, and strands is a natural wildlife sanctuary, and thanks to a policy of balanced land use—"use without abuse"—the watery wilderness is devoted to recreation as well as to research and preservation. Bald cypress trees that may look dead are actually dormant, with green needles springing to life in the spring. The preserve allows—in limited areas—hiking, hunting, and off-road vehicles (airboat, swamp buggy, four-wheel drive) by permit. Compared with Everglades National Park, the preserve is less developed and hosts fewer visitors, and that makes it ideal for naturalists, birders, and hikers.

Several scenic drives branch out from the Tamiami Trail; a few lead to camping areas and roadside picnic spots. Aside from the Oasis Visitor Center, a popular springboard for viewing alligators, the newer Nathaniel P. Reed Center features a platform for watching manatees. Both

Native plants along the Turner River Canoe Trail hem in paddlers on both sides, and alligators lurk nearby.

centers, along the Tamiami Trail between Miami and Naples, feature a 25-minute film on Big Cypress.

### PARK ESSENTIALS

**Admission Fees.** It's free to visit the preserve.

**Admission Hours.** The park is open 24/7, year-round. The Oasis Visitor Center is open Tuesday through Saturday. The Nathaniel P. Reed Visitor Center is open every day but December 25.

**CONTACTS Big Cypress National Preserve.** ⊠ *Ochopee* ☎ *239/695–2000* ⊕ *www. nps.gov/bicy/index.htm.*

##  Sights

### HISTORIC SIGHTS

#### Ochopee Post Office

**OTHER ATTRACTION | FAMILY |** A must-see for a souvenir photo, the smallest post office in the United States is a former shed for irrigation pipes on the Tamiami Trail. Blink and you'll risk missing it. You can support this quaint and historical

outpost by purchasing a postcard of the little shack and mailing it off to a history buff. You can also mail packages and buy money orders here. ⊠ *38000 Tamiami Trail E, Ochopee* ☎ *239/695–2099* ⊘ *Closed Sun.*

### SCENIC DRIVES

#### Loop Road

**SCENIC DRIVE |** To see the best variety of wildlife in Big Cypress, including alligators, raccoons, and softshell turtles, follow the 24-mile Loop Road, south of US 41 and west of Shark Valley. Bring binoculars for bird-watching as there are swallow-tailed kites and red-shouldered hawks here as well. Afterward, stop at the H. P. Williams Roadside Park, west of the Oasis Visitor Center, for a picnic, taking time to walk along the boardwalk to spy gators, turtles, and garfish in the river waters of the cypress swamp. ⊠ *Oasis Visitor Center, 52105 Tamiami Trail E, Ochopee* ☎ *239/695–4111* ⊕ *www.nps. gov/bicy/learn/historyculture/loop-road. htm.*

## SCENIC SPOTS

### ★ Big Cypress Gallery

ART GALLERY | FAMILY | Clyde Butcher's Big Cypress Gallery is a wonderful spot for finding a postcard, a calendar, or a more serious piece of art. Butcher, a big guy with an even bigger beard, is known for his stunning photography of landscapes and his knowledge of the 'glades; his famed black-and-white images from deep within the Everglades and Big Cypress have been compared to Ansel Adams's portraits of the American West. Out back, Butcher also rents a bungalow ($295 per night, October–April) and a cottage ($350 per night, year-round). ■TIP→ Look into Butcher's private eco and photo swamp tours. After all, "to know the swamp, you have to get into the swamp," he says. ⊠ 52388 Tamiami Trail, Ochopee ☎ 239/695–2428 ⊕ clydebutcher.com/galleries.

### TRAILS

### Florida National Scenic Trail

TRAIL | Florida's 1,500-mile hiking trail starts in Big Cypress National Preserve and stretches all the way to the western tip of the Panhandle, at Gulf Islands National Seashore. It's broken up into smaller trails of 6 to 28 miles each. Two 5-mile trails, Concho Billie and Fire Prairie, can be accessed in Big Cypress off Turner River Road. Pick up maps and a hiking permit at the Oasis Visitor Center. Moderate. ⊠ Oasis Visitor Center, 52105 Tamiami Trail E, Ochopee ☎ 850/523–8501 ⊕ www.fs.usda.gov/fnst.

### Turner River Paddling Trail

TRAIL | Spanning Big Cypress National Preserve to the north and Everglades National Park to the south, this moderately difficult paddling trail winds through almost 10 miles of Turner River marked by cypress, sawgrass prairie, and mangrove trees. Save at least five to seven hours for a full trip. If you're in Big Cypress, you can access the trail on U.S. 41 west of Turner River Road. If you're accessing from Everglades City, enter at the NPS Gulf District Ranger Station or Chokoloskee Island. Moderate. ■TIP→ There are four additional paddling trails within Big Cypress. ⊠ U.S. 41, Ochopee ✛ West of Turner River Rd. ☎ 239/695–4758 ⊕ www.nps.gov/bicy/planyourvisit/canoetrails.htm.

### VISITOR CENTERS

### Nathaniel P. Reed Visitor Center

VISITOR CENTER | FAMILY | The welcome center on the preserve's western side has abundant information and educational features, as well as restrooms, picnic facilities, and a 70-seat auditorium. An outdoor breezeway showcases an interactive Big Cypress watershed exhibit, illustrating Florida's water flow. It's a convenient place to stop when crossing from either coast. ■TIP→ Love manatees? The boardwalk overlooking the canal behind the welcome center can be a good spot for viewing the intriguing mammals. (Legend has it that they were once mistaken for mermaids by thirsty or love-starved sailors.) ⊠ 33000 Tamiami Trail E, Ochopee ☎ 239/695–4757 ⊕ www.nps.gov/bicy/planyourvisit/npr-vc.htm ☜ Free.

### Oasis Visitor Center

VISITOR CENTER | FAMILY | The big attraction at the Oasis Visitor Center, on the east side of Big Cypress Preserve, is the observation deck for viewing fish, birds, and other wildlife, such as gators. The native plants in a small butterfly garden attract winged wonders. Inside the visitor center, you'll find an exhibition gallery, the Florida National Parks Association

## Picnic Areas

H. P. Williams Roadside Park on Turner River Road is a good spot to stop for picnic tables, a toilet, and a boardwalk that leads to views of cypress swamp. See if you can spot egrets and alligators during your break—just don't try to feed them.

bookshop, and a theater showing an informative film on the swamp. (Leashed pets are allowed, but not on the boardwalk deck.) The off-road vehicle permit office is also located at the Oasis Visitor Center. ✉ *52105 Tamiami Trail E, Ochopee* ☎ *239/695–4111* 🌐 *www.nps.gov/bicy/planyourvisit/oasis-visitor-center.htm* 🎫 *Free.*

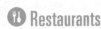

## 🍴 Restaurants

**Joanie's Blue Crab Café**
**$$ | SEAFOOD | FAMILY** | West of the nation's tiniest post office, you'll find this red barn of a place dishing out catfish, frog legs, gator, grouper, burgers, salads, and (no surprise here) an abundance of soft-shell crabs and crab cakes. Entrées are reasonably priced, and peanut butter pie makes for a solid finish. **Known for:** fresh seafood; live music; patio dining. [$] *Average main: $15* ✉ *39395 Tamiami Trail E, Ochopee* ✥ *Less than a mile west of Ochopee Post Office* ☎ *239/695–2682* 🌐 *www.facebook.com/joaniesbluecrabcafe* 🕒 *Hrs vary seasonally; call to confirm.*

## 🏃 Activities

There are three types of trails—walking (including part of the extensive Florida National Scenic Trail), paddling, and bicycling. All three trail types are easily accessed from the Tamiami Trail near the Nathaniel P. Reed Visitor Center, and one boardwalk trail departs from the center. Canoe, kayak, and bike equipment can be rented from outfitters in Everglades City, 24 miles west, and Naples, 40 miles west.

Hikers can tackle the Florida National Scenic Trail, which begins in the preserve and is divided into segments of 6½ to 28 miles each. Two 5-mile trails, Concho Billie and Fire Prairie, can be accessed off Turner River Road, a few miles east. Turner River Road and Birdon Road form a 17-mile gravel loop drive that's excellent for birding. Bear Island has about 32 miles of scenic, flat, looped trails that are ideal for bicycling. Most trails are hard-packed lime rock, but a few miles are gravel. Cyclists share the road with off-road vehicles, most plentiful from mid-November through December.

### CAMPING

There are eight campgrounds in Big Cypress where you can set up tents or park your RV under the stars—ones that may seem especially bright thanks to the park's designation by the International Dark-Sky Association (IDA) as an International Dark Sky Park. We suggest the Midway and Monument Lake sites if amenities like drinking water and restrooms are important to you. Rental per night is $24 for tents, $30 for RVs. Make reservations in advance at 🌐 *www.recreation.gov.*

### RANGER PROGRAMS

From the Oasis Visitor Center you can get in on the seasonal ranger-led or self-guided activities, such as campfire and wildlife chats, hikes, slough slogs, and canoe excursions. The 8-mile Turner River Paddling Trail begins nearby and crosses through Everglades National Park before ending in Chokoloskee Bay, near Everglades City. Rangers lead 4-hour canoe trips and 2-hour swamp walks in season; call for days and times. Bring shoes and long pants for swamp walks, and be prepared to wade at least knee-deep in water. Ranger program reservations are accepted up to 14 days in advance. The programs are free to the public.

# Biscayne National Park

*About 35 miles south of Miami.*

Occupying 172,000 acres along the southern portion of Biscayne Bay, south of Miami and north of the Florida Keys, Biscayne National Park is 95% submerged, making it a wonderland for water activities such as boating, snorkeling, and kayaking. Contained within are four distinct zones, or ecosystems: Biscayne Bay, undeveloped upper Florida Keys, coral reefs, and coastal mangrove forest. Mangroves line the shores of the mainland much like they do elsewhere along South Florida's protected waters.

Biscayne Bay serves as a lobster sanctuary and a nursery for fish, sponges, crabs, and other sea life. Manatees and sea turtles frequent its warm, shallow waters. The park hosts legions of boaters and landlubbers (novices) gazing in awe across the bay.

## GETTING HERE

To reach Biscayne National Park from south of Homestead, take U.S. Highway 1 and turn right on SW 344th Street (Palm Drive, the last light before the Florida Turnpike entrance). After about 4 miles, the road curves to the north near the Homestead Speedway. Turn right on SW 328th Street (North Canal Drive) heading east. Continue for 4 miles to the end of the road. The park entrance is on the left just before the entrance to Herbert Hoover Marina in Homestead Bayfront Park.

From the north, take the Florida Turnpike south to Exit 6 (Speedway Boulevard). Turn left from the exit ramp and continue south to SW 328th Street (North Canal Drive). Turn left on 328th Street and continue for 4 miles to the end of the road. The park entrance is on the left right before the entrance to Herbert Hoover Marina in Homestead Bayfront Park.

## PARK ESSENTIALS

**Admission Fees.** There's no fee to enter Biscayne National Park, and you don't pay a fee to access the islands, but there's a $35 overnight camping fee for each stay at Elliott Key or Boca Chita Key. A solid selection of authorized park concessioners charge for day trips to the coral reefs and islands.

**Admission Hours.** The park is open daily, year-round.

**CONTACTS Biscayne National Park.**
✉ *9700 S.W. 328th St., Sir Lancelot Jones Way, Homestead* ☎ *305/230–1144* ⊕ *www.nps.gov/bisc.*

 # Sights

About 8 miles off the coast, 44 tiny keys stretch 18 nautical miles north to south, reachable only by boat. No mainland commercial transportation operates to the islands, and only a handful are accessible: Elliott, Boca Chita, Adams, and Sands Keys. The rest are wildlife refuges or have rocky shores or waters too shallow for boats. December through April, when the mosquito population is less aggressive, is the best time to explore.

## SCENIC SPOTS

### Adams Key

**ISLAND | FAMILY |** Named Adams Key as early as the 1860s, the history of this minor key far exceeds its size. Roughly a century ago, as Miami began its transformation into a winter resort, some of the nation's most noted figures looked down the coast and saw the strand of islands that made up the Upper Keys. Conveniently close to, but comfortably removed from, the busy pace of Miami, Adams Key became the home of the exclusive Cocolobo Cay Club, a private resort for the rich and famous that welcomed presidents Harding, Hoover, Johnson, and Nixon. It was an executive trend that might have continued had Hurricane Andrew not leveled what remained of the club in 1992.

The club relied on brothers Sir Lancelot and King Arthur Jones, who had developed a thriving pineapple and lime farm on adjacent Porgy Key and knew the bay's best fishing spots. This inside information made the brothers indispensable to the club's well-heeled guests.

Arguably less elegant today than in its heyday, the island has picnic areas with grills, restrooms, dockage, and a short trail running along the shore through a

hardwood hammock. Accessible only by private boat, it's fine for a day trip since no overnight docking is available—although that's an option you'll find at nearby Elliott and Boca Chita Keys. ⊠ *Biscayne National Park ✛ 9 miles west of Convoy Point* ⊕ *www.nps.gov/bisc/planyourvisit/adamskey.htm.*

### Boca Chita Key

ISLAND | FAMILY | Echoes of the past ring across Boca Chita, which is listed on the National Register of Historic Places for its 10 historic structures. The park's most visited island was purchased in 1937 by Mark C. Honeywell, founder and CEO of today's global conglomerate, and became a hip hangout, of sorts, when Honeywell invited his fellow entrepreneurs and industrialists to enjoy elegant island living and boisterous parties. Honeywell sold Boca Chita in 1942 after his wife was injured on the island and died before she could reach proper medical care. It was later enveloped into the collection of islands comprising Biscayne National Park.

Still here are a pavilion, a chapel, a 65-foot-high ornamental lighthouse (make arrangements with a ranger to climb it), and a garage that Honeywell built. Today's parties, however, consist of soirees held aboard yachts that tie up in the small harbor or more basic affairs amid tents pitched in the primitive campground. A half-mile hiking trail curves around the island's south side. Note that pets aren't allowed here, and there is no potable water (or sinks or showers) but rather just portable toilets. A $35 overnight (6 pm to 6 am) docking fee covers a campsite. ⊠ *Biscayne National Park* ⊕ *www.nps.gov/bisc/planyourvisit/bocachita.htm.*

### Elliott Key

ISLAND | FAMILY | At 7 miles long from north to south, the park's largest key has a history that includes legends of pirates as well as the actual presence of pioneers, who began cultivating farms here in the late 1800s. In the 1950s, developers envisioned creating a tropical city called "Islandia" on this key. But it was the idea of creating a causeway needed to open the island to homes, as well as hotels and other businesses, that marked a turning point in the battle between developers and preservationists and ultimately led to the creation of Biscayne National Park. Today, without a hotel in sight, Elliott Key is a popular destination for boaters and campers.

A highlight here is a 30-foot-wide sandy shoreline, the park's only swimming beach, situated a mile north of the harbor on the island's west (bay) side. In addition to having a mile-long hiking trail, Elliott Key is home to the so-called Spite Highway, a clear-cut scar that runs approximately 6 miles down the center of the island. Carved out of spite by developers in their quest to turn the lush key into a commercial haven, the meaning has changed as nature continues to spite those developers by slowly and steadily reclaiming the land.

Overnight guests tie up their boats at one of the harbor's 33 slips or pitch tents at the campground, which has restrooms, picnic tables, grills, fresh drinking water, and cold showers. Either way, the fee is $35 per evening. Leashed pets are allowed in developed areas only, not on trails. ⊠ *Biscayne National Park* ⊕ *www.nps.gov/bisc/planyourvisit/elliottkey.htm.*

## VISITOR CENTER

### ★ Dante Fascell Visitor Center

VISITOR CENTER | FAMILY | From the wide veranda of Biscayne National Park's mainland visitor center, you can soak up views of the mangroves and the bay before signing up for tours, snorkeling excursions, and ranger programs. The compact but very informative collection in the small museum offers insights into the park's natural, geological, and human history. Restrooms with showers, a gift shop, picnic tables, grills, and children's activities are also found here. ⊠ *Convoy*

*Point, 9700 S.W. 328th St., Sir Lancelot Jones Way, Homestead* ☎ *305/230–1144* ⊕ *www.nps.gov/bisc* ✉ *Free.*

## 🏃 Activities

Biscayne is a hub for boating, diving, snorkeling, canoeing, birding, and, to some extent (if you have a private boat), camping. Elliott Key is the best place to hike; two trails tunnel through the island's tropical hardwood hammock.

Biscayne's corals range from soft, flagellant fans, plumes, and whips found chiefly in shallow patch reefs to the hard brain corals, elkhorn, and staghorn forms that can withstand depths and heavier shoreline wave action.

### BOATING
#### ★ Biscayne National Park Institute
**BOAT TOURS** | One of the most enriching ways to experience the national park is on a Biscayne National Park Institute boat tour or diving excursion. Although adventures vary in length, all of them put you in the knowledgeable hands of a park staffer, who will teach you about this Florida ecosystem and its history.

Among the offerings are the naturalist-led Paddle the Mangroves & Seagrass Meadows kayak tour (1.5 hours, $39); the Snorkel Experience/Island Visit (3.5 hours, $199), which explores a reef, a shipwreck, or mangrove sites and is limited to 12 or fewer people; and the Heritage of Biscayne Cruise (3.5 hours, $79), a guided pontoon-boat cruise that covers the natural and human history of the major islands, with a leisurely stop on Boca Chita.

Longer excursions include the immersive Scuba Eco-Adventure (6 hours, $298), which is open to certified divers with previous experience, and the Sail, Paddle, Snorkel & Island Visit (6 hours, $199), which features snorkeling in calm waters and along the fringes of mangroves, as well as stops at Boca Chita or Adams

## Biscayne in One Day

Most visitors come to snorkel or dive. Divers should plan to spend the morning on the water and the afternoon exploring the visitor center. The opposite is true for snorkelers, as snorkel trips (and one-tank shallow-dive trips) depart in the afternoon. If you want to hike, turn to the trails at Elliott Key—just be sure to apply insect repellent (and sunscreen, too, no matter what time of year).

Key. Tours can be booked online in advance; check-in and departure are from the Dante Fascell Visitor Center. ✉ *Dante Fascell Visitor Center, 9700 S.W. 328th St., Sir Lancelot Jones Way, Homestead* ☎ *786/335–3644* ⊕ *www.biscaynenationalparkinstitute.org.*

### BIRD-WATCHING
More than 170 species of birds have been identified in and around the park. Expect to see flocks of brown pelicans patrolling the bay—suddenly rising, then plunging beak first to capture prey in the water. White ibis probe exposed mudflats for small fish and crustaceans. Although all the keys are excellent for birding, Jones Lagoon (south of Adams Key, between Old Rhodes Key and Totten Key) is outstanding. It's approachable only by nonmotorized craft.

### DIVING AND SNORKELING
Diving is great year-round, but it's best in the summer, when calmer winds and seas result in clearer waters. Living tropical coral reefs are the highlight here; some are the size of a table, others as large as a football field. Glass-bottom-boat rides showcase this underwater wonderland, but you really should get in the water to fully appreciate it.

A diverse population of colorful fish—angelfish, parrotfish, porkfish, wrasses, and many more—hang out in the reefs. Shipwrecks from the 18th century are evidence of the area's international maritime heritage, and a Maritime Heritage Trail has been developed to link six of the major shipwrecks and underwater cultural sites, including the Fowey Rocks Lighthouse, built in 1878. Sites, including a 19th-century wooden sailing vessel, have been plotted with GPS coordinates and marked with buoys.

# Everglades City

*36 miles southeast of Naples and 85 miles west of Miami.*

Aside from a chain gas station or two, Everglades City retains its Old Florida authenticity. High-rises (other than an observation tower named for pioneer Ernest Hamilton) are nowhere to be found along this western gateway to Everglades National Park. The ramshackle town attracts adventure seekers heading to the park for the thrill of canoeing, fishing, and bird-watching. Airboat tours, though popular, operate at a limited capacity within the park because of the environmental damage they cause to the mangroves. The Everglades Seafood Festival, launched in 1970 and held the first full weekend of February, draws huge crowds for delights from the sea, music, and craft displays.

The town is small, fishing-oriented, and unhurried, making it excellent for boating, bicycling, or just strolling around. You can pedal along the waterfront on a 2-mile strand out to Chokoloskee Island.

 Sights

### Collier-Seminole State Park

**STATE/PROVINCIAL PARK | FAMILY** | At Collier-Seminole State Park, opportunities to try biking, birding, hiking, camping, and canoeing in Everglades territory are plentiful. This makes the 7,000-plus-acre park a prime introduction to the elusive mangrove swampland. The campground sites come complete with electricity, water, a grill, and a picnic table. Leashed pets are allowed. Alternatively, there are "primitive" campsites accessible by foot or canoe. Of historical interest, a Seminole War blockhouse has been recreated to hold the interpretive center, and one of the "walking dredges"—a towering black machine invented to carve the Tamiami Trail out of the muck—stands silent on the grounds. Kayaks and canoes can be launched into the Blackwater River here. Bring your own, or rent a canoe from the park. The Friends of Collier-Seminole State Park organization offers guided canoe trips from December to March; reservations are recommended. ⊠ *20200 Tamiami Trail E* ☎ *239/394–3397* ⊕ *www. floridastateparks.org/parks-and-trails/collier-seminole-state-park* ⊠ *$5 per vehicle; $4 for solo driver; $2 for pedestrians or bikers; camping starts at $22 per night.*

### Fakahatchee Strand Preserve State Park

**STATE/PROVINCIAL PARK | FAMILY** | The 2,500-foot-long boardwalk at Big Cypress Bend takes visitors fairly quickly through this swamp forest, providing an opportunity to see rare plants, nesting eagles, and Florida's largest swath of coexisting native royal palms—unique to Fakahatchee Strand—with bald cypress under the forest canopy. Fakahatchee Strand is also considered the orchid and bromeliad capital of the continent, with 44 native orchids and 14 native bromeliads, many blooming most extravagantly in hotter months. It's particularly famed for ghost orchids that are visible on guided hikes. Keep an eye out for white-tailed deer, black bears, bobcats, and the Florida panther. For park nature on parade, take the 6-mile stretch of Janes Memorial Scenic Drive (between the visitor center and East Main) that's open to traffic; the rest of the drive is open only to hikers and bikers. ⊠ *137 Coastline Dr.* ☎ *239/695–4593*

🌐 *www.floridastateparks.org/parks-and-trails/fakahatchee-strand-preserve-state-park* 🎫 *$3 per vehicle; $2 per person for bicyclists and pedestrians.*

**Florida Panther National Wildlife Refuge**
**WILDLIFE REFUGE** | **FAMILY** | Though most of this 26,000-acre refuge is off-limits to the public to protect endangered Florida panthers, it has two short loop trails in a region lightly traveled by panthers, where visitors can get a feel for the wet prairies, tropical hammocks, and pine uplands where panthers roam and wild orchids thrive. The 1.3-mile trail is rugged and often thigh-high underwater during summer and fall; it's closed when completely flooded. The shorter trail meanders through a hardwood hammock, is wheelchair-accessible, and open year-round. For both, bring drinking water and insect repellent. Sightings are rare, but you may spot deer, black bears, and the occasional panther—or their tracks. In spring the refuge and its nonprofit host an Open House event, in which areas normally closed to public access are open for buggy tours, swamp hikes, birding tours, and plant ID walks. ✉ *12085 State Rd. 29 S* ☎ *239/657–8001* 🌐 *www.fws.gov/refuge/Florida_Panther* 🎫 *Free.*

**Museum of the Everglades**
**HISTORY MUSEUM** | **FAMILY** | At this Collier County museum, you can learn about early Native Americans, pioneers, entrepreneurs, and anglers who played pivotal roles in southwest Florida development. Exhibits of artifacts and photographs, as well as a short film, detail the tremendous feat of building the Tamiami Trail across mosquito-ridden, gator-infested Everglades wetlands. Permanent displays and monthly shows rotate works by local and regional artists in the Pauline Reeves Gallery. The small museum, listed on the National Register of Historic Places, is housed in the 1927 Laundry Building, which was once used for washing linens from the Rod & Gun Club until it closed during World War II. ✉ *105 W. Broadway* ☎ *239/252–5026* 🌐 *www.evergladesmuseum.org* 🎫 *Free* 🕒 *Closed Sun. and Mon.*

## 🍴 Restaurants

**City Seafood**
**$$** | **SEAFOOD** | **FAMILY** | Gems from the sea are delivered fresh from the owners' boats to this rustic haven. Enjoy breakfast, lunch, or an early dinner outdoors to watch pelicans, gulls, tarpon, manatees, and the occasional gator play off the dock on the Barron River. **Known for:** sustainable stone crab in season; waterfront hangout; wrapping and shipping fresh seafood. [$] *Average main: $15* ✉ *702 Begonia St., Everglades City* ☎ *239/695–4700* 🌐 *www.cityseafood1.com.*

**HavAnnA Cafe**
**$$** | **CUBAN** | Cuban and Caribbean specialties are a welcome alternative to the typical seafood houses in the Everglades City area. This cheery eatery—3 miles south of Everglades City on Chokoloskee Island—has a dozen or so tables inside and more seating on the porch amid plenty of greenery. Jump-start your day with *café con leche* and a pressed-egg sandwich, or try a Havana omelet. **Known for:** café con leche; the Cuban sandwich; charming patio dining. [$] *Average main: $18* ✉ *191 Smallwood Dr., Chokoloskee* 🌐 *havannacafe.com/* 🕒 *Closed Apr.–Oct.*

**Triad Seafood Market & Café**
**$$** | **SEAFOOD** | **FAMILY** | Along the Barron River, seafood houses, fishing boats, and crab traps populate one shoreline, while mangroves line the other. Some seafood houses added picnic tables and eventually grew into restaurants, like the family-owned Triad Seafood Market & Café. **Known for:** coveted grouper sandwiches; outdoor dining; all-you-can-eat stone crab feasts. [$] *Average main: $15* ✉ *401 W. School Dr., Everglades City* ☎ *239/695–2662* 🌐 *triadseafoodmarketcafe.com* 🕒 *Closed seasonally; call for hours.*

##  Hotels

### ★ The Ivey House Everglades Adventures Hotel

$ | B&B/INN | What was once a boardinghouse built for crews working on the Tamiami Trail in 1928 is now the top spot to stay in town for adventurers on assorted budgets. **Pros:** plush rooms by Everglades standards; kayak tours can be booked on site; affordable. **Cons:** not on water; some small rooms; no pets. Ⓢ *Rooms from: $134 ⊠ 605 Buckner Ave. N, Everglades City ☎ 239/323–9836 ⊕ iveyhouse.com ➲ 18 rooms ⦙⦿⦙ Free Breakfast.*

##  Activities

### BOATING AND CANOEING

On the Gulf Coast, be sure to explore the nooks, crannies, and mangrove islands of Chokoloskee Bay and **Ten Thousand Islands National Wildlife Refuge,** as well as the rivers near Everglades City. The **Turner River Paddling Trail,** popular even during the holidays, is a pleasant day trip with almost guaranteed bird and alligator sightings; it passes through mangrove tunnels, dwarf cypress, coastal prairie, and freshwater slough ecosystems of Everglades National Park and Big Cypress National Preserve.

### SCENIC FLIGHTS

**Wings Aero Tours**

SKYDIVING | Wings' flightseeing tours of Ten Thousand Islands National Wildlife Refuge, Fakahatchee Strand Preserve State Park, Big Cypress National Preserve, Everglades National Park, and Everglades City are available seasonally, November to May. Hop aboard an Alaskan bush plane to see sawgrass prairies, Native American shell mounds, alligators, manatees, dolphins, and wading birds from above. Captains provide passengers with headsets to keep them informed about the sights below. Flight tours can also be booked to see Marco Island and Key West, among other hot spots. ⊠ *Everglades Airpark, 650 E.C. Airpark Rd., Everglades City ☎ 907/441–5736 ⊕ www.wingsaerotours.com ➲ From $150 per adult or $50 each for 3–4 adults.*

# Florida City

*2 miles southwest of Homestead on U.S. 1.*

Florida's Turnpike ends in Florida City, the southernmost town of Miami–Dade County's mainland. This is the point where thousands of vehicles spill onto U.S. 1 and eventually west to Everglades National Park, east to Biscayne National Park, or south to the Florida Keys. As the last outpost before 18 miles of mangroves and water, this stretch of U.S. 1 is lined with fast-food eateries, service stations, hotels, bars, and dive shops. Hotel rates increase significantly during NASCAR races at the nearby Homestead–Miami Speedway. Like Homestead, Florida City is rooted in agriculture, with expanses of farmland west of Krome Avenue and a huge farmers' market that ships produce nationwide.

### GETTING HERE AND AROUND

From Miami, take the Florida Turnpike south for about 40 miles until it ends at U.S. 1. The trip will take at least 45 minutes to an hour depending on traffic.

## ⊙ Sights

### Tropical Everglades Visitor Center

VISITOR CENTER | Managed by the nonprofit Tropical Everglades Visitor Association, this pastel-pink information center with teal signage offers abundant printed material, plus tips from volunteer experts on exploring South Florida, especially Homestead, Florida City, and the Florida Keys. ⊠ *160 S.E. 1st Ave., Florida City ☎ 305/245–9180 ⊕ tropicaleverglades. com.*

## 🍴 Restaurants

**Capri Restaurant**
$$ | **ITALIAN** | **FAMILY** | This family-owned enterprise has been a magnet for affordable Italian-American classics since 1958. Eat pasta, crunchy-crust pizza, steak, prime rib, and a multitude of locally inspired desserts amid redbrick walls in the classic Capri dining room. **Known for:** large salad buffet; family-friendly environment; staples like lasagna. [$] *Average main: $20* ✉ *935 N. Krome Ave., Florida City* ☎ *305/247–1542* 🌐 *www.dinecapri.com* 🕒 *Dinner only on Sat. Closed Sun.*

**Farmers' Market Restaurant**
$ | **SEAFOOD** | This quaint eatery is inside the farmers' market on the edge of town, and it's big on serving fresh vegetables and seafood. A family of anglers runs the place, so fish and shellfish are only hours from the ocean. **Known for:** early hours for breakfast; seafood-centric menu; using fresh produce from the market. [$] *Average main: $13* ✉ *300 N. Krome Ave., Ste. 17, Florida City* ☎ *305/242–0008* 🌐 *www.facebook.com/floridacityfarmersmarketrestaurant.*

**Rosita's Mexican Restaurant**
$ | **MEXICAN** | This delightful hole-in-the-wall Mexican spot boasts authenticity you can't get at the Tex-Mex chains. Breakfast, lunch, and dinner entrées, served all day, range from Mexican eggs, enchiladas, and taco salad to stewed beef and fried pork chops. **Known for:** authentic Mexican cuisine; a brisk take-out business; breakfast served all day. [$] *Average main: $11* ✉ *199 W. Palm Dr., Homestead* ☎ *305/246–3114* 🌐 *rositasmexicanrestaurantfl.com.*

## 🛏 Hotels

**Best Western Gateway to the Keys**
$ | **HOTEL** | For easy access to Everglades and Biscayne National Parks, as well as the Keys, you'll be well situated at this relatively modern, two-story motel close to Florida's Turnpike. **Pros:** conveniently located; free Wi-Fi and breakfast; attractive poolscape. **Cons:** traffic noise; books up fast in high season; no pets. [$] *Rooms from: $120* ✉ *411 S. Krome Ave., Florida City* ☎ *305/246–5100* 🌐 *www.bestwestern.com* 🛏 *114 rooms* 🍴 *Free Breakfast.*

**Fairway Inn**
$ | **HOTEL** | This two-story motel, with a waterfall pool and some of the area's lowest rates, is close to the Tropical Everglades Visitor Association. **Pros:** affordable; conveniently located; nice pool. **Cons:** plain, small rooms; no pets allowed; dated decor. [$] *Rooms from: $75* ✉ *100 S.E. 1st Ave., Florida City* ☎ *305/248–4202* 🌐 *fairwayinnflorida.com* 🛏 *160 rooms* 🍴 *Free Breakfast.*

**Quality Inn Florida City**
$ | **HOTEL** | Nestled in a complex of hotels, gas stations, and eateries just off U.S. 1, this two-story Quality Inn has a friendly front-desk staff offering tips on Everglades and Keys adventures or race action at the nearby track. **Pros:** conveniently located; modern decor; affordable rates. **Cons:** no elevator; noisy location; no pets allowed. [$] *Rooms from: $75* ✉ *333 S.E. 1st Ave., Florida City* ☎ *786/465–7600* 🌐 *www.choicehotels.com* 🛏 *123 rooms* 🍴 *Free Breakfast.*

**Travelodge by Wyndham**
$ | **HOTEL** | This affordable hotel is close to Florida's Turnpike, Everglades and Biscayne national parks, and Homestead-Miami Speedway. **Pros:** conveniently located; nice heated outdoor pool; no frills, but clean and comfortable. **Cons:** busy location; some small rooms; no pets allowed. [$] *Rooms from: $70* ✉ *409 S.E. 1st Ave., Florida City* ☎ *305/482–1961, 877/257–2297 international* 🌐 *www.wyndhamhotels.com* 🛏 *88 rooms* 🍴 *Free Breakfast.*

## 🛍 Shopping

**Robert Is Here Fruit Stand and Farm**

**FOOD | FAMILY |** This historic stand and farm sells more than 100 types of jams, jellies, honeys, and salad dressings along with farm-fresh veggies and dozens of tropical fruits. The list of rare finds includes carambola, lychee, eggfruit, sapodilla, and tamarind. Try them in a smoothie or milk shake. ⊠ *19200 S.W. 344th St., Homestead* ☎ *305/246–1592* ⊕ *www.robertishere.com.*

# Homestead

*40 miles southwest of Miami.*

Homestead has established itself as a destination for tropical agritourism and ecotourism. At the confluence of Miami and the Keys, as well as Everglades and Biscayne National Parks, the area is less than an hour from Miami and has the added dimension of shopping centers, residential development, hotel chains, and the Homestead–Miami Speedway. The historic downtown is a preservation-driven Main Street. Krome Avenue is lined with restaurants, an arts complex, antiques shops, and low-budget accommodations. West of Krome Avenue, miles of fields grow fresh fruits and vegetables. Some are harvested commercially, and others beckon with "U-pick" signs. Stands selling farm-fresh produce and nurseries that grow and sell orchids and tropical plants abound.

In addition to its agricultural legacy, the town has an eclectic flavor, attributable to its population mix: descendants of pioneer farmers, professionals escaping the Miami mania, and retirees.

## 👁 Sights

**Coral Castle Museum**

**HISTORIC SIGHT | FAMILY |** Driven by unrequited love, Latvian immigrant Ed Leedskalnin (1887–1951) fashioned this attraction along Dixie Highway in the early 1900s out of massive slabs of coral rock, a feat he likened to building the pyramids. You can learn how he populated this fantasy world on his property with an imaginary wife and three children, studied astronomy, and created a simple home and elaborate courtyard without formal engineering education and with mostly handmade tools. Highlights of this National Register of Historic Places site, originally named Rock Gate, include a working sundial, a banquet table shaped like Florida, and other quirky coral sculptures. Fun fact: Billy Idol wrote, recorded, and shot the video for his song "Sweet Sixteen" on the grounds of Coral Castle as a tribute to Ed. Candidly, among locals, it's known as a tourist trap. ⊠ *28655 S. Dixie Hwy.* ☎ *305/248–6345* ⊕ *coralcastle.com* 🖭 *$18* 🕐 *Closed Mon. to Wed.*

**★ Knaus Berry Farm**

**FARM/RANCH | FAMILY |** South Florida locals count down the days until the seasonal opening (from November to April) of this Homestead bakery and U-pick strawberry farm, owned and operated by the Knaus family since 1956. Line up early for a box of legendary, gooey cinnamon rolls and a milkshake, and walk it off by picking a bag of fresh strawberries and tomatoes to take home. ◼ **TIP➔ The Farm Store is cash only.** ⊠ *15980 S.W. 248th St., Homestead* ☎ *305/247–0668* ⊕ *knausberryfarm.com* 🕐 *Closed Sun. and May–Oct.*

**Schnebly Redland's Winery**

**WINERY |** Homestead's tropical bounty is transformed into wine at this flourishing enterprise that started producing wines with lychee, mango, guava, and other local fruits as a way to eliminate waste from family groves each year. Over the course of a few decades, the winery expanded to include a tasting room, a full-service restaurant, and a lush plaza picnic area landscaped in coral rock, tropical plants, and waterfalls. It's also home to popular beer brand Miami Brewing Company. ✉ *30205 S.W. 217th Ave., Homestead* ☎ *305/242–1224* ⊕ *www.schneblywinery.com* ⊠ *Weekend tours $16 per person.*

#  Restaurants

### ★ Casita Tejas

**$ | MEXICAN |** Free-flowing chips and salsa are placed on the brightly colored plastic tablecloths the moment you take a seat at this family-run, authentic Mexican spot open since 1987. The massive menu is filled with hearty plates, each accompanied by a portion of Mexican rice and refried beans. **Known for:** nachos, burritos, and lunch specials; great service; huge portions. $ *Average main: $12* ✉ *27 N Krome Ave,, Homestead* ☎ *305/248–8224* ⊕ *casitatejas.com.*

### Chefs on the Run

**$$ | CARIBBEAN |** Chef and owner Jodrick I. Ujaque cooks with flavors inspired by his Puerto Rican roots at this Caribbean-American gastropub. From various versions of mofongo (seasoned mashed plantains) topped with different proteins to a burger menu with more than a dozen options, this spot is a favorite among locals. **Known for:** large portions; Caribbean-inspired bowls; plenty of vegan options. $ *Average main: $16* ✉ *10 E Mowry Dr., Homestead* ⊕ *chefsontheruninhomestead.com* ☾ *Closed Sun. and Mon.; No dinner except Fri. and Sat.*

### Royal Palm Grill and Deli

**$ | AMERICAN | FAMILY |** This popular "breakfast all day, every day" enterprise has two locations, only a few blocks apart, to accommodate a steady stream of customers who come for everything from omelets and pancakes to biscuits and gravy, plus salads, steaks, and seafood. **Known for:** early hours; breakfast all day; retro decor and vibe. $ *Average main: $10* ✉ *806 N. Krome Ave., Homestead* ☎ *305/246–5701* ⊕ *royalpalmhomestead.com* ☾ *No dinner.*

### Shiver's BBQ

**$ | BARBECUE | FAMILY |** Piggin' out since the 1950s, Shiver's BBQ is celebrated near and far for its slowly smoked pork, beef, and chicken. Be forewarned as you settle in at the communal tables; this spot is no place to cut calories. **Known for:** hickory-smoked barbecue; baby back ribs; takeout service. $ *Average main: $19* ✉ *28001 S. Dixie Hwy., Homestead* ☎ *305/248–2272* ⊕ *shiversbbq.com.*

### White Lion Cafe

**$$ | AMERICAN |** Although the antiques shop within White Lion Cafe's cottage is now history, this comfort-food haven, with outdoor seating, remains embellished with reminders of the past. From a 1950s-era wooden wall phone to a metal icebox and a Coca-Cola machine, you'll also find a mounted jackalope watching over a wide list of specials (Homestead crab cakes, burgers, fried chicken, and meat loaf). **Known for:** comfort food; patio dining; kitschy decor. $ *Average main: $18* ✉ *146 N.W. 7th St., Homestead* ⊕ *whitelioncafe.com* ☾ *Closed Sun. and Mon.*

### Yardie Spice

**$ | JAMAICAN |** This beloved Jamaican spot serves stews, jerk chicken, and oxtail, plus a few vegan options. You can select from nearly a dozen plates that each feature rice, salad, and plantains. **Known for:** jerk chicken salad; griot (fried pork chunks); flavorful side dishes. $ *Average main: $12* ✉ *255 S Krome Ave., Homestead* ☎ *786/439–5138* ⊕ *www.yardiespicehomestead.com* ☾ *Closed Sun.*

#  Hotels

### The Hotel Redland

**$ | HOTEL |** Of downtown Homestead's smattering of mom-and-pop lodges, this historic inn is by far the most desirable. **Pros:** historic charm; conveniently located; excellent dining. **Cons:** traffic noise; small rooms; potentially haunted. $ *Rooms from: $150* ✉ *5 S. Flagler Ave.,*

Homestead ☎ 305/246–1904 ⊕ www. cityhallbistromartinibar.com ⇥ 13 rooms ⑩ No Meals.

## 🏃 Activities

**Homestead Bayfront Park**

WATER SPORTS | FAMILY | Boaters, anglers, and beachgoers give high praise to this recreational area with a natural atoll pool and beach, a marina, the La Playa Grill Seafood & Bar restaurant, a playground, and a picnic pavilion with grills, showers, and restrooms. ⊠ 9698 S.W. 328th St., Homestead ☎ 305/230–3033 ⊕ www. miamidade.gov/parks/homestead-bay-front.asp ⊠ $7 per car on weekends; $5 per car on weekdays.

**Homestead–Miami Speedway**

AUTO RACING | FAMILY | Buzzing more than 300 days a year, the 600-acre speedway has 65,000 grandstand seats, club seating, and two tracks—a 2.21-mile road course and a 1.5-mile oval. ⊠ 1 Ralph Sanchez Speedway Blvd., Homestead ☎ 305/230–5000, 866/409–7223 ticket office ⊕ www.homesteadmiamispeedway.com.

# Tamiami Trail

*U.S. 41, between Naples and Miami.*

There's a long stretch of U.S. 41 (originally known as the Tamiami Trail) that traverses the Everglades, Big Cypress National Preserve, and Fakahatchee Strand Preserve State Park while connecting Florida's west coast to Miami. The road was conceived in 1915 to link Miami to Fort Myers and Tampa, but when it finally became a reality in 1928, it cut through the Everglades and altered the natural flow of water as well as the lives of the Miccosukee tribe, who were making a living fishing, hunting, farming, and frogging here.

The landscape is surprisingly varied, changing from hardwood hammocks to

## Croc or Gator?

You can tell you're looking at a crocodile, not an alligator, if you can see its lower teeth sticking up over the upper lip when those powerful jaws are shut. Gators are darker in color—a grayish black—compared with the lighter tan shades of crocodiles. Alligator snouts form a U-shape and are also wider than the snouts of their long, thin crocodilian counterparts (V-shape). South Florida is the only place in the world where the two coexist in the wild.

pinelands, then abruptly to tall cypress trees dripping with Spanish moss and back to sawgrass marsh. Slow down to take in the scenery and you'll likely be rewarded with glimpses of alligators sunning themselves along the banks of roadside canals and hundreds of water-birds, especially in winter. The man-made portion of the landscape includes Native American villages and airboats parked at roadside enterprises. Between Miami and Naples the road goes by several names, including the Tamiami Trail, U.S. 41, Ninth Street in Naples, and, at the Miami end, Southwest 8th Street/Calle Ocho.

■ TIP➜ **This is where you will find the only national park–approved Everglades airboat tours: Coopertown, Everglades Safari Park, and Gator Park. Other airboat tours do not take you inside the park and are generally frowned upon by environmentalists.**

## 👁 Sights

**Everglades Safari Park**

THEME PARK | FAMILY | A perennial favorite with tour operators, this family-run park has been in business since 1968 on a wild plot of land just 15 miles from overdeveloped west Miami. It has an arena for alligator wrestling shows with

Are baby alligators more to your liking than their parents? You can pet one at Gator Park.

seating for up to 300 people. Before and after the show, get a closer look at both American alligators and American crocodiles on Gator Island, follow a jungle trail, walk through a small wildlife museum, or board an airboat for a 40-minute ride on the River of Grass (fee is included in park admission). The park also has a restaurant, a gift shop, and an observation platform overlooking the lush vegetation in the surrounding Everglades. Smaller, private airboats can be chartered for tours lasting 40 minutes to two hours. Check online for discounts and count on free parking. ■ TIP→ **This is one of three businesses authorized by the National Park Service to conduct airboat tours inside Everglades National Park.** ✉ *26700 S.W. 8th St., Miami* ☎ *305/226–6923* ⊕ *www. evergladessafaripark.com* ✇ *$39.*

### Gator Park

**THEME PARK | FAMILY** | At Gator Park, you can really get to know alligators and even touch a baby gator during the park's wildlife show. You can also meet turtles, macaws, and peacocks. Native snakes

also reside nearby, including the black pine snake, brooks king snake, Florida king snake, and red rat snake. The park, open rain or shine, also provides educational airboat tours through Everglades National Park, as well as a gift shop and restaurant serving swamp fare like burgers, gator tail, and sausage. Tickets include admission, a group airboat ride, and an alligator wrestling show. Private tours are available. ■ TIP→ **Gator Park is authorized by the National Park Service to give airboat rides inside Everglades National Park.** ✉ *24050 S.W. 8th St., Miami* ☎ *305/559–2255, 800/559–2205 international* ⊕ *gatorpark.com* ✇ *$27.99 online ($29.99 at gate).*

## 🍽 Restaurants

### Coopertown Restaurant

**$$ | AMERICAN | FAMILY** | Make a pit stop at Coopertown Restaurant for local flavor and delicacies sourced straight from the swamp. This eatery opened in the early 1960s as a sandwich stand, and it has long been a favorite among the famous and the humbly hungry. **Known for:** catfish and shrimp; fried alligator; old-fashioned charm. $ *Average main: $15* ✉ *Coopertown Airboat Rides & Restaurant, 22700 S.W. 8th St., Miami* ☎ *305/226–6048* ⊕ *coopertownairboats.com* ⊙ *No dinner.*

##  Hotels

### Miccosukee Casino & Resort

$ | RESORT | Like an oasis on the horizon of endless sawgrass, this nine-story resort on the edge of the Everglades can't help attracting attention—even if you're not a fan of 24-hour gaming action. **Pros:** casino; relatively modern; golf course. **Cons:** smoke-filled lobby; limited parking; stark contrast to its surroundings. $ *Rooms from: $140* ✉ *500 S.W. 177th Ave., Miami* ☎ *305/222–4600, 877/242–6464 International* ⊕ *miccosukee.com/mcr* ↪ *302 rooms* ⊙ *No Meals.*

##  Activities

### BOAT TOURS

Many Everglades-area tours operate only in season, roughly November to April.

### Buffalo Tiger Airboat Tours

BOATING | FAMILY | A former chief of Florida's Miccosukee tribe founded this Shark Valley tour operation that operates in Miccosukee tribal lands. Savvy guides narrate the trip to an old Miccosukee camp on the north side of the Tamiami Trail from the Native American perspective. Don't worry about airboat noise, they shut off the engines three times during informative talks and photo opportunities. The standard tours are 45 minutes, and longer private tours are available. Reservations are not required for standard tours, and credit cards are now accepted at this outpost, but it's cheaper to purchase online in advance. ✉ *29701 S.W. 8th St., West Miami-Dade* ☎ *305/559–5250* ⊕ *buffalotigerboats.com* ▥ *Standard tours from $27.50 per person. Private tours from $366 per group of 4.*

### Coopertown Airboat Tours

BOATING | FAMILY | Coopertown is the oldest airboat operator in the Everglades. The nearly 75-year-old business, which is attached to a restaurant with the same name, offers 35- to 40-minute tours that take you 9 miles into the fragile ecosystem to see hammocks and alligator holes, red-shouldered hawks, and turtles. You can also book longer private charters with the company. ■TIP→ **Coopertown is one of only three companies authorized by the National Park Service to give airboat tours inside Everglades National Park.** ✉ *22700 S.W. 8th St., Miami* ☎ *305/226–6048* ⊕ *coopertownairboats.com* ▥ *From $20 (if purchased online).*

### Everglades Alligator Farm

WILDLIFE-WATCHING | FAMILY | More than 2,000 alligators live within the Everglades Alligator Farm. It's the oldest of its kind in South Florida and offers alligator shows, encounters, and airboat rides outside national park boundaries. It's a working farm, and feedings for 500 hungry gators are at noon and 3 pm. ■TIP→ **While this farm works with the Florida Fish and Wildlife Conservation Commission to ensure its animals are cared for, there are ethical concerns regarding alligator interactions.** ✉ *40351 S.W. 192nd Ave., Homestead* ☎ *305/247–2628* ⊕ *www.everglades.com* ▥ *$31, including airboat tour.*

### Wooten's Airboat Tours

BOATING | FAMILY | Convenient for travelers coming from southwest Florida, this classic Florida roadside attraction offers airboat tours and swamp buggy rides through private grasslands outside Big Cypress Swamp, educational sessions in the animal sanctuary, and live alligator shows. Some packages include an airboat ride, swamp buggy adventure, and sanctuary access. ✉ *32330 Tamiami Trail E, Ochopee* ☎ *239/695–2781* ⊕ *www.wootenseverglades.com* ▥ *Tours from $30; alligator show from $9.*

# THE FLORIDA KEYS

Updated by
Sara Liss

| ◉ Sights | 🍴 Restaurants | 🛏 Hotels | 🛍 Shopping | 🍸 Nightlife |
|----------|---------------|----------|-------------|-------------|
| ★★★★☆ | ★★★☆☆ | ★★★☆☆ | ★★★☆☆ | ★★★☆☆ |

# WELCOME TO THE FLORIDA KEYS

## TOP REASONS TO GO

★ **John Pennekamp Coral Reef State Park:** A perfect introduction to the Florida Keys, this nature reserve offers snorkeling, diving, camping, and kayaking. An underwater highlight is the massive *Christ of the Deep* statue.

★ **Viewing the underwater world:** Whether you scuba dive, snorkel, or ride a glass-bottom boat, don't miss gazing at the coral reef and its colorful denizens.

★ **Sunset at Mallory Square:** Sure, it's touristy, but just once while you're here, you've got to witness the circuslike atmosphere of this nightly celebration.

★ **Duval crawl:** Shop, eat, drink, repeat. Key West's Duval Street and the nearby streets make a good day's worth of window-shopping and people-watching.

★ **Getting on the water:** From angling for trophy-size fish to zipping out to the Dry Tortugas, a boat trip is in your future. It's really the whole point of the Keys.

**1 Key Largo.** The first Key reachable by car, it's a prime spot for diving and snorkeling.

**2 Islamorada.** Sportfishing in deep offshore waters and backcountry reigns.

**3 Conch Key and Duck Key.** Sleepy Conch Key is great place to fish. Upscale Duck Key has beautiful marina resort.

**4 Grassy Key.** Known for natural wonders like Curry Hamock State Park.

**5 Marathon.** Most activity in the Middle Keys revolves around this bustling town.

**6 Bahia Honda Key.** One of the top beaches in Florida, with fine sand and clear water.

**7 Big Pine Key.** Laid-back community that's home to an impressive wildlife refuge.

**8 Little Torch Key.** A good jumping-off point for divers headed to Looe Key Reef.

**9 Key West.** The ultimate in Keys wildness, this party town is for the open-minded.

**10 Dry Tortugas National Park.** Take a day trip to snorkel at these islands off Key West.

*Gulf of*

**THE LOWER KEYS**

Big Torch Key
Little Torch Key
Cudjoe Key
Mud Keys

Key West
**Key West**
Key West International Airport

Stock Island
Boca Chica Key
Saddlebunch Keys
Big Coppitt Key
Sugarloaf Key

←10 TO DRY TORTUGAS NATIONAL PARK

Everglades National Park

TO MIAMI

Homestead

Whitewater Bay

Card Sound Bridge

CAPE SABLE

Barnes Sound

Flamingo

Key Largo 1

THE UPPER KEYS

Florida Bay

Tavernier

John Pennekamp Coral Reef State Park

Mexico

Windley Key

Plantation Key

Islamorada 2

Upper Matecumbe Key

National Key Deer Refuge

THE MIDDLE KEYS

Layton

Lower Matecumbe Key

Long Key Channel

Craig Key

Marathon Airport 4 3

Conch Key

Marathon 5

Duck Key

Vaca Key

Grassy Key

Far Deer Key

Pigeon Key

7 6

Seven Mile Bridge

Little Duck Key

Bahia Honda Key

Big Pine Key

Ramrod Key

Summerland Key

ATLANTIC OCEAN

Straits of Florida

0          10 mi

0          10 km

# SEAFOOD IN THE FLORIDA KEYS

Fresh seafood from the Gulf

Fish. It's what's for dinner in the Florida Keys. The Keys' runway between the Gulf of Mexico or Florida Bay and Atlantic warm waters means fish of many fins. Restaurants take full advantage by serving it fresh, whether you caught it or a local fisherman did.

Menus at colorful waterfront shacks such as **Snapper's** (✉ *139 Seaside Ave., Key Largo* ☎ *305/852–5956*) in Key Largo and **Half Shell Raw Bar** (✉ *231 Margaret St., Key West* ☎ *305/294–7496*) range from basic raw, broiled, grilled, or blackened fish to some Bahamian and New Orleans–style interpretations. Other seafood houses dress up their fish in creative styles, such as **Pierre's** (✉ *MM 81.5 BS, Islamorada* ☎ *305/664–3225*) hogfish meunière, or yellowtail snapper with pear-ricotta pasta at **Café Marquesa** (✉ *600 Fleming St., Key West* ☎ *305/292–1244*). Try a Keys-style breakfast of "grits and grunts"—fried fish and grits—at the **Stuffed Pig** (✉ *3520 Overseas Hwy., Marathon* ☎ *305/743–4059*).

## BUILT-IN FISH

You know it's fresh when you see a fish market upon entering a restaurant. It happens frequently in the Keys. You can even peruse the seafood and pick the fish you want.

Many of the Keys' best restaurants are found in marina complexes, where the fishermen bring their catches. Try those in **Stock Island** (north of Key West) and at **Keys Fisheries Market & Marina** (✉ *MM 49 BS, end of 35th St., Marathon* ☎ *305/743–4353, 866/743–4353*).

## CONCH

One of the tastiest legacies of the Keys' Bahamian heritage (and most mispronounced), conch (pronounced *konk*) shows up on nearly every menu in some shape or form. It's so prevalent in local diets that natives refer to themselves as Conchs. Conch fritters are the most popular culinary manifestations, followed by cracked (pounded, breaded, and fried) conch, and conch salad, a ceviche-style refresher. Since the harvesting of queen conch is now illegal, most of the islands' conch comes from the Bahamas.

Stone crabs

## FLORIDA LOBSTER

Where are the claws? Stop looking for them: Florida spiny lobsters don't have any. The sweet tail meat, however, makes up for the loss. Divers harvest these crustaceans from late July through March. Check with local dive shops on restrictions, and then get ready for a fresh feast. Restaurants serve them broiled with drawn butter or in dishes such as lobster Benedict, lobster spring rolls, lobster Reuben, and lobster tacos.

## GROUPER

Once central to Florida's trademark seafood dish—fried grouper sandwich—its populations have been overfished in recent years, meaning that the state has exerted more control over bag regulations and occasionally closes grouper fishing on a temporary basis during the winter season. Some restaurants have gone antigrouper to try to bring back the abundance, but most grab it when they can. Black grouper is the most highly prized variety.

## STONE CRAB

In season October 15 through May 15, it gets its name from its rock-hard shell. Fishermen take only one claw, which can regenerate in a sustainable manner. Connoisseurs prefer them chilled with tangy mustard sauce. Some restaurants give you a choice of hot claws and drawn butter, but this means the meat will be cooked twice, because it's usually boiled or steamed as soon as it's taken from its crab trap.

Conch fritters

## YELLOWTAIL SNAPPER

The preferred species of snappers, it's more plentiful in the Keys than in any other Florida waters. As pretty as it is tasty, its mild, sweet, and delicate meat lends itself to any number of preparations, and it's available pretty much year-round. Chefs top it with everything from Key lime beurre blanc to mango chutney. **Ballyhoo's** in Key Largo (⊠ *MM 97.8* ☎ *305/852–0822*) serves it 10 different ways.

Your Keys experience begins on your 18-mile drive south on "The Stretch," a portion of U.S. 1 with a specially colored blue median that takes you from Florida City to Key Largo. The real magic starts at Mile Marker 113, where the Florida Keys Scenic Highway begins. As the only All-American Road in Florida, it is a destination unto itself, one that crosses 42 bridges over water, including the Seven Mile Bridge—with its stunning vistas—and ends in Key West. Look for crocodiles, alligators, and bald eagles along the way.

Key West has a Mardi Gras mood with Fantasy Festival, a Hemingway look-alike contest, and the occasional threat to secede from the Union. It's an island whose eclectic natives, known as "Conchs," mingle well with visitors (of the spring-break variety as well as those seeking to escape reality for a while) on this scenic, sometimes raucous 4x2-mile island paradise.

Although life elsewhere in the island chain isn't near as offbeat, it is as diverse. Overflowing bursts of bougainvillea, shimmering waters, and mangrove-lined islands can be admired throughout. The one thing most visitors don't admire much in the Keys are their beaches. They're not many, and they're not what you'd expect. The reason? The coral reef.

It breaks up the waves and prevents sand from being dumped on the shores. That's why the beaches are mostly rough sand, as it's crushed coral. Think of it as a trade-off: the Keys have the only living coral reef in the United States, but that reef prevents miles of shimmering sands from ever arriving.

In season, a river of traffic gushes southwest on this highway. But that doesn't mean you can't enjoy the ride as you cruise along the islands. Gaze over the silvery blue-and-green Atlantic and its living coral reef, with Florida Bay, the Gulf of Mexico, and the backcountry on your right (the Keys extend southwest from the mainland). At a few points the ocean and Gulf are as much as 10 miles apart; in most places, however, they're from 1 to 4 miles apart, and on the narrowest landfill islands they're separated only by the road.

While the views can be mesmerizing, to appreciate the Keys you need to get off the highway, especially in more developed regions like Key Largo, Islamorada, and Marathon. Once you do, rent a boat, anchor, and then fish, swim, or marvel at the sun, sea, and sky. Or visit one of the many sandbars, which are popular places to float the day away. Ocean-side, dive or snorkel spectacular coral reefs or pursue grouper, blue marlin, mahimahi, and other deepwater game fish. Along Florida Bay's coastline, kayak to secluded islands through mangrove forests, or seek out the bonefish, snapper, snook, and tarpon that lurk in the shallow grass flats and mangrove roots of the backcountry.

With virtually no distracting air pollution or obstructive high-rises, sunsets are a pure, unadulterated spectacle that each evening attract locals and visitors to any waterfront.

The Keys were only sparsely populated until the early 20th century. In 1905, however, railroad magnate Henry Flagler began building the extension of his Florida railroad south from Homestead to Key West. His goal was to establish a Miami–Key West rail link to his steamships that sailed between Key West and Havana, just 90 miles across the Straits of Florida. The railroad arrived at Key West in 1912, and remained a lifeline of commerce until the Labor Day hurricane of 1935 washed out much of its roadbed. The Overseas Highway, built over the railroad's old roadbeds and bridges, was completed in 1938.

### MAJOR REGIONS

As the doorstep to the islands' coral reefs and blithe spirit, **the Upper Keys** introduce all that's sporting and sea-oriented about the Keys. They stretch from Key Largo, 56 miles south of Miami

International Airport, to the Long Key Channel (MM 105–65). Centered on the town of Marathon, **the Middle Keys** hold most of the chain's historic and natural attractions outside Key West. They go from Conch (pronounced *konk*) Key through Marathon to the south side of the Seven Mile Bridge, including Pigeon Key (MM 65–40). The Middle Keys make a fitting transition from the Upper Keys to the Lower Keys not only geographically but also mentally. Crossing Seven Mile Bridge prepares you for the slow pace and don't-give-a-damn attitude you'll find a little farther down the highway. Pressure drops another notch when you reach **the Lower Keys**, the most laid-back part of the region, where key-deer viewing and fishing reign supreme. The Lower Keys go from Little Duck Key west through Big Coppitt Key (MM 40–9). Finally, **Key West** lies 150 miles from Miami and encompasses MM 9–0.

# Planning

## When to Go

**Low Season:** Low season is July through October, though holidays and festivals can cause rates to rise to high-season levels. The summer months tend to be the cheapest time to visit, when daily downpours, high humidity, and temperatures in the 90s turn off many visitors.

**Shoulder Season:** From April through June, winter crowds taper off, hotel rates become reasonable, and the weather is remarkably pleasant, with highs in the 80s and less rain than in the deep summer months.

**High Season:** Peak season is generally from November through mid-April, when temps are cooler and "snowbirds," or visitors from northern states, fly down to escape cold weather.

# Getting Here and Around

## AIR

The number of passengers using Key West International Airport (EYW) each year is approaching 1 million. Its most recent renovation includes a beach where travelers can catch their last blast of rays after clearing security. You can fly nonstop to Key West from Atlanta (Delta), Fort Lauderdale (United), Miami (American), and Tampa (American, United).

There are both bus and shuttle services from MIA to the Keys. The Lower Keys Shuttle runs between Key West and Marathon, offering cheap service and multiple stops.

Greyhound Lines' special Keys shuttle departs twice a day (times vary) from MIA's lower level Concourse E and makes stops throughout the Keys. Fares run from around $25 for Key Largo (Mile Marker 99.6) or Islamorada (Burger King, Mile Marker 82) to around $49 for Key West (3535 S. Roosevelt, Key West International Airport).

Keys Shuttle runs scheduled service six times a day in 15-passenger vans (nine passengers maximum) between Miami and Fort Lauderdale airports and Key West with stops throughout the Keys for $110 per person sharing rides.

**CONTACTS Greyhound.** ✉ *3439 S Roosevelt Blvd., Key West* ☎ *800/231–2222* ⊕ *www.greyhound.com.* **Keys Shuttle.** ✉ *1333 Overseas Hwy., Marathon* ☎ *888/765–9997* ⊕ *www.keysshuttle. com.*

## BOAT AND FERRY

Boaters can travel to and through the Keys either along the Intracoastal Waterway (5-foot draft limitation) through Card, Barnes, and Blackwater Sounds and into Florida Bay, or along the deeper Atlantic Ocean route through Hawk Channel, a buoyed passage. Refer to NOAA Nautical Charts Nos. 11451, 11445, and 11441. The Keys are full of marinas that welcome transient visitors, but they don't have enough slips for everyone. Make reservations, and ask about channel and dockage depth—many marinas are quite shallow.

Key West Express operates air-conditioned ferries between the Key West Terminal (Caroline and Grinnell streets) and Marco Island and Fort Myers Beach. The trip takes at least four hours each way and costs $130 one-way, and from $165 round-trip (a $6 convenience fee is added to all online bookings). Ferries depart from Fort Myers Beach at 8 am and from Key West at 6 pm. The Marco Island ferry departs at 8 am (the return trip leaves Key West at 5 pm). A photo ID is required for each passenger. Reservations are recommended.

**CONTACT Key West Express.** ✉ *100 Grinnell St., Key West* ☎ *239/463–5733* ⊕ *www.keywestexpress.net.*

## BUS

The City of Key West Department of Transportation has six color-coded bus routes traversing the island from 6:30 am to 11:30 pm. Stops have signs with the international bus symbol. Schedules are available on buses and at hotels, visitor centers, and shops. The fare is $2 one-way.

The Lower Keys Shuttle bus runs from Marathon to Key West ($4 one way), with scheduled stops along the way. Miami Dade Transit provides daily bus service from Mile Marker 50 in Marathon to the Florida City Walmart Supercenter on the mainland. The bus stops at major shopping centers as well as on demand anywhere along the route during daily round-trips on the hour from 6 am to 10 pm. The cost is $2 one-way, exact change required.

## CAR

By car from Miami International Airport, follow signs to Coral Gables and Key West, which puts you on LeJeune Road, then Route 836 west. Take the Homestead Extension of Florida's Turnpike south (toll road), which ends at Florida City and connects to the Overseas Highway (U.S. 1). Tolls from the airport run approximately $3. Payment is collected via SunPass, a prepaid toll program, or with Toll-By-Plate, a system that photographs each vehicle's license plate and mails a monthly bill for tolls, plus a $2.50 administrative fee, to the vehicle's registered owner.

Vacationers traveling in their own cars can obtain a mini-SunPass sticker via mail before their trip for $4.99 and receive the cost back in toll credits and discounts. The pass also is available at many major Florida retailers and turnpike service plazas. It works on all Florida toll roads and many bridges. For details on purchasing a mini-SunPass, call or visit the website.

For visitors renting cars in Florida, most major rental companies have programs allowing customers to use the Toll-By-Plate system. Tolls, plus varying service fees, are automatically charged to the credit card used to rent the vehicle (along with a hefty service charge in most cases). For details, including pricing options at participating rental-car agencies, check the program website. Under no circumstances should motorists attempt to stop in high-speed electronic tolling lanes. Travelers can contact Florida's Turnpike Enterprise for more information about the all-electronic tolling on Florida's Turnpike.

The alternative from Florida City is Card Sound Road (Route 905A), which has a (cash-only) bridge toll of $1. SunPass isn't accepted. Continue to the only stop sign and turn right on Route 905, which rejoins the Overseas Highway 31 miles south of Florida City.

Except in Key West, a car is essential for visiting the Keys. The best Keys road map, published by the Homestead–Florida City Chamber of Commerce, can be obtained for $5.50 from the Tropical Everglades Visitor Association.

**CONTACTS Florida's Turnpike Enterprise.** ☎ *800/749–7453* ⊕ *www.floridasturnpike. com.* **SunPass.** ☎ *888/865–5352* ⊕ *www. sunpass.com.*

### THE MILE MARKER SYSTEM
Getting lost in the Keys is almost impossible once you understand the unique address system. Many addresses are simply given as a mile marker (MM) number. The markers are small, green, rectangular signs along the side of the Overseas Highway (U.S. 1). They begin with Mile Marker 126, 1 mile south of Florida City, and end with Mile Marker 0, in Key West. Keys residents use the abbreviation BS for the bay side of Overseas Highway and OS for the ocean side. From Marathon to Key West, residents may refer to the bay side as the gulf side.

## Hotels

Throughout the Keys, the types of accommodations are remarkably varied, from 1950s-style motels to cozy inns to luxurious resorts. Most are on or near the ocean, so water sports are popular. Key West's lodging portfolio includes historic cottages, restored Conch houses, and large resorts. Some larger properties throughout the Keys charge a mandatory daily resort fee, which can cover equipment rental, fitness-center use, and other services, on top of state and county taxes. Some guesthouses and inns don't welcome children.

## Restaurants

The variety of restaurants in the Keys is vast, but if you were to ask a visitor what is typical, you would probably hear about the colorful seaside fish houses, some with more character than others. Seafood comes so fresh that you'll be spoiled for life. Pay special attention to local catches—especially snapper, mahimahi, grouper, lobster, and stone crab. Florida spiny lobster is local and fresh from August to March and stone crabs from mid-October to mid-May.

Also keep an eye out for authentic Key lime pie. The real McCoy has yellow filling in a graham-cracker crust and tastes pleasantly tart. (If it's green, just say no.) Cuban and Bahamian styles influence local cuisine, so be sure to sample some black beans and rice and conch fritters.

Restaurants may close for a two- to four-week vacation during the slow season—between mid-September and mid-November.

*Hotel and restaurant reviews have been shortened. For full information, visit Fodors.com. Hotel prices cited are the lowest cost of a standard double room in high season. Restaurant prices are the average cost of a main course at dinner, or if dinner is not served, at lunch.*

## What It Costs in U.S. Dollars

| $ | $$ | $$$ | $$$$ |
|---|---|---|---|
| **RESTAURANTS** | | | |
| under $20 | $20–$25 | $26–$35 | over $35 |
| **HOTELS** | | | |
| under $200 | $200–$300 | $301–$400 | over $400 |

## Visitor Information

There are several separate tourism offices in the Florida Keys, and you can use Visit Florida's website (⊕ *www.visit-florida.com*) for general information and referrals to local agencies.

# Key Largo

*56 miles south of Miami International Airport (between MM 107 and 91).*

The first of the Upper Keys reachable by car, 30-mile-long Key Largo is the largest island in the chain. Key Largo—named Cayo Largo (Long Key) by the Spanish—makes a great introduction to the region. This is the gateway to the Keys, and an evening of fresh seafood and views of the sunset on the water will get you in the right state of mind.

The history of Largo reads much like that of the rest of the Keys: a succession of native people, pirates, wreckers, and developers. The first settlement on Key Largo was named Planter, back in the days of pineapple and, later, key lime plantations. For a time it was a convenient shipping port, but when the railroad arrived Planter died on the vine. Today, three communities—North Key Largo, Key Largo, and the separately incorporated city of Tavernier—make up the whole of Key Largo.

### GETTING HERE AND AROUND

Key Largo is 56 miles south of Miami International Airport, with its mile markers ranging from 106 to 91. The island runs northeast–southwest, with the Overseas Highway (U.S. 1), divided by a median most of the way, running down the center. If the highway is your only glimpse of the island, you're likely to feel barraged by its tacky commercial side. Make a point of driving Route 905 in North Key Largo and down side streets to get a better feel for it.

### VISITOR INFORMATION

Stop by the Key Largo Chamber of Commerce for information or some colorful gifts (it sells a surprising selection of women's clothing). Divers take note: the Florida Keys National Marine Sanctuary has an office in Key Largo.

**CONTACTS Florida Keys National Marine Sanctuary.** ⊠ *MM 95.23 BS, 95230 Overseas Hwy, Key Largo* ☎ *305/852–7717* ⊕ *floridakeys.noaa.gov.* **Key Largo Chamber of Commerce.** ⊠ *MM 106 BS, 10600 Overseas Hwy., Key Largo* ☎ *305/451–4747, 800/822–1088* ⊕ *www.keylargochamber. org.*

## ◉ Sights

### Dagny Johnson Key Largo Hammock Botanical State Park

**OTHER ATTRACTION | FAMILY |** American crocodiles, mangrove cuckoos, white-crowned pigeons, mahogany mistletoe, wild cotton, and 100 other rare critters and plants inhabit these 2,400 acres, between Crocodile Lake National Wildlife Refuge and the waters of Pennekamp Coral Reef State Park. The park is also a user-friendly place to explore the largest remaining stand of the vast West Indian tropical hardwood hammock and mangrove wetland that once covered most of the Keys. ⊠ *Rte. 905 OS, North Key Largo ✛ ½ mile north of Overseas Hwy.* ☎ *305/451–1202* ⊕ *www. floridastateparks.org/parks-and-trails/ dagny-johnson-key-largo-hammock-botanical-state-park* ⌨ *$3 (exact change needed for the honor box).*

### Dolphins Plus Bayside

**OTHER ATTRACTION | FAMILY |** Programs begin with a get-acquainted session beneath a tiki hut. After that, you slip into the water for some frolicking with your new dolphin pals. Options range from a shallow-water swim to a hands-on structured swim with a dolphin. You can also shadow a trainer—it's $350 for a half day or a hefty $630 for a full day. ⊠ *MM 101.9 BS, 101900 Overseas Hwy., Key Largo* ☎ *305/451–4060, 866/860–7946* ⊕ *www. dolphinsplus.com* ⌨ *Admission only $20, interactive programs from $59.*

### ★ Dolphins Plus Marine Mammal Responder

**OTHER ATTRACTION | FAMILY |** This nonprofit focuses on marine mammal conservation, and you can help it by participating in one of the educational offerings. One popular option is the Connect to Protect, an immersive water program that begins with an educational briefing, after which you enter the deep-water lagoon to interact with the dolphins. Prefer to stay mostly dry? Opt for the tour of the facility or the general admission, which provides unlimited viewing of the dolphin lagoons, trainer talks, and educational exhibits. ⊠ *MM 99, 31 Corrine Pl., Key Largo* ☎ *305/453–4321* ⊕ *www.connecttoprotect.org* ⌨ *Programs from $59.*

### Florida Keys Wild Bird Center

**WILDLIFE REFUGE | FAMILY |** Have a nose-to-beak encounter with ospreys, hawks, herons, and other unreleasable birds at this bird rehabilitation center. The birds live in spacious screened enclosures along a boardwalk running through some of the best waterfront real estate in the Keys. ⊠ *MM 93.6 BS, 93600 Overseas Hwy., Key Largo* ☎ *305/852–4486* ⊕ *www.keepthemflying.org* ⌨ *Free, donations accepted.*

### Jacobs Aquatic Center

**POOL | FAMILY |** Take the plunge at one of three swimming pools: an eight-lane, 25-meter lap pool with two diving boards; a 3- to 4-foot-deep pool accessible to people with mobility challenges; and an interactive children's play pool with a waterslide, pirate ship, waterfall, and sloping zero-entry instead of steps. Because so few of the motels in Key Largo have pools, it remains a popular destination for visiting families. ⊠ *Key Largo Community Park, 320 Laguna Ave., at St. Croix Pl., Key Largo* ☎ *305/453–7946* ⊕ *www.jacobsaquaticcenter.org* ⌨ *$10 weekdays, $12 weekends.*

## Did You Know?

The bronze *Christ of the Deep* (also called *Christ of the Abyss*) statue of Jesus Christ underwater near John Pennekamp Coral Reef State Park is modeled after one in the Mediterranean Sea near where Italian Dario Gonzatti died while scuba diving.

## Beaches

**★ John Pennekamp Coral Reef State Park**

**BEACH | FAMILY** | This state park is on everyone's list for easy access to the best diving and snorkeling in Florida. The underwater treasure encompasses 78 nautical square miles of coral reefs and sea-grass beds. It lies adjacent to the Florida Keys National Marine Sanctuary, which contains 40 of the 52 species of coral in the Atlantic Reef System and nearly 600 varieties of fish, from the colorful parrotfish to the demure cocoa damselfish. Whatever you do, get in the water. Snorkeling and diving trips ($39 and $90, respectively; equipment extra) and glass-bottom-boat rides to the reef ($32) are available, weather permitting. One of the most popular snorkel trips is to see *Christ of the Deep*, the 2-ton underwater statue of Jesus. The park also has nature trails, two man-made beaches, picnic shelters, a snack bar, and a campground. **Amenities:** food and drink; parking (fee); showers; toilets; water sports. **Best for:** snorkeling; swimming. ✉ *MM 102.5 OS, 102601 Overseas Hwy., Key Largo* ☎ *305/451–1202 for park, 305/451–6300 for excursions* 🌐 *pennekamppark.com* 🎫 *$4 for 1 person in vehicle, $8 for 2–8 people, $2 for pedestrians and cyclists or extra people (plus a 50¢ per-person county surcharge).*

## Restaurants

**Alabama Jack's**

$ | **SEAFOOD** | Calories be damned—the conch fritters here are heaven on a plate. Come early for dinner (Jack's closes by 6:30, when the mosquitos start biting), and come hungry; the free-form fritters are large and loaded with flavor. **Known for:** heavenly conch fritters; unique setting (about a 30-minute drive from Key Largo); live music. [$] *Average main: $11* ✉ *58000 Card Sound Rd., Key Largo* ☎ *305/248–8741* 🌐 *www.facebook.com/realalabamajacks.*

**★ The Buzzard's Roost**

$$ | **SEAFOOD** | The views are nice at this waterfront restaurant, but the food is what gets your attention. Burgers, fish tacos, and seafood baskets are lunch faves. **Known for:** marina views; daily chef's specials; Sunday brunch with live steel drums. [$] *Average main: $21* ✉ *Garden Cove Marina, 21 Garden Cove Dr., Key Largo* ☎ *305/453–3746* 🌐 *www.buzzardsroostkeylargo.com.*

**★ Calusa**

$$$ | **CARIBBEAN** | Nestled on the third floor of the main building of Baker's Cay Resort, this waterfront spot offers panoramic views of the Gulf and a creative menu of Creole-Caribbean-inspired dishes. Start off with a round of craft cocktails (the Dark Rum Sazerac is a popular one), and then head to a table on the multilevel balcony for a dinner of Keys pink shrimp and lobster pasta or local mahimahi with miso-honey glaze. **Known for:** spectacular views; creative cocktails; whole fried fish. [$] *Average main: $28* ✉ *Baker's Cay Resort, MM 97 BS, 97000 Overseas Hwy., 3rd fl., Key Largo* ☎ *305/852–5553* 🌐 *www.bakerscay.com.*

**★ Italian Food Company**

$ | **ITALIAN** | **FAMILY** | Authentic southern Italian cuisine, with freshly made Neapolitan (Naples-style) pizza, pastas, and desserts is the focus here. A nicely landscaped garden with a cute Fiat decked out in the colors of the Italian flag should alert you to founders Tony and Isis Wright's obsession with detail. **Known for:** friendly service; Neopolitan pizza; a second location in Islamorada. [$] *Average main: $17* ✉ *98070 Overseas Hwy., Key Largo* ☎ *305/440–2700* 🌐 *italianfoodcompany.com* 🕒 *Closed Tues.*

**Jimmy Johnson's Big Chill**

$$ | **SEAFOOD** | Owned by former NFL coach Jimmy Johnson, this waterfront establishment offers three experiences: the best sports bar in the Upper Keys, an all-glass dining room with a waterfront deck, and an enormous outdoor tiki

bar with entertainment seven nights a week. There's even a pool and cabanas where (for a fee) you can spend the day sunning. **Known for:** the place to watch a game; fantastic bay views; brick-oven chicken wings with rosemary. $ *Average main: $24* ✉ *MM 104 BS, 104000 Overseas Hwy., Key Largo* ☎ *305/453–9066* ⊕ *www.jjsbigchill.com.*

### Key Largo Conch House

$ | **AMERICAN** | This family-owned restaurant in a Victorian-style home tucked into the trees is worth seeking out. Seven varieties of Benedict, including conch, are brunch favorites, while lunch and dinner menus highlight local seafood like lionfish (when available) and yellowtail snapper. **Known for:** shrimp and grits; all-season outside dining; seafood tacos. $ *Average main: $16* ✉ *MM 100.2, 100211 Overseas Hwy., Key Largo* ☎ *305/453–4844* ⊕ *www.keylargoconchhouse.com* ⊙ *Closed Thurs.*

### Mrs. Mac's Kitchen

$ | **SEAFOOD** | **FAMILY** | Locals pack the counters and booths at this tiny eatery, where license plates decorate the walls, to dine on everything from blackened prime rib to crab cakes. Every night is themed, including Meatloaf Monday, Italian Wednesday, and Seafood Sensation (offered Friday and Saturday). **Known for:** a second location a half mile south with a full liquor bar; champagne breakfast; being a stop on the Florida Keys Food Tour. $ *Average main: $17* ✉ *MM 99.4 BS, 99336 Overseas Hwy., Key Largo* ☎ *305/451–3722, 305/451–6227* ⊕ *www.mrsmacskitchen.com* ⊙ *Closed Sun.*

### Sal's Ballyhoo's

$$ | **SEAFOOD** | **FAMILY** | Occupying a 1930s conch house with outdoor seating right alongside U.S. 1 under the sea-grape trees, this local favorite is all about the fish: yellowtail snapper, tuna, and mahimahi. Choose your favorite, then choose your preparation, such as the Hemingway, with a Parmesan crust,

crabmeat, and key lime butter. **Known for:** spicy corn muffins; fish and fried-tomato sandwich; grilled avocado appetizer. $ *Average main: $24* ✉ *MM 97.8 median, 97800 Overseas Hwy., Key Largo* ☎ *305/852–0822* ⊕ *www.ballyhoosrestaurant.com.*

### Snappers

$$ | **SEAFOOD** | In a lively waterfront setting, Snappers has live music, Sunday brunch (including a build-your-own Bloody Mary bar), killer rum drinks, and seating alongside the fishing dock. The crab cakes are famous, as is the Bahamian cocktail sauce that accompanies them. **Known for:** grouper Oscar style; deep-fried gator bites doused in blue-cheese dressing; happening vibe and a local crowd. $ *Average main: $20* ✉ *MM 94.5 OS, 139 Seaside Ave., Key Largo* ☎ *305/852–5956* ⊕ *www.snapperskeylargo.com.*

### ★ Sol by the Sea

$$ | **CARIBBEAN** | This is the spot you might imagine when you think of dining by the water in the Keys. The Caribbean-influenced menu includes things like lobster and shrimp cakes, fried whole fish (the presentation is a photo op), and catch of the day served with fried plantains and rice and beans. **Known for:** picturesque spot; unique key lime dessert; Caribbean-influenced seafood. $ *Average main: $25* ✉ *Playa Largo Resort, MM 97 BS, 97540 Overseas Hwy., Key Largo* ☎ *305/853–1001* ⊕ *www.playalargoresort.com.*

### Sundowners

$$$ | **AMERICAN** | If it's a clear night and you can snag a reservation, this restaurant will treat you to a sherbet-hued sunset over Florida Bay. Try the key lime seafood, a happy combo of sautéed shrimp, lobster, and crabmeat swimming in a tangy sauce spiked with Tabasco served over penne or rice. **Known for:** bacon-wrapped scallops; sunset views; choose your fish, choose your

preparation. $ *Average main: $29 ⊠ MM 104 BS, 103900 Overseas Hwy., Key Largo ☎ 305/451–4502 ⊕ sundowners-keylargo.com.*

##  Coffee and Quick Bites

### Key Largo Fisheries Backyard Cafe
$ | **AMERICAN** | This waterfront café serves locally sourced seafood, soups, and salads in a casual setting—specifically, the back of Key Largo Fisheries. Order at the counter, find a picnic table on the covered patio, and watch the boats come in as your food is prepared. **Known for:** fresh seafood; easy to-go ordering; happy hour. $ *Average main: $16 ⊠ 1313 Ocean Bay Dr., Ste. A, Key Largo ☎ 305/451–3784 ⊕ www.keylargofisheries.com/cafe.*

## Hotels

### Azul del Mar
$$ | **B&B/INN** | The dock points the way to beautiful sunsets at this adults-only boutique hotel, which has been transformed from a run-down mom-and-pop place into a waterfront gem. **Pros:** high-quality linens; good location; sophisticated design. **Cons:** small beach; could use a refresh; minimum stays during holidays. $ *Rooms from: $299 ⊠ MM 104.3 BS, 104300 Overseas Hwy., Key Largo ☎ 305/451–0337, 888/253–2985 ⊕ www.azulkeylargo.com ⤳ 6 units ⦿ No Meals.*

### ★ Baker's Cay Resort Key Largo, Curio Collection by Hilton
$$$ | **RESORT** | **FAMILY** | Nestled within a "hardwood hammock" (localese for uplands habitat where hardwood trees such as live oak grow) near the southern border of Everglades National Park, this sprawling, 13-acre resort is not to be missed. **Pros:** you never have to leave the resort; pretty pools with waterfalls; 21-slip marina for all your boating needs. **Cons:** some rooms overlook the parking lot; pools are near the highway; high per-night resort fee. $ *Rooms from: $399 ⊠ MM 97 BS, 97000 Overseas Hwy., Key Largo ☎ 305/852–5553, 888/871–3437 ⊕ www.keylargoresort.com ⤳ 200 rooms ⦿ No Meals.*

### ★ Bungalows Key Largo
$$$$ | **ALL-INCLUSIVE** | This 12-acre, adults-only hideaway has charming free-standing bungalows (some of which are waterfront) that are outfitted with a front porch with Adirondack chairs, a sitting area with a couch, and a private patio with an outdoor soaking tub, shower, and seating area. **Pros:** only all-inclusive resort in the Keys; relaxing atmosphere; a lavish spa. **Cons:** gratuities are charged separately; two-night minimum stay; extra fees for early arrival and late checkout. $ *Rooms from: $990 ⊠ MM 99, 99010 Overseas Hwy., Key Largo ☎ 305/363–2830 ⊕ bungalowskeylargo.com ⤳ 135 suites ⦿ All-Inclusive.*

### Largo Resort
$$$$ | **RESORT** | Behind 10-foot, dark-wood Kong gates is a Bali-inspired world, where tranquility washes over you like a rain shower. **Pros:** unrivaled privacy; free kayaks and paddleboards; weekday special rates. **Cons:** no food or drinks on site for purchase; removed from sights; quietude isn't for everyone. $ *Rooms from: $500 ⊠ MM 101.7 BS, 101740 Overseas Hwy., Key Largo ☎ 305/451–0424 ⊕ www.largoresort.com ⤳ 6 bungalows ⦿ No Meals.*

### ★ Kona Kai Resort
$$ | **RESORT** | Brilliantly colored bougainvillea, coconut palm, and guava trees—and a botanical garden of other rare species—make this 2-acre adult hideaway one of the prettiest places to stay in the Keys. **Pros:** friendly staff; free use of sports equipment; spa-like pool area. **Cons:** expensive; some rooms are very close together; no restaurant on site. $ *Rooms from: $299 ⊠ MM 97.8 BS, 97802 Overseas Hwy., Key Largo ☎ 305/852–7200, 800/365–7829 ⊕ www.konakairesort.com ⤳ 13 rooms ⦿ Free Breakfast.*

### The Pelican

**$ | HOTEL | FAMILY |** This 1950s throwback recalls the days when parents packed the kids into the station wagon and headed to no-frills seaside motels. **Pros:** free use of kayaks and a canoe; well-maintained dock; reasonable rates. **Cons:** some rooms are small; basic accommodations and amenities; road noise with some units. *$ Rooms from: $159 ⊠ MM 99.3, 99340 Overseas Hwy., Key Largo ☎ 305/451–3576, 877/451–3576 ⊕ www.pelicankeylargo.com ⇨ 32 units ⦿ Free Breakfast.*

### ★ Playa Largo Resort & Spa, Autograph Collection

**$$$ | RESORT | FAMILY |** At this luxurious, 14-acre, bayfront retreat, you'll find one of the nicest beaches in the Keys, as well as water sports galore, bocce, tennis, basketball, and a fitness center with inspiring pool views. **Pros:** comfortable rooms, most with balconies; large pool; nightly sunset celebration. **Cons:** hefty resort fee; pool can get crowded; luxury will cost you. *$ Rooms from: $399 ⊠ MM 97.4, 97450 Overseas Hwy., Key Largo ☎ 305/853–1001 ⊕ playalargoresort.com ⇨ 178 units ⦿ No Meals.*

### Reefhouse Resort & Marina

**$$$ | RESORT | FAMILY |** Set on 17 acres overlooking Blackwater Sound, this hotel has been given a much-needed refresh, including the rooms, which span traditional and two-bedroom suite-style accommodations. **Pros:** lots of activities; dive shop on property; free Wi-Fi. **Cons:** rooms facing highway can be noisy; thin walls; chain-hotel feel. *$ Rooms from: $359 ⊠ MM 103.8 BS, 103800 Overseas Hwy., Key Largo ☎ 305/453–0000, 866/849–3753 ⊕ www.opalcollection.com/reefhouse ⇨ 153 rooms ⦿ No Meals.*

### Seafarer Resort and Beach

**$ | HOTEL | FAMILY |** At this basic, budget lodging it's all about staying on the water for a song. **Pros:** kitchen units available; complimentary kayak use; cheap rates. **Cons:** can hear road noise in some rooms; some complaints about cleanliness; decor could use an upgrade. *$ Rooms from: $149 ⊠ MM 97.6 BS, 97684 Overseas Hwy., Key Largo ☎ 305/852–5349 ⊕ www.seafarerkeylargo.com ⇨ 15 units ⦿ Free Breakfast.*

 **Nightlife**

### Breezer's Tiki Bar

**BARS |** Mingle with locals over cocktails and catch amazing sunsets from the comfort of an enclosed, air-conditioned bar. Floor-to-ceiling doors can be opened on cool days and closed on hot days. *⊠ Reefhouse Resort & Marina, MM 103.8 BS, 103800 Overseas Hwy., Key Largo ☎ 305/453–0000.*

### ★ C&C Wood Fired Eats

**WINE BARS |** Although it's only open till 10, this is still a place to see and be seen. It's dark and a little mysterious, and the wine, wood-fired pizzas, cheese pairings, meats, and fondues are five-star worthy. Sit at the bar, on a couch, or at a high-top, and be transported to somewhere other than a typical, tropical Keys venue. The daily happy hour offers a "pizza and pitcher" special that's a hit with locals. *⊠ MM 9.2, 99201 Overseas Hwy., Key Largo ☎ 305/451–0995 ⊕ candcwoodfiredeats.com.*

### Caribbean Club

**BARS |** Walls plastered with Bogart memorabilia remind customers that the classic 1948 Bogart-Bacall flick *Key Largo* has a connection with this watering hole. Although no food is served, and the floors are bare concrete, this landmark draws boaters, curious visitors, and local barflies to its humble barstools and pool tables. But the real magic is around back, where you can grab a seat on the deck and catch a postcard-perfect sunset. Live music draws revelers Thursday through Sunday. *⊠ MM 104 BS, 104080 Overseas Hwy., Key Largo ☎ 305/451–4466 ⊕ caribbeanclubkl.com.*

### Skipper's Dockside
**CAFÉS | FAMILY |** Marina views are among the many charms of this fun place in the heart of Key Largo. Sit outside under the tiki, in a brightly colored Adirondack chair by the firepits, or inside amid driftwood walls and prize catches. No matter: what you'll remember is the fresh, everything-made-in-house food. ⊠ *MM 100 OS, 528 Caribbean Dr., Key Largo* ☎ *305/453–9794* ⊕ *www.skippersdockside.com.*

##  Shopping

### Key Lime Products
**OTHER SPECIALTY STORE |** Go into olfactory overload—you'll find yourself sniffing every single bar of soap and scented candle inside this key lime treasure trove. Take home some key lime juice (super-easy pie-making directions are right on the bottle), marmalade, candies, sauces, and even key lime shampoo. ⊠ *MM 95.2 BS, 95231 Overseas Hwy., Key Largo* ☎ *305/853–0378, 800/870–1780* ⊕ *www.keylimeproducts.com.*

### ★ Keys Chocolates & Ice Cream
**CHOCOLATE | FAMILY |** The only chocolate factory in the Keys specializes in key lime truffles. In addition to fine white, milk, and dark Belgian-chocolate confections (the salted turtles, a fan favorite, are worth every calorie), you'll find cupcakes and ice cream. Chocolate-making classes are also available for kids and adults, and a small gift area showcases local art, jewelry, hot sauces, and other goodies. ⊠ *MM 100 BS, 100471 Overseas Hwy., Key Largo* ☎ *305/453–6613* ⊕ *www.keylargochocolates.com.*

### ★ Old Road Gallery
**ART GALLERIES |** This shop is filled with ceramics, bronze and copper creations, and jewelry—all made by local artists—but it's the secret sculpture garden that really makes this place unique. Further, owner-artists Cindy and Dwayne King genuinely embody the joyful spirit of the Florida Keys. ⊠ *88888 Old Hwy.,* *Tavernier* ⊹ *In the median between Overseas Hwy. and Old Hwy.* ☎ *305/852–8935* ⊕ *www.oldroadgallery.com.*

##  Activities

### BIKING
#### Bubba's
**BIKING |** Bubba's organizes one-week custom biking tours through the Keys along the Heritage Trail. A van accompanies tours to carry luggage and tired riders. Former police officer Bubba Barron also hosts a weeklong ride down the length of the Keys every November. Riders can opt for tent camping or motel-room accommodations. Meals are included, but bike rentals are extra. ⊠ *Key Largo* ☎ *321/759–3433* ⊕ *www.bubbaspamperedpedalers.com* 🖫 *From $1,210 per person, double occupancy.*

### BOATING
#### Everglades Eco-Tours
**BOATING | FAMILY |** For more than 30 years, Captain Sterling has operated Everglades and Florida Bay ecology tours and sunset cruises. With his expert guidance, you can see dolphins, manatees, and birds from a pontoon boat equipped with PVC chairs. Bring your own food and drinks; each tour has a maximum of six people. ⊠ *Sundowners Restaurant, MM 104 BS, 103900 Overseas Hwy., Key Largo* ☎ *305/853–5161, 888/224–6044* ⊕ *www.captainsterling.com* 🖫 *From $59.*

#### M. V. *Key Largo Princess*
**BOATING | FAMILY |** Two-hour glass-bottom-boat trips and pricier sunset cruises on a 70-foot motor yacht with a large glass viewing area depart from the Holiday Inn docks three times a day. ■TIP➔ **Purchase tickets online to save big.** ⊠ *Holiday Inn, MM 100 OS, 99701 Overseas Hwy., Key Largo* ☎ *305/451–4655, 877/648–8129* ⊕ *www.keylargoprincess.com* 🖫 *$30.*

## CANOEING AND KAYAKING

You can paddle for a few hours or the whole day, on your own or with a guide. Some outfitters even offer overnight trips. The **Florida Keys Overseas Paddling Trail,** part of a statewide system, runs from Key Largo to Key West. You can paddle the entire distance, 106 miles on the Atlantic side, which takes 9 to 10 days.

### Coral Reef Park Co.

CANOEING & ROWING | FAMILY | At John Pennekamp Coral Reef State Park, this operator has a fleet of canoes and kayaks for gliding around the 2½-mile mangrove trail or along the coast. Powerboat rentals are also available. ⊠ *MM 102.5 OS, 102601 Overseas Hwy., Key Largo* ☎ *305/451–6300* ⊕ *www.pennekamp-park.com* ⊠ *Rentals from $20 per hr.*

### Florida Bay Outfitters

CANOEING & ROWING | FAMILY | Rent canoes, sea kayaks, or Hobie Eclipses from this company, which matches equipment to your skill level and also sets up self-guided trips on the Florida Keys Overseas Paddling Trail and helps with trip planning. ⊠ *MM 104 BS, 104050 Overseas Hwy., Key Largo* ☎ *305/451–3018* ⊕ *www.paddlefloridakeys.com* ⊠ *From $15.*

## FISHING

### Sailors Choice

FISHING | Fishing excursions depart twice daily (half-day trips are cash only), but the company also does private charters. The 65-foot boat leaves from the Holiday Inn docks. Rods, bait, and license are included. ⊠ *Holiday Inn Resort and Marina, MM 100 OS, 99701 Overseas Hwy., Key Largo* ☎ *305/451–1802, 305/451–0041* ⊕ *www.sailorschoicefishingboat.com* ⊠ *From $45.*

## SCUBA DIVING AND SNORKELING

### Amy Slate's Amoray Dive Resort

SCUBA DIVING | This outfit makes diving easy. Stroll down to the full-service dive shop (PADI, TDI, and BSAC certified), then onto a 45-foot catamaran.

Certification courses are also offered. ⊠ *MM 104.2 BS, 104250 Overseas Hwy., Key Largo* ☎ *305/451–3595, 800/426–6729* ⊕ *www.amoray.com* ⊠ *From $85.*

### Conch Republic Divers

SCUBA DIVING | Book diving instruction as well as scuba and snorkeling tours of Upper Keys wrecks and reefs. Two-location dives are the standard; tanks and weights cost $20 extra. ⊠ *MM 90.8 BS, 90800 Overseas Hwy., Key Largo* ☎ *305/852–1655, 800/274–3483* ⊕ *www.conchrepublicdivers.com* ⊠ *From $80.*

### Coral Reef Park Co.

SCUBA DIVING | At John Pennekamp Coral Reef State Park, this company gives 3½-hour scuba and 2½-hour snorkeling tours of the park. In addition to the great location and the dependability, it's also suited for water adventurers of all levels. ⊠ *MM 102.5 OS, 102601 Overseas Hwy., Key Largo* ☎ *305/451–6300* ⊕ *www.pennekamppark.com* ⊠ *From $30.*

### Horizon Divers

SCUBA DIVING | Horizon offers customized diving and snorkeling trips aboard a 45-foot catamaran. ⊠ *105.8, 105800 Overseas Hwy., Key Largo* ☎ *305/453–3535, 800/984–3483* ⊕ *www.horizondivers.com* ⊠ *Snorkeling from $50, diving from $85.*

### Island Ventures

SCUBA DIVING | If you like dry British humor and no crowds, this is the operator for you. It specializes in small groups for snorkeling or dive trips, no more than 10 people per boat. Scuba trips are two tanks and two locations and include tanks and weights; ride-alongs pay just $35. Choose morning or afternoon. ⊠ *Jules Undersea Lodge, 51 Shoreland Dr., Key Largo* ☎ *305/451–4957* ⊕ *www.islandventure.com* ⊠ *Snorkel trips $45, diving $85.*

### ★ Quiescence Diving Services

SCUBA DIVING | This operator limits groups to six to ensure personal attention and offers day, twilight (when sea creatures are most active), and night dives, as well as organized snorkeling excursions. ⊠ *MM 103.5 BS, 103680 Overseas Hwy., Key Largo* ☎ *305/451–2440* ⊕ *keylargodiving.com* ⊠ *Snorkel trips $55, diving from $89.*

# Islamorada

*Between MM 90.5 and 70.*

Early maps show Islamorada as encompassing only Upper Matecumbe Key. But the incorporated "Village of Islands" is made up of a string of islands that the Overseas Highway crosses, including Plantation Key, Windley Key, Upper Matecumbe Key, Lower Matecumbe Key, Craig Key, and Fiesta Key.

Islamorada (locals pronounce it *eye*-la-mor- *ah*-da) is one of the world's top fishing destinations. For nearly 100 years, seasoned anglers have fished these clear, warm waters teeming with trophy fish. It's also known for sophisticated resorts and restaurants that meet the needs of those in search of luxury, but there's still plenty for those who want something more casual and affordable.

## GETTING HERE AND AROUND
Most visitors arrive in Islamorada by car. If you're flying into Miami International Airport or Key West International Airport, you can easily rent a car (make a reservation) to make the drive.

## VISITOR INFORMATION
**CONTACT Islamorada Chamber of Commerce & Visitors Center.** ⊠ *MM 87.1 BS, 87100 Overseas Hwy., Upper Matecumbe Key* ☎ *305/664–4503, 800/322–5397* ⊕ *www.islamoradachamber.com.*

 Sights

**Florida Keys Memorial/Hurricane Monument**
MONUMENT | On Monday, September 2, 1935, more than 400 people perished when the most intense hurricane to

make landfall in the United States swept through this area of the Keys. Two years later, the Florida Keys Memorial was dedicated in their honor. Native coral rock, known as keystone, covers the 18-foot obelisk monument that marks the cremated remains of some 300 of the storm victims. ⊠ *MM 81.8, 81831 Old State Hwy. 4A, Upper Matecumbe Key* ⊕ *In front of the public library and just south of the Cheeca Lodge entrance* ⊠ *Free.*

★ **Founders Park**
CITY PARK | FAMILY | Amenities at this gem of a public park include a palm-shaded beach, pool, marina, skate park, tennis, and places to rent a boat or learn to sail. If you're staying in Islamorada, admission is free; otherwise, it costs $8 (cash only) to enter. ⊠ *MM 87 BS, 87000 Overseas Hwy., Plantation Key* ☎ *305/853–1685* ⊕ *www.islamorada.fl.us/departments/parks_and_recreation/founders_park.php.*

★ **History of Diving Museum**
HISTORY MUSEUM | FAMILY | This museum plunges into the history of man's thirst for undersea exploration. Amid its 13 galleries of interactive and other interesting displays are a submarine and helmet re-created from the film *20,000 Leagues Under the Sea*. Vintage U.S. Navy equipment, diving helmets from around the world, and early scuba gear explore 4,000 years of diving history. Nifty scavenger hunt printouts make this fun for little ones. ⊠ *MM 83 BS, 82990 Overseas Hwy., Upper Matecumbe Key* ☎ *305/664–9737* ⊕ *www.divingmuseum.org* ⊠ *$15.*

**Robbie's Marina**
MARINA/PIER | FAMILY | Silver-sided tarpon—huge, prehistoric-looking denizens of the not-so-deep—congregate around the docks at this authentic local marina. Children (and many adults) pay $4.50 for a bucket of sardines to feed them and $2.50 each for dock admission. You can also grab a bite to eat indoors or out; shop at a slew of artisans' booths; or charter a boat, kayak, or other watercraft.

✉ *MM 77.5 BS, 77522 Overseas Hwy., Lower Matecumbe Key* ☎ *305/664–8070, 877/664–8498* 🌐 *www.robbies.com.*

**Theater of the Sea**

**OTHER ATTRACTION | FAMILY** | The second-oldest marine-mammal center in the world doesn't attempt to compete with more modern, more expensive parks. Even so, it's among the better attractions north of Key West, especially if you have kids in tow. In addition to seeing marine-life exhibits and shows, you can make reservations for up-close-and-personal encounters like a swim with a dolphin or sea lion or stingray and turtle feedings (which include general admission). Stop for lunch at the grill, shop in the extensive gift shop, or sunbathe and swim at the private beach. ✉ *MM 84.5 OS, 84721 Overseas Hwy., Windley Key* ☎ *305/664–2431* 🌐 *www.theaterofthesea.com* 🎫 *$45, interaction programs from $65.*

## Beaches

**Anne's Beach**

**BEACH | FAMILY** | On Lower Matecumbe Key this popular village park is named for a local environmental activist. Its "beach" (really a typical Keys-style sand flat with a gentle slope) is best enjoyed at low tide. The nicest feature here is the elevated, wooden, ½-mile boardwalk that meanders through a natural wetland hammock. Covered picnic areas along the way give you places to linger and enjoy the view. Restrooms are at the north end. Weekends are packed with Miami day-trippers as it's the only public beach until you reach Marathon. **Amenities:** parking (no fee); toilets. **Best for:** partiers; snorkeling; swimming; windsurfing. ✉ *MM 73.5 OS, Lower Matecumbe Key* ☎ *305/853–1685.*

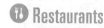

## Restaurants

**Bitton Bistro Café**

**$ | FRENCH** | Authentic French food is on the menu at this supercasual eatery run by chef-owner Michel Bitton. The gelatos and homemade French pastries might be famous, but don't miss the opportunity to savor his daily quiches, fresh salads with Dijon vinaigrette, rustic soups, and French baguette sandwiches. **Known for:** oversize crepes; freshly made gelato; wide assortment of macarons. [$] *Average main: $12* ✉ *MM 82 OS, 82245 Overseas Hwy., Upper Matecumbe Key* ☎ *305/396–7481* 🌐 *facebook.com/BittonBistroCafe* 💳 *No credit cards* 🕓 *No dinner.*

★ **Chef Michael's**

**$$$$ | SEAFOOD** | This local favorite makes big waves with fresh seafood that's prepared with tropical flair. Carnivores can feast on prime-grade beef, which is carved in-house and has the kind of marbling that just melts in your mouth. **Known for:** watermelon mint sangria; fresh catch "Juliette" with shrimp and scallops; intimate tropical dining. [$] *Average main: $38* ✉ *MM 81.7, 81671 Overseas Hwy., Upper Matecumbe Key* ☎ *305/664–0640* 🌐 *www.foodtotalkabout.com* 🕓 *No lunch Mon.–Sat.*

**Green Turtle Inn**

**$$ | SEAFOOD** | This circa-1947 landmark—with its vintage neon sign, wood-paneled walls, and period photos—is a slice of Florida Keys history. Breakfast options include French toast made with challah bread and Captain Morgan batter or Keys Benedict with a blue crab cake; at lunch, opt for lobster mac and cheese. **Known for:** excellent conch chowder; outstanding pound cake; huge homemade sticky buns. [$] *Average main: $24* ✉ *MM 81.2 OS, 81219 Overseas Hwy., Upper Matecumbe Key* ☎ *305/664–2006* 🌐 *www.greenturtlekeys.com* 🕓 *Closed Mon.*

**Hungry Tarpon**

**$ | SEAFOOD | FAMILY** | This is part of the colorful, bustling Old Florida scene at Robbie's Marina, so you know that the seafood here is fresh and top quality. The extensive menu seems as if it's bigger than the dining space, which consists of a few tables and counter seating indoors, plus tables out back under the mangrove trees. **Known for:** insanely good Bloody Marys with a beef-stick straw; heart-of-the-action location; biscuits and gravy. [$] *Average main: $19* ✉ *MM 77.5 BS, 77522 Overseas Hwy., Lower Matecumbe Key* ☎ *305/664–0535* 🌐 *www.hungrytarpon.com.*

**Islamorada Fish Company**

$ | **SEAFOOD** | **FAMILY** | Owned by Bass Pro Shops and housed in an open-air, oversize tiki hut on Florida Bay, this restaurant offers a quintessential Keys dining experience. Menu highlights include cracked conch beaten until tender and then fried, and fresh-catch Portofino blackened perfectly and topped with Key West shrimp and a brandied lobster sauce. **Known for:** tourist hot spot; great views; afternoon fish and shark feedings in its private lagoon. [$] *Average main: $18* ✉ *MM 81.5 BS, 81532 Overseas Hwy., Upper Matecumbe Key* ☎ *305/664–9271* 🌐 *www.islamoradafishco.com.*

**Island Grill**

$ | **SEAFOOD** | Don't be fooled by appearances; this waterfront shack takes island breakfast, lunch, and dinner up a notch. Tempting options include the famed "original tuna nachos," lobster rolls, and a nice selection of seafood and sandwiches. **Known for:** eclectic seafood options; slow service; nice views. [$] *Average main: $14* ✉ *MM 85.5 OS, 85501 Overseas Hwy., Islamorada* ☎ *305/664–8400* 🌐 *www.keysislandgrill.com.*

**Marker 88**

$$$ | **SEAFOOD** | A few yards from Florida Bay, this popular seafood restaurant has large picture windows that offer great sunset views, though most patrons dine outside on the sand. Chef Bobby Stoky serves such irresistible entrées as onion-crusted mahimahi and house-smoked sea-salt-and-black-pepper-encrusted rib eye. **Known for:** a gathering place for locals and visitors; fantastic fresh-fish sandwich; extensive wine list. [$] *Average main: $34* ✉ *MM 88 BS, 88000 Overseas Hwy., Plantation Key* ☎ *305/852–9315* 🌐 *www.marker88.info.*

**Morada Bay Beach Café**

$$$ | **ECLECTIC** | **FAMILY** | This bayfront restaurant wins high marks for its surprisingly stellar cuisine, tables in the sand, and tiki torches that bathe the evening in romance. Seafood takes center stage, but you can always get roasted organic chicken or prime rib. **Known for:** feet-in-the-sand dining; full-moon parties; intoxicating sunset views. [$] *Average main: $27* ✉ *MM 81 BS, 81600 Overseas Hwy., Upper Matecumbe Key* ☎ *305/664–0604* 🌐 *www.moradabay.com.*

★ **Pierre's Restaurant**

$$$$ | **FRENCH** | One of the Keys' most elegant restaurants, Pierre's marries colonial style with modern food trends and lets you taste the world from its romantic verandas. French chocolate, Australian lamb, Hawaiian fish, Florida lobster—whatever is fresh and in season will be masterfully prepared and beautifully served. **Known for:** romantic spot for that special night out; seasonally changing menu; full-moon parties. [$] *Average main: $43* ✉ *MM 81.5 BS, 81600 Overseas Hwy., Upper Matecumbe Key* ☎ *305/664–3225* 🌐 *www.moradabay.com* ⏲ *No lunch.*

## Coffee and Quick Bites

**Bayside Gourmet**

$ | **ITALIAN** | **FAMILY** | This tiny counter-service restaurant is the best-kept secret in Islamorada, with the tastiest and most affordable ($11) grouper Reuben sandwich in the Keys. It's a small place—with six tables inside, a bar overlooking the kitchen, and an outdoor patio—and most diners are locals. **Known for:** excellent key lime pie; microbrews; seafood omelets. [$] *Average main: $17* ✉ *MM 82.7 BS, 82758 Overseas Hwy., Upper Matecumbe Key* ☎ *305/735–4471* 🌐 *baysidegourmet.com.*

## Hotels

**Amara Cay Resort**

$$ | **RESORT** | At this simple yet chic resort, spacious rooms evoke well-to-do bachelor pads, complete with a counter and stools, wine chiller, minimalistic furniture, and artwork. **Pros:** free local shuttle; use of kayaks, bikes, paddleboards; oceanfront zero-entry pool. **Cons:** pricey $40 daily resort fee; living areas of rooms lack seating; no on-site spa. [$] *Rooms from: $299* ✉ *MM 80 OS, 80001 Overseas Hwy., Upper Matecumbe Key* ☎ *305/664–0073* 🌐 *www.amaracayresort.com* 🛏 *110 rooms* 🍴 *No Meals.*

**Casa Morada**

$$$ | **B&B/INN** | This relic from the 1950s has been restyled into a suave, design-forward, all-suites property with outdoor showers and whirlpool tubs in some of the suites. **Pros:** private island connected by footbridge; adults only; complimentary use of bikes, kayaks, paddleboards, and snorkel gear. **Cons:** dinner off property; beach is small and inconsequential; minimum two-night stay on weekends. [$] *Rooms from: $400* ✉ *MM 82 BS, 136 Madeira Rd., Upper Matecumbe Key* ☎ *305/664–0044, 888/881–3030* 🌐 *www.casamorada.com* 🛏 *16 suites* 🍴 *Free Breakfast.*

★ **Cheeca Lodge & Spa**

$$$$ | **RESORT** | **FAMILY** | One of the most storied and luxurious resorts in the Keys, this legendary property still packs in more amenities than any other we can think of. **Pros:** everything you need is on site; designer rooms; water-sports center on property. **Cons:** expensive rates; expensive resort fee; can get busy. [$] *Rooms from: $410* ✉ *MM 82 OS, 81801 Overseas Hwy., Upper Matecumbe Key* ☎ *305/664–4651, 800/327–2888* 🌐 *www.cheeca.com* 🛏 *214 rooms* 🍴 *No Meals.*

**Chesapeake Beach Resort**

$$ | **RESORT** | **FAMILY** | Modern conveniences and a retro look are among the hallmarks of this boutique hotel on the beach. **Pros:** oceanfront location; reasonable prices; private porches or balconies. **Cons:** no dining on site; $25 resort fee per night; no spa. [$] *Rooms from: $210* ✉ *MM 83.5, 83409 Overseas Hwy., Upper Matecumbe Key* ☎ *305/664–4662, 800/338–3395* 🌐 *www.chesapeake-resort.com* 🛏 *52 rooms* 🍴 *No Meals.*

**Drop Anchor**

$$ | **HOTEL** | Immaculately maintained, this place has the feel of an old friend's beach house, and it's easy to find the one- or two-bedroom units, as they are painted in an array of Crayola colors. **Pros:** bright and colorful; very clean; laid-back charm. **Cons:** noise from the highway; beach is for fishing, not swimming; simplicity isn't for everyone. [$] *Rooms from: $200* ✉ *MM 85 OS, 84959 Overseas Hwy., Windley Key* ☎ *305/664–4863, 888/664–4863* 🌐 *www.dropanchorresort.com* 🛏 *18 suites* 🍴 *No Meals.*

**Islander Resort**

$$ | **RESORT** | **FAMILY** | Here you get to choose between a self-sufficient town home on the bay side or an oceanfront resort with on-site restaurants and oodles of other amenities. **Pros:** spacious rooms; nice kitchens; eye-popping views. **Cons:** pricey; no dining at bayside location; some activities have a fee. [$] *Rooms from: $300* ✉ *MM 82.1 OS, 82200 Overseas Hwy., Upper Matecumbe Key* ☎ *305/664–0082* 🌐 *www.islanderfloridakeys.com* 🛏 *114 rooms* 🍴 *No Meals.*

★ **The Islands of Islamorada**

$$$ | **HOTEL** | Situated right on the Atlantic, this luxury club resort has waterfront villas and hotel suites, all nestled along 600 feet of private shoreline. **Pros:** private marina; luxurious facilities and amenities; 24-hour gym. **Cons:** limited number of units means it's often booked solid; luxury comes at a price; lacks a full-service restaurant. [$] *Rooms from: $399* ✉ *MM 82 OS, 82885 Old Hwy., Windley Key* ☎ *866/540–5520*

🌐 *theislandsofislamorada.com* 🛏 *30 units* 🍴 *Free Breakfast.*

**La Siesta Resort & Marina**
$$$ | **RESORT** | **FAMILY** | With 6 acres of oceanfront property, accommodations that range from studio units to a glamorous three-bedroom waterfront home, and staffers who go the extra mile, this resort has everything a visitor to the Keys could want. **Pros:** free use of kayaks, paddleboards, bicycles, and fishing rods; free Wi-Fi; access to sister properties. **Cons:** $40 nightly resort fee; bar-café only open until 7; not a swimming beach. [$] *Rooms from: $399* ✉ *MM 80.2 OS, 80241 Overseas Hwy., Upper Matecumbe Key* ☎ *305/664–2132, 855/335–1078 reservations* 🌐 *www.lasiestaresort.com* 🛏 *53 rooms* 🍴 *Free Breakfast.*

**The Moorings Village**
$$$$ | **HOTEL** | At this tropical retreat, the embodiment of the laid-back Keys, hammocks sway between towering trees and aqua-green waves lap manicured sand. **Pros:** romantic setting; good dining options with room-charging privileges; beautiful views. **Cons:** no room service; $25 daily resort fee for activities; must cross the highway to walk or drive to its restaurants. [$] *Rooms from: $800* ✉ *MM 81.6 OS, 123 Beach Rd., Upper Matecumbe Key* ☎ *305/664–4708* 🌐 *www.themooringsvillage.com* 🛏 *17 cottages* 🍴 *No Meals.*

**Postcard Inn Beach Resort & Marina**
$$ | **RESORT** | The boathouse-chic units at this storied property have white wooden accents, faux-wood–tiled floors, and a comfy daybed. **Pros:** large private beach; heated pools; on-site restaurants, including Ciao Hound Italian Kitchen & Bar. **Cons:** rooms near tiki bar are noisy; minimum stay required during peak times; some rooms overlook a parking lot. [$] *Rooms from: $267* ✉ *MM 84 OS, 84001 Overseas Hwy., Islamorada* ☎ *305/664–2321* 🌐 *www.holidayisle.com* 🛏 *145 rooms* 🍴 *No Meals.*

## Nightlife

**Hog Heaven**
**BARS** | Come by boat or car to this oceanfront restaurant and sports bar, where you can soak in the views dockside or relax in the air-conditioning. Munch on fresh fish sandwiches or barbecue dishes while you shoot pool, catch the big game on large flat-screens, or dance to a live band or DJ. Late night can get a bit wild and loud. ✉ *MM 85.3 OS, 85361 Overseas Hwy., Windley Key* ☎ *305/664–9669* 🌐 *www.hogheavensportsbar.com.*

**The Lorelei Restaurant and Cabana Bar**
**BARS** | A larger-than-life mermaid guides you to the kind of place you fantasize about during those long, cold winters up north. It's all about good drinks, tasty pub grub, and beautiful sunsets set to live bands playing island tunes and light rock nightly. Dining is all outdoors, on a deck or under the trees. Service is slow, sometimes even nonexistent. ✉ *MM 82 BS, 81924 Overseas Hwy., Upper Matecumbe Key* ☎ *305/664–2692* 🌐 *www.loreleicabanabar.com.*

**Ziggie & Mad Dog's**
**BARS** | The area's glam celebrity hangout, Ziggie & Mad Dog's serves appetizers with its happy-hour drink specials. Its wine list and outrageous steaks have become legendary. ✉ *MM 83 BS, 83000 Overseas Hwy., Upper Matecumbe Key* ☎ *305/664–3391* 🌐 *www.ziggieandmaddogs.com.*

## Shopping

**Bass Pro Shops - World Wide Sportsman**
**SPORTING GOODS** | This two-level retail center sells upscale and everyday fishing equipment, resort clothing, sport-fishing art, and other gifts. It's worth a stop to climb aboard the *Pilar*, a replica of Hemingway's boat installed in the middle of the store. ✉ *MM 81.5 BS, 81576 Overseas Hwy., Upper Matecumbe Key*

Kayak ready to be used on a beach in the Florida Keys

☎ *305/664–4615, 800/327–2880* ⊕ *www. basspro.com.*

### ★ Casa Mar Village

**MALL** | What was once a row of worn-down buildings is now a merry mix of gift shops and galleries. By day, these colorful stores glisten at their canal-front location; by nightfall, they're lit up like a lovely Christmas town. ✉ *MM 90 OS, 90775 Old Hwy., Plantation Key* ⊕ *www. casamarvillage.com.*

### Rain Barrel Village

**CRAFTS** | You can't miss the giant sculpture of Betsy the lobster in front of this eclectic spot. Set in a tropical garden of shady trees, native shrubs, and orchids, the crafts village has shops selling the work of local and national artists, as well as resident artists who sell work from their own studios. ✉ *MM 86.7 BS, 86700 Overseas Hwy., Plantation Key* ☎ *305/852–3084* ⊕ *rainbarrelvillage.com.*

### Redbone Gallery

**CRAFTS** | This gallery stocks hand-stitched clothing, giftware, and jewelry, in addition to works of art by watercolorists C. D. Clarke and Julie Joyce and painters Luther Hall, Stephen Left, Tim Borski, and Jorge Martinez, among others. Proceeds benefit cystic fibrosis research. It's in the Morada Way Arts and Cultural District. ✉ *MM 81.5 OS, 200 Morada Way, Upper Matecumbe Key* ☎ *305/664–2002* ⊕ *www.redbone.org.*

##  Activities

### BOATING

#### Early Bird Fishing Charters

**FISHING** | Captain Ross knows these waters well, and he'll hook you up with whatever is in season—mahimahi, sailfish, tuna, and wahoo, to name a few—while you cruise on a comfy and stylish 43-foot custom Willis charter boat. The salon is air-conditioned for those hot summer days, and everything but booze and food is included. ✉ *Bud N' Mary's Marina, MM 79.8 OS, 79851 Overseas Hwy., Upper Matecumbe Key* ☎ *305/942–3618* ⊕ *www.fishearlybird.*

com ☎ 4 hrs $850, 6 hrs $1,100, 8 hrs $1,300.

### Keys Boat Rental

**BOATING** | You can rent both fishing and deck boats here (from 18 to 29 feet) by the day or the week. Free local delivery with seven-day rentals from each of its locations is available. ⊠ *MM 85.9 BS and 99.7 OS, 85920 Overseas Hwy., Plantation Key* ☎ *305/664–9404, 877/453–9463* ⊕ *www.keysboatrental.com* ☎ *Rentals from $240 per day.*

### Robbie's Boat Rentals

**BOATING** | This full-service company will even give you a crash course on how not to crash your boat. The rental fleet includes an 18-foot skiff with a 90-horsepower outboard and a 21-foot deck boat with a 130-horsepower engine. Robbie's also rents snorkeling gear (there's good snorkeling nearby) and sells bait, drinks, and snacks. Want to hire a guide who knows the local waters and where the fish lurk? Robbie's offers offshore-fishing trips, patch-reef trips, and party-boat fishing. Backcountry flats trips are a specialty. ⊠ *MM 77.5 BS, 77522 Overseas Hwy., Lower Matecumbe Key* ☎ *305/664–9814, 877/664–8498* ⊕ *www.robbies.com* ☎ *From $185 per day.*

## FISHING

### ★ Bamboo Charters

**FISHING** | A world-class fisherman and guide who studied to be a marine biologist, Captain Matt know his stuff, whether you want a calm day in the shallow waters or a day at the reef catching snapper, grouper, or anything else with fins. ⊠ *Angler House Marina MM 80.5, 80500 Overseas Hwy., Upper Matecumbe Key* ☎ *305/394–0000* ⊕ *www.bamboocharters.com.*

### Captain Ted Wilson

**FISHING** | Go into the backcountry for bonefish, tarpon, redfish, snook, and shark aboard a 17-foot boat that accommodates up to three anglers. Choose four-, six-, or eight-hour trips or evening tarpon-fishing excursions. Rates are for one or two anglers. There's a $75 charge for an additional person. ⊠ *Bud N' Mary's Marina, MM 79.9 OS, 79851 Overseas Hwy., Upper Matecumbe Key* ☎ *305/942–5224* ⊕ *www.captaintedwilson.com* ☎ *Half-day and evening trips from $450.*

### Florida Keys Fly Fish

**FISHING** | Like other top fly-fishing and light-tackle guides, Captain Geoff Colmes helps his clients land trophy fish in the waters around the Keys, from Islamorada to Flamingo in the Everglades. ⊠ *105 Palm La., Plantation Key* ☎ *305/393–1245* ⊕ *www.floridakeysflyfish.com* ☎ *From $550.*

### Florida Keys Outfitters

**FISHING** | Long before fly-fishing became popular, Sandy Moret was fishing the Keys for bonefish, tarpon, and redfish. Now he attracts anglers from around the world on a quest for the big catch. ⊠ *Green Turtle, MM 81.2, 81219 Overseas Hwy., Upper Matecumbe Key* ☎ *305/664–5423* ⊕ *www.floridakeysoutfitters.com* ☎ *Half-day trips from $550.*

### Miss Islamorada

**FISHING** | This 65-foot party boat offers full-day fishing trips. Bring your lunch or buy one from the dockside deli. ⊠ *Bud N' Mary's Marina, MM 79.8 OS, 79851 Overseas Hwy., Upper Matecumbe Key* ☎ *305/664–2461, 800/742–7945* ⊕ *www.budnmarys.com* ☎ *$70.*

## KAYAKING

### The Kayak Shack

**KAYAKING** | You can rent kayaks for trips to Indian Key (about 20 minutes one-way) and Lignumvitae Key (about 45 minutes one-way), two favorite destinations for paddlers. ⊠ *Robbie's Marina, MM 77.5 BS, 77522 Overseas Hwy., Lower Matecumbe Key* ☎ *305/664–4878* ⊕ *www.kayakthefloridakeys.com* ☎ *From $40 for single, $55 for double; guided trips from $45.*

## Did You Know?

The coral making up the
Barrier Reef is living and
provides an ecosystem for
small marine creatures.
Bumping against or
touching the coral can kill
these creatures as well as
damage the reef itself.

## SCUBA DIVING AND SNORKELING
### Florida Keys Dive Center
**SCUBA DIVING** | Dive from John Pennekamp Coral Reef State Park to Alligator Reef with this outfitter. It has two 46-foot Coast Guard–approved dive boats, offers scuba training, and is one of the few Keys dive centers to offer nitrox and trimix (mixed-gas) diving. ✉ *MM 90.5 OS, 90451 Overseas Hwy., Plantation Key* ☎ *305/852–4599, 800/433–8946* ⊕ *www. floridakeysdivecenter.com* ⌕ *Snorkeling from $38, diving from $84.*

### Islamorada Dive Center
**SCUBA DIVING** | This one-stop dive shop has a resort, pool, restaurant, lessons, twice-daily dive and snorkel trips, and the newest fleet in the Keys. Take a daytrip with a two-tank dive or a one-tank night trip with their equipment or yours. Snorkel and spearfishing trips are also available. ✉ *MM 84 OS, 84001 Overseas Hwy., Windley Key* ☎ *305/664–3483, 800/327–7070* ⊕ *www.islamoradadivecenter.com* ⌕ *Snorkel trips from $45, diving from $85.*

### San Pedro Underwater Archaeological Preserve State Park
**SCUBA DIVING** | This site includes the remains of a Spanish treasure-fleet ship that sank in 1733. Resting in only 18 feet of water, its ruins are visible to snorkelers as well as divers and attract a colorful array of fish. ✉ *MM 85.5 OS, Islamorada* ☎ *305/664–2540* ⊕ *www. floridastateparks.org/parks-and-trails/ san-pedro-underwater-archaeological-preserve-state-park.*

# Conch Key and Duck Key

*Conch Key: between MM 63 and 60. Duck Key: at MM 61.*

Fishing dominates Conch Key's economy, and many residents are descendants of immigrants from the mainland South. There are a few lodging options here for those exploring Marathon or taking advantage of the water sports on the more upscale Duck Key, which is just across the causeway from Conch Key and has one of the region's nicest marina resorts, Hawks Cay, as well as a boating-oriented residential community.

##  Restaurants

### ★ Angler & Ale
**$$$** | **SEAFOOD** | **FAMILY** | If you're a fan of vibrant coastal decor and fresh local seafood, you'll gush over this restaurant and bar overlooking the water and Hawks Cay Marina. The menu is varied with options that include burgers as well as grilled fish, the cocktails are creative, and there are more than a dozen beers on tap. **Known for:** locally sourced seafood like grouper cheeks and Key West pink shrimp; pricey menu; family friendliness. $ *Average main: $30* ✉ *Hawks Cay Resort, MM 61 OS, 540 Duck Key Dr., Duck Key* ☎ *305/209–9991* ⊕ *www. hawkscay.com.*

### Sixty-One Prime
**$$$$** | **AMERICAN** | This elegant, fine-dining restaurant in Hawks Cay Resort serves steaks and seafood. Chefs work with local farmers and fishermen to find what's fresh and in season, then create a menu that will wow your palate (and your wallet). **Known for:** naturally raised certified Black Angus beef; nightly changing menu; attentive service. $ *Average main: $36* ✉ *Hawks Cay Resort, MM 61 OS, 61 Hawks Cay Blvd., Duck Key* ☎ *305/743–7000, 888/432–2242* ⊕ *www.hawkscay. com* ⊙ *No lunch.*

## 🛏 Hotels

### ★ Hawks Cay Resort
**$$$** | **RESORT** | **FAMILY** | The 60-acre, Caribbean-style retreat with a full-service spa and six restaurants has plenty to keep the kids occupied (and adults happy). **Pros:** great activities for families; restful spa; full-service marina and dive shop. **Cons:** no real beach; far from Marathon's

attractions; resort-wide tram gets busy, so plan to wait or walk far. $ *Rooms from: $315* ✉ *MM 61 OS, 61 Hawks Cay Blvd., Duck Key* ☎ *305/743–7000, 888/432–2242* ⊕ *www.hawkscay.com* ⇗ *431 units* ⓧ *No Meals.*

## Activities

### Dolphin Connection
**OTHER ATTRACTION | FAMILY** | Hawks Cay Resort's Dolphin Connection offers three programs, including Dockside Dolphins, a 30-minute encounter from the dry training docks; Dolphin Discovery, an in-water program that lasts about 45 minutes and lets you kiss, touch, and feed the dolphins; and Trainer for a Day, a three-hour session with the animal training team. ✉ *Hawks Cay Resort, MM 61 OS, 61 Hawks Cay Blvd., Duck Key* ☎ *305/289–9975* ⊕ *www.dolphinconnection.com* ⟋ *From $79.*

### Fish 'n Fun
**BOATING** | Get out on the water on 19- to 26-foot powerboats. Rentals can be for a half or full day. The company also offers free delivery in the Middle Keys. ✉ *Duck Key Marina, MM 61 OS, 1149 Greenbriar Rd., Duck Key* ☎ *305/743–2275, 800/471–3440* ⊕ *www.fishnfunrentals.com* ⟋ *From $225.*

# Grassy Key

*Between MM 60 and 57.*

Local lore has it that this sleepy little key was named not for its vegetation—mostly native trees and shrubs—but for an early settler by the name of Grassy. A few families operating small fishing camps and roadside motels primarily inhabit the key. Although there's no marked definition between Marathon and Grassy Key, making it feel sort of like a suburb, sights tend toward the natural, including a worthwhile dolphin attraction and a small state park.

GETTING HERE AND AROUND
Most visitors arrive by air and drive here from Miami International or Key West International Airports. Rental cars are readily available at both and, in the long run, are the best way to reach and tour the Middle Keys.

##  Sights

### ★ Curry Hammock State Park
**STATE/PROVINCIAL PARK | FAMILY** | On the ocean and bay sides of the Overseas Highway are 260 acres of upland hammock, wetlands, and mangroves. On the bay side, there's a trail through thick hardwoods to a rocky shoreline. The ocean side is more developed, with a sandy beach, a clean bathhouse, picnic tables, a playground, grills, and a 28-site campground with electric and water hookups. Locals consider the paddling trails under canopies of arching mangroves among the best kayaking spots in the Keys. Manatees frequent the area, and it's a great place for watching herons, egrets, ibises, plovers, and sanderlings. Raptors are often seen in the park, too, especially during migration periods. ✉ *MM 57 OS, 56200 Overseas Hwy., Grassy Key* ☎ *305/289–2690* ⊕ *www.floridastateparks.org/parks-and-trails/curry-hammock-state-park* ⟋ *$5 for up to 2 people, $1 per additional person* ⟋ *Campsites are $36 per night.*

### Dolphin Research Center
**OTHER ATTRACTION | FAMILY** | The 1963 movie *Flipper* popularized the notion of humans interacting with dolphins, and Milton Santini, the film's creator, opened this center, which is home to a colony of dolphins and sea lions. The nonprofit center has educational sessions and programs that allow you to greet the dolphins from dry land or play with them in their watery habitat. You can even paint a T-shirt with a dolphin—you pick the paint, the dolphin "designs" your shirt. ✉ *MM 59 BS, 58901 Overseas Hwy.,*

*Grassy Key ☎ 305/289–1121 information, 305/289–0002 reservations 🌐 www.dolphins.org 🎟 $28.*

## 🍴 Restaurants

**★ Hideaway Café**

**$$$ | AMERICAN** | It's easy to miss this café tucked between Grassy Key and Marathon, but when you find it (upstairs at Rainbow Bend Resort), expect it to be filled with locals who appreciate a well-planned menu, lovely ocean view, and quiet evening away from the crowds. For starters, dig into escargots à la Edison (sautéed with vegetables, pepper, cognac, and cream) before feasting on specialties, such as a rarely found chateaubriand for one or a seafood medley combining the catch of the day with scallops and shrimp. **Known for:** seclusion and quiet; amazing escargots; hand-cut steaks and fresh fish. [$] *Average main: $30 ✉ Rainbow Bend Resort, MM 58 OS, 57784 Overseas Hwy., Grassy Key ☎ 305/289–1554 🌐 www.hideawaycafe.net ⏲ No lunch.*

## 🛏 Hotels

**★ Grassy Flats**

**$$ | RESORT | FAMILY** | Owned by retired professional kiteboarder Matt Sexton, this relaxed, eco-friendly resort and beach club is popular with water-sports enthusiasts, who make regular visits to its sibling property, The Lagoon, for wakeboarding sessions. **Pros:** peaceful atmosphere; no resort fee; complimentary paddleboards and kayaks. **Cons:** not close to sights in Marathon; Conch House rooms close to highway; limited food options. [$] *Rooms from: $299 ✉ MM 59, 58182 Overseas Hwy., Grassy Key ☎ 305/998–4590 🌐 www.grassyflats.com 🔑 33 units 🍴 No Meals.*

## 🏃 Activities

**The Lagoon on Grassy Key**

**WATER SPORTS | FAMILY** | This 50-acre, water-sports complex is home to Keys Cable Park, Bongos Beer Garden, and The Lagoon Saloon surf shop. Keys Cable Park specializes in wakeboarding, with additional activities including stand-up paddleboarding, efoil (electric hydrofoil) boarding, and kayaking. Bongos, a locals' favorite venue with live music and a weekend brunch, has a laid-back feel with hammock chairs and lawn games. The Lagoon Saloon, living up to its "Surf, Sail, Swim, and Swill" motto, sells the latest in wind, surf, skate, and lifestyle clothing and accessories and has beer on tap at the register. *✉ MM 59, 59300 Overseas Hwy., Grassy Key ☎ 305/414–8245 🌐 ridethelagoon.com 🎟 $35.*

# Marathon

*Between MM 53 and 47.5.*

New Englanders founded this former fishing village in the early 1800s. The community on Vaca Key subsequently served as a base for pirates, salvagers (also known as "wreckers"), spongers, and, later, Bahamian farmers who eked out a living growing cotton and other crops. More Bahamians arrived in the hope of finding work building the railroad. According to local lore, Marathon was renamed when a worker commented that it was a marathon task to position the tracks across the 6-mile-long island.

During the building of the railroad, Marathon developed a reputation for lawlessness that rivaled that of the Old West. It is said that to keep the rowdy workers from descending on Key West for their off-hours endeavors, residents would send boatloads of liquor up to Marathon. Needless to say, things have quieted down considerably since then.

### Did You Know?

Dolphins in Florida
are predominantly of
the Atlantic bottlenose
variety. These playful
and smart creatures love
to leap out of the water
and synchronize their
movements with others.
By swimming next to
boats, dolphins can
conserve energy.

Still, Marathon is a bustling town, at least compared to other communities in the Keys. As it leaves something to be desired in the charm department, Marathon may not be your first choice of places to stay, but water-sports types will find plenty to enjoy, and its historic and natural attractions merit a visit. Surprisingly good dining options abound, so you'll definitely want to stop for a bite even if you're just passing through on the way to Key West. And the sprawling new Isla Bella Beach Resort has drawn plenty of visitors to Marathon looking for an upscale getaway in the Keys.

Marathon hosts fishing tournaments throughout the year (practically monthly), a huge seafood festival in March, and lighted boat parades around the holidays.

### GETTING HERE AND AROUND

SuperShuttle charges $190 per passenger for trips from Miami International Airport to the Upper Keys. To go farther into the Keys, you must book an entire 11-person van, which costs about $300 to Marathon. Reserve trips to the airport 24 hours ahead.

Miami-Dade Transit provides daily bus service from Mile Marker 50 in Marathon to the Florida City Walmart Supercenter on the mainland. The bus stops at major shopping centers as well as on demand anywhere along the route during round trips on the hour from 6 am to 10 pm. The cost is $2 one way, exact change required. The Key West Transit bus runs from Marathon to Key West ($4 one way), with scheduled stops along the way.

### VISITOR INFORMATION

**CONTACT Greater Marathon Chamber of Commerce and Visitor Center.** ⊠ MM 53.5 BS, 12222 Overseas Hwy., Marathon ☎ 305/743–5417, 800/262–7284 ⊕ www. floridakeysmarathon.com.

##  Sights

### Crane Point Museum, Nature Center, and Historic Site

**HISTORY MUSEUM | FAMILY |** Tucked away from the highway behind a stand of trees, Crane Point is part of a 63-acre tract that contains the last-known undisturbed thatch-palm hammock. The facility includes the Museum of Natural History of the Florida Keys, which has displays about local wildlife, a seashell exhibit, and a marine-life display that makes you feel like you're at the bottom of the sea. Kids love the replica 17th-century galleon; the pirate dress-up room; and the re-created Cracker House filled with insects, sea-turtle exhibits, and children's activities. On the 1-mile loop trail, visit the Laura Quinn Wild Bird Center and the remnants of a Bahamian village, site of the restored George Adderly House. It is the oldest surviving example of Bahamian tabby (a concrete-like material created from sand and seashells) construction outside Key West. A boardwalk crosses wetlands, rivers, and mangroves before ending at Adderly Village. From November to Easter, docent-led tours are available. Bring good walking shoes and bug repellent. ⊠ MM 50.5 BS, 5550 Overseas Hwy., Marathon ☎ 305/743–9100 ⊕ www.cranepoint.net ⊠ $14.95.

### ★ Florida Keys Aquarium Encounters

**AQUARIUM | FAMILY |** This isn't your typical large-city aquarium. It's more hands-on and personal, and it's all outdoors with several tiki huts to house the encounters and provide shade as you explore, rain or shine. Plan to spend at least two to three hours here. You'll find a 200,000-gallon aquarium and plenty of marine encounters (extra cost), as well as guided tours, viewing areas, and a predator tank. The Coral Reef encounter ($95 snorkel, $130 regulator) lets you dive without hearing the theme from *Jaws* in your head (although you can see several sharks on the other side of the glass). Touch tanks have unique critters like slipper lobsters. Hungry? The on-site Eagle Ray Café serves up wings, fish tacos, salads, burgers, and more. Note that general admission is required, even if you've signed up for a marine encounter. ⊠ *MM 53 BS, 11710 Overseas Hwy., Marathon* ☎ *305/407–3262* ⊕ *www.floridakeysaquariumencounters.com* 🖻 *$27.50.*

### Pigeon Key

**OTHER ATTRACTION | FAMILY |** There's much to like about this 5-acre island under the Old Seven Mile Bridge. You might even recognize it from a season finale of the TV show *The Amazing Race.* You can reach it via a restored train that departs from the gift shop, which is in a trailer at Mile Marker 47.5. Once there, tour the island on your own, or join a guided tour to explore the buildings that formed the early-20th-century work camp for the Overseas Railroad, which linked the mainland to Key West in 1912. Later, the island became a fish camp, a state park, and then government-administration headquarters. Exhibits in a small museum recall the history of the Keys, the railroad, and railroad baron Henry M. Flagler. The train ride with tour lasts two hours. ■TIP➔ **Bring your own snorkel gear and dive flag and you can snorkel right from the shore; pack a picnic lunch, too.** ⊠ *MM 47.5 BS, 2010 Overseas Hwy., Pigeon Key* ✛ *Between the Marriott and Hyatt Place* ☎ *305/743–5999* ⊕ *pigeonkey.net* 🖻 *$25.*

### ★ Seven Mile Bridge and Old Seven Mile Bridge

**BRIDGE | FAMILY |** This is one of the most photographed images in the Keys. Actually measuring slightly less than 7 miles, it connects the Middle and Lower Keys and is believed to be the world's longest segmental bridge, with 39 expansion joints separating its various concrete sections. Each April, runners gather in Marathon for the annual Seven Mile Bridge Run.

The expanse running parallel to the Seven Mile Bridge is what remains of the Old Seven Mile Bridge, an engineering and architectural marvel in its day that's now on the National Register of Historic Places. Once proclaimed the Eighth Wonder of the World, it rested on a record 546 concrete piers. A $44 million renovation, begun in 2017, is part of a 30-year, $77-million restoration and maintenance agreement between the Keys' Monroe County, Marathon municipal officials, and the Florida Department of Transportation. No cars are allowed on the old bridge, but the oft-photographed, 2.2-mile span is open to pedestrians and serves as the gateway to historic Pigeon Key, an islet nestled beneath the "Old Seven" that was once home to about 400 workers constructing the railroad. ⊠ *Marathon.*

### The Turtle Hospital

**WILDLIFE REFUGE | FAMILY |** Each year, more than 100 injured creatures are admitted to the world's first state-certified veterinary hospital for sea turtles. Guided 90-minute tours take you into recovery and surgical areas. In the "hospital bed" tanks, you can see recovering patients and others that are permanent residents due to their injuries. After the tour, you can feed some of the residents. Call ahead—space is limited and tours are sometimes canceled due to medical emergencies. The turtle ambulance out front makes for a memorable souvenir photo. ⊠ *MM 48.5 BS, 2396 Overseas Hwy., Marathon* ☎ *305/743–2552* ⊕ *www.turtlehospital.org* 🖻 *$30.*

## 🏖 Beaches

### ★ Sombrero Beach

**BEACH | FAMILY |** One of the best beaches in the Keys has shaded picnic areas overlooking a coconut palm–lined grassy stretch and the Atlantic. Roped-off areas allow swimmers, boaters, and windsurfers to share the narrow cove. Facilities include grills, a large playground, a pier, a volleyball court, and a paved, lighted bike path off the Overseas Highway. Sunday afternoons draw lots of local families toting coolers. The park is accessible for those with disabilities and allows leashed pets. Turn east at the traffic light in Marathon and follow signs to the end. **Amenities:** showers; toilets. **Best for:** swimming; windsurfing. ⊠ *MM 50 OS, Sombrero Beach Rd., Marathon* ☎ *305/743–0033* ⬚ *Free.*

## 🍴 Restaurants

### Fish Tales Market and Eatery

$ | **SEAFOOD** | This no-frills, roadside eatery has a loyal local following, an unfussy ambience, a couple of outside picnic tables, and friendly service. Signature dishes include snapper on grilled rye with coleslaw and melted Muenster cheese, a fried-fish burrito, George's crab cake, and tomato-based conch chowder. **Known for:** luscious lobster bisque; fresh and affordable seafood and meat market; affordable specials. $ *Average main: $14* ⊠ *MM 52.5 OS, 11711 Overseas Hwy., Marathon* ☎ *305/743–9196, 888/662–4822* ⬀ *www.floridalobster.com* ⊘ *Closed weekends.*

### Herbie's Bar and Chowder House

$ | **SEAFOOD** | This shack-like spot has been the go-to for quick, affordable comfort food since the 1940s. You'll find all the Old Keys staples—conch, lobster tail, fried oysters, and fresh fish—as well as cheeseburgers and filet mignon. **Known for:** great craft-beer selection; crispy conch fritters; good key lime pie. $ *Average main: $14* ⊠ *MM 50.5, 6350 Overseas Hwy., Marathon* ☎ *305/743–6373* ⬀ *www.herbiesrestaurant.com* ⊘ *Closed Sun.–Tues.*

### Key Colony Inn

$$ | **ITALIAN** | The inviting aroma of an Italian kitchen pervades this family-owned favorite. For lunch there are fish and steak entrées served with fries, salad, and bread in addition to Italian specialties; dinner features veal Oscar and other traditional dishes, as well as specialties like seafood *Italiano*, a dish of scallops and shrimp sautéed in garlic

butter and served with marinara sauce over linguine. **Known for:** friendly and attentive service; Italian specialties; Sunday brunch (November through April). $ *Average main: $20* ⊠ *MM 54 OS, 700 W. Ocean Dr., Marathon* ☎ *305/743–0100* ⬀ *www.kcinn.com.*

### Keys Fisheries

$ | **SEAFOOD** | **FAMILY** | You can't miss the enormous tiki bar on stilts, but the walk-up window on the ground floor is the heart of this warehouse-turned-restaurant. The huge lobster Reuben served on thick slices of toasted bread is the signature dish, and the adults-only upstairs tiki bar offers a sushi and raw bar for eat-in only. **Known for:** seafood market; marina views; fish-food dispensers (25¢) so you can feed the tarpon. $ *Average main: $16* ⊠ *MM 49 BS, 3390 Gulfview Ave., at the end of 35th St., Marathon* ⊹ *Turn onto 35th St. from Overseas Hwy.* ☎ *305/743–4353, 866/743–4353* ⬀ *www. keysfisheries.com.*

### Lazy Days South

$$ | **SEAFOOD** | Tucked into Marathon Marina, ½ mile north of the Seven Mile Bridge, this restaurant offers views just as spectacular as its highly lauded food. The offerings at this spinoff of an Islamorada favorite range from fried or sautéed conch and a coconut-fried fish du jour sandwich to seafood pastas and beef tips over rice. **Known for:** water views; delicious seafood entrées; hook and cook. $ *Average main: $22* ⊠ *MM 47.3 OS, 725 11th St., Marathon* ☎ *305/289–0839* ⬀ *www.lazydayssouth.com.*

### ★ Mahina

$$ | **ITALIAN** | Dishes such as ahi poke and lobster-crusted mahimahi nod to executive chef Pavy Keomaniboth's native Hawaii. The spectacular indoor–outdoor setting features coconut palms strung with lights and panoramic sunset views. **Known for:** Hawaiian-inspired dishes and cocktails; romantic; extensive wine list. $ *Average main: $24* ⊠ *Isla Bella Resort, MM 47 OS, 1 Knights Key Blvd.,*

*Marathon ☎ 786/638–8106 🌐 www.islabellabeachresort.com.*

**Sunset Grille and Raw Bar**

$$ | **SEAFOOD** | Treat yourself to a seafood lunch or dinner at this vaulted tiki hut at the foot of the Seven Mile Bridge. For lunch, try the Voodoo grouper sandwich topped with mango-guava mayo (and wear your swimsuit if you want to take a dip in the pool afterward); dinner specialties include a Brie-stuffed filet mignon and coconut curry lobster. **Known for:** weekend pool parties and barbecues; pricey dinner specials; a swimming pool for patrons. [$] *Average main: $24* ✉ *MM 47 OS, 7 Knights Key Blvd., Marathon* ☎ *305/396–7235* 🌐 *www.sunsetgrille7milebridge.com.*

## Coffee and Quick Bites

**The Stuffed Pig**

$ | **AMERICAN** | With only nine tables and a counter inside, this place is always full. The kitchen whips up daily lunch specials like seafood platters or pulled pork with hand-cut fries, but the all-day breakfast is the main draw. **Known for:** local twists on breakfast standards; large portions; cash only. [$] *Average main: $11* ✉ *MM 49 BS, 3520 Overseas Hwy., Marathon* ☎ *305/743–4059* 🌐 *www.thestuffedpig.com* 💳 *No credit cards* 🕘 *No dinner.*

## Hotels

**Glunz Ocean Beach Hotel and Resort**

$$ | **HOTEL** | The Glunz family got it right when they purchased this former time-share property and put a whole lot of love into ensuring it achieved its full ocean-front potential—from the bottom-floor rooms, you can walk out your back door and your feet are in the sand, or you can also chill at the oceanfront tiki bar or one of two heated pools. **Pros:** friendly staff; nice private beach; excellent free Wi-Fi. **Cons:** small elevator; no interior corridors; not cheap. [$] *Rooms from: $300* ✉ *MM 53.5 OS, 351 E. Ocean Dr., Marathon* ☎ *305/289–0525* 🌐 *www.glunzoceanbeachhotel.com* 🔑 *46 units* 🍴 *No Meals.*

★ **Isla Bella Beach Resort**

$$ | **RESORT** | **FAMILY** | Combining Caribbean luxury with Keys charm, this glamorous 24-acre resort is a destination unto itself with five pools, rooms along a sandy waterfront, toes-in-the-sand dining, and amenities like kids activities, resort bikes, and morning yoga. **Pros:** secluded setting; spacious rooms; full-service spa and marina. **Cons:** no real beach; a hefty resort fee; some balconies lack privacy. [$] *Rooms from: $250* ✉ *MM 47 OS, 1 Knights Key Blvd., Marathon* ☎ *305/481–9451* 🌐 *www.islabellabeachresort.com* 🔑 *199 rooms* 🍴 *No Meals.*

★ **Tranquility Bay**

$$$$ | **RESORT** | **FAMILY** | Ralph Lauren could have designed the rooms at this stylish, luxurious resort on a nice beach. **Pros:** secluded setting; tiki bar on the beach; main pool is nice and big. **Cons:** a bit sterile; no privacy on balconies; cramped building layout. [$] *Rooms from: $425* ✉ *MM 48.5 BS, 2600 Overseas Hwy., Marathon* ☎ *305/289–0888, 866/643–5397* 🌐 *www.tranquilitybay.com* 🔑 *102 rooms* 🍴 *No Meals.*

## Activities

### BIKING

**Bike Marathon Bike Rental**

**BIKING** | "Have bikes, will deliver" could be the motto of this company, which will transport beach cruisers (as well as helmets, baskets, and locks) to your hotel door. It also rents kayaks. There's no physical location, but services are available Monday through Saturday 9–4 and Sunday 9–2. ✉ *Marathon* ☎ *305/743–3204* 🌐 *www.bikemarathonbikerentals.com* 🎟 *$69 per wk.*

### BOATING

**Captain Pip's**

**BOATING** | This operator rents 18- to 24-foot outboards as well as snorkeling gear. Ask about multiday deals, or try one of the accommodation packages and walk right from your bay-front room to your boat. ⊠ *MM 47.5 BS, 1410 Overseas Hwy., Marathon* ☎ *305/743–4403, 800/707–1692* ⊕ *www.captainpips.com* ⬦ *Rentals from $199 per day.*

### FISHING

#### Marathon Lady

**FISHING** | Morning, afternoon, and night, fish for mahimahi, grouper, and other tasty catches aboard this 73-footer, which departs on half-day excursions from the Vaca Cut Bridge (Mile Marker 53), north of Marathon. Join the crew for night fishing ($55) from 6:30 to midnight from Memorial Day to Labor Day. ⊠ *MM 53 OS, 11711 Overseas Hwy., at 117th St., Marathon* ☎ *305/743–5580* ⊕ *www.marathonlady.net* ⬦ *From $45.*

#### Sea Dog Charters

**FISHING** | Captain Jim Purcell, a deep-sea specialist for ESPN's *The American Outdoorsman,* provides one of the best values in Keys fishing. His company offers half- and full-day offshore, reef and wreck, and backcountry fishing trips, as well as fishing and snorkeling trips aboard 30- to 37-foot boats. The per-person cost for a half-day trip is the same regardless of whether or not your group fills the boat, and it includes bait, light tackle, ice, coolers, and fishing licenses. If you prefer an all-day private charter on a 37-foot boat, he offers those, too, for up to six people. A fuel surcharge may apply. ⊠ *MM 47.5 BS, 1248 Overseas Hwy., Marathon* ☎ *305/743–8255* ⊕ *www.seadogcharters.net* ⬦ *From $60.*

### SCUBA DIVING AND SNORKELING

Many dive operators head to Sombrero Reef and Lighthouse, the most popular down-under destination in these parts; some also go to Looe Key Reef. For a shallow dive and some lobster nabbing, Coffins Patch, off Key Colony Beach, is good, and wrecks like the *Thunderbolt* serve as artificial reefs.

#### Spirit Snorkeling

**SNORKELING** | **FAMILY** | Join regularly scheduled snorkeling excursions to Sombrero Reef and its Lighthouse on this company's comfortable catamaran. It also offers sunset cruises and private charters. ⊠ *MM 47.5 BS, 1410 Overseas Hwy., Slip No. 1, Marathon* ☎ *305/289–0614* ⊕ *www.captainpips.com* ⬦ *From $49.*

#### Tilden's Scuba Center

**SCUBA DIVING** | Since the mid-1980s, Tilden's Scuba Center has been providing lessons, gear rental, and snorkel, scuba, and Snuba adventures. Look for the huge, colorful angelfish sculpture outside the building. ⊠ *MM 49.5 BS, 4650 Overseas Hwy., Marathon* ☎ *305/743–7255, 888/728–2235* ⊕ *www.tildensscubacenter.com* ⬦ *From $60 for snorkel trips; from $70 for dive trips.*

# Bahia Honda Key

*Between MM 38.5 and 36.*

All of Bahia Honda Key is devoted to its eponymous state park, which keeps it in a pristine state. Besides the park's outdoor activities, it offers an up-close view of the original railroad bridge.

### GETTING HERE AND AROUND

Bahia Honda Key is near the southern terminus of the Seven Mile Bridge. A two-lane road travels its 2-mile length. It is 32 miles north of Key West and served by Key West Transit buses.

##  Sights

#### ★ Bahia Honda State Park

**STATE/PROVINCIAL PARK** | **FAMILY** | Most first-time visitors to the region are dismayed by the lack of beaches—but then they discover Bahia Honda Key. The 524-acre park sprawls across both sides of the highway, giving it 2½ miles of fabulous sandy coastline. Beaches include Sandspur and Loggerhead Beaches on the Atlantic side and Calusa Beach, which

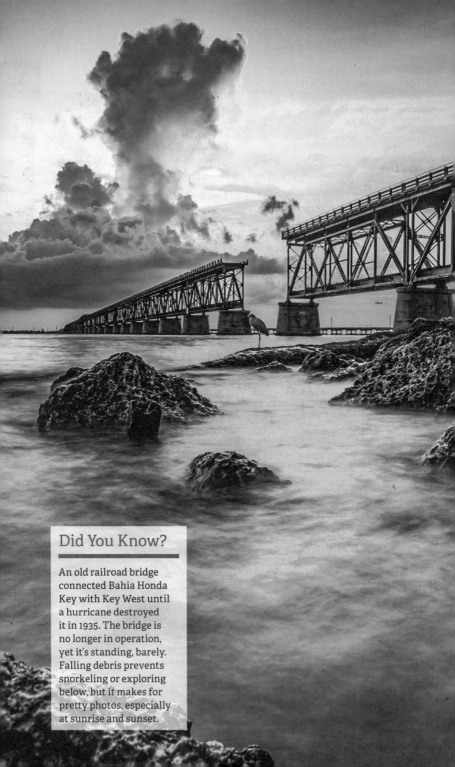

## Did You Know?

An old railroad bridge connected Bahia Honda Key with Key West until a hurricane destroyed it in 1935. The bridge is no longer in operation, yet it's standing, barely. Falling debris prevents snorkeling or exploring below, but it makes for pretty photos, especially at sunrise and sunset.

faces the Gulf of Mexico. The snorkeling isn't bad, either; there's underwater life (soft coral, queen conchs, random little fish) just a few hundred feet offshore. Seasonal ranger-led nature programs take place at or depart from the Sand and Sea Nature Center. There are rental cabins and a campground, snack bar, gift shop, and 19-slip marina, as well as facilities for renting kayaks and arranging snorkeling tours. Get a panoramic view of the island from what's left of the railroad—the Bahia Honda Rail Bridge. ✉ *MM 37 OS, 36850 Overseas Hwy., Bahia Honda Key* ☎ *305/872–2353* 🌐 *www.floridastateparks.org/park/Bahia-Honda* 🎫 *From $5.*

## Beaches

**Loggerhead Beach**
**BEACH | FAMILY** | What is sometimes called "the Oceanside Beach" offers an excellent view of Henry Flagler's old railroad bridge. A small rock island not far from shore is easy enough to kayak around (rentals are available elsewhere in Bahia Honda State Park), and there are plenty of snorkeling opportunities in the clear waters. This beach doesn't have picnic pavilions, and its comparative lack of amenities makes it less crowded and more rustic than other park beaches. **Amenities:** parking (no fee). **Best for:** solitude; swimming; walking. ✉ *MM 37 OS, 36850 Overseas Hwy., Bahia Honda Key* ☎ *305/872–2353* 🌐 *www.floridastateparks.org/park/Bahia-Honda* 🎫 *From $5.*

★ **Sandspur Beach**
**BEACH | FAMILY** | Of Bahia Honda State Park's three beaches, which also include Calusa and Loggerhead, Sandspur is the largest. It's also regularly declared the best beach in the Florida Keys, and you'll be hard pressed to argue. The sand is baby-powder soft, and the aqua water is warm, clear, and shallow. Mild currents here and at the other beaches make them great for swimming, even with small fry. **Amenities:** food and drink; parking (no fee); showers; toilets; water sports. **Best for:** snorkeling; swimming. ✉ *MM 37 OS, 36850 Overseas Hwy., Bahia Honda Key* ☎ *305/872–2353* 🌐 *www.floridastateparks.org/park/Bahia-Honda* 🎫 *From $5.*

## Hotels

**Bahia Honda State Park Cabins**
**$ | HOTEL** | Elsewhere you'd pay big bucks for the wonderful views available at these three cabins, each of which has two two-bedroom units with full kitchens and baths, as well as air-conditioning (but no television, radio, or phone). **Pros:** great Florida Bay views; beachfront camping; affordable rates. **Cons:** books up fast; area can be buggy; need to bring toiletries. [$] *Rooms from: $163* ✉ *MM 37 OS, 36850 Overseas Hwy., Bahia Honda Key* ☎ *305/872–2353, 800/326–3521* 🌐 *www.reserveamerica.com* 🛏 *6 cabins* 🍴 *No Meals.*

## Activities

**Bahia Honda Dive Shop**
**SNORKELING | FAMILY** | The concessionaire at Bahia Honda State Park manages a 19-slip marina; rents wet suits, snorkel equipment, and corrective masks; and operates twice-daily offshore-reef snorkel trips. You can also rent kayaks and beach chairs here. ✉ *MM 37 OS, 36850 Overseas Hwy., Bahia Honda Key* ☎ *305/872–3210* 🌐 *www.bahiahondapark.com* ☞ *Kayak rentals from $10 per hr; snorkel tours from $30.*

# Big Pine Key

*Between MM 32–30.*

Welcome to the Keys' most natural holdout, where wildlife refuges protect rare and endangered animals. Here you swap the commercialism of the Upper Keys for an authentic backcountry atmosphere.

How could things get more casual than Key Largo, you might wonder? Find out by exiting U.S. 1 to explore the habitat of the charmingly diminutive Key deer or cast a line from No Name Key Bridge.

Tours explore the expansive waters of the National Key Deer Refuge and Great White Heron National Wildlife Refuge, one of the first such refuges in the country. Along with Key West National Wildlife Refuge, it encompasses more than 200,000 acres of water and more than 8,000 acres of land on 49 small islands. Besides its namesake bird, Great White Heron National Wildlife Refuge provides habitat for uncounted species of birds and three species of sea turtles. It is the only U.S. breeding site for the endangered hawksbill turtle.

### GETTING HERE AND AROUND

Most people rent a car to get to Big Pine Key so they can also explore Key West and other parts of the chain.

### VISITOR INFORMATION

**CONTACT Lower Keys Chamber of Commerce.** ⊠ *31020 Overseas Hwy., Big Pine Key* ☎ *305/872–2411, 800/872–3722* ⊕ *www.lowerkeyschamber.com.*

##  Sights

### National Key Deer Refuge

**WILDLIFE REFUGE | FAMILY |** This 84,824-acre refuge was established in 1957 to protect the dwindling population of the Key deer, one of more than 22 animals and plants federally classified as endangered or threatened. The Key deer, which stands about 30 inches at the shoulders and is a subspecies of the Virginia white-tailed deer, once roamed throughout the Lower and Middle Keys, but hunting, destruction of their habitat, and a growing human population caused their numbers to decline to 27 by the middle of the last century. The deer have made a comeback, increasing their numbers to approximately 750. The best place to see them in the refuge is at the

end of Key Deer Boulevard and on No Name Key, a sparsely populated island just east of Big Pine Key. Mornings and evenings are the best time to spot them. Deer may turn up along the road at any time of day, so drive slowly. They wander into nearby yards to nibble tender grass and bougainvillea blossoms, but locals do not appreciate tourists driving into their neighborhoods after them. Feeding them is against the law and puts them in danger.

A quarry left over from railroad days, Blue Hole is the largest body of fresh water in the Keys. From the observation platform and nearby walking trail, you might see the resident alligators, turtles, and other wildlife. There are two well-marked trails, recently revamped: the Jack Watson Nature Trail (0.6 miles), named after an environmentalist and the refuge's first warden, and the Fred C. Mannillo Wildlife Trail (0.2 miles), one of the most wheelchair-accessible places to see an unspoiled pine-rockland forest and wetlands. The visitor center has exhibits on Keys biology and ecology. The refuge also provides information on Key West National Wildlife Refuge and Great White Heron National Wildlife Refuge. Accessible only by water, both are popular with kayak outfitters. ⊠ *Visitor Center–Headquarters, Big Pine Shopping Center, MM 30.5 BS, 28950 Watson Blvd., Big Pine Key* ☎ *305/872–2239* ⊕ *www.fws.gov/ nationalkeydeer* ⊠ *Free* ☉ *Visitor center closed Sun. and Mon.*

## 🍴 Restaurants

### No Name Pub

**$ | AMERICAN |** This honky-tonk has been around since 1936, delighting the inveterate locals and the intrepid vacationers who come for the excellent pizza, cold beer, and *interesting* companionship. The decor, such as it is, amounts to the autographed dollar bills that cover every inch of the place. **Known for:** shrimp pizza and fish sandwich; fried grouper sandwiches;

conch chowder. $ *Average main: $15* ⌧ *MM 30 BS, 30813 Watson Blvd., Big Pine Key* ✛ *From U.S. 1, turn west on Wilder Rd., left on South St., right on Ave. B, right on Watson Blvd.* ☎ *305/872–9115* ⊕ *www.nonamepub.com.*

##  Hotels

### Big Pine Key Resort

$ | **HOTEL | FAMILY** | There's a congenial atmosphere at this lively, family-owned lodge-campground-marina—a happy mix of tent campers (who have the fabulous waterfront real estate), RVers (who look pretty permanent), and motel dwellers who like to mingle at the rooftop pool and play poker. **Pros:** local fishing crowd; nice pool; great price. **Cons:** RV park is too close to motel; deer will eat your food if you're camping; some rooms could use updating. $ *Rooms from: $159* ⌧ *MM 33 OS, 33000 Overseas Hwy., Big Pine Key* ☎ *305/872–2351* ⊕ *www.covecommunities.com/rv-resorts/florida/big-pine-key-resort* ⬳ *16 rooms* ⦿ *No Meals* ☞ *To protect Key deer, no dogs allowed.*

### Deer Run on the Atlantic

$$ | **B&B/INN** | Wildlife, including the endangered Key deer, roams the grounds of this bed-and-breakfast, which has four guest rooms, all with ocean views, cathedral ceilings, king beds, private baths, small porches, and calming decor. **Pros:** quiet neighborhood; vegan, organic breakfasts; free state park pass and use of bikes, kayaks, and beach towels. **Cons:** no children or pets allowed; a little hard to find; may be too secluded for some. $ *Rooms from: $200* ⌧ *MM 33 OS, 1997 Long Beach Dr., Big Pine Key* ☎ *305/872–2015* ⊕ *www.deerrunfloridabb.com* ⬳ *4 rooms* ⦿ *Free Breakfast.*

##  Activities

### BIKING

A good 10 miles of paved roads run from Mile Marker 30.3 bay side, along Wilder Road, across the bridge to No Name Key, and along Key Deer Boulevard into the National Key Deer Refuge. On the way you might see some Key deer. Stay off the trails that lead into wetlands, where fat tires can damage the environment.

### Big Pine Bicycle Center

**BIKING | FAMILY** | Owner Marty Baird is an avid cyclist who enjoys sharing his knowledge of great places to ride. He's also skilled at selecting the right bike for the journey, and he knows his repairs, too. His old-fashioned, single-speed, fat-tire cruisers rent by the half or full day. Helmets, baskets, and locks are included. ⌧ *MM 30.9 BS, 31 County Rd., Big Pine Key* ☎ *305/872–0130* ⊕ *www.facebook.com/bigpinebikes* ⬳ *From $25.*

### FISHING

### Captain Hook's Big Pine Key

**BOATING | FAMILY** | Glass-bottom-boat excursions venture into the backcountry and out onto the Atlantic Ocean. The five-hour Out Island Excursion and Picnic emphasizes nature and Keys history; in addition to close encounters with birds, sea life, and vegetation, there's a fish cookout on an island. Snorkel and fishing equipment, food, and drinks are included. This is one of the few nature outings in the Keys with wheelchair access. Deep-sea charter rates for up to six people can be arranged for a half or full day. The outfitter also offers flats fishing in the Gulf of Mexico. Dive excursions head to the wreck of the 110-foot *Adolphus Busch Sr.,* and scuba and snorkel trips to Looe Key Reef, prime scuba and snorkeling territory, aboard glass-bottom boats. ⌧ *MM 29.6 BS, 29675 Overseas Hwy., Big Pine Key* ☎ *305/872–9863, 800/654–9560* ⊕ *www.captainhooks.com* ⬳ *From $38.*

### KAYAKING

There's nothing like the vast expanse of pristine waters and mangrove islands preserved by national refuges from here to Key West. The mazelike terrain can be confusing, so it's wise to hire a guide at least the first time out.

**Big Pine Kayak Adventures**

**KAYAKING | FAMILY** | There's no excuse to skip a water adventure with this convenient kayak rental service, which delivers them to your lodging or anywhere between the Seven Mile Bridge and Stock Island. The company, headed by *The Florida Keys Paddling Guide* author, Bill Keogh, will rent you a kayak and then ferry you—called taxi-yakking—to remote islands with clear instructions on how to paddle back on your own. Rentals are by the half day or full day. Three-hour group kayak tours, which are the cheapest option, explore the mangrove forests of the Key Deer and Great White Heron National Wildlife Refuges. More expensive four-hour custom tours transport you to exquisite backcountry areas teeming with wildlife. Kayak fishing charters are also popular. Paddleboard ecotours, rentals, and yoga are also available. ✉ *Old Wooden Bridge Fishing Camp, 1791 Bogie Dr., Big Pine Key* ✣ *From MM 30, turn right at traffic light, continue on Wilder Rd. toward No Name Key; the fishing camp is just before the bridge with a big yellow kayak on the sign out front* ☎ *305/872–7474* 🌐 *www.keyskayaktours.com* 🎟 *From $50.*

# Little Torch Key

*Between MM 29 and 10.*

Little Torch Key and its neighbor islands, Ramrod Key and Summerland Key, are good jumping-off points for divers headed for Looe Key Reef. The islands also serve as a refuge for those who want to make forays into Key West but not stay in the thick of things. Sugarloaf Key and Cudjoe Key have a few dining spots.

The undeveloped backcountry at your door makes Little Torch Key an ideal location for fishing and kayaking. Nearby Ramrod Key, which also caters to divers bound for Looe Key, derives its name from a ship that wrecked on nearby reefs in the early 1800s.

## 🍴 Restaurants

**★ The Dining Room at Little Palm Island Resort**

**$$$$ | ECLECTIC** | The restaurant at the exclusive Little Palm Island Resort—its dining room and adjacent outdoor terrace lit by candles and warmed by live music—is one of the most romantic spots in the Keys. It's open to nonguests on a reservations-only basis, but no one under 16 is allowed on the island. **Known for:** oceanfront tables in the sand; Key deer meandering by your table; Latin and Caribbean flavors. [$] *Average main: $65* ✉ *MM 28.5 OS, 28500 Overseas Hwy., Little Torch Key* ☎ *305/872–2551* 🌐 *www.littlepalmisland.com.*

**The Fish Camp at Geiger Key Marina**

**$ | AMERICAN** | There's a strong hint of the Old Keys at this oceanside marina restaurant, where local fishermen stop for breakfast before heading out to catch the big one, and everyone shows up on Sunday for the barbecue from 4 to 9. "On the backside of paradise," as the sign says, its tiki structures overlook quiet mangroves at an RV park marina. Locals usually outnumber tourists. **Known for:** local hangout; casual atmosphere on the water; conch fritters loaded with conch. [$] *Average main: $16* ✉ *MM 10, 5 Geiger Key Rd., off Boca Chica Rd., Geiger Key* ☎ *305/296–3553, 305/294–1230* 🌐 *www.geigerkeymarina.com.*

**Mangrove Mama's**

**$$ | SEAFOOD | FAMILY** | This could be the prototype for a Keys restaurant, given its shanty appearance, lattice trim, and roving sort of indoor-outdoor floor plan. Then there's the seafood, from the ubiquitous fish sandwich (fried, grilled, broiled, or blackened) to the lobster Reubens, crab cakes, and coconut shrimp. **Known for:** pizza; award-winning conch chowder; slow service. [$] *Average main:*

$20 ⊠ MM 20 BS, 19991 Overseas Hwy.,
Sugarloaf Key ☎ 305/745–3030 ⊕ www.
mangrovemamasrestaurant.com.

### ★ My New Joint

$ | **AMERICAN** | Atop the famed Square
Grouper restaurant is a secret spot that
locals love and smart travelers seek out
for its tapas and well-stocked bar. Sit at
a high-top table or on a sofa, and savor
made-from-scratch small plates you
won't soon forget, like salted caramel
puffs or chicken lollipops. **Known for:** craft
cocktails and 170 types of beer; cheese
or chocolate fondue; raw bar. $ *Average
main: $15* ⊠ *MM 22.5 OS, 22658 Over-
seas Hwy., Cudjoe Key* ☎ 305/745–8880
⊕ www.mynewjoint420lounge.com
☾ *Closed Sun. and Mon. No lunch.*

### ★ Square Grouper Bar and Grill

$$ | **SEAFOOD** | In an unassuming ware-
house-like building on U.S. 1, chef-owner
Lynn Bell is creating seafood magic. For
starters, try the flash-fried conch with
wasabi drizzle or homemade smoked-fish
dip. **Known for:** everything made fresh,
in-house; long lines in season; outstand-
ing seafood. $ *Average main: $25* ⊠ *MM
22.5 OS, 22658 Overseas Hwy., Cudjoe
Key* ☎ 305/745–8880 ⊕ www.square-
grouperbarandgrill.com ☾ *Closed Sun.;
Mon. May–Dec.; and Sept.*

## ● Coffee and Quick Bites

### Baby's Coffee

$ | **AMERICAN** | The aroma of rich, roasting
coffee beans arrests you at the door of
"the Southernmost Coffee Roaster in
America." Buy beans by the pound or
coffee by the cup, along with sandwiches
and sweets. Locals swear it's the best
coffee in the Keys and beyond. **Known
for:** best coffee in the Keys; gluten-free,
vegan, and vegetarian specialty foods;
excellent service. $ *Average main: $8*
⊠ *MM 15 OS, 3180 Overseas Hwy.,
Sugarloaf Key* ☎ 305/744–9866, 800/523–
2326 ⊕ www.babyscoffee.com.

##  Hotels

### ★ Little Palm Island Resort & Spa

$$$$ | **RESORT** | *Haute tropicale* best
describes this wildly luxurious private-is-
land retreat, and "second mortgage"
might explain how some can afford the
extravagant prices, but for those who
can, it's worth the price. **Pros:** secluded
setting; heavenly spa; easy wildlife view-
ing. **Cons:** expensive; might be too quiet
for some; accessible only by boat or
seaplane. $ *Rooms from: $1,500* ⊠ *MM
28.5 OS, 28500 Overseas Hwy., Little
Torch Key* ☎ 305/872–2524, 800/343–
8567 ⊕ www.littlepalmisland.com ⇨ 30
suites ✵ Free Breakfast ☞ No one under
age 16 allowed on island.

### Looe Key Reef Resort & Dive Center

$ | **HOTEL** | If your Keys vacation is all
about diving, you won't mind the no-frills,
basic motel rooms with dated furniture at
this scuba-obsessed operation because
it's the closest place to the stellar reef
to stay. **Pros:** guests get discounts on
dive and snorkel trips; inexpensive rates;
casual Keys atmosphere. **Cons:** some
reports of uncleanliness; unheated
pool; close to the road. $ *Rooms from:
$159* ⊠ *MM 27.5 OS, 27340 Overseas
Hwy., Little Torch Key* ☎ 305/872–2215,
877/816–3483 ⊕ www.diveflakeys.com
⇨ 24 rooms ✵ No Meals.

### Parmer's Resort

$ | **HOTEL** | Almost every room at this
budget-friendly option has a view of
South Pine Channel, with the lovely curl
of Big Pine Key in the foreground. **Pros:**
bright rooms; pretty setting; good value.
**Cons:** a bit out of the way; housekeep-
ing costs extra; little shade around the
pool. $ *Rooms from: $165* ⊠ *MM 28.7
BS, 565 Barry Ave., Little Torch Key*
☎ 305/872–2157 ⊕ www.parmersresort.
com ⇨ 47 units ✵ Free Breakfast.

Activities

## KAYAKING

**Sugarloaf Marina**

KAYAKING | FAMILY | Rates for one-person kayaks are based on an hourly or daily rental. Two-person kayaks are also available. Delivery is free for rentals of three days or more. The folks at the marina can also hook you up with an outfitter for a day of offshore or backcountry fishing. There's also a well-stocked ship store. ✉ *MM 17 BS, 17015 Overseas Hwy., Sugarloaf Key* ☎ *305/745-3135* ⊕ *www.sugarloafkeymarina.com* ☒ *From $15 per hr.*

## SCUBA DIVING AND SNORKELING

This is the closest you can get on land to Looe Key Reef, which is where local dive operators love to head. In 1744 the HMS *Looe*, a British warship, ran aground and sank on one of the most beautiful coral reefs in the Keys. Today, the key owes its name to the ill-fated ship.

The 5.3-square-nautical-mile reef, part of the Florida Keys National Marine Sanctuary, has strands of elkhorn coral on its eastern margin, as well as purple sea fans and abundant sponges and sea urchins. On its seaward side, it drops almost vertically 50 to 90 feet. In its midst, the Shipwreck Trail plots the location of nine historic wreck sites in 14 to 120 feet of water. Buoys mark the sites, and underwater signs tell the history of each site and what marine life to expect.

Snorkelers and divers will find the sanctuary a quiet place to observe reef life—except in July, when the annual Underwater Music Festival pays homage to Looe Key's beauty and promotes reef awareness with six hours of music broadcast via underwater speakers. Dive shops, charters, and private boats transport about 500 divers and snorkelers to hear the spectacle, which includes classical, jazz, New Age, and Caribbean music, as well as a little Jimmy Buffett. There are even underwater Elvis impersonators.

**Looe Key Reef Resort & Dive Center**

SCUBA DIVING | FAMILY | This center, the closest dive shop to Looe Key Reef, offers two affordable trips daily, at 8 am and 12:45 pm (for divers, snorkelers, or bubble watchers). The maximum depth is 30 feet, so snorkelers and divers go on the same boat. Call to check for availability for wreck and night dives. The dive boat, a 45-foot catamaran, is docked at the full-service Looe Key Reef Resort. ✉ *MM 27.5 OS, 27340 Overseas Hwy., Little Torch Key* ☎ *305/872-2215, 877/816-3483* ⊕ *looekeyreefresort.com* ☒ *From $40.*

# Key West

Situated 150 miles from Miami and 90 miles from Havana, this end-of-the-line community has never been like anywhere else. Even after it was connected to the rest of the country—by the railroad in 1912 and by the highway in 1938—it maintained a strong sense of detachment.

The United States acquired Key West from Spain in 1821, along with the rest of Florida. The Spanish had named the island Cayo Hueso, or Bone Key, after the Native American skeletons they found on its shores. In 1823, President James Monroe sent Commodore David S. Porter to chase pirates away. For three decades, the primary industry in Key West was wrecking—rescuing people and salvaging cargo from ships that foundered on the nearby reefs. According to some reports, when pickings were lean the wreckers hung out lights to lure ships aground. Their business declined after 1849, when the federal government began building lighthouses.

In 1845, the army began construction on Fort Taylor, which kept Key West on the Union side during the Civil War. After the fighting ended, an influx of Cubans unhappy with Spain's rule brought the cigar industry here. Fishing, shrimping, and sponge gathering became important industries, as did pineapple canning. Throughout much of the 19th century and into the 20th, Key West was Florida's wealthiest city per capita. But in 1929, the local economy began to unravel. Cigar making moved to Tampa, Hawaii dominated the pineapple industry, and the sponges succumbed to blight. Then the Depression hit, and within a few years half the population was on relief.

Tourism began to revive Key West, but that came to a halt when a hurricane knocked out the railroad bridge in 1935. To help the tourism industry recover from that crushing blow, the government offered incentives for islanders to turn their charming homes—many of them built by shipwrights—into guesthouses and inns. That wise foresight has left the town with more than 100 such lodgings, a hallmark of Key West vacationing today. In the 1950s, the discovery of "pink gold" in the Dry Tortugas boosted the economy of the entire region. Catching Key West shrimp required a fleet of up to 500 boats and flooded local restaurants with some of the sweetest shrimp alive. The town's artistic community found inspiration in the colorful fishing boats.

Key West reflects a diverse population: Conchs (natives, many of whom trace their ancestry to the Bahamas), freshwater Conchs (longtime residents who migrated from somewhere else years ago), Cuban immigrants, recent refugees from the urban sprawl of mainland Florida, military personnel, and an assortment of vagabonds, drifters, and dropouts in search of refuge. The island was once a gay vacation hot spot, and it remains a decidedly gay-friendly destination. Some of the once-renowned gay guesthouses, however, no longer cater to an exclusively gay clientele. Key Westers pride themselves on their tolerance of all people, all sexual orientations, and even all animals. Most restaurants allow pets, and it's not surprising to see stray cats, dogs, and even chickens roaming freely through the dining rooms. The chicken issue is one that government officials periodically try to bring to an end, but the colorful fowl continue to strut and crow, particularly in the vicinity of Old Town's Bahamian Village.

As a tourist destination, Key West has a lot to sell—an average temperature of 79°F, 19th-century architecture, and a laid-back lifestyle. Yet much has been lost to those eager for a buck. Duval Street is starting to resemble a shopping mall with name-brand storefronts, garish T-shirt shops, and tattoo shops with sidewalk views of the inked action. Cruise ships dwarf the town's skyline and fill the streets with day-trippers gawking at the hippies with dogs in their bike baskets, and the oddball lot of locals.

## WHEN TO GO

Key West has a growing calendar of festivals and artistic and cultural events—including the Conch Republic Celebration in April and the Halloween Fantasy Fest in October. December brings festivity in the form of a lighted boat parade at the Historic Seaport and New Year's Eve revelry that rivals any in the nation. Few cities of its size—a mere 2 miles by 4 miles—celebrate with the *joie de vivre* of this one.

## GETTING HERE AND AROUND
### AIR

You can fly directly to Key West on a limited number of flights, most of which connect at other Florida airports. But a lot of folks fly into Miami or Fort Lauderdale and drive down or take the bus.

### BOAT

Key West Express operates air-conditioned ferries between the Key West Terminal (Caroline and Grinnell streets) and Marco Island, and Fort Myers Beach. The trip from Fort Myers Beach takes at least four hours each way and costs $95 one-way, $155 round-trip. Ferries depart from Fort Myers Beach at 8 am and from Key West at 6 pm. The Marco Island ferry costs $95 one-way and $155 round-trip and departs at 8 am. A photo ID is required for each passenger. Reservations are recommended and can save money.

## BUS AND SHUTTLE

Greyhound Lines runs a special Keys Shuttle up to twice a day (depending on the day of the week) from Miami International Airport (departing from Concourse E, lower level) that stops throughout the Keys. Fares run about $45 (web fare) to $57 for Key West. Keys Shuttle runs scheduled service three times a day in 15-passenger vans between Miami Airport and Key West with stops throughout the Keys for $70 to $90 per person. SuperShuttle charges $102 per passenger for trips from Miami International Airport to the Upper Keys. To go farther into the Keys, you must book an entire 11-person van, which costs about $350 to Key West. You need to place your request for transportation back to the airport 24 hours in advance. Uber is also available throughout the Keys and from the airport.

## LOCAL BUSES

Between Mile Markers 4 and 0, Key West is the one place in the Keys where you could conceivably do without a car, especially if you plan on staying around Old Town. If you've driven the 106 miles down the chain, you're probably ready to abandon your car in the hotel parking lot anyway. Trolleys, buses, bikes, scooters, and feet are more suitable alternatives. When your feet tire, catch a rickshaw-style pedicab ride, which will run you about $1.50 a minute. But to explore the beaches, New Town, and Stock Island, you'll need a car or taxi.

The City of Key West Department of Transportation has six color-coded bus routes traversing the island from 5:30 am to 11:30 pm. Stops have signs with the international bus symbol. Schedules are available on buses and at hotels, visitor centers, shops, and online. The fare is $2 one-way. Its Lower Keys Shuttle bus runs between Marathon to Key West ($4 one-way), with scheduled stops along the way.

## HOTELS

Historic cottages, restored century-old Conch houses, and large resorts are among the offerings in Key West, the majority charging between $100 and $300 a night. Quaint guesthouses, the town's trademark, offer a true island experience in residential neighborhoods near Old Town's restaurants, shops, and clubs. In high season, December through April, you'll be hard-pressed to find a decent room for less than $200, and most places raise prices considerably during holidays and festivals. Many guesthouses and inns do not welcome children under 16, and most do not permit smoking indoors. Most tariffs include an expanded continental breakfast and, often, an afternoon glass of wine or snack.

## LODGING ALTERNATIVES

The Key West Lodging Association is an umbrella organization for dozens of local properties. Vacation Rentals Key West lists historic cottages, homes, and condominiums for rent. Rent Key West Vacations specializes in renting vacation homes and condos for a week or longer. Vacation Key West lists all kinds of properties throughout Key West. In addition to these local agencies, ⊕ airbnb.com and ⊕ vrbo.com have many offerings in Key West.

**CONTACTS Key West Vacations.**
☎ 888/775–3993 ⊕ www.keywestvacations.com. **Lodging Association of the Florida Keys and Key West.** ✉ 818 White St., Ste. 8, Historic Seaport ☎ 800/492–1911 ⊕ www.keyslodging.org. **Rent Key West Vacations.** ✉ 1075 Duval St., Suite C11, Key West ☎ 305/294–0990, 800/833–7368 ⊕ www.rentkeywest.com. **Vacation Key West.** ✉ Key West Ferry Terminal, 100 Grinnell St., Key West ☎ 305/295–9500, 800/595–5397 ⊕ www.vacationkw.com.

## NIGHTLIFE

Rest up: much of what happens in Key West occurs after dark. Open your mind and take a stroll. Scruffy street performers strum next to dogs in sunglasses. Characters wearing parrots or iguanas try to sell you your photo with their pet. Brawls tumble out the doors of Sloppy Joe's. Drag queens strut across stages. And margaritas flow like a Jimmy Buffett tune.

## RESTAURANTS

Bring your appetite, a sense of daring, and a lack of preconceived notions about propriety. A meal in Key West can mean overlooking the crazies along Duval Street, watching roosters and pigeons battle for a scrap of food that may have escaped your fork, relishing the finest in what used to be the dining room of a 19th-century Victorian home, or gazing out at boats jockeying for position in the marina, not to mention the selection of hole-in-the-wall places that couldn't be any more colorful. And that's just the diversity of the setting. Seafood dominates local menus, but the treatment afforded that fish or crustacean can range from Cuban and New World to Asian and continental. Tropical fruits and citrus figure prominently on the menus, too, and mango, papaya, and passion fruit are often featured in beverages.

## TOURS

### ★ Conch Tour Train

**BUS TOURS | FAMILY |** The Conch Tour Train is a 90-minute narrated tour of Key West, traveling 14 miles through Old Town and around the island. Board at Mallory Square or Angela Street and Duval Street depot every half hour from 9 to 4:30. Discount tickets are available online. ✉ *303 Front St., Historic Seaport* ☎ *305/294–5161, 888/916–8687* ⊕ *www.conchtourtrain.com* 🎟 *$40.*

### Historic Florida Keys Foundation

**WALKING TOURS |** In addition to publishing several good guides on Key West, the foundation conducts tours of the City Cemetery on Tuesday and Thursday at 9:30 am. ✉ *Old City Hall, 510 Greene St., Key West* ☎ *305/292–6718* ⊕ *www.historicfloridakeys.org* 🎟 *$15.*

### Key West Promotions

**WALKING TOURS |** If you're not entirely a do-it-yourselfer, Key West Promotions offers a variety of pub tours, from the famous Duval Crawl to a chilling, haunted, and "spirited" adventure. ✉ *424 Greene St., Key West* ☎ *305/294–7170* ⊕ *www.keywestwalkingtours.com.*

### Lloyd's Original Tropical Bike Tour

**BICYCLE TOURS | FAMILY |** Explore the natural, noncommercial side of Key West at a leisurely pace, stopping on backstreets and in backyards of private homes to sample native fruits and view indigenous plants and trees with a 45-year Key West veteran. The behind-the-scenes tours run two hours and include a bike rental. ✉ *601 Truman Ave., Key West* ☎ *305/428–2678* ⊕ *www.lloydstropicalbiketour.com* 🎟 *$49.*

### Old Town Trolley

**BUS TOURS | FAMILY |** Old Town Trolley operates trolley-style buses, departing from Mallory Square every 30 minutes from 9 to 4:30, for 90-minute narrated tours of Key West. The smaller trolleys go places the larger Conch Tour Train won't fit, and you can ride a second consecutive day for an additional $24. You may disembark at any of 13 stops and reboard a later trolley. You can save nearly $4 by booking online. It also offers package deals with Old Town attractions. ✉ *1 Whitehead St., Old Town* ☎ *305/296–6688, 855/623–8289* ⊕ *www.trolleytours.com/key-west* 🎟 *$58.*

## VISITOR INFORMATION

**CONTACTS Greater Key West Chamber of Commerce.** ✉ *510 Greene St., 1st fl., Key West* ☎ *305/294–2587, 800/527–8539* ⊕ *www.keywestchamber.org.*

# Old Town

The heart of Key West, the historic Old Town area runs from White Street to the waterfront. Beginning in 1822, wharves, warehouses, chandleries, ship-repair facilities, and eventually, in 1891, the U.S. Custom House, sprang up around the deep harbor to accommodate the navy's large ships and other sailing vessels. Wreckers, merchants, and sea captains built lavish houses near the bustling waterfront.

A remarkable number of these fine Victorian and pre-Victorian structures has been restored to their original grandeur and now serve as homes, guesthouses, shops, restaurants, and museums. These, along with the dwellings of famous writers, artists, and politicians who've come to Key West over the past 175 years, are among the area's approximately 3,000 historic structures.

Old Town also has the city's finest restaurants and hotels, lively street life, and popular nightspots. The Historic Seaport is worth a stroll to check out its restaurants, bars, and galleries and to sign up for a boat tour.

##  Sights

### Audubon House & Tropical Gardens

**GARDEN** | If you've ever seen an engraving by ornithologist John James Audubon, you'll understand why his name is synonymous with birds. See his works in this three-story house, which was built in the 1840s for Captain John Geiger and is filled with period furniture. It now commemorates Audubon's 1832 stop in Key West while he was traveling through Florida to study birds. After an introduction by a docent, you can do a self-guided tour of the house and gardens. An art gallery sells lithographs of the artist's famed portraits. ⊠ *205 Whitehead St., Old Town* ☎ *305/294–2116, 877/294–2470* ⊕ *www. audubonhouse.com* ☜ *$15.*

### ★ The Ernest Hemingway Home & Museum

**HISTORIC HOME** | Amusing anecdotes spice up the guided tours of Ernest Hemingway's home, built in 1851 by the town's most successful wrecker. While living here between 1931 and 1942, Hemingway wrote about 70% of his life's work, including classics like *For Whom the Bell Tolls*. Few of his belongings remain aside from some books, and there's little about his actual work, but photographs help you visualize his day-to-day life. The famous six-toed descendants of Hemingway's cats—many named for actors, artists, authors, and even a hurricane— have free rein of the property. Tours begin every 10 minutes and take 30 minutes; then you're free to explore on your own. Be sure to find out why there is a urinal in the garden! ⊠ *907 Whitehead St., Old Town* ☎ *305/294–1136* ⊕ *www.hemingwayhome.com* ☜ *$17.*

### ★ Florida Keys Eco-Discovery Center

**OTHER MUSEUM** | **FAMILY** | While visiting Fort Zachary Taylor Historic State Park, stop in at this colorful, 6,400-square-foot, interactive attraction, where you can experience a variety of Florida Keys habitats from pinelands, beach dunes, and mangroves to the deep sea. Walk through a model of the *Aquarius*—a unique, underwater, National Oceanic and Atmospheric Administration (NOAA) laboratory 9 miles off Key Largo—to virtually discover what lurks in the ocean's depths. Touch-screen computer displays, a dramatic movie, a 2,500-gallon aquarium, and live underwater web cameras show off North America's only contiguous barrier coral reef. You'll leave with a new understanding of the native animals and unique plants of the Florida Keys. ⊠ *35 E. Quay Rd., Old Town* ✛ *At end of Southard St. in Truman Annex* ☎ *305/809–4750* ⊕ *eco-discovery.com* ☜ *Free (donations accepted)* ⊗ *Closed Sun. and Mon.*

# Hemingway Was Here

In a town where Pulitzer Prize–winning writers are almost as common as coconuts, Ernest Hemingway stands out. Many bars and restaurants around the island claim that he ate or drank there.

Hemingway came to Key West in 1928 at the urging of writer John Dos Passos and rented a house with his second wife, Pauline Pfeiffer. They spent winters in the Keys and summers in Europe and Wyoming, occasionally taking African safaris. Along the way, they had two sons, Patrick and Gregory. In 1931, Pauline's wealthy uncle Gus gave the couple the house at 907 Whitehead Street. Now known as the Ernest Hemingway Home and Museum, it's Key West's number one tourist attraction. Renovations included the addition of a pool and a tropical garden.

In 1935, when the visitor bureau included the house in a tourist brochure, Hemingway promptly built the brick wall that surrounds it today. He wrote of the visitor bureau's offense in a 1935 essay for *Esquire*, saying, "The house at present occupied by your correspondent is listed as number eighteen in a compilation of the forty-eight things for a tourist to see in Key West. So there will be no difficulty in a tourist finding it or any other of the sights of the city, a map has been prepared by the local F.E.R.A. authorities to be presented to each arriving visitor. This is all very flattering to the easily bloated ego of your correspondent but very hard on production."

During his time in Key West, Hemingway penned some of his most important works, including *A Farewell to Arms, To Have and Have Not, Green Hills of Africa*, and *Death in the Afternoon*. His rigorous schedule consisted of writing almost every morning in his second-story studio above the pool, then promptly descending the stairs at midday. By afternoon and evening he was ready for drinking, fishing, swimming, boxing, and hanging around with the boys.

One close friend was Joe Russell, a craggy fisherman and owner of the rugged bar Sloppy Joe's, originally at 428 Greene Street but now at 201 Duval Street. Russell was the only one in town who would cash Hemingway's $1,000 royalty check. Russell and Charles Thompson introduced Hemingway to deep-sea fishing, which became fodder for his writing.

Hemingway stayed in Key West for 11 years before leaving Pauline for his third wife. Pauline and the boys stayed on in the house, which sold in 1951 for $80,000, 10 times its original cost.

★ **Fort Zachary Taylor Historic State Park**
**MILITARY SIGHT | FAMILY |** Construction of the redbrick fort began in 1845 but was halted during the Civil War. Even though Florida seceded from the Union, Yankee forces used the fort as a base to block Confederate shipping. More than 1,500 Confederate vessels were detained in Key West's harbor. The fort, completed in 1866, was also used in the Spanish-American War. Take a 30-minute guided walking tour of this National Historic Landmark at noon and 2 or do a self-guided tour anytime between 8 and 5. One of the park's most popular features is its man-made beach, a rest stop for migrating birds in the spring and fall;

See the typewriter Hemingway used at his home office in Key West. He lived here from 1931 to 1942.

there are also picnic areas, hiking and biking trails, and a kayak launch. ✉ *Old Town* ✛ *End of Southard St., through Truman Annex* ☏ *305/292–6713* ⊕ *www. floridastateparks.org/park/Fort-Taylor* ☑ *From $5.*

### Harry S. Truman Little White House

**HISTORIC HOME** | Renovations to this circa-1890 landmark have restored the home and gardens to the Truman era, down to the wallpaper pattern. A free photographic review of visiting dignitaries and presidents—John F. Kennedy, Jimmy Carter, and Bill Clinton are among the chief executives who passed through here—is on display in the back of the gift shop. Engaging 45-minute tours, conducted every 20 minutes, start with an excellent 10-minute video on the history of the property and Truman's visits. On the grounds of Truman Annex, a 103-acre former military parade grounds and barracks, the home served as a "winter White House" for presidents Truman, Eisenhower, and Kennedy. Entry is cheaper when purchased in advance online; tickets bought on-site add sales tax. ■**TIP**➔ **The house tour does require climbing steps. Note that you can also do a free self-guided botanical tour of the grounds with a brochure from the museum store.** ✉ *111 Front St., Old Town* ☏ *305/294–9911* ⊕ *www.trumanlittle-whitehouse.com* ☑ *$24* ☞ *Last tour at 4:30 pm.*

### Historic Seaport at the Key West Bight

**MARINA/PIER** | What was once a funky—in some places even seedy—part of town is now a 20-acre historic district with restored structures containing waterfront restaurants, open-air bars, museums, clothing stores, and water-sports concessions. It's all linked by the 2-mile waterfront Harborwalk, which runs between Front and Grinnell Streets, passing big ships, schooners, sunset cruises, fishing charters, and glass-bottom boats. This is where the locals go for great music and good drinks. ✉ *Historic Seaport* ⊕ *www. keywesthistoricseaport.com.*

## The Key West Butterfly & Nature Conservatory

GARDEN | FAMILY | This air-conditioned refuge for butterflies, birds, and humans gladdens the soul with hundreds of colorful wings—more than 45 species of butterflies alone—in a lovely glass-encased bubble. Waterfalls, artistic benches, paved pathways, birds, and lush, flowering vegetation elevate this above most butterfly attractions. The gift shop and gallery are worth a visit on their own. ✉ 1316 Duval St., Old Town ☎ 305/296–2988, 800/839–4647 ⊕ www. keywestbutterfly.com 🔗 $15.

## Key West Lighthouse & Keeper's Quarters

LIGHTHOUSE | FAMILY | For the best view in town, climb the 88 steps to the top of this 1847 lighthouse. The 92-foot structure has a Fresnel lens, which was installed in the 1860s at a cost of $1 million. The keeper lived in the adjacent 1887 clapboard house, which now exhibits vintage photographs, ship models, nautical charts, and artifacts from all along Key West's reefs. A kids' room is stocked with books and toys. ✉ 938 Whitehead St., Old Town ☎ 305/294–0012 ⊕ www.kwahs.com 🔗 $17.

## ★ Key West Museum of Art & History

ART MUSEUM | When Key West was designated a U.S. port of entry in the early 1820s, a customhouse was established. Salvaged cargoes from ships wrecked on the reefs were brought here, setting the stage for Key West to become—for a time—the richest city in Florida. The imposing redbrick-and-terra-cotta Richardsonian Romanesque–style building became a museum and art gallery in 1999. Smaller galleries have long-term and changing exhibits about the history of Key West, including a Hemingway room and a permanent Henry Flagler exhibit that commemorates the arrival of Flagler's railroad in Key West in 1912. ✉ 281 Front St., Old Town ☎ 305/295–6616 ⊕ www.kwahs.com 🔗 $13.

## Key West Shipwreck Treasure Museum

HISTORY MUSEUM | FAMILY | Much of Key West's history, early prosperity, and interesting architecture come from ships that ran aground on its coral reef. Artifacts from the circa-1856 Isaac Allerton, which yielded $150,000 worth of wreckage, comprise the museum portion of this multifaceted attraction. Actors and films add a bit of Disneyesque drama. The final highlight is climbing to the top of the 65-foot lookout tower, a reproduction of the 20 or so towers used by Key West wreckers during the town's salvaging heyday. ✉ 1 Whitehead St., Old Town ☎ 305/292–8990 ⊕ www.keywestshipwreck.com 🔗 $18.

## Mallory Square and Pier

MARINA/PIER | For cruise-ship passengers, this is the disembarkation point for an attack on Key West. For practically every visitor, it's the requisite venue for a nightly sunset celebration that includes street performers—human statues, sword swallowers, tightrope walkers, musicians, and more—plus craft vendors, conch-fritter fryers, and other regulars who defy classification. With all the activity, don't forget to watch the main show: a dazzling tropical sunset. ✉ Old Town.

## ★ Mel Fisher Maritime Museum

OTHER MUSEUM | FAMILY | In 1622, a flotilla of Spanish galleons laden with riches left Havana en route to Spain, but it foundered in a hurricane 40 miles west of the Keys. In 1985, diver Mel Fisher recovered items from two of the lost ships, including the Nuestra Señora de Atocha, said to carry the mother lode of the treasure, and the Santa Margarita. Fisher's adventures tracking these fabled hoards and battling the state of Florida for rights are as amazing as the loot you'll see, touch, and learn about in this museum. Artifacts include a 77.76-carat natural emerald worth almost $250,000. Changing second-floor exhibits cover other aspects of Florida maritime history.

# Key West Old Town

**KEY**

- **1** Sights
- **1** Restaurants
- **1** Quick Bites
- **1** Hotels

✉ *200 Greene St., Old Town* ☎ *305/294–2633* 🌐 *www.melfisher.org* 🎟 *$17.50.*

**The Southernmost Point**
**OTHER ATTRACTION | FAMILY** | Possibly the most photographed site in Key West (even though the actual geographic southernmost point in the continental United States lies across the bay on a naval base, where you see a satellite dish), this is a must-see. Have your picture taken next to the big striped buoy that's been marking the southernmost point in the continental United States since 1983. A plaque next to it honors Cubans who lost their lives trying to escape to America, and other signs tell Key West history. ✉ *Whitehead and South Sts., Old Town.*

## Beaches

**Dog Beach**
**BEACH | FAMILY** | Next to Louie's Backyard restaurant, this tiny beach—the only one in Key West where dogs are allowed unleashed—has a shore that's a mix of sand and rocks. **Amenities:** none. **Best for:** walking. ✉ *Vernon and Waddell Sts., Old Town* 🎟 *Free.*

★ **Fort Zachary Taylor Beach**
**BEACH | FAMILY** | This beach in the historic state park with the same name is the best and safest place to swim in Key West. There's an adjoining picnic area with barbecue grills and shade trees, a snack bar, and rental equipment, including snorkeling gear. A café serves sandwiches and other munchies. Water shoes are recommended since the bottom is rocky here. **Amenities:** food and drink; showers; toilets; water sports. **Best for:** snorkeling; swimming. ✉ *Old Town* ✣ *End of Southard St., through Truman Annex* ☎ *305/292–6713* 🌐 *www.fortzacharytaylor.com* 🎟 *From $5.*

★ **Higgs Beach and Astro City Playground**
**BEACH | FAMILY** | This Monroe County park, with its groomed pebbly sand, is a popular sunbathing spot. A nearby grove of Australian pines provides shade, and the West Martello Tower provides shelter should a storm suddenly sweep in. Kayak and beach-chair rentals are available, as is a volleyball net. The beach also has the largest AIDS memorial in the country and a cultural exhibit commemorating the gravesite of 295 enslaved Africans who died after being rescued from three South America–bound slave ships in 1860. An athletic trail with 10 fitness stations is also available. Hungry? Grab a bite to eat at Salute!, the on-site restaurant. Across the street, Astro City Playground is popular with young children. **Amenities:** parking; toilets; water sports. **Best for:** snorkeling; swimming. ✉ *Atlantic Blvd. between White and Reynolds Sts., Old Town* 🎟 *Free.*

## Restaurants

**Azur Restaurant**
**$$$ | ECLECTIC** | In a contemporary setting with indoor and outdoor seating, welcoming staff serve original, eclectic dishes that stand out from those at the hordes of Key West restaurants. Key lime–stuffed French toast and yellowtail snapper Benedict make breakfast a pleasant wake-up call; the crab cake BLT commands notice on the lunch menu. **Known for:** homemade gnocchi; a nice variety of fish specials at dinner; daily brunch. [$] *Average main: $26* ✉ *425 Grinnell St., Old Town* ☎ *305/292–2987* 🌐 *www.azurkeywest.com.*

**Blue Heaven**
**$$ | CARIBBEAN** | The outdoor dining area here is often referred to as "the quintessential Keys experience," and it's hard to argue. There's much to like about this historic Caribbean-style restaurant where Hemingway refereed boxing matches and customers cheered for cockfights. **Known for:** shrimp and grits; lobster Benedict with key lime hollandaise; the wait for a table and lack of parking. [$] *Average main: $24* ✉ *729 Thomas St., Old Town*

☎ *305/296–8666* 🌐 *www.blueheavenkw.com* 🕓 *Closed for 6 wks after Labor Day.*

**★ B.O.'s Fish Wagon**

$ | **SEAFOOD** | What started out as a fish house on wheels appears to have broken down on the corner of Caroline and William Streets and is today one of Key West's junkyard-chic dining institutions. Step up to the window and order a grouper sandwich fried or grilled and topped with key lime sauce. **Known for:** lots of Key West charm; Friday-night jam sessions; all seating on picnic tables in the yard. [$] *Average main: $18* ✉ *801 Caroline St., Old Town* ☎ *305/294–9272* 🌐 *bosfishwagon.com.*

**★ Café Marquesa**

$$$ | **EUROPEAN** | You'll find seven or more inspired entrées on a changing menu each night, including anything from yellowtail snapper to seared duck breast. End your meal on a sweet note with chocolate pot de crème and homemade ice cream. **Known for:** relaxed but elegant setting; good wine and martini lists; desserts worth ordering. [$] *Average main: $30* ✉ *600 Fleming St., Old Town* ☎ *305/292–1244* 🌐 *marquesa.com/cafe-marquesa* 🕓 *No lunch.*

**Café Solé**

$$$ | **FRENCH** | This little corner of France hides behind a high wall in a residential neighborhood. Inside, French training intertwines with local ingredients, creating delicious takes on classics, including a must-try conch carpaccio and some of the best bouillabaisse that you'll find outside Marseilles. **Known for:** hogfish in several different preparations; intimate, romantic atmosphere; award-winning key lime pie. [$] *Average main: $28* ✉ *1029 Southard St., Old Town* ☎ *305/294–0230* 🌐 *www.cafesole.com.*

**Conch Republic Seafood Company**

$$ | **SEAFOOD** | **FAMILY** | Because of its location where the fast ferry docks, Conch Republic does a brisk business. It's huge, open-air, and on the water, and the menu is ambitious, offering more than just standard seafood fare. **Known for:** "Royal Reds" peel-and-eat shrimp; no reservations; live music most nights. [$] *Average main: $25* ✉ *631 Greene St., at Elizabeth St., Historic Seaport* ☎ *305/294–4403* 🌐 *www.conchrepublicseafood.com.*

**El Meson de Pepe**

$ | **CUBAN** | This is the place to dine—alfresco or in the dining room—on refined Cuban classics. Begin with a megasize mojito while you browse the expansive menu offering *tostones rellenos* (green plantains with different traditional fillings), ceviche, and more. **Known for:** authentic plantain chips; Latin band during the nightly sunset celebration; touristy atmosphere. [$] *Average main: $19* ✉ *Mallory Sq., 410 Wall St., Old Town* ☎ *305/295–2620* 🌐 *www.elmesondepepe.com.*

**El Siboney**

$ | **CUBAN** | At this family-style restaurant, the dining room bustles, the food is traditional *cubano,* the prices are reasonable, and the sangria is *muy buena.* There are well-seasoned black beans, a memorable paella, traditional *ropa vieja,* and local seafood served grilled, stuffed, or breaded. **Known for:** memorable paella and traditional dishes; wine and beer only; cheaper than more touristy options close to Duval. [$] *Average main: $11* ✉ *900 Catherine St., Old Town* ☎ *305/296–4184* 🌐 *www.elsiboneyrestaurant.com.*

**Four Marlins Oceanfront Dining**

$$$ | **SEAFOOD** | Inspired by an Ernest Hemingway photograph of a family fishing trip in Key West, this oceanfront spot pays homage to pristine seafood that's served alongside views that will make you feel like you're on a luxury liner. While the indoor dining room has a bright and airy feel with nautical decor, the outdoor patio is the spot to reserve, a fitting backdrop to dishes of wood-roasted oysters with smoky lemon, Key West pink shrimp, or grits and vegetable island

curry. **Known for:** well-trained staff; craft cocktails; fabulous key lime pie. [$] *Average main: $31* ✉ *The Reach Key West Hotel, 1435 Simonton St., Old Town* ☎ *305/293–6250.*

### Half Shell Raw Bar

$ | SEAFOOD | FAMILY | Smack-dab on the docks, this legendary place gets its name from the oysters, clams, and peel-and-eat shrimp that are the stars of its sea-food-based menu. It's not clever recipes or fine dining (or even air-conditioning) that packs 'em in; it's fried fish, po'boy sandwiches, and seafood combos. **Known for:** daily happy hour with food and drink deals; few nonseafood options; good people-watching spot. [$] *Average main: $16* ✉ *Lands End Village at Historic Seaport, 231 Margaret St., Historic Seaport* ☎ *305/294–7496* ⊕ *www.halfshellrawbar.com.*

### Jimmy Buffett's Margaritaville

$ | AMERICAN | If you must have your cheeseburger in paradise, it may as well be here. The first of Buffett's line of chain eateries, it belongs in Key West more than anywhere else, but, quite frankly, it's more about the name, music, and attitude (and margaritas) than the food. **Known for:** pricey Caribbean bar food; good and spicy conch chowder; raucous party atmosphere most of the time. [$] *Average main: $18* ✉ *500 Duval St., Old Town* ☎ *305/292–1435* ⊕ *www.margaritavillekeywest.com.*

### ★ Latitudes

$$$ | ECLECTIC | Take the short boat ride to lovely Sunset Key for lunch or dinner on the beach, where the magical views are matched by a stellar menu. At dinner, start with the crispy lobster-crab cakes, then move on to one of the creative entrées, such as seared scallops with spiced butternut squash. **Known for:** amazing sunset views; sophisticated atmosphere and expensive food; lobster bisque. [$] *Average main: $32* ✉ *Sunset Key Guest Cottages, 245 Front St., Old Town* ☎ *305/292–5300, 888/477–7786*

⊕ *www.sunsetkeycottages.com/latitudes-key-west* ☞ *Reservations are required for the ferry: no reservation, no ride.*

### Louie's Backyard

$$$$ | ECLECTIC | Feast your eyes on a steal-your-breath-away view and beautifully presented dishes prepared by executive chef Doug Shook. Once you get over sticker shock on the seasonally changing menu, settle in on the outside deck and enjoy dishes like cracked conch with mango chutney, lamb chops with sun-dried-tomato relish, and tamarind-glazed duck breast. **Known for:** fresh, pricey seafood and steaks; affordable lunch menu; late night drinks at the Afterdeck Bar, directly on the water. [$] *Average main: $38* ✉ *700 Waddell Ave., Old Town* ☎ *305/294–1061* ⊕ *www.louiesbackyard.com.*

### Mangia Mangia

$$ | ITALIAN | This longtime favorite serves large portions of homemade pastas that can be matched with any of the home-made sauces. Tables are arranged in a brick garden hung with twinkling lights and in a cozy, casual dining room in an old house. **Known for:** extensive wine list with a nice range of prices; gluten-free and organic pastas; outdoor seating in the garden. [$] *Average main: $24* ✉ *900 Southard St., Old Town* ☎ *305/294–2469* ⊕ *www.mangia-mangia.com* ☽ *No lunch.*

### ★ Nine One Five

$$$ | ECLECTIC | Twinkling lights draped along the lower- and upper-level porches of a 100-year-old Victorian home set an unstuffy and comfortable stage here. If you like to sample and sip, you'll appreciate the variety of small-plate selections and wines by the glass. **Known for:** fun place to people-watch; intimate and inviting atmosphere; light jazz during dinner. [$] *Average main: $32* ✉ *915 Duval St., Old Town* ☎ *305/296–0669* ⊕ *www.915duval.com* ☽ *No lunch Mon. and Tues.*

### Salute! on the Beach

$$ | **ITALIAN** | Sister restaurant to Blue Heaven, this colorful establishment sits on Higgs Beach, giving it one of the island's best lunch views—and a bit of sand and salt spray on a windy day. The intriguing menu is Italian with a Caribbean flair and will not disappoint. **Known for:** amazing water views; casual, inviting atmosphere; pricey slice of key lime pie. $ Average main: $22 ⊠ Higgs Beach, 1000 Atlantic Blvd., Old Town ☎ 305/292–1117 ⊕ www.saluteonthebeach.com.

### ★ Santiago's Bodega

$ | **SPANISH** | Picky palates will be satisfied at this funky, dark, and sensuous tapas restaurant, which is well off the main drag and is a secret spot for local foodies in the know. Small plates include yellowfin tuna ceviche with hunks of avocado and mango or filet mignon with creamy Gorgonzola butter. **Known for:** legendary bread pudding; homemade white or red sangria; a favorite with local chefs. $ Average main: $16 ⊠ Bahama Village, 207 Petronia St., Old Town ☎ 305/296–7691 ⊕ www.santiagosbodega.com.

### Sarabeth's Key West

$$ | **AMERICAN** | Named for the award-winning jam-maker and pastry chef Sarabeth Levine, this locally owned restaurant serves all-day breakfast, best enjoyed in the picket-fenced front yard of a circa-1870 synagogue. Lemon ricotta pancakes, pumpkin waffles, and homemade jams make the meal. **Known for:** brunch and dessert; daily specials; key lime pie French toast. $ Average main: $20 ⊠ 530 Simonton St., at Souhard St., Old Town ☎ 305/293–8181 ⊕ www.sarabethskw.com ♥ Closed Mon. and Tues.

### Seven Fish

$$$$ | **SEAFOOD** | This local hot spot has a casual Key West vibe and an eclectic menu. The specialty is the local fish of the day (like snapper with creamy Thai curry), but you might also try the tropical shrimp salsa, wild-mushroom quesadilla, or old-fashioned meat loaf with real mashed potatoes. **Known for:** fresh seafood; busy spot requiring reservations; amazing foccacia. $ Average main: $36 ⊠ 921 Truman Ave., Old Town ☎ 305/296–2777 ⊕ www.7fish.com ♥ Closed Tues. No lunch.

##  Coffee and Quick Bites

### ★ La Grignote

$ | **FRENCH** | **FAMILY** | This is the place to satisfy any French-pastry craving—from the made-from-scratch croissants to the cookies, muffins, coconut macarons, and of course, breads. A lovely patio is the perfect backdrop for breakfasts of brioche French toast, quiches with fresh salads, and a croque madame oozing with bechamel and poached eggs. **Known for:** ham-and-cheese croissants; friendly owners; French breakfasts. $ Average main: $11 ⊠ 1211 Duval St., Old Town ☎ 305/916–5445 ⊕ lagrignotecafe.com ♥ Closed Mon.

## Hotels

### Ambrosia Key West

$$$ | **B&B/INN** | **FAMILY** | If you desire personal attention, a casual atmosphere, and a dollop of style, stay at these twin inns spread out on nearly 2 acres. **Pros:** spacious rooms; breakfast served poolside; great location. **Cons:** on-street parking can be tough to come by; a little too spread out; high windows in some rooms let in the early morning light. $ Rooms from: $385 ⊠ 615, 618, 622 Fleming St., Old Town ☎ 305/296–9838, 800/535–9838 ⊕ www.ambrosiakeywest.com ⇥ 20 rooms ☉ Free Breakfast.

### Azul Key West

$$ | **B&B/INN** | The ultramodern, nearly minimalistic redo of this classic, circa-1903 Queen Anne mansion—an adults-only property—offers a break from the sensory overload of Key West's other abundant Victorian guesthouses. **Pros:** lovely building; marble-floored baths; luxurious linens. **Cons:** on a busy

street; modern isn't for everyone; staff not on site. $ *Rooms from: $289* ✉ *907 Truman Ave., Old Town* ☎ *305/296–5152, 888/253–2985* ⊕ *www.dwellkeywest. com/key-west-vacation-rentals/azul* ⇆ *11 rooms* ⦿ *Free Breakfast.*

### Casa Marina, Curio Collection by Hilton

$$$ | RESORT | FAMILY | This luxurious property is on the largest private beach in Key West, and it has the same richly appointed lobby with beamed ceilings, polished pine floor, and original art as it did when it opened in 1920 on New Year's Eve. Guest rooms are stylishly decorated in neutral colors that evoke a certain comfortable crispness. **Pros:** huge beach; on-site dining, bars, and water sports; away from the crowds. **Cons:** long walk to central Old Town; expensive resort fee; spa is across the street in a separate building. $ *Rooms from: $399* ✉ *1500 Reynolds St., Old Town* ☎ *305/296–3535, 866/203–6392* ⊕ *www.casamarinaresort. com* ⇆ *311 rooms* ⦿ *No Meals.*

### Crowne Plaza La Concha

$$$ | HOTEL | History and franchises can mix, as this 1920s-vintage hotel proves with its handsome atrium lobby and sleep-conducive rooms. **Pros:** location is everything; good on-site restaurant and wine bar; free Wi-Fi. **Cons:** high-traffic area; rooms are small, bathrooms are smaller; expensive valet-only parking. $ *Rooms from: $350* ✉ *430 Duval St., Old Town* ☎ *305/296–2991* ⊕ *www. laconchakeywest.com* ⇆ *178 rooms* ⦿ *No Meals.*

### Eden House

$$ | HOTEL | From the vintage metal rockers on the street-side porch to the old neon hotel sign in the lobby, this 1920s rambling Key West mainstay hotel is high on character, low on gloss. **Pros:** free parking; hot tub is actually hot; daily happy hour around the pool. **Cons:** pricey for older rooms; brown towels take getting used to; parking is first-come, first-served. $ *Rooms from: $225* ✉ *1015 Fleming St., Old Town* ☎ *305/296–6868,*

*800/533–5397* ⊕ *www.edenhouse.com* ⇆ *44 rooms* ⦿ *No Meals.*

### ★ The Gardens Hotel

$$$$ | HOTEL | Built in 1875, this gloriously shaded property was a labor of love from the get-go, and it covers a third of a city block in Old Town. **Pros:** luxurious bathrooms; secluded garden seating; free Wi-Fi. **Cons:** hard to get reservations; expensive; nightly secure parking fee. $ *Rooms from: $415* ✉ *526 Angela St., Old Town* ☎ *305/294–2661, 800/526–2664* ⊕ *www.gardenshotel.com* ⇆ *20 suites* ⦿ *Free Breakfast.*

### H2O Suites

$$$$ | HOTEL | Take the plunge at this swanky, luxurious, adults-only (age 25 and up) hotel, where half the one-bedroom suites have a private plunge pool. **Pros:** on-site garage parking; rooms have the most flattering lighting—ever; beachchair setup at nearby South Beach. **Cons:** pricey resort fee; smoking is allowed outdoors; long walk to the happening side of Duval Street. $ *Rooms from: $499* ✉ *1212 Simonton St., Old Town* ☎ *305/296–3432* ⊕ *www.h2osuites.com* ⇆ *22 suites* ⦿ *No Meals.*

### Island City House Hotel

$$$ | B&B/INN | FAMILY | A private garden with brick walkways, tropical plants, and a canopy of palms sets this convivial guesthouse apart from the pack. **Pros:** lush gardens; knowledgeable staff; bike rentals on site. **Cons:** spotty Wi-Fi service; front desk is staffed only 8 am–8 pm; no parking. $ *Rooms from: $320* ✉ *411 William St., Old Town* ☎ *305/294–5702, 800/634–8230* ⊕ *www.islandcityhouse. com* ⇆ *24 suites* ⦿ *No Meals.*

### Key West Bed and Breakfast/The Popular House

$ | B&B/INN | There are accommodations for every budget here, but the owners reason that budget travelers deserve as pleasant an experience (and as lavish a tropical continental breakfast) as their well-heeled counterparts. **Pros:** lots of art;

tiled outdoor shower; hot tub and sauna area is a welcome hangout. **Cons:** some rooms are small; four rooms have shared baths; historic homes have thinner walls. $ *Rooms from: $145* ✉ *415 William St., Old Town* ☎ *305/296–7274, 800/438–6155* ⊕ *www.keywestbandb.com* ↦ *10 rooms* ⧈ *Free Breakfast.*

### La Pensione

$$ | **B&B/INN** | Hospitality and period furnishings make this 1891 home, once owned by a cigar executive, a wonderful glimpse into Key West life in the late 19th century. **Pros:** pine-paneled walls; first-come, first-served parking included; some rooms have wraparound porches. **Cons:** street-facing rooms are noisy; rooms do not have TVs; rooms accommodate only two people. $ *Rooms from: $258* ✉ *809 Truman Ave., Old Town* ☎ *305/292–9923, 800/893–1193* ⊕ *www.lapensione.com* ↦ *9 rooms* ⧈ *Free Breakfast.*

### The Marker

$$$ | **RESORT** | The Marker is a welcome and luxurious option on the waterfront in Old Town, with conch-style architecture and an authentic Keys aesthetic. **Pros:** convenient Old Town location; large private balconies; three saltwater pools, including one for adults only. **Cons:** hefty resort and parking fees nightly; "locals welcome" policy means pool chairs can be hard to come by; lots of walking if your room isn't near the amenities. $ *Rooms from: $400* ✉ *200 William St., Old Town* ☎ *305/501–5193* ⊕ *www.themarkerkeywest.com* ↦ *96 rooms* ⧈ *No Meals.*

### ★ Marquesa Hotel

$$$ | **HOTEL** | In a town that prides itself on its laid-back luxury, this complex of four restored 1884 houses stands out. **Pros:** room service; romantic atmosphere; turndown service. **Cons:** street-facing rooms can be noisy; expensive rates; no elevator. $ *Rooms from: $395* ✉ *600 Fleming St., Old Town* ☎ *305/292–1919,*

*800/869–4631* ⊕ *www.marquesa.com* ↦ *27 rooms* ⧈ *No Meals* ☞ *No children under age 14 allowed.*

### The Mermaid & the Alligator

$$ | **B&B/INN** | An enchanting combination of.flora and fauna makes this 1904 Victorian house a welcoming retreat. **Pros:** hot plunge pool; massage pavilion; island-get-away feel. **Cons:** minimum stay required (length depends on season); dark public areas; plastic lawn chairs. $ *Rooms from: $278* ✉ *729 Truman Ave., Old Town* ☎ *305/294–1894, 800/773–1894* ⊕ *www.kwmermaid.com* ↦ *9 rooms* ⧈ *Free Breakfast.*

### NYAH: Not Your Average Hotel

$$$ | **B&B/INN** | From its charming white picket fence, it may look similar to other Victorian-style Key West B&Bs, but that's where the similarities end, as this adults-only property's minimalistic rooms (all with upscale, private baths) have customizable sleeping arrangements: up to six can stay in one room, and all get their own bed. **Pros:** central location; perfect for traveling with a group of friends; free daily happy hour. **Cons:** small rooms, even smaller closets; street parking only; no toiletries provided. $ *Rooms from: $349* ✉ *420 Margaret St., Old Town* ☎ *305/296–2131* ⊕ *www.nyahotels.com* ↦ *36 rooms* ⧈ *Free Breakfast* ☞ *Age 18 and over only.*

### ★ Ocean Key Resort & Spa

$$$$ | **RESORT** | This full resort—relatively rare in Key West—has large, tropical-look rooms and excellent on-site amenities, including a pool and bar overlooking Sunset Pier and a Thai-inspired spa. **Pros:** well-trained staff; lively pool scene; fantastic location at the busy end of Duval. **Cons:** daily valet parking and resort fee; too bustling for some; rooms are starting to show their age. $ *Rooms from: $495* ✉ *0 Duval St., Old Town* ☎ *305/296–7701, 800/328–9815* ⊕ *www.oceankey.com* ↦ *100 rooms* ⧈ *No Meals.*

Sunset Key cottages are right on the water's edge, far away from the action of Old Town.

**Pier House Resort & Spa**

$$$$ | **RESORT** | This upscale resort, near Mallory Square in the heart of Old Town, offers a wide range of amenities, including a beach and comfortable, traditionally furnished rooms. **Pros:** beautiful beach; free Wi-Fi; nice spa and restaurant. **Cons:** lots of conventions; poolside rooms are small; not really suitable for children under 16. [$] *Rooms from: $470* ✉ *1 Duval St., Old Town* ☎ *305/296–4600, 800/327–8340* 🌐 *www.pierhouse.com* 🛏 *145 rooms* 🍴 *No Meals.*

**The Reach Key West, Curio Collection by Hilton**

$$$ | **RESORT** | **FAMILY** | Embracing Key West's only natural beach, this full-service, luxury resort offers stylish rooms—all with balconies and modern amenities—and access to the spa, pools, and other facilities at the nearby Casa Marina resort. **Pros:** removed from Duval hubbub; great sunrise views; pullout sofas in most rooms. **Cons:** expensive resort fee; high rates; lacks the grandeur you'd expect of a resort property. [$] *Rooms from: $399* ✉ *1435 Simonton St., Old Town* ☎ *305/296–5000, 888/318–4316* 🌐 *www.reachresort.com* 🛏 *150 rooms* 🍴 *No Meals.*

★ **Santa Maria Suites**

$$$$ | **RESORT** | It's odd to call this a hidden gem when it sits on a prominent corner just one block off Duval, but a concrete facade keeps this luxurious find well secluded from the outside world. **Pros:** amenities galore; front desk concierge services; private parking lot. **Cons:** daily resort fee; poolside units must close curtains for privacy; only two-bedroom units available. [$] *Rooms from: $549* ✉ *1401 Simonton St., Old Town* ☎ *866/726–8259, 305/296–5678* 🌐 *www.santamariasuites.com* 🛏 *35 suites* 🍴 *No Meals.*

★ **Southernmost Beach Resort**

$$$ | **HOTEL** | **FAMILY** | Rooms at this hotel on the quiet end of Duval—a 20-minute walk from downtown—are modern and sophisticated, and although the area around it gets some car and foot traffic, the property is far enough from the hubbub that you can relax but close enough

that you can participate if you wish. **Pros:** pool attracts a lively crowd; access to nearby properties and beach; free Wi-Fi. **Cons:** can get crowded around the pool and public areas; expensive nightly resort fee; beach is across the street. $ *Rooms from: $359* ✉ *1319 Duval St., Old Town* ☎ *305/296–6577, 800/354–4455* ⊕ *www. southernmostbeachresort.com* ⤴ *118 rooms* ⦿ *No Meals.*

### Speakeasy Inn

$ | **B&B/INN** | During Prohibition, Raul Vasquez made this place popular by smuggling in rum from Cuba; today, its reputation is for having reasonably priced rooms within walking distance of the beach. **Pros:** good location; all rooms have kitchenettes; first-come, first-served free parking. **Cons:** no pool; on busy Duval; rooms are fairly basic. $ *Rooms from: $189* ✉ *1117 Duval St., Old Town* ☎ *305/296–2680* ⊕ *www.speakeasyinn. com* ⤴ *7 suites* ⦿ *Free Breakfast.*

### ★ Sunset Key Cottages

$$$$ | **RESORT** | **FAMILY** | This luxurious, private-island retreat with its own beach feels completely cut off from the world, yet it's just a 10-minute ride—via a free, 24-hour ferry—from the action in Mallory Square. **Pros:** all units have kitchens; roomy verandas; excellent Latitudes restaurant. **Cons:** luxury doesn't come cheap; beach shore is rocky; launch runs only every 30 minutes. $ *Rooms from: $780* ✉ *245 Front St., Old Town* ☎ *305/292–5300, 888/477–7786* ⊕ *www. opalcollection.com/sunset-key-cottages* ⤴ *40 cottages* ⦿ *Free Breakfast.*

### Winslow's Bungalows

$$$ | **HOTEL** | Part of the Kimpton Hotel brand, this 1854, Grand Bahama–style house on the National Register of Historic Places is in the center of Key West, just two blocks off Duval Street, and features vibrant gardens, three private pools, and an outdoor bar. **Pros:** walking distance to clubs and bars; some rooms have private outdoor spaces; free Wi-Fi. **Cons:** over a mile to the sunset

end of Duval Street; pool faces a busy street; $20 daily parking fee. $ *Rooms from: $359* ✉ *725 Truman Ave., Old Town* ☎ *305/294–5229, 800/549–4430* ⊕ *www.kimptonkeywest.com/key-west-hotels/winslows-bungalows* ⤴ *85 rooms* ⦿ *Free Breakfast.*

##  Nightlife

### Aqua

**BARS** | Key West's largest gay bar, Aqua hosts karaoke contests, dancing, and live entertainment at three bars, including one outside on the patio. For an evening like no other, come see the Aquanettes at their "Reality Is a Drag" show. ✉ *711 Duval St., Old Town* ☎ *305/294–0555* ⊕ *www.aquakeywest.com.*

### ★ Capt. Tony's Saloon

**BARS** | When it was the original Sloppy Joe's in the mid-1930s, Hemingway was a regular. Later, a young Jimmy Buffett sang here and made this watering hole famous in his song "Last Mango in Paris." Captain Tony was even voted mayor of Key West. Yes, this place is a beloved landmark. Stop in and take a look at the "hanging tree" that grows through the roof, listen to live music seven nights a week, and play some pool. ✉ *428 Greene St., Old Town* ☎ *305/294–1838* ⊕ *www. capttonyssaloon.com.*

### Durty Harry's

**BARS** | This megasize entertainment complex is home to eight different bars and clubs, both indoor and outdoor. Their motto is "Eight Famous Bars, One Awesome Night," and they're right. You'll find pizza, dancing, live music, Rick's Key West, and the infamous Red Garter strip club. ✉ *208 Duval St., Old Town* ☎ *305/296–5513* ⊕ *www.facebook.com/ rickskeywest.*

### Garden of Eden

**BARS** | Perhaps one of Duval's more unusual and intriguing watering holes, the Garden of Eden sits atop the Bull & Whistle saloon and has a clothing-optional

Sloppy Joe's is one must-stop on most Key West visitors' bar-hop stroll, also known as the Duval Crawl.

policy. Most drinkers are lookie-loos, but some actually bare it all, including the barmaids. ✉ *224 Duval St., Old Town* ☎ *305/396–4565* ⊕ *bullkeywest.com/ garden-of-eden.*

### ★ Green Parrot Bar

**BARS** | Pause for a libation in the open air and breathe in the spirit of Key West. Built in 1890 as a grocery store, this property has been many things to many people over the years. It's touted as the oldest bar in Key West, and the sometimes rowdy saloon has locals outnumbering out-of-towners, especially on nights when bands play. ✉ *601 Whitehead St., at Southard St., Old Town* ☎ *305/294–6133* ⊕ *www.greenparrot. com.*

### Hog's Breath Saloon

**LIVE MUSIC** | Belly up to the bar for a cold mug of the signature Hog's Breath Lager at this infamous joint, a must-stop on the Key West bar crawl. Live bands play daily 1 pm–2 am (except when the game's on TV). You never know who'll stop by and perhaps even jump on stage for an impromptu concert (can you say Kenny Chesney?). ✉ *400 Front St., Old Town* ☎ *305/296–4222* ⊕ *www.hogsbreath. com.*

### Mangoes

**BARS** | On a busy corner right on bustling Duval Street, it's the perfect spot for people-watching and being part of the action. Find a seat at the bar, especially at happy hour, for half-price appetizers and drink deals. ✉ *700 Duval St., corner of Angela St., Old Town* ☎ *305/294–8002* ⊕ *www. mangoeskeywest.com.*

### Margaritaville

**LIVE MUSIC** | A youngish, touristy crowd mixes with aging Parrot Heads. It's owned by former Key West resident and recording star Jimmy Buffett, who has been known to perform here. The drink of choice is, of course, a margarita, made with Jimmy's own brand of Margaritaville tequila. There's live music nightly, as well as lunch and dinner. ✉ *500 Duval St., Old Town* ☎ *305/292–1435* ⊕ *www.margaritavillekeywest.com.*

### Pier House

BARS | The party begins at the Beach Bar, with live entertainment daily to celebrate sunset on the beach, and then moves to the Chart Room. It's small and odd, but there are free hot dogs and peanuts, and its history is intriguing. ⊠ *1 Duval St., Old Town* ☎ *305/296–4600, 800/327–8340* ⊕ *www.pierhouse.com.*

### Schooner Wharf Bar

BARS | This open-air waterfront bar and grill retains its funky Key West charm and hosts live entertainment daily. Its margaritas rank among Key West's best, as does the bar itself, voted Best Local's Bar six years in a row. For great views, head up to the second floor and be sure to order up some fresh seafood and fritters and Dark and Stormy cocktails. ⊠ *202 William St., Old Town* ☎ *305/292–3302* ⊕ *www.schoonerwharf.com.*

### ★ Sloppy Joe's

BARS | There's history and good times at the successor to a famous 1937 speakeasy named for its founder, Captain Joe Russell. Decorated with Hemingway memorabilia and marine flags, the bar is full and noisy all the time. A Sloppy Joe's T-shirt is a de rigueur Key West souvenir, and the gift shop sells them like crazy. Grab a seat (if you can), and be entertained by the bands—and the parade of people in constant motion. ⊠ *201 Duval St., Old Town* ☎ *305/294–5717* ⊕ *www.sloppyjoes.com.*

### Two Friends Patio Lounge

BARS | Love karaoke? Get it out of your system at Two Friends Patio Lounge, where your performance gets a live Internet feed via the bar's Karaoke Cam. The singing starts at 8:30 most nights. The Bloody Marys are famous. ⊠ *512 Front St., Old Town* ☎ *305/296–3124* ⊕ *www.twofriends.com.*

## 🛍 Shopping

### ARTS AND CRAFTS

### Alan S. Maltz Gallery

ART GALLERIES | The owner, declared the state's official wildlife photographer by the Fish & Wildlife Foundation of Florida, captures the state's nature and character in stunning portraits. Spend four figures for large-format images on canvas or save on small prints and closeouts. ⊠ *1210 Duval St., Old Town* ☎ *305/294–0005* ⊕ *www.alanmaltz.com.*

### Art at 830

ART GALLERIES | This inviting gallery carries a little bit of everything, from pottery to paintings and jewelry to sculptures. Most outstanding is its selection of glass art, particularly the jellyfish lamps. Take time to admire all that is here. ⊠ *830 Caroline St., Old Town* ☎ *305/295–9595* ⊕ *www.art830.com.*

### Gallery on Greene

ART GALLERIES | This is the largest gallery–exhibition space in Key West, and it showcases 37 museum-quality artists. It prides itself on being the leader in the field of representational fine art, painting, sculptures, and reproductions from the Florida Keys and Key West. You can see the love immediately from gallery curator Nancy Frank, who aims to please everyone from the casual buyer to the established collector. ⊠ *606 Greene St., Old Town* ☎ *305/294–1669* ⊕ *www.galleryongreene.com.*

### Gingerbread Square Gallery

ART GALLERIES | The oldest private art gallery in Key West represents local and internationally acclaimed artists on an annually changing basis, in media ranging from paintings to art glass. ⊠ *1207 Duval St., Old Town* ☎ *305/296–8900* ⊕ *www.gingerbreadsquaregallery.com.*

### Key West Pottery

CERAMICS | You won't find any painted coconuts here, but you will find a collection of contemporary tropical ceramics. Wife-and-husband owners Kelly Lever and Adam Russell take real pride in this working studio that, in addition to their own creations, features artists from around the country. ✉ *1203 Duval St., Old Town* ☎ *305/900–8303* ⊕ *www. keywestpottery.com.*

★ **Wyland Gallery**

ART GALLERIES | Painter, sculptor, and photographer Robert Wyland is world renowned for his marine-life art pieces and conservation efforts. You'll get your first glimpse of his work as you enter the Keys: he chose the Bimini Blue paint for the concrete safety walls that stretch from the mainland to Key Largo. At Mile Marker 99.2, you can't miss *Keys to the Seas,* one of his famed "whaling wall" murals; *Florida's Radiant Reef* is in Marathon, at Mile Marker 55.5; *Florida's Living Reef* is in Key West at the foot of William Street (Guy Harvey helped on this one). This gallery carries many incredible works by Wyland and other marine-life artists. You might not be able to afford anything, but viewing the art is the equivalent of exploring underwater without getting your hair wet. ✉ *623 Duval St., Old Town* ☎ *305/292–4998* ⊕ *www.wylandgalleries-ofthefloridakeys.com.*

### BOOKS

**Key West Island Bookstore**

BOOKS | This home away from home for the large Key West writers' community carries new, used, and rare titles. It specializes in Hemingway, Tennessee Williams, and South Florida mystery writers. ✉ *513 Fleming St., Old Town* ☎ *305/294–2904* ⊕ *www.keywestisland-books.com.*

### CLOTHING AND FABRICS

**Fairvilla Megastore**

OTHER SPECIALTY STORE | Don't leave town without a browse through the legendary shop. Although it's not really a clothing store, you'll find an astonishing array of fantasy wear and outlandish costumes

(check out the pirate section), as well as other "adult" toys. (Some of the products may make you blush.) ✉ *520 Front St., Old Town* ☎ *305/292–0448* ⊕ *www. fairvilla.com.*

★ **Kino Sandals**

SHOES | A pair of Kino sandals was once a public declaration that you'd been to Key West. The attraction? You can watch these inexpensive items being made. The factory has been churning out several styles since 1966. Walk up to the counter, grab a pair, try them on, and lay down some cash. It's that simple. ✉ *107 Fitzpatrick St., Old Town* ☎ *305/294–5044* ⊕ *www.kinosandalfactory.com.*

### FOOD AND DRINK

**Fausto's Food Palace**

FOOD | Since 1926 Fausto's has been the spot to catch up on the week's gossip and to chill out in summer—it has groceries, organic foods, marvelous wines, a sushi chef on duty 8 am–3 pm, and box lunches and dinners-by-the-pound to go. There are two locations you can shop at in Key West (the other is at 1105 White Street) plus an online store. ✉ *522 Fleming St., Old Town* ☎ *305/296–5663* ⊕ *www.faustos.com.*

★ **Kermit's Key West Key Lime Shoppe**

FOOD | You'll see Kermit himself standing on the corner every time a trolley passes, pie in hand. He carries many key lime products—from barbecue sauce to jelly beans—and his key lime pie is the best on the island. Once you try it, perhaps frozen on a stick and dipped in chocolate, you may consider quitting your job and moving here. Savor every bite in the patio-garden area, or come for breakfast or lunch in the on-site café. Note, too, that Kermit's frozen pies, topped with a special long-lasting whipped cream instead of meringue, travel well. There's a smaller second location on the corner of Duval and Front Streets. ✉ *200 Elizabeth St., Old Town* ☎ *305/296–0806, 800/376–0806* ⊕ *www.keylimeshop.com.*

## GIFTS AND SOUVENIRS
### Cayo Hueso y Habana Historeum
SOUVENIRS | Part museum, part shopping center, this circa-1879 warehouse includes a hand-rolled-cigar shop, one-of-a-kind souvenirs, a Cuban restaurant, and exhibits that tell of the island's Cuban heritage. Outside, a memorial garden pays homage to the island's Cuban ancestors. ✉ *Mallory Sq., 410 Wall St., Old Town* ☎ *305/293–7260.*

## SHOPPING CENTERS
### Bahama Village
SHOPPING CENTER | Where to start your shopping adventure? This cluster of spruced-up shops, restaurants, and vendors is responsible for the restoration of the colorful historic district where Bahamians settled in the 19th century. The village lies roughly between Whitehead and Fort Streets and Angela and Catherine Streets. Hemingway frequented the bars, restaurants, and boxing rings in this part of town. ✉ *Old Town* ✛ *Between Whitehead and Fort Sts. and Angela and Catherine Sts.*

# New Town

The Overseas Highway splits as it enters Key West, the two forks rejoining to encircle New Town, the area east of White Street to Cow Key Channel. The southern fork runs along the shore as South Roosevelt Boulevard (Route A1A) and skirts Key West International Airport, while the northern fork runs along the north shore as North Roosevelt Boulevard and turns into Truman Avenue once it hits Old Town. Part of New Town was created with dredged fill. The island would have continued growing this way had the Army Corps of Engineers not determined in the early 1970s that it was detrimental to the nearby reef.

# ◉ Sights

### Fort East Martello Museum and Gardens
ART MUSEUM | This redbrick Civil War fort never saw a lick of action during the war. Today it serves as a museum, operated by the Key West Art & Historical Society, with exhibits about the 19th and 20th centuries, including relics from the USS *Maine*, cigar factory and shipwrecking displays, and a collection of Stanley Papio's "junk art" sculptures and Cuban folk artist Mario Sanchez's chiseled and painted wooden carvings of historic Key West street scenes. You can climb to the top of the citadel tower. ✉ *3501 S. Roosevelt Blvd., New Town* ☎ *305/296–3913* ⊕ *www.kwahs.com* ✉ *$16.*

# ⬆ Beaches

### Rest Beach/C. B. Harvey Memorial Park
BEACH | This beach and park were named after Cornelius Bradford Harvey, former Key West mayor and commissioner. Adjacent to Higgs Beach, it has half a dozen picnic areas across the street, dunes, a pier, and a wheelchair and bike path. **Amenities:** none. **Best for:** walking. ✉ *Atlantic Blvd., east side of White St. Pier, New Town* ✉ *Free.*

### ★ Smathers Beach
BEACH | This wide beach has nearly 1 mile of nice white sand, plus beautiful coconut palms, picnic areas, and volleyball courts, all of which make it popular with the spring-break crowd. Trucks along the road rent rafts, windsurfers, and other beach "toys." **Amenities:** food and drink; parking; toilets; water sports. **Best for:** partiers. ✉ *S. Roosevelt Blvd., New Town* ✉ *Free.*

# 🍴 Restaurants

### Tavern N Town
$$$ | ECLECTIC | At this handsome restaurant, lovely aromas waft from the wood-fired oven in the open kitchen. Among the popular choices on the dinner menu,

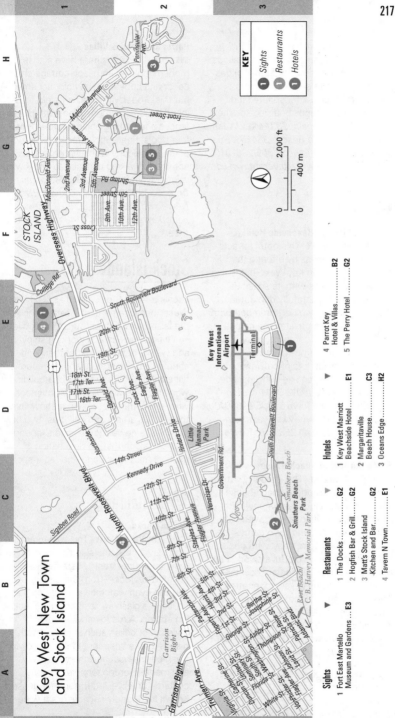

# Key West New Town and Stock Island

217

**KEY**

- ① Sights
- ① Restaurants
- ① Hotels

2,000 ft
400 m

0
0

**Sights** ▶

1 Fort East Martello
Museum and Gardens ... **E3**

**Restaurants** ▶

1 The Docks .................. **G2**
2 Hogfish Bar & Grill ...... **G2**
3 Matt's Stock Island
Kitchen and Bar .......... **G2**
4 Tavern N Town .......... **E1**

**Hotels** ▶

1 Key West Marriott
Beachside Hotel .......... **E1**
2 Margaritaville
Beach House .............. **C3**
3 Oceans Edge ............. **H2**
4 Parrot Key
Hotel & Villas ............ **B2**
5 The Perry Hotel .......... **G2**

which has both small plates and full entrées, are lemon-crusted sea scallops, rack of Colorado lamb, and small pizzas (including a white seafood version). **Known for:** upscale atmosphere (and prices); popular happy hour; noise when busy. [$] *Average main: $33* ✉ *Key West Marriott Beachside Resort, 3841 N. Roosevelt Blvd., New Town* ☎ *305/296–8100, 800/546–0885* 🌐 *www.tavernntown.com* ⏲ *No lunch.*

## Hotels

**Key West Marriott Beachside Hotel**
$$$$ | **HOTEL** | **FAMILY** | This hotel attracts convention business by offering the biggest ballroom in Key West, but it also appeals to families with its spacious, impeccably and tastefully decorated rooms and one-, two-, or three-bedroom condo units. **Pros:** private tanning beach; poolside cabanas; complimentary shuttle to Old Town and airport. **Cons:** no swimming at its beach; lots of conventions and conferences; cookie-cutter facade. [$] *Rooms from: $409* ✉ *3841 N. Roosevelt Blvd., New Town* ☎ *305/296–8100, 800/546–0885* 🌐 *www.keywestmarriottbeachside.com* 🛏 *258 units* 🍴 *No Meals.*

★ **Margaritaville Beach House**
$$ | **RESORT** | **FAMILY** | This property, which definitely has a modern-beach-house feel, features a lagoon-style pool with a waterfall; lush landscaping with pathways, hammocks, and lawn games; and Jimmy Buffet–inspired flair with poolside entertainment and colorful artwork. **Pros:** friendly staff; complimentary cocktail at check-in; all rooms have kitchenettes. **Cons:** not directly on beach; not all rooms have balconies; hefty daily resort fee. [$] *Rooms from: $220* ✉ *2001 S. Roosevelt Blvd., New Town* ☎ *305/292–9800* 🌐 *www.margaritavilleresorts.com/margaritaville-beach-house-key-west* 🛏 *184 rooms* 🍴 *No Meals.*

**Parrot Key Hotel & Villas**
$$$ | **HOTEL** | Rooms here have a crisp, modern look—with beach-cottage chic decor and upbeat pastel color schemes—but this property maintains its old-fashioned beach community feel with picket fences and rocking-chair porches. **Pros:** four pools; finely appointed units; patio, porch, or balcony with all rooms. **Cons:** not within walking distance to Old Town; valet only; hefty resort fee. [$] *Rooms from: $339* ✉ *2801 N. Roosevelt Blvd., New Town* ☎ *305/809–2200* 🌐 *www.parrotkeyresort.com* 🛏 *148 rooms* 🍴 *No Meals.*

# Stock Island

Locals refer to Stock Island as "Old Key West" because parts of it reflect the way the island was before tourism took over. You'll find marinas and working shipyards and waterfronts, the last of their kind, for shrimpers, lobstermen, and commercial fishermen. You'll spy some boatbuilding workshops as well. A laid-back vintage vibe, a monthly art stroll that showcases the island's artists and galleries, two of Key West's newer hotels, and a legendary fish saloon that's a destination in itself all make this under-the-radar spot well worth a visit.

## Restaurants

★ **The Docks**
$$$ | **SEAFOOD** | **FAMILY** | This restaurant with views of Stock Island's working marina features fresh, sustainably sourced seafood—from the dining room, you can even watch bivalves being plated on ice in a glass-enclosed oyster-shucking station. A rustic-upcycled, island-style decor belies such sophisticated dishes as the snapper "Philly" sandwich, fresh-off-the-boat ceviche specials, and made-to-order *zeppoles* (cream-, custard-, or jelly-filled fritters) for dessert. **Known for:** friendly service; great wine

list; super-fresh seafood. $ *Average main: $27 ⊠ 6840 Front St., Stock Island* ☎ *305/396–7049 ⊕ thedocksstockisland. com.*

### Hogfish Bar & Grill
$ | **SEAFOOD** | It's worth a drive to Stock Island for a meal at this down-to-earth spot, where hogfish is, of course, the specialty. Favorites include the "Killer Hogfish Sandwich," which is served on Cuban bread (be sure to sprinkle it with one of the house hot sauces), as well as the hogfish tacos, gator bites, lobster BLT or pot pie, pulled-pork sandwich, and barbecued ribs. **Known for:** pricey fish sandwiches; a taste of local life; fried grouper cheeks. $ *Average main: $17 ⊠ 6810 Front St., Stock Island* ☎ *305/293–4041 ⊕ www.hogfishbar. com.*

### ★ Matt's Stock Island Kitchen & Bar
$$ | **SEAFOOD** | This casual-yet-stylish haven of "American coastal comfort food" has garnered local and national accolades for its eclectic seafood-focused menu and industrial-cool design. The crab beignets are a must, as is the Southern-style fried chicken with bacon salt fries and barbecue ribs. **Known for:** fresh catch of the day; marina views; sophisticated seafood dishes. $ *Average main: $24 ⊠ Perry Hotel, 7001 Shrimp Rd., Stock Island* ☎ *305/294–3939 ⊕ www.perrykey-west.com.*

##  Hotels

### ★ Oceans Edge
$$ | **HOTEL** | **FAMILY** | Set on 20 acres, this luxury resort unfurls along a marina with both Atlantic and Gulf views. **Pros:** all rooms have waterfront views; suites include kitchenettes; complimentary shuttle bus to downtown. **Cons:** not walking distance to Old Town; not near a beach; only one restaurant on site. $ *Rooms from: $230 ⊠ 5950 Peninsular Ave., Stock Island* ☎ *305/809–8204*

⊕ *www.oceansedgekeywest.com* ↷ *175 rooms* ❑I *No Meals.*

### The Perry Hotel
$ | **HOTEL** | This industrial-chic stunner— where spacious, airy rooms juxtapose crisp white linens with furnishings and fixtures in rich chocolate-browns and shades of gray—has made off-the-beaten-path Stock Island a Key West destination. **Pros:** free shuttle to Old Town; direct access to fishing; home to a sophisticated restaurant. **Cons:** 5 miles from Duval Street; limited number of suites; marina slip owners have access to the pool. $ *Rooms from: $170 ⊠ 7001 Shrimp Rd., Stock Island* ☎ *305/296–1717 ⊕ www.perrykeywest.com* ↷ *100 rooms* ❑I *No Meals.*

# Activities

Unlike the rest of the region, Key West isn't known primarily for outdoor pursuits. But everyone should devote at least half a day to relaxing on a boat tour, heading out on a fishing expedition, or pursuing some other adventure at sea. The ultimate excursion is a boat or seaplane trip to Dry Tortugas National Park for snorkeling and exploring Fort Jefferson.

Other excursions cater to nature lovers, scuba divers, snorkelers, and folks who just want to get out in or on the water and enjoy the scenery and sunset. For those who prefer land-based recreation, biking is the way to go. Hiking is limited, but walking the streets of Old Town provides plenty of exercise.

## BIKING
### A&M Rentals
**BIKING** | **FAMILY** | This outfit rents beach cruisers with large baskets, scooters, and electric minicars and has a second location on South Street. ⊠ *523 Truman Ave., Old Town* ☎ *305/294–0399 ⊕ www. amscooterskeywest.com* 🚲 *Bicycles from $15, scooters from $35, electric cars from $139.*

## FISHING

### Key West Bait & Tackle

**FISHING** | Prepare to catch a big one with this outfitter's live bait, frozen bait, and fishing equipment. Rod and reel rentals start at $15 for a day ($5 each additional day). Stop by the on-site Live Bait Lounge, where you can sip a $3.25 ice-cold beer while telling fish tales. ✉ *241 Margaret St., Historic Seaport* ☎ *305/292–1961* ⊕ *www.keywest-baitandtackle.com.*

### ★ Key West Pro Guides

**FISHING | FAMILY** | This outfitter offers four-, five-, six-, or eight-hour private charters, and you can choose from more than a dozen captains. Trips include flats, backcountry, reef, offshore fishing, and excursions to the Dry Tortugas. Whatever your fishing pleasure, the captains will hook you up. ✉ *31 Miriam St., Stock Island* ☎ *866/259–4205* ⊕ *www.keywest-proguides.com* ⌨ *From $500.*

## GOLF

### Key West Golf Club

**GOLF** | Key West isn't a major golf destination, but there is one course on Stock Island designed by Rees Jones that will downright surprise you with its water challenges and tropical beauty. It's also the only "Caribbean" golf course in the United States, boasting 200 acres of unique Florida foliage and wildlife. Hole 8 is the famous "Mangrove Hole," which will give you stories to tell. It's a 143-yard par 3 that is played completely over a mass of mangroves with their gnarly, intertwined roots and branches. Bring extra balls and book your tee time early in peak season. Nike rental clubs are available. ✉ *6450 E. College Rd., Stock Island* ☎ *305/294–5232* ⊕ *www.keywestgolf.com* ⌨ *$75* ⛳ *18 holes, 6500 yards, par 70.*

## KAYAKING

### Key West Eco Tours

**KAYAKING | FAMILY** | The sail-kayak-snorkel excursions offered by this company take you into backcountry flats and mangrove forests without the crowds. The 4½-hour trips include a light lunch, equipment, and even dry camera bags. Private sunset sails, backcountry boating adventures, kayak, and paddleboard tours are available, too. ✉ *231 Margaret St., Historic Seaport* ☎ *305/294–7245* ⊕ *www.keywestecotours.com* ⌨ *From $65.*

### Lazy Dog

**KAYAKING | FAMILY** | Take a two-hour backcountry mangrove ecotour or a four-hour guided sea kayak–snorkel tour around the mangrove islands just east of Key West. Costs include transportation, bottled water, a snack, and supplies, including snorkeling gear. Paddleboard tours, PaddleYoga, and PaddleFit classes are also available, as are maps and rentals for self-touring. ✉ *5114 Overseas Hwy., Stock Island* ☎ *305/295–9898* ⊕ *www.lazydog.com* ⌨ *From $50.*

## SAILING

### ★ Bluesail Yachting

**SAILING | FAMILY** | Bluesail offers everything from multi-day boat charters to four-hour private sunset sails complete with chef-made appetizers, wine, and beer. Its vessels have multi-occupancy cabins, full bathrooms, air-conditioning, and fully enclosed living spaces. The company is also an accredited American Sailing Association sailing school. ✉ *7005 Shrimp Rd., Stock Island* ☎ *813/601–5243* ⊕ *www.bluesailcharter.com* ⌨ *$1,500.*

### Classic Harbor Line

**SAILING** | The *Schooner America 2.0* is refined and elegant, with comfortable seating that makes it a favorite for sails between November and April. Its two-hour sunset cruises are especially popular—with both locals and visitors. Reserve well in advance. ✉ *202-R Williams St., Historic Seaport* ☎ *305/293–7245* ⊕ *www.sail-keywest.com* ⌨ *Day sails from $44, sunset sails from $76.*

### Dancing Dolphin Spirit Charters

**BOATING | FAMILY** | Victoria Impallomeni-Spencer, a wilderness guide and

Aerial view of Dry Tortugas National Park, known for its stellar snorkeling and hexagon-shape Fort Jefferson.

environmental marine science walking encyclopedia, invites up to six nature lovers aboard the *Imp II,* a 25-foot Aquasport, for four- and seven-hour eco-tours that frequently include encounters with wild dolphins. ✉ *Hurricane Hole Marina, MM 4 OS, 5130 Overseas Hwy., Stock Island* ☎ *305/304–7562, 305/745–9901* ⊕ *www.dancingdolphinspirits.com* ✈ *From $600.*

### ★ Sebago Watersports

**SAILING | FAMILY |** A one-stop-shop for all your sailing and snorkeling adventure needs, this popular company offers catamaran and schooner excursions, Key West sunset sails, snorkel trips to the living reef, parasailing, and more. Sebago's ships are spacious and state-of-the-art, with an experienced, friendly crew. ✉ *205 Elizabeth St., Historic Seaport* ☎ *305/294–5687* ⊕ *keywestsebago.com* ✈ *From $50.*

### Wind & Wine Sunset Sail

**SAILING |** Set sail on a historic 65-foot schooner and catch Key West's famous sunset as you drink wines from around the world (eight are presented during each sailing, three whites, four reds, and a champagne). Nosh on nibbles like Gouda and crackers, Brie and apples, and sausage rounds. Beer is also available. ✉ *Margaritaville Marina, 245 Front St., Old Town* ☎ *305/304–7999* ⊕ *www. dangercharters.com* ✈ *$85.*

## SCUBA DIVING AND SNORKELING

### Captain's Corner

**DIVING & SNORKELING | FAMILY |** This PADI-certified dive shop has classes in several languages and twice-daily snorkel and dive trips to reefs and wrecks aboard a 60-foot dive boat, the *Sea Eagle.* Weights, belts, masks, and fins are included in the rates. ✉ *125 Ann St., Old Town* ☎ *305/296–8865* ⊕ *www.captain-scorner.com* ✈ *From $45.*

### Dive Key West

**DIVING & SNORKELING | FAMILY |** In business for more than 40 years and dedicated to coral reef preservation, this full-service dive center offers snorkel excursions and scuba trips, instruction, gear rental, sales, and repair. ✉ *3128 N. Roosevelt*

Blvd., New Town ☎ 305/296–3823
⊕ www.divekeywest.com ⊠ Snorkeling
from $69, scuba from $249.

★ **Honest Eco Tours**
**SNORKELING | FAMILY** | Honest Eco's four-hour Dolphin Watch & Snorkel Tours take place aboard SQUID, a lithium-ion-battery-powered hybrid charter boat. You can watch wild dolphins as they play, sleep, hunt, and mate in Key West's calm, turquoise waters, and spend some time snorkeling in a tranquil spot. ⊠ 231 Margaret St., Historic Seaport ☎ 305/294–6306 ⊕ honesteco.org ☜ $99.

**Snuba of Key West**
**SCUBA DIVING | FAMILY** | If you've always wanted to dive but never found the time to get certified, Snuba is for you. You can dive safely using a regulator tethered to a floating air tank with a simple orientation. ⊠ Garrison Bight Marina, Palm Ave. between Eaton St. and N. Roosevelt Blvd., New Town ☎ 305/292–4616 ⊕ www.snubakeywest.com ☜ From $109.

# Excursion to Dry Tortugas National Park

*70 miles southwest of Key West.*

The Dry Tortugas lie in the central time zone. Key West Seaplane pilots like to tell their passengers that they land 15 minutes before they take off. If you can't do the time-consuming and (by air, at least, expensive) trip, the national park operates an interpretive center in the Historic Seaport at Old Key West Bight.

**GETTING HERE AND AROUND**
The *Yankee Freedom III* ferryboat departs from a marina in Old Town and does day-trips to Garden Key. Key West Seaplane Adventures has half- and full-day trips to the Dry Tortugas, departing from the Key West airport.

**CONTACTS Key West Seaplane Adventures.**
⊠ 3471 S. Roosevelt Blvd., New Town ☎ 305/615–7429 ⊕ keywestseaplanecharters.com. **Yankee Freedom III.** ⊠ Ticket booth, 240 Margaret St., Historic Seaport ☎ 305/294–7009, 800/634–0939 ⊕ www.drytortugas.com.

 **Sights**

★ **Dry Tortugas National Park**
**NATIONAL PARK | FAMILY** | This park, 70 miles off the shores of Key West, consists of seven small islands. Most people spend their time on Garden Key, touring the 19th-century Fort Jefferson, the largest brick building in the Western Hemisphere, then heading out to snorkel on the protected reef. The brick fort acts like a gigantic, almost 16-acre reef. Around its moat walls, coral grows and schools of snapper, grouper, and wrasse hang out.

Serious snorkelers and divers head out farther offshore to epic formations, including Palmata Patch, one of the few surviving concentrations of elkhorn coral in the Keys. Day-trippers congregate on the sandy beach to relax in the sun and enjoy picnics. Overnight tent campers have use of restroom facilities and achieve a total getaway from noise, lights, and civilization in general.

The park has signposted a self-guided tour that takes about 45 minutes. You should budget more time if you're into photography because the scenic shots are hard to pass up. Ranger-guided tours are also available at certain times. Check in at the visitor center for a schedule. ⊠ Key West ☎ 305/242–7700 ⊕ www.nps.gov/drto ☜ $15.

Chapter 6

# FORT LAUDERDALE AND BROWARD COUNTY

Updated by
Amber Love Bond

⊙ Sights
★★★★☆

🕐 Restaurants
★★★★☆

🛏 Hotels
★★★★☆

🛍 Shopping
★★★☆☆

🍸 Nightlife
★★★☆☆

# WELCOME TO FORT LAUDERDALE AND BROWARD COUNTY

## TOP REASONS TO GO

★ **Blue waves:** The cerulean waters of the Atlantic Ocean hugging Broward County's entire coast form a 23-mile stretch of picturesque beaches between Miami–Dade and Palm Beach Counties.

★ **Inland waterways:** More than 300 miles of inland waterways, including the historic New River and Intracoastal in downtown Fort Lauderdale, create what's known as the "Venice of America."

★ **Everglades adventures:** The untamed landscape of the Everglades—home to alligators, crocodiles, colorful birds, and other elusive wildlife—is a short trip from beachfront luxury.

★ **Emerging arts scene:** Experience the local contemporary art scene as it grows into a major force in the region.

★ **Cruise gateway:** A dozen supermodern terminals serve about 4 million cruisers and ferry guests a year at Port Everglades, one of the busiest cruise ports in the country.

Along Florida's Gold Coast, Fort Lauderdale and Broward County present a delightful middle ground between the posh Palm Beaches and the extravagance of Miami. From downtown Fort Lauderdale, it's about a four-hour drive to Orlando or Key West, but Broward's allure is undeniable. From oceanside to inland, the county's sprawling geography encompasses 31 communities with a resident population of roughly 2 million.

**1 Downtown and Las Olas.** The eclectic hub of town is known for its arts and nightlife scenes and is complemented by Las Olas Boulevard's boutiques, sidewalk cafés, and restaurants.

**2 Fort Lauderdale Beach.** Fort Lauderdale's 23 miles of sparkling beaches are lined with restaurants and hotels.

**3 Intracoastal and Inland Fort Lauderdale.** Even if you're not on the beach, you're likely still near the water: waterways and canals that weave through town are big among the boating community.

**4 Wilton Manors and Oakland Park.** Wilton Manors is a progressive area with independent shops and nightlife venues.

**5 Western Suburbs and Beyond.** The suburbs are just as bustling, if not more, than the city center, but out west you're essentially on the edge of the Everglades.

**6 Lauderdale-by-the-Sea.** North of Fort Lauderdale on State Road A1A, old-school seaside charm draws families and cost-conscious travelers to a more low-rise, low-key beach alternative to Fort Lauderdale.

**7 Pompano Beach.** Explore shipwrecks and coral reefs on a scuba diving adventure off the shore of this beach town, just north of Lauderdale-by-the-Sea.

**8 Hollywood.** From the beachside Broadwalk to historic Young Circle (now ArtsPark at Young Circle), this South Broward destination provides grit and good times in a laid-back manner.

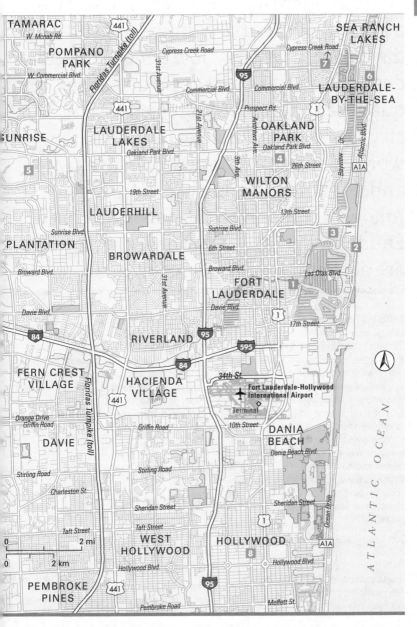

It was only a matter of time before the sun-soaked streets of Fort Lauderdale faced an identity crisis. What was once a hotbed of dive bars, diners, and all-day beach parties is now a more upscale destination with a deeper focus on quality in the pursuit of leisure. The city has more notable eateries and world-class hotel brands than ever, and, fortunately, the upscaling doesn't follow Miami's over-the-top lead. Fort Lauderdale is still a place where flip-flops are acceptable, if not encouraged.

Along the Strip and west to the Intracoastal, many of the mid-century modern boutique properties are trying to preserve the neighborhood's vintage design aesthetic. Somehow Greater Fort Lauderdale gracefully melds disparate eras into nouveau nirvana, seasoned with a lot of sand. This could be the result of its massive territory: Broward County encompasses more than 1,100 square miles of land—ranging from dense residential enclaves to agricultural farms and subtropical wilds. But it's the county's beautiful beaches and some 3,000 hours of sunshine each year that make all this possible.

Fort Lauderdale was named for Major William Lauderdale, who built a fort in 1838 during the Second Seminole War. It was incorporated in 1911 with only 175 residents but grew quickly during the Florida boom of the 1920s, and it became a popular spring break destination in the 1960s. Today's population is more than 182,000, and the suburbs continue to grow. Of Broward County's 31 municipalities and unincorporated areas, Fort Lauderdale is the largest. And now showstopping hotels, a hot food scene, and a burgeoning cultural platform accompany the classic beach lifestyle.

# Planning

## When to Go

Peak season is Thanksgiving through April, when cultural events (performing arts, visual art displays, concerts, and other outdoor entertainment) go full throttle. Expect extreme heat and humidity along with rain in the summer.

Hurricanes come most notably in August and September. Tee times are harder to get on weekends year-round. Regardless of season, remember that Fort Lauderdale sunshine will burn even on a cloudy day.

# Getting Here and Around

## AIR

Fort Lauderdale–Hollywood International Airport (FLL) serves more than 36 million passengers a year with nonstop flights to over 125 U.S. and international cities. FLL is 3 miles south of downtown Fort Lauderdale—just off U.S. 1 (South Federal Highway) between Fort Lauderdale and Hollywood, and near Port Everglades and Fort Lauderdale Beach. Other options include Miami International Airport (MIA), which is about 32 miles southwest, and the far less chaotic Palm Beach International Airport (PBI), which is about 50 miles north.

**AIRPORT INFORMATION Fort Lauderdale–Hollywood International Airport.** (*FLL*) ✉ *Fort Lauderdale* ☎ *866/435–9355* ⊕ *www.broward.org.* **Miami International Airport.** (*MIA*) ✉ *Miami* ☎ *305/876–7000* ⊕ *www.miami-airport.com.* **Palm Beach International Airport.** (*PBI*) ✉ *Palm Beach* ☎ *561/471–7400* ⊕ *www.pbia.org.*

## BUS

Broward County Transit (BCT) operates Bus Route 1 between the airport and its main terminal at Broward Boulevard and Northwest First Avenue in downtown Fort Lauderdale. Service from the airport (Rental Car Center, Stop 7) is every 15 to 30 minutes and begins at 5:38 am on weekdays, 6:04 am Saturday, and 6:44 am Sunday; the last bus leaves the airport at 11:44 pm on weekdays, 11:44 pm Saturday, and 9:44 pm Sunday. The one-way cash fare is $2 (exact change). BCT also covers the county on fixed routes to four transfer terminals: Broward Central Terminal, West Regional Terminal, Lauderhill Transit Center, and Northeast Transit Center. The fare for an all-day bus pass is $5 (exact change). Service starts around 4:30 am and continues to 12:40 am, except on Sunday.

■TIP→ **Exercise caution at the Northwest 1st Avenue stop, day or night. Better yet, take an Uber, Lyft, or taxi to and from the airport.**

**BUS CONTACTS Broward County Transit.** (*BCT*) ☎ *954/357–8400* ⊕ *www.broward.org/BCT.*

## CAR

Renting a car to get around Broward County is highly recommended. Traditional cabs are unreliable and expensive; ride-hailing apps such as Uber and Lyft are a cheaper, better option. Public transportation is not a realistic option for most travelers, but the Sun Trolley can be sufficient for some visitors who don't need or wish to explore beyond the downtown core and beaches.

By car, access to Broward County from north or south is via Florida's Turnpike, Interstate 95, U.S. 1, or U.S. 441. Interstate 75 (Alligator Alley, requiring a toll despite being part of the nation's interstate-highway system) connects Broward with Florida's west coast and runs parallel to State Road 84 within the county. East–west Interstate 595 runs from westernmost Broward County and connects Interstate 75 with Interstate 95 and U.S. 1, providing easy access to the airport and seaport. State Road A1A, designated a Florida Scenic & Historic Coastal Byway by the state's Department of Transportation, runs parallel to the beach.

## TRAIN

Amtrak provides daily service to Fort Lauderdale and stops in Deerfield Beach and Hollywood.

All three of the region's airports link to Tri-Rail, a commuter train operating daily through Palm Beach, Broward, and Miami–Dade counties.

The modern, privately operated Brightline high-speed train service connects downtown Miami, Fort Lauderdale, and West Palm Beach. The trip from downtown Miami to Fort Lauderdale takes about 30 minutes; it's another 30 minutes to West Palm Beach.

**CONTACTS Brightline.** ⊠ *Miami Central Station, 600 NW 1st Ave., Downtown* ☎ *888/448–8491* ⊕ *www.gobrightline. com.*

## Hotels

A collection of luxury beachfront hotels—the Atlantic Hotel & Spa, Four Seasons, Hilton Fort Lauderdale Beach Resort, the Ritz-Carlton, the W—welcomes travelers to the "Luxe Lauderdale" corridor. These seriously sophisticated places to stay are increasingly popular as smaller retro spots are disappearing. You can also find hotel chains along the Intracoastal Waterway. If you want to be *on* the beach, be sure to ask when booking your room, as many hotels on the inland waterways or on A1A advertise "waterfront" accommodations.

## Restaurants

Greater Fort Lauderdale offers one of the best and most diverse dining scenes of any U.S. city its size. There are more than 4,000 eateries in Broward offering everything from new American and South American to Pan-Asian cuisines. Go beyond the basics, and you'll find an endless supply of hidden gems.

*Restaurant prices are the average cost of a main course at dinner or, if dinner is not served, at lunch. Hotel prices are the lowest cost of a standard double room in high season. Hotel and restaurant reviews have been shortened. For full information, visit Fodors.com.*

| What It Costs in U.S. Dollars | | | |
|---|---|---|---|
| $ | $$ | $$$ | $$$$ |
| **RESTAURANTS** | | | |
| under $15 | $15–$20 | $21–$30 | over $30 |
| **HOTELS** | | | |
| under $200 | $200–$300 | $301–$400 | over $400 |

# Fort Lauderdale

Like most of southeast Florida, Fort Lauderdale has long been revitalizing. Despite wariness of overdevelopment, city leaders have allowed a striking number of glittering high-rises and new hotels. Nostalgic locals and frequent visitors fret over the diminishing vision of sailboats bobbing in waters near downtown; however, Fort Lauderdale remains the yachting capital of the world, and the water toys don't seem to be going anywhere.

Sharp demographic changes are also altering the face of Greater Fort Lauderdale with increasingly cosmopolitan communities. Young professionals and families are settling into Fort Lauderdale proper, whereas longtime residents are heading north for more space. Downtown Fort Lauderdale's burgeoning arts district, cafés, and nightlife venues continue to the main drag of Las Olas Boulevard, where boutiques and restaurants dot the pedestrian-friendly street. Farther east is the sparkling shoreline. There are myriad neighborhoods to the north and south of Las Olas Boulevard that all offer their own brand of charm.

### GETTING HERE AND AROUND
The Fort Lauderdale metro area is laid out in a grid system, and only a few waterways and bridges interrupt the relatively straight path of streets and roads. Nomenclature is important here: streets, roads, courts, and drives run

east–west; avenues, terraces, and ways run north–south; boulevards can (and do) run any which way. For visitors, Las Olas Boulevard is one of the most important east–west passageways.

The city's road system suffers from traffic overload. Interstate 595 connects the city and suburbs and provides a direct route to the Fort Lauderdale–Hollywood International Airport and Port Everglades, but lanes slow to a crawl during rush hours. The Intracoastal Waterway is the nautical equivalent of an interstate highway; it provides easy boating access to local hot spots as well as neighboring waterfront communities.

To bounce around for free, catch a multicolor LauderGO! Community Shuttle (formerly Sun Trolley). There are five routes and each operates on its own fixed schedule. Luggage is not allowed, so this isn't a viable option for airport transportation.

Yellow Cab covers most of Broward County, but it's very expensive. You can book by phone, text, app, or website, and all Yellow Cab vehicles accept major credit cards. The Uber and Lyft rideshare services give more attention to the passenger experience and charge cheaper rates, hence their significant presence in the area.

**CONTACTS LauderGO! Community Shuttle.** ⊕ *www.fortlauderdale.gov.* **Yellow Cab Broward.** ✉ *Fort Lauderdale* ☎ *954/777–7777* ⊕ *www.yellowcabbroward.com.*

## TOURS

The labyrinthine waterways of Fort Lauderdale are home to thousands of privately owned vessels, but you don't need to be or know a boat owner to play on the water. To fully understand this city of canals (aka the Venice of America) spanning more than 300 miles of inland waterways, you must see it from the water. Kick back on a boat tour or hop on a free LauderGO! Water Trolley.

### *Carrie B* Cruises
**BOAT TOURS** | Board the *Carrie B,* a 112-foot paddle wheeler, for a 90-minute sightseeing tour of the New River, the Intracoastal Waterway, and Port Everglades. Cruises depart at 11 am, 1 pm, and 3 pm daily from October through April; Thursday–Monday between May and September. The cost is $27.95 plus tax. Book ahead online for discounts. ✉ *440 N. New River Dr. E, Fort Lauderdale* ☎ *888/238–9805* ⊕ *www.carriebcruises.com.*

### ★ *Jungle Queen* Riverboats
**BOAT TOURS** | **FAMILY** | The kitschy *Jungle Queen* and *River Queen* riverboats cruise through the heart of Fort Lauderdale on the New River. It's an old-school experience that dates back to 1935, when the company launched its tours, and the touristy charm is a big part of the fun. There are several types of sightseeing tours that leave at various times of day—from morning cruises to dinner cruises with entertainment—and prices start at around $25 per person. Check the website for details and availability. ✉ *Bahia Mar Yachting Center, 801 Seabreeze Blvd., Fort Lauderdale* ☎ *954/462–5596* ⊕ *www.junglequeen.com.*

### ★ Water Taxi
**BOAT TOURS** | **FAMILY** | At once a sightseeing tour and a mode of transportation, the Water Taxi is a smart way to experience most of Fort Lauderdale and Hollywood's waterways. There are 11 scheduled stops, plus on-demand whistle stops, and the system has two connected routes: the Fort Lauderdale and the Hollywood Express. The Fort Lauderdale route runs from around 10 am to 10 pm; the Hollywood Express route starts at 9 am and runs every other hour. It's possible to cruise all day while taking in the sights. Captains and crew share fun facts and white lies about the city's history, as well as quirky tales about celebrity homes. A day pass is $35. ✉ *904 E. Las Olas Blvd., Fort Lauderdale* ☎ *954/467–6677* ⊕ *watertaxi.com.*

# Downtown and Las Olas

The jewel of downtown is the Riverwalk Arts & Entertainment District, where Broadway shows, ballet, and theater take place at the Broward Center for the Performing Arts on the riverfront. A cluster of cultural entities is within a five-minute walk: the Museum of Discovery and Science, History Fort Lauderdale, and NSU Art Museum (part of Nova Southeastern University). Restaurants, sidewalk cafés, bars, and nightclubs flourish along the downtown extension of Las Olas, and its main presence brings a more upscale atmosphere. Riverwalk ties these two areas together with a 2-mile stretch along the New River's north and south banks, though the commercial success of this section has been tepid. Tropical gardens with benches and interpretive displays line the walk on the north, with boat landings on the south side.

##  Sights

### ⭐ FATVillage (Flagler + Art + Technology)
**NEIGHBORHOOD** | **FAMILY** | Inspired by Miami's Wynwood Arts District, Flagler + Art + Technology (or Food + Art + Technology) Village encompasses several square blocks of a formerly blighted warehouse district in downtown Fort Lauderdale. It's now thriving with a slew of production studios, art studios, and loft-style apartments. On the last Saturday of the month (except in December), FATVillage hosts an evening art walk, in which businesses display contemporary artworks by local talent and food trucks gather. There are libations, of course, and the warehouse district erupts into a giant, culture-infused street party. ⊠ *FATVillage, 521 N.W. 1st Ave., Downtown* ☎ *954/760–5900* ⊕ *www.fatvillage.com.*

### Historic Stranahan House Museum
**HISTORIC SIGHT** | **FAMILY** | The city's oldest surviving structure was once home to businessman Frank Stranahan, who arrived from Ohio in 1892. With his wife, Ivy, the city's first schoolteacher, he befriended and traded with the Seminole tribe. In 1901 he built a store that would later become his home after serving as a post office, a general store, and a restaurant. The couple's tale is filled with ups and downs. Their home remains Fort Lauderdale's principal link to its brief history and has been on the National Register of Historic Places since 1973. Guided tours are about an hour long and are offered a few times a day; however, calling ahead for availability is a good idea. Self-guided tours of the museum are not allowed. ⊠ *335 S.E. 6th Ave., Downtown* ☎ *954/524–4736* ⊕ *www. stranahanhouse.org* ⊠ *$12* ◔ *Closed holidays.*

### ⭐ Las Olas Boulevard
**STREET** | **FAMILY** | What Lincoln Road is to South Beach, Las Olas Boulevard is to Fort Lauderdale. Regarded as the heart and soul of Broward County, Las Olas has historically been the premier street for restaurants, art galleries, museums, shopping, dining, and strolling. Lined with high-rises in the downtown area and original boutiques and ethnic eateries along 10 blocks of the main stretch, it's also home to beautiful mansions and traditional Florida homes along the Intracoastal Waterway to the east, which typify the modern-day aesthetic of Fort Lauderdale. The ocean appears beyond the residential swath, and that's where you see that the name "Las Olas" (Spanish for "The Waves") begins to make more sense. It's a pedestrian-friendly thoroughfare, but it's not closed to vehicular traffic at any point. ⊠ *E. Las Olas Blvd., Downtown* ⊕ *www.lasolasboulevard.com.*

### Museum of Discovery and Science and AutoNation IMAX Theater
**SCIENCE MUSEUM** | **FAMILY** | There are dozens of interactive exhibits here to entertain children—and adults—through the wonders of science and Florida's

delicate ecosystem. The state-of-the-art 7D theater takes guests on a virtual tour of aviation technology, while the EcoDiscovery Center comes with an Everglades Airboat Adventure ride, resident otters, and an interactive Florida storm center. The 300-seat AutoNation IMAX theater is part of the complex and shows mainstream and educational films, some in 3D, on the biggest screen in South Florida with a rare high-tech laser projection system. ✉ *401 S.W. 2nd St., Fort Lauderdale* ☎ *954/467–6637 museum, 954/463–4629 IMAX* 🌐 *mods.org* 🎟 *Museum $27, IMAX tickets from $12.*

**★ NSU Art Museum**

**ART MUSEUM | FAMILY** | Led by visionary director and chief curator Bonnie Clearwater, the NSU Art Museum's international exhibition programming ignites downtown Fort Lauderdale. Part of Nova Southeastern University, the 83,000-square-foot modernist building, designed by architect Edward Larrabee Barnes, opened in 1986. The interior holds an impressive permanent collection of more than 7,000 works, including the country's largest collection of paintings by American realist William Glackens and pivotal works by female and multicultural artists, avant-garde CoBrA artists, and a wide array of Latin American masters.

**■ TIP→ The lobby-level Museum Café is a cool hangout with art-inspired gifts.** ✉ *1 E. Las Olas Blvd., Downtown* ☎ *954/525–5500* 🌐 *nsuartmuseum.org* 🎟 *$12* 🕒 *Closed Mon.*

**Riverwalk**

**CITY PARK | FAMILY** | Along the inlets of downtown Fort Lauderdale is Riverwalk, a tropical waterfront trail lined with 10 parks plus museums and restaurants. Great for a leisurely stroll or a fun-filled day with family, it often hosts activities like dog-training classes, cycle tours, events and festivals. ✉ *888 E. Las Olas Blvd., Fort Lauderdale* ☎ *954/468-1541* 🌐 *www.goriverwalk.com.*

## 🍴 Restaurants

**Big City Tavern**

**$$$ | MODERN AMERICAN | FAMILY** | A must-visit Las Olas landmark, Big City Tavern mingles Asian entrées like shrimp pad Thai with Italian four-cheese ravioli and an American grilled-chicken Cobb salad. The crispy flatbread changes every day. **Known for:** eclectic menu; weekend brunch; fun bar scene. [$] *Average main: $26* ✉ *609 E. Las Olas Blvd., Downtown* ☎ *954/727–0307* 🌐 *www.bigcitylasolas.com.*

**Casa Sensei**

**$$$$ | ASIAN FUSION** | This waterfront restaurant along the Himmarshee Canal offers Pan-Asian-Latin fusion dishes, including a full sushi bar and a plethora of comfort dishes like pad Thai, lo mein, and kimchi fried rice. Diners can opt to enjoy their meal as part of a gondola ride leaving from the restaurant's dock. **Known for:** waterfront dining; creative cocktails; romantic atmosphere. [$] *Average main: $32* ✉ *1200 E. Las Olas Blvd., Suite 101, Downtown* ☎ *954/530–4176* 🌐 *casasensei.com.*

**The Floridian**

**$$ | AMERICAN | FAMILY** | No matter the hour at this classic 24-hour diner, you can order no-nonsense breakfast favorites like oversize omelets with biscuits, toast, or English muffins. Good hangover eats abound, but don't expect anything exceptional besides the location and the low prices. **Known for:** breakfast anytime; low prices; always open. [$] *Average main: $15* ✉ *1410 E. Las Olas Blvd., Downtown* ☎ *954/463–4041* 🌐 *thefloridiandiner.com.*

**★ The Katherine**

**$$$ | FUSION** | Beloved South Florida chef Timon Balloo named this restaurant after his wife, who can be seen chatting with guests while refilling their drinks. The constantly evolving menu is inspired by the chef's Chinese-Indian-Trinidadian heritage but always features a fresh pasta, a daily ceviche, and some kind

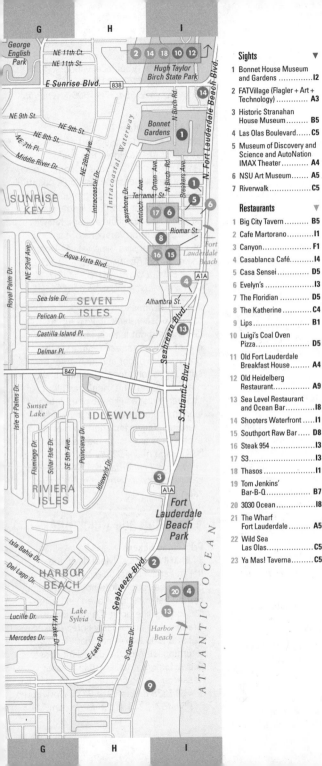

## Sights ▼

1 Bonnet House Museum and Gardens ..............I2
2 FATVillage (Flagler + Art + Technology) .............A3
3 Historic Stranahan House Museum .........B5
4 Las Olas Boulevard......C5
5 Museum of Discovery and Science and AutoNation IMAX Theater ...........A4
6 NSU Art Museum .......A5
7 Riverwalk .................C5

## Restaurants ▼

1 Big City Tavern ..........B5
2 Cafe Martorano...........I1
3 Canyon....................F1
4 Casablanca Café.........I4
5 Casa Sensei .............D5
6 Evelyn's .................I3
7 The Floridian ............D5
8 The Katherine ...........C4
9 Lips ......................B1
10 Luigi's Coal Oven Pizza......................D5
11 Old Fort Lauderdale Breakfast House........A4
12 Old Heidelberg Restaurant..............A9
13 Sea Level Restaurant and Ocean Bar............I8
14 Shooters Waterfront ....I1
15 Southport Raw Bar .....D8
16 Steak 954 .................I3
17 S3............................I3
18 Thasos ....................I1
19 Tom Jenkins' Bar-B-Q................B7
20 3030 Ocean ................I8
21 The Wharf Fort Lauderdale .........A5
22 Wild Sea Las Olas...................C5
23 Ya Mas! Taverna.........C5

## Quick Bites ▼

1 Gran Forno Bakery .....D5
2 Kilwins Fort Lauderdale-Las Olas...................C5

## Hotels ▼

1 The Atlantic Hotel & Spa.....................I2
2 B Ocean Resort...........I7
3 Bahia Mar Fort Lauderdale Beach, A DoubleTree by Hilton Hotel .............I6
4 Fort Lauderdale Marriott Harbor Beach Resort & Spa ..............I8
5 Four Seasons Fort Lauderdale ...........I3
6 Hilton Fort Lauderdale Beach Resort.............I3
7 Hyatt Centric Las Olas.................A5
8 Kimpton Shorebreak Fort Lauderdale Beach Resort.............I3
9 Lago Mar Beach Resort & Club ....................I9
10 Pelican Grand Beach Resort.............I1
11 Pineapple Point ..........E4
12 Residence Inn by Marriott Fort Lauderdale Intracoastal/ Il Lugano...................I1
13 The Ritz-Carlton, Fort Lauderdale ...........I4
14 Sonesta Fort Lauderdale ...........I1
15 W Fort Lauderdale........I3

of jerk meat paired with fresh veggies. **Known for:** great natural wine selection; clam chowder fries and Thai-style crab rice; cozy atmosphere with funky music. [$] *Average main: $23* ✉ *723 E. Broward Blvd., Fort Lauderdale* ☎ *754/216–0690* 🌐 *www.thekatherinerestaurant.com* 🕒 *Closed Mon. and Tues.*

### ★ Luigi's Coal Oven Pizza

$$ | **PIZZA** | **FAMILY** | One of the best little pizza joints in South Florida, Luigi's Coal Oven Pizza runs the full gamut of pizzas, phenomenal salads with fresh dressings, classics like eggplant parmigiana, and oven-baked chicken wings. For the Margherita Napoletana, the quality and flavors of the crust, cheese, and sauce are the result of Luigi's century-old recipe from Naples. **Known for:** traditional Neopolitan-style pizza; intimate dining room; coal-fired oven. [$] *Average main: $19* ✉ *1415 E. Las Olas Blvd., Downtown* ☎ *954/522–8888* 🌐 *www.luigiscoaloven-pizza.com.*

### ★ Old Fort Lauderdale Breakfast House

(*OB House*)

$$$ | **AMERICAN** | Locals can't get enough of OB House's commitment to quality; you'll find only fresh and organic ingredients here. Try cheesy grits, mega-pancakes with real Vermont maple syrup, or the free-range-egg omelets with wild-caught mahimahi. **Known for:** organic ingredients; fun breakfast options; unique renovation of an old post office. [$] *Average main: $23* ✉ *333 Himmarshee St., Downtown* ☎ *954/530–7520* 🌐 *www.o-bhouse.com* 🕒 *Closed Mon.*

### The Wharf Fort Lauderdale

$$ | **MODERN AMERICAN** | Situated on 1¼ acres of the city's historic New River waterfront, this nautical-themed space with communal tables and two large bars is surrounded by five local pop-up restaurants and Rivertail, by award-winning chef José Mendin. Nightly events and activities make this the go-to spot for Sunday Funday and hanging out with friends. **Known for:** live music; fun atmosphere; great local vendors. [$] *Average main: $15* ✉ *20 W. Las Olas Blvd., Downtown* ☎ *954/372–7606* 🌐 *wharfftl.com.*

### Wild Sea Las Olas

$$$$ | **SEAFOOD** | In the heart of Las Olas at the Riverside Hotel, this seafood restaurant and bar keeps things simple with a small menu focused on a beautiful raw bar and ever-changing preparations of diverse catches from Florida, Hawaiian, and New England waters. **Known for:** worldly interpretations of seafood; raw bar; extensive wine list. [$] *Average main: $43* ✉ *Riverside Hotel, 620 E. Las Olas Blvd., Downtown* ☎ *954/467–2555* 🌐 *www.wildseaonlasolas.com.*

### Ya Mas! Taverna

$$$ | **MEDITERRANEAN** | Take a trip to Greece without leaving Las Olas at this quaint Mediterranean restaurant, its bright white decor and lush greenery setting the tone for casual indoor and outdoor dining. The menu has plenty of shareable dishes like whipped feta and labneh, grilled octopus, and a whole branzino. **Known for:** short-rib moussaka; excellent falafel; large mezze platters. [$] *Average main: $23* ✉ *1103 E. Las Olas Blvd., Fort Lauderdale* ☎ *954/306-8388* 🌐 *www.yamastaverna.com* 🕒 *Closed Mon.*

## ☕ Coffee and Quick Bites

### Gran Forno Bakery

$ | **BAKERY** | **FAMILY** | Most days, the Italian sandwiches, specialty breads, and pastries sell out before noon at this aptly named bakery ("large oven" in Italian). Customers line up in the morning to get Gran Forno's hot artisanal breads like ciabatta (800 loaves are made a day), returning later for the decadent desserts. **Known for:** great Italian-style breads; desserts; strong coffee. [$] *Average main: $14* ✉ *1235 E. Las Olas Blvd., Downtown* ☎ *954/467–2244* 🌐 *granforno.com.*

### Kilwins Fort Lauderdale–Las Olas

$ | AMERICAN | FAMILY | The sweet smell of waffle cones wafts into the Las Olas air from this old-fashioned confectionery chain that also sells hand-paddled fudge and scoops of homemade ice cream. **Known for:** creamy Mackinac Island fudge; ice cream and waffle cones; sea salt–caramel fudge. $ *Average main: $7* ✉ *Kilwins Fort Lauderdale-Las Olas, 809 E. Las Olas Blvd., Downtown* ☎ *954/523–8338* ⊕ *www.kilwins.com.*

##  Hotels

### Hyatt Centric Las Olas

$ | HOTEL | FAMILY | Located inside Fort Lauderdale's tallest skyscraper and featuring views of the city, neighboring Bubier Park, and the Riverwalk, this nautical-chic hotel has an eighth-floor pool complete with cozy indoor-outdoor cabanas. **Pros:** walking distance of Las Olas nightlife; on-site restaurant; easy garage parking. **Cons:** no beach access; lack of views from pool; limited outdoor seating at restaurant. $ *Rooms from: $120* ✉ *100 E. Las Olas Blvd., Downtown* ☎ *954/353–1234* ⊕ *www.hyatt.com* ⇌ *238 rooms* ⦿ *No Meals.*

### Pineapple Point

$$ | B&B/INN | Tucked a few blocks behind Las Olas Boulevard in the residential neighborhood of Victoria Park, clothing-optional Pineapple Point is a magnificent maze of posh tropical cottages and dense foliage catering to the LGBTQ+ community and is nationally renowned for its stellar service. **Pros:** superior service; luxurious and tropical setting; lots of amenities. **Cons:** difficult to find at first; cancellations or changes require 14-day notice; rates can get high during season. $ *Rooms from: $300* ✉ *315 N.E. 16th Terr., Downtown* ☎ *954/527–0094, 888/844–7295* ⊕ *www.pineapplepoint. com* ⇌ *25 rooms* ⦿ *Free Breakfast.*

##  Nightlife

The majority of Fort Lauderdale nightlife takes place near downtown, beginning on Himmarshee Street (Second Street) and continuing on to the riverfront, and then to Las Olas Boulevard. The downtown area tends to draw a younger demographic somewhere between college-aged and late twenties. On Himmarshee Street, a dozen rowdy bars and clubs, ranging from the divey to the sophisticated, entice a wide range of partygoers. Toward East Las Olas Boulevard, near the financial towers and boutique shops, upscale bars cater to the more professional crowd.

### ★ Glitch Bar

THEMED ENTERTAINMENT | This casual spot has old-school arcade games, pinball, occasional DJs, and craft cocktails often named after pop-culture references. Come for the games (ranging from classics like Ms. Pac-Man and Galaga to Killer Queen, the world's only 10-player strategy arcade game) and stay for drinks and friendly bartenders. Those looking for something to soak up the alcohol can enjoy a selection of muffuletta sandwiches made to order. ✉ *905 N.E. 5th Ave., Downtown* ☎ *954/616–5762* ⊕ *www. glitchbar.com.*

### Laser Wolf

BARS | Far from the main drag of Fort Lauderdale's nightlife district, Laser Wolf celebrates the urban grit on the other side of the tracks as an artsy, hipster, craft-beer bar. It's located on the railroad tracks in a cool indoor-outdoor space and might be the most popular bar for locals because of its great drinks, music, and overall vibe. Motto: "Yes beer. No jerks."

■ TIP → **Drive or Uber it here. It's best not to walk from other bars off Las Olas and Himmarshee due to distance and safety concerns.** ✉ *901 Progresso Dr., No. 101, Downtown* ☎ *954/667–9373* ⊕ *laserwolf. bar.*

### ★ No Man's Land

**COCKTAIL LOUNGES** | Easy to miss, in a shopping center next to a Chinese take-out spot, No Man's Land is a sultry bar that welcomes guests with heavy velvet drapery and an old-school Zoltar fortune teller machine. The cocktails are whimsical and tiki-esque, and the bar offers live music (including a Monday Jazz night) and fancy bar bites like deviled eggs topped with caviar and smoked foie gras. ✉ *Victoria Park Shoppes, 666 N. Federal Hwy., Fort Lauderdale* ☎ *954/368–2616* ⊕ *nomanslandftl.com.*

### Stache

**DANCE CLUBS** | Inspired by the Roaring '20s, this speakeasy-style drinking den and nightclub infuses party-hard downtown Fort Lauderdale with some class and pizzazz. Expect awesome craft cocktails, inclusive of bespoke ice cubes for old-school drinks like Manhattans and Sidecars. Late night on Friday and Saturday, anticipate great music and a fun crowd. The 5,000-square-foot bar opens at 7 am on weekdays to serve coffee. ✉ *109 S.W. 2nd Ave., Downtown* ☎ *954/449–1025* ⊕ *stacheftl.com.*

##  Performing Arts

### ★ Broward Center for the Performing Arts

**ARTS CENTERS** | **FAMILY** | Fort Lauderdale's 2,700-seat architectural gem offers more than 500 events annually, including Broadway-style musicals, plays, dance, symphony, opera, rock, film, lectures, comedy, and children's theater. The theaters are state-of-the-art, and dining venues are available, including the restaurant Marti's New River Bistro and the Intermezzo Lounge. An elevated walkway connects the centerpiece of the complex to a parking garage across the street. ✉ *201 S.W. 5th Ave., Downtown* ☎ *954/462–0222* ⊕ *www.browardcenter. org.*

### Revolution Live

**ARTS CENTERS** | If a charming dive bar were a concert venue, this would be it. The intimate venue for live rock, electronic, funk, and more houses both indoor and outdoor stages featuring rising-star performers, local acts, and popular indie bands. Many big names, including Lady Gaga and Panic! at the Disco, performed here before breaking out as stars. ✉ *100 S.W. 3rd Ave., Downtown* ☎ *954/449– 1025* ⊕ *www.jointherevolution.net.*

##  Shopping

### ★ Las Olas Boulevard

**NEIGHBORHOODS** | **FAMILY** | Las Olas Boulevard is the epicenter of Fort Lauderdale's lifestyle. Not only are 50 of the city's best boutiques, dozens of top restaurants, and eclectic art galleries found along this landscaped street, but Las Olas links the growing downtown area with Fort Lauderdale's beautiful beaches. ✉ *E. Las Olas Blvd., Downtown* ☎ *954/258–8382* ⊕ *lasolasboulevard.com.*

# Fort Lauderdale Beach

## ⊚ Sights

### ★ Bonnet House Museum & Gardens

**GARDEN** | **FAMILY** | This 35-acre subtropical estate endures as a tribute to Old South Florida. Prior to its "modern" history, the grounds had already seen 4,000 years of activity when settler Hugh Taylor Birch purchased the site in 1895. Birch gave it to his daughter Helen as a wedding gift when she married Frederic Bartlett, and the newlyweds built a charming home for a winter residence in 1920. Years after Helen died, Frederic married his second wife, Evelyn, and the artistically gifted couple embarked on a mission to embellish the property with personal touches and surprises that are still evident today. This historic place is a must-see for its architecture, artwork, and horticulture. While admiring the fabulous gardens,

Fort Lauderdale's picture-perfect beach is Blue Wave certified by the Clean Beaches Coalition.

look out for playful monkeys swinging from the trees. ⊠ *900 N. Birch Rd., Beachfront* ☎ *954/563–5393* ⊕ *www. bonnethouse.org* ✉ *$20 house tour, $10 gardens only; $4 tram tour* ⊙ *Closed Mon.*

##  Beaches

### ★ Fort Lauderdale Beach

**BEACH | FAMILY |** The same stretch of sand that once welcomed America's wild spring breakers is now miles of beach-side sophistication. It remains gloriously open and uncluttered when compared to other major beaches along the Florida coastline; walkways line both sides of the road, and traffic is trimmed to two gently curving northbound lanes. Fort Lauderdale Beach unofficially begins between B Ocean Resort and the DoubleTree by Hilton Bahia Mar Resort, starting with the quiet Fort Lauderdale Beach Park, where picnic tables and palm trees rule. Going north, a younger crowd gravitates toward the section near Las Olas Boulevard. The beach is actually most crowded from

here to Beach Place, home to Marriott's vacation rentals and touristy places like Hooters and Fat Tuesday (and a beach-themed CVS). An LGBTQ crew soaks up the sun along Sebastian Street Beach, just north of the Ritz-Carlton. Families with children enjoy hanging out between Seville Street and Vistamar Street, between the Westin Fort Lauderdale Beach and The Atlantic Hotel and Spa. High-spirited dive bars dot the Strip and epitomize its "anything goes" attitude. **Amenities:** food and drink; lifeguards; parking (fee). **Best for:** partiers; sunrise; swimming; walking; windsurfing. ⊠ *SR A1A, from Holiday Dr. to Sunrise Blvd., Beachfront* ⊕ *myfortlauderdalebeach. com.*

### Harbor Beach

**BEACH | FAMILY |** The posh Harbor Beach community includes Fort Lauderdale's most opulent residences on the Intra-coastal Waterway. Due east of this community, a stunning beach has adopted the name of its surroundings. The Harbor Beach section has some of the only private beaches in Fort Lauderdale, and most of this beach belongs to hotels like the Marriott Harbor Beach Resort & Spa and Lago Mar Beach Resort & Club. (To be clear: Only hotel guests have access.) Such status allows the hotels to provide guests with full-service amenities and dining options on their own slices of heaven. **Amenities:** water sports. **Best for:** solitude; swimming; walking. ✉ *S. Ocean La. and Holiday Dr., Beachfront.*

## 🍴 Restaurants

If you want to stop for a bite to eat or a drink before or after visiting Bonnet House, consider **Casablanca Café** (✉ *3049 Alhambra Street*) or **Steak 954** (✉ *W Fort Lauderdale, 401 N. Fort Lauderdale Beach Boulevard*).

**Casablanca Café**

$$$ | **ECLECTIC** | **FAMILY** | The menu at this piano bar and restaurant offers a global hodgepodge of American, Mediterranean, and Asian flavors, with a specific focus on eclectic preparations of Florida fish. The food isn't particularly good, but the atmosphere at this historic home is excellent. **Known for:** dining with ocean views; historic setting in Jova House; popular piano bar. [$] *Average main: $28* ✉ *3049 Alhambra St., Beachfront* ☎ *954/764–3500* 🌐 *casablancacafeonline.com.*

★ **Evelyn's**

$$$$ | **MIDDLE EASTERN** | Rooted in the area's history and named after the nearby Bonnet House's owner, the late Evelyn Bartlett, this trendy new restaurant serves coastal Florida cuisine with Middle Eastern influences. Begin the meal with grand mezze (smoked eggplant, hummus, charred red pepper spread, and pickled veggies) served with fresh-made pita before moving on to larger plates like wood-smoked octopus and pomegranate-glazed salmon. **Known for:** plush seating with water views; homemade Jerusalem bagel with spreads; perfectly plated dishes. [$] *Average main: $37* ✉ *Four Seasons Fort Lauderdale, 525 N. Fort Lauderdale Beach Blvd., Fort Lauderdale* ☎ *754/336–3100* 🌐 *fourseasons.com/fortlauderdale/dining/restaurants/evelyns.*

**Sea Level Restaurant and Ocean Bar**

$$$ | **SEAFOOD** | **FAMILY** | You have to take the road less traveled to find Sea Level, a haven for fresh seafood. The indoor-outdoor restaurant overlooks the ocean from sea level at Marriott's Harbor Beach Resort & Spa, and its seasonal menu wows with daily specials and cocktails featuring ingredients from the chef's organic garden. **Known for:** the freshest seafood; outdoor dining; good cocktail menu. [$] *Average main: $25* ✉ *Fort Lauderdale Marriott Harbor Beach Resort and Spa, 3030 Holiday Dr., Beachfront* ☎ *954/765–3041* 🌐 *www.marriott.com.*

**Steak 954**

$$$$ | **MODERN AMERICAN** | It's not just the steaks that impress at Stephen Starr's superstar spot inside the W Fort Lauderdale, the seafood selections shine, too. Order as many dishes as possible, like the lobster and crab-coconut ceviche, the red snapper tiradito, and the Colorado lamb chops. **Known for:** high-quality (and expensive) steaks and seafood; outdoor dining; Sunday brunch. [$] *Average main: $55* ✉ *W Fort Lauderdale, 401 N. Fort Lauderdale Beach Blvd., Beachfront* ☎ *954/414–8333* 🌐 *steak954.com.*

**S3**

$$$ | **FUSION** | S3 stands for the fabulous trio of sun, surf, and sand, paying homage to its prime beachfront location. The menu features a variety of Japanese-inspired raw dishes, sushi rolls, and dishes with a New American focus. **Known for:** eclectic Asian and American flavors; solid selection of wine and cocktails; drawing both locals and visitors. [$] *Average main: $29* ✉ *Hilton Fort Lauderdale Beach Resort, 505 N. Fort Lauderdale Beach Blvd., Beachfront* 🌐 *s3restaurant.com.*

★ **3030 Ocean**

$$$$ | **SEAFOOD** | 3030 Ocean's unpredictable menus are guided by award-winning chef Adrienne Grenier's perfectionist flair. Her interpretation of modern American seafood focuses on balancing complex flavors to enhance her fresh ingredients—without subtracting from their integrity. **Known for:** ever-changing menu; locally sourced seafood; consistently good food. [$] *Average main: $45* ✉ *Fort Lauderdale Marriott Harbor Beach Resort and Spa, 3030 Holiday Dr., Beachfront* ☎ *954/765–3030* 🌐 *www.3030ocean.com.*

## Hotels

**The Atlantic Hotel & Spa**

$$$ | **HOTEL** | **FAMILY** | In addition to a relaxing spa, a restaurant, and a sleek fifth-floor pool overlooking the Atlantic, this towering oceanfront hotel has fantastic views of the ocean from its beds (unless, of course, you select a city view). **Pros:** oceanfront property; en suite kitchenettes; pet-friendly, a rare find in Fort Lauderdale. **Cons:** dated decor in the rooms; expensive parking; issues with service. [$] *Rooms from: $320* ✉ *601 N. Fort Lauderdale Beach Blvd., Beachfront* ☎ *954/516–1720* 🌐 *www.atlantichotelfl.com* 🛏 *104 rooms* 🍴 *No Meals.*

**B Ocean Resort**

$$ | **HOTEL** | This iconic riverboat-shaped landmark, once the Yankee Clipper, is chic yet functional, and the unobstructed ocean views and beach access set it apart from neighboring properties. **Pros:** retro mermaid show in swimming pool; proximity to beach; excellent gym. **Cons:** daily resort fee; beach umbrellas are an additional fee; not all rooms have balconies. [$] *Rooms from: $200* ✉ *1140 Seabreeze Blvd., Beachfront* ☎ *954/564–1000* 🌐 *www.bhotelsandresorts.com/b-ocean* 🛏 *484 rooms* 🍴 *No Meals.*

**Bahia Mar Fort Lauderdale Beach, A DoubleTree by Hilton Hotel**

$$ | **HOTEL** | **FAMILY** | This nicely situated resort has identical rooms in both its marina building and its tower building; however, the latter offers superior views. **Pros:** crosswalk from hotel to beach; on-site yacht center; water taxi stop. **Cons:** busy location; small bathrooms; high rates during events. [$] *Rooms from: $215* ✉ *801 Seabreeze Blvd., Beachfront* ☎ *954/764–2233* 🌐 *www.bahiamarhotel.com* 🛏 *296 rooms* 🍴 *No Meals.*

★ **Fort Lauderdale Marriott Harbor Beach Resort & Spa**

$$$$ | **RESORT** | **FAMILY** | Sitting on a quarter-mile of private beach, this property shines with the luxe personality of a top-notch island resort. **Pros:** private beachfront; all rooms have balconies; great eateries. **Cons:** Wi-Fi isn't free; expensive parking; large resort feel. [$] *Rooms from: $450* ✉ *3030 Holiday Dr., Beachfront* ☎ *954/525–4000* 🌐 *www.marriott.com* 🛏 *650 rooms* 🍴 *No Meals.*

★ **Four Seasons Fort Lauderdale**

$$$$ | **HOTEL** | **FAMILY** | Mid-century modern meets luxury yacht at the new Four Seasons, its curved architecture mimicking the front of a ship and its interior as airy and luxurious as the best of the brand. **Pros:** large bathrooms; on-site concierge can help plan activities and dining reservations; water views from every room. **Cons:** size restrictions for pets; narrow valet driveway; no hot tub. [$] *Rooms from: $650* ✉ *525 N. Fort Lauderdale Beach Blvd., Fort Lauderdale* ☎ *754/336–3100* 🌐 *fourseasons.com/fortlauderdale* 🛏 *189 rooms* 🍴 *No Meals.*

**Hilton Fort Lauderdale Beach Resort**

$$ | **HOTEL** | **FAMILY** | This oceanfront sparkler features tasteful, large suites and a fabulous sixth-floor pool deck. **Pros:** fun pool; most rooms have balconies; great spa. **Cons:** not pet-friendly; expensive valet parking; beach umbrellas not included in resort fee. [$] *Rooms from: $330* ✉ *505 N. Fort Lauderdale Beach Blvd.,*

Lago Mar Resort and Club in Fort Lauderdale has its own private beach on the Atlantic Ocean.

*Beachfront* ☎ *954/414–2222* 🌐 *www.hilton.com* 🛏 *374 suites* 🍴 *No Meals.*

**Kimpton Shorebreak Fort Lauderdale Beach Resort**

**$$$** | **HOTEL** | Tucked between downtown and the beach, this tropical hidden gem boasts secret pathways, courtyards, and plenty of art deco decor, making it dreamy and photogenic. **Pros:** pet-friendly amenities at no extra cost; daily social hour with complimentary wine; plenty of wellness offerings. **Cons:** limited food options; not oceanfront; no bathtubs. [$] *Rooms from: $340* ✉ *2900 Riomar St., Intracoastal and Inland* ☎ *954/908–7301* 🌐 *ihg.com* 🛏 *96 rooms* 🍴 *No Meals.*

**Lago Mar Beach Resort & Club**

**$$$** | **RESORT** | **FAMILY** | The sprawling family-friendly Lago Mar retains its sparkle and authentic Florida feel thanks to committed owners. **Pros:** secluded setting with swimming lagoon and access to a private beach; no resort fee; free valet and self-parking. **Cons:** not easy to find; far from restaurants and beach action; crowded during holidays, including Spring Break. [$] *Rooms from: $350* ✉ *1700 S. Ocean La., Beachfront* ☎ *954/523–6511* 🌐 *lagomar.com* 🛏 *204 rooms* 🍴 *No Meals.*

**Pelican Grand Beach Resort**

**$$$** | **RESORT** | **FAMILY** | This bright yellow Key West–style Noble House property fuses a heritage seaside charm with understated luxury. **Pros:** incredible spa; directly on the beach; romantic restaurant. **Cons:** small fitness center; nothing notable within walking distance; small property. [$] *Rooms from: $350* ✉ *2000 N. Ocean Blvd., Beachfront* ☎ *954/568–9431* 🌐 *www.pelicanbeach.com* 🛏 *159 rooms* 🍴 *No Meals.*

★ **The Ritz-Carlton, Fort Lauderdale**

**$$$$** | **HOTEL** | Twenty-four dramatically tiered, glass-walled stories rise from the sea, forming a resort that's helping to revive a golden age of luxury travel. **Pros:** prime beach location; exceptional service; organic spa treatments. **Cons:** expensive valet parking; cancel at least 14 days in advance or get hit with a two-night penalty; extra-busy poolscape.

$ *Rooms from: $750* ⊠ *1 N. Fort Lauderdale Beach Blvd., Beachfront* ☎ *954/465–2300* ⊕ *www.ritzcarlton.com/FortLauderdale* ⇌ *192 rooms* ⦿ *No Meals.*

### Sonesta Fort Lauderdale

**$$ | HOTEL | FAMILY |** Sonesta Fort Lauderdale merges trendiness with affordability in its 13-story U-shaped tower overlooking the ocean. **Pros:** all rooms have ocean views; trendy but affordable; nighttime firepits. **Cons:** small pool area; no balconies; small driveway and expensive valet. $ *Rooms from: $279* ⊠ *999 N. Fort Lauderdale Beach Blvd., Beachfront* ☎ *954/315–1460* ⊕ *www.sonesta.com/FortLauderdale* ⇌ *240 rooms* ⦿ *No Meals.*

### W Fort Lauderdale

**$$ | HOTEL |** Fort Lauderdale's trendiest hotel has a glamorous poolscape, uber-modern rooms and suites, and dramatic views from every direction. **Pros:** amazing pool; pet-friendly; great restaurants. **Cons:** party atmosphere not for everyone; can be hard to navigate the property; Wi-Fi isn't free. $ *Rooms from: $300* ⊠ *435 N. Fort Lauderdale Beach Blvd., Beachfront* ☎ *954/414–8200* ⊕ *www.marriott.com* ⇌ *329 rooms* ⦿ *No Meals.*

## ▼ Nightlife

Given its roots as a beachside party town, it's hard to believe that Fort Lauderdale Beach offers very few options in terms of nightlife. A few dive bars are at opposite ends of the main strip, near Sunrise Boulevard and Route A1A, as well as Las Olas Boulevard and A1A. On the main thoroughfare between Las Olas and Sunrise, a few high-end bars at the beach's showstopping hotels have become popular, namely those at the W Fort Lauderdale.

### McSorley's Beach Pub

**PUBS |** This modern take on a classic Irish pub offers standard pub fun—from a jukebox to 35 beers on tap—but remains wildly popular thanks to its location right across from Fort Lauderdale Beach. Indeed, it's one of the few places on the beach to get an affordable drink and attracts its fair share of tourists and locals. Upstairs, the pub has a second lounge that's far clubbier, as well as a rooftop terrace, and downstairs features a game room with pool, beer pong, and more. ⊠ *837 N. Fort Lauderdale Beach Blvd., Beachfront* ☎ *954/565–4446* ⊕ *www.mcsorleysftl.com.*

### The World Famous Parrot

**PUBS | FAMILY |** A venerable Fort Lauderdale hangout, this dive bar–sports bar is particularly popular with Philadelphia Eagles fans and folks reminiscing about the big hair and spray tans of '80s Fort Lauderdale (aka its heyday). This place is stuck in the past, but it's got great bartenders, wings, chicken fingers, poppers, and skins. 'Nuff said. ⊠ *911 Sunrise La., Beachfront* ☎ *954/563–1493* ⊕ *www.theparrotlounge.com.*

### The Wreck Bar

**THEMED ENTERTAINMENT |** Travel back in time to the '50s at this "under the sea" dive bar and seafood eatery at B Ocean Resort, where huge aquariums and a porthole show off live mermaids, who perform an underwater series of tangos and group ensembles dressed in sparkling fishtails. These late-night, aqua burlesque shows take place in the pool on Friday and Saturday. ⊠ *B Ocean Resort, 1140 Seabreeze Blvd., Beachfront* ☎ *954/524–5551* ⊕ *www.boceanresort.com/dining/the-wreck-bar/.*

## 🏃 Activities

### BIKING

Among the most popular routes are Route A1A and Bayview Drive, especially in early morning before traffic builds, and a seven-mile bike path that parallels State Road 84 and the New River and leads to Markham Park, which has mountain-bike trails.

■ TIP→ **Alligator alert: Do not dangle your legs from seawalls.**

## Broward BCycle

BIKING | FAMILY | The big-city trend of bike-sharing is alive and well in Broward County. With more than 20 station locations in six cities, from as far south as Hallandale to as far north as Pompano Beach, bikes can be rented for as little as 30 minutes or as long as a week, and can be picked up and dropped off at any and all stations in Broward County. Most stations are found downtown and along the beach. Electric bikes are available at select stations. Download the BCycle app for up-to-date station availability. Please note that helmets are not provided at the kiosks. ⊕ *broward.bcycle.com.*

## FISHING

### Bahia Mar Yachting Center

BOATING | FAMILY | If you're interested in a saltwater charter, check out the offerings on the A Dock at the marina of the Bahia Mar Fort Lauderdale. Sportfishing and drift fishing bookings can be arranged. Snorkeling and diving outfitter Sea Experience also leaves from here, as does the famous *Jungle Queen* steamboat. In addition, the Water Taxi makes regular stops here. ✉ *801 Seabreeze Blvd., Beachfront* ☎ *954/627–6309* ⊕ *bahiamaryachtingcenter.com.*

## SCUBA DIVING AND SNORKELING

### ★ Sea Experience

SCUBA DIVING | FAMILY | The *Sea Experience I* leaves daily at 10:15 am and 2:15 pm for glass-bottom-boat-and-snorkeling combination trips through offshore reefs. Beginner and advanced scuba-diving experiences are available as well. ✉ *Bahia Mar Fort Lauderdale Beach–A DoubleTree by Hilton Hotel, 801 Seabreeze Blvd., Beachfront* ☎ *954/770–3483* ⊕ *www.seaxp.com.*

## SPAS

Most of Fort Lauderdale's upscale spas are located within elegant beachfront hotels, yet they remain open to the public. During low season (August and September), top spas offer $99 treatments as a seasonal promotion.

### AWAY Spa, W Fort Lauderdale

SPAS | The AWAY Spa at the W Fort Lauderdale features a menu of full-service body and beauty treatments broken down into five categories: quick fix tune-ups, detoxes, massages, face-focused treatments, body buffing, and polish and glow. Each service starts off with a "Bright Elixir" shot served complimentary upon arrival to help cleanse and energize. There's also a Glam Station equipped for everything from touch-ups to full-face makeup and hair styling. There are several traditional massage rooms, but those looking to work out the kinks without stepping into a changing room can take advantage of state-of-the-art express massage chairs in a Quick Fix Booth with 10-, 25-, or 50-minute options. ✉ *W Fort Lauderdale, 401 N. Fort Lauderdale Beach Blvd., Beachfront* ☎ *954/414–8232* ⊕ *www.marriott.com.*

### The Ritz-Carlton Spa, Fort Lauderdale

SPAS | The Ritz-Carlton's expansive 8,500-foot hideaway is focused on tranquility and relaxation, from the layout of the treatment rooms to the magical hands of Fort Lauderdale's top therapists. Massage options run the gamut, including Swedish, aromatherapy, hot stone, couples, deep tissue, hydrotherapy, reflexology, Thai, and prenatal. Dermatologist-developed skin-care treatments, anti-cellulite and anti-aging treatments, facials, manicures, and pedicures are also on the menu. Go for the Intuitive Ocean treatment for an intense detoxification with help from the marine mud, seaweed, and sea salt. ✉ *The Ritz-Carlton Spa, Fort Lauderdale, 1 N. Fort Lauderdale Beach Blvd., Beachfront* ☎ *954/302–6490* ⊕ *www.ritzcarlton.com.*

### Spa Atlantic

SPAS | Spa Atlantic exudes a relaxed glamour and offers perfected core spa services in its 10,000-square-foot space outfitted with separate spaces for men and women, relaxation rooms, Jacuzzis, saunas, and steam rooms. Many treatments are rooted in Asia, the Middle East, and the Mediterranean, with a holistic approach aiming to connect the mind and soul. Body treatments include a wide variety of massages, baths, body wraps, and body glows (exfoliation). Other beauty treatments offered include skin-care enhancements, anti-aging treatments, facials, manicures, pedicures, waxing, hair, and makeup. ✉ *The Atlantic Hotel and Spa, 601 N. Fort Lauderdale Beach Blvd., Beachfront* ☎ *954/567–8085* 🌐 *www.atlantichotelfl.com/spa-atlantic.*

## Intracoastal and Inland Fort Lauderdale

### Beaches

**★ Hugh Taylor Birch State Park**

**BEACH | FAMILY** | North of the bustling beachfront at Sunrise Boulevard, quieter sands run parallel to Hugh Taylor Birch State Park, an exquisite patch of Old Florida. The 180-acre subtropical oasis forms a barrier island between the Atlantic Ocean and the Intracoastal Waterway—surprisingly close to the urban core. Lush vegetation includes mangroves, and there are lovely nature trails through the hammock system. Visit the Birch House Museum, enjoy a picnic, play volleyball, or grab a canoe, kayak, or stand-up paddleboard. **Amenities:** toilets; water sports. **Best for:** solitude; walking. ✉ *3109 E. Sunrise Blvd., Intracoastal and Inland* ☎ *954/564–4521* 🌐 *www.floridastateparks.org/parks-and-trails/hugh-taylor-birch-state-park* 🎟 *From $4 single driver or motorcycle; $2 per pedestrian or bicyclist.*

### Restaurants

**★ Cafe Martorano**

**$$$$ | ITALIAN** | This Italian-American restaurant, serving hearty portions of the classics, is hard to miss thanks to the flashy cars that valet from its unassuming strip mall location. Loved by locals and sometimes even celebrities, it could be confused for a lounge after 10 pm on weekends, when owner Steve Martorano often DJs from the open kitchen's counter. **Known for:** famous meatball and salad; fresh pasta dishes; indulgent desserts. [$] *Average main: $35* ✉ *3343 E. Oakland Park Blvd., Intracoastal and Inland* ☎ *954/561–2554* 🌐 *cafemartorano.com.*

**Canyon**

**$$$ | SOUTHWESTERN** | Inside this magical enclave, a Southwestern fusion of Central and South American flavors and a twist of Asian influence are on the menu. Pair the fresh seafood or wild game with a robust selection of tequilas, a few mezcals, or a bottle from the decent wine list. **Known for:** locally sourced ingredients; long waits; large selection of tequilas. [$] *Average main: $28* ✉ *1818 E. Sunrise Blvd., Intracoastal and Inland* ✥ *At N.E. 18th Ave.* ☎ *954/765–1950* 🌐 *www.canyonfl.com* 🕒 *Closed Sun.*

**Old Heidelberg Restaurant**

**$$$ | GERMAN | FAMILY** | Old Heidelberg is like a Bavarian mirage on State Road 84, with a killer list of German specialties and beers on tap. Classics like bratwurst, knockwurst, kielbasa, and spaetzle dovetail nicely with four types of Wiener schnitzel. **Known for:** kitschy decor; huge selection of German imports on tap; extensive menu of German favorites. [$] *Average main: $25* ✉ *900 W. State Rd. 84, Intracoastal and Inland* ☎ *954/463–6747* 🌐 *www.heidelbergfl.com* 🕒 *No lunch weekends.*

**★ Shooters Waterfront**

**$$$ | AMERICAN | FAMILY** | Fresh, coastal-inspired dishes are enjoyed alfresco at this dockside restaurant, where each of the three bar areas and massive lounge get gorgeous Intracoastal views. Munch on the expected seaside starters like coconut shrimp, crispy calamari, and smoked fish dip before moving onto flatbreads, sushi, or one of the many entrées served at both lunch and dinner. **Known for:** mahimahi sandwich; great cocktails; scenic weekend brunch. $ *Average main: $29 ⊠ 3033 N.E. 32nd Ave., Intracoastal and Inland ☎ 954/566–2855 ⊕ www. shooterswaterfront.com.*

### Southport Raw Bar
**$$ | SEAFOOD |** You can't go wrong at this unpretentious dive, where seafood reigns. Feast on raw or steamed clams, raw oysters, and peel-and-eat shrimp. **Known for:** affordable prices; fresh seafood; open late on weekends. $ *Average main: $19 ⊠ 1536 Cordova Rd., Intracoastal and Inland ☎ 954/525–2526 ⊕ www.southportrawbar.com.*

### Thasos
**$$$$ | GREEK | FAMILY |** Traditional Greek cuisine with a modern twist is served family-style at this bright-white restaurant, where the fish is beyond fresh and the grape leaves are stuffed to the brim. The vibrant setting is made complete with great service and a reasonably priced wine list. **Known for:** private dining area for groups; live Greek music; great lamb chops. $ *Average main: $33 ⊠ 3330 E. Oakland Park Blvd., Intracoastal and Inland ☎ 954/200–6006 ⊕ www. thasosrestaurant.com ⊘ Closed Mon.*

### Tom Jenkins' Bar-B-Q
**$ | BARBECUE | FAMILY |** Big portions of dripping barbecue are dispensed at this chill spot for eat-in or take-out. Dinners come with two sides from a list that includes baked beans, collards, and mac and cheese. **Known for:** ample portions; very reasonable prices; good sides. $ *Average main: $12 ⊠ 1236 S. Federal Hwy., Intracoastal and Inland ☎ 954/522–5046 ⊕ tomjenkinsbbq.net ⊘ Closed Sun. and Mon.*

##  Hotels

### Residence Inn by Marriott Fort Lauderdale Intracoastal/Il Lugano
**$ | HOTEL |** This clean, modern hotel has studios and suites with fully equipped kitchens and private balconies with Intracoastal views, plus amenities including a pool and fitness center. **Pros:** docking is available to guests; pet-friendly; bike rentals available. **Cons:** lacks character of other properties; "business traveler" vibes; not on the beach. $ *Rooms from: $154 ⊠ 3333 N.E. 32nd Ave., Intracoastal and Inland ☎ 954/564–4400 ⊕ www. marriott.com ⊅ 105 rooms ⦿ Free Breakfast.*

##  Nightlife

Bars and pubs along Fort Lauderdale's Intracoastal cater to the city's large boating community along with its young professional population. Heading inland along Sunrise Boulevard, the bars around The Galleria mall tend to attract singles.

### Blue Martini Fort Lauderdale
**BARS |** A hot spot for the wild set, Blue Martini's menu is filled with tons of unconventional martini creations. The drinks are usually very good and the scene is fun for everyone, even those who aren't single and looking to mingle. ⊠ *The Galleria at Fort Lauderdale, 2432 E. Sunrise Blvd., Intracoastal and Inland ☎ 954/653–2583 ⊕ fortlauderdale.bluemartini.com.*

##  Activities

### BIRD-WATCHING
#### Evergreen Cemetery
**BIRD WATCHING | FAMILY |** North of Fort Lauderdale's 17th Street Causeway sits an unexpected haven for bird-watchers. It's the city's oldest cemetery (established 1910), and the shade from its gumbo-limbo trees and strangler figs doubles as a place of repose for Bahama mockingbirds and other species flying

through Broward. Warblers are big here, and there are occasional sightings of red-eyed vireos, northern water thrushes, and scarlet tanagers across 11 acres on Cliff Lake. ✉ *1300 S.E. 10th Ave., Intracoastal and Inland* ☎ *954/745–2140* 🌐 *www.parks.fortlauderdale.gov/programs/cemeteries.*

### SCUBA DIVING AND SNORKELING

**Lauderdale Diver**

**SCUBA DIVING | FAMILY** | This dive center facilitates daily trips on a bevy of hard-core dive boats up and down Broward's shoreline (they don't have their own boats, but they work with a handful of preferred outfitters). A variety of snorkeling, reef-diving, and wreck-diving trips is offered as well as scuba-diving lessons. ✉ *2830 W State Rd. 84, Suite 107, Intracoastal and Inland* ☎ *954/467–2822* 🌐 *lauderdalediver.com.*

### TENNIS

**Jimmy Evert Tennis Center**

**LOCAL SPORTS | FAMILY** | This grande dame of Fort Lauderdale's public tennis facilities is where legendary champ Chris Evert learned her two-handed backhand under the watchful eye of her father, Jimmy, who was the center's tennis pro for nearly four decades. There are 18 lighted clay courts and three hard courts. ✉ *Holiday Park, 701 N.E. 12th Ave., Intracoastal and Inland* ☎ *954/828–5378* 🌐 *www.parks.fortlauderdale.gov* 🎟 *$15 per day for nonresidents.*

# Wilton Manors and Oakland Park

North of Fort Lauderdale, Wilton Manors is the hub of gay life in the greater Fort Lauderdale area and has several popular restaurants and bars. Oakland Park, immediately to the north, also has several restaurants that are worth a visit.

## 🍴 Restaurants

**Lips**

**$$$ | AMERICAN** | The '90s are still alive and well at Lips. The hit restaurant and drag-show bar is a hot spot for groups celebrating birthdays, bachelorette parties, and other milestones requiring glitz and glamour. **Known for:** drag performances while you dine; Sunday brunch; raucous celebrations. [$] *Average main: $23* ✉ *1421 E. Oakland Park Blvd., Oakland Park* ☎ *954/567–0987* 🌐 *www.fladragshow.com* 🕒 *Closed Mon.*

## 🍸 Nightlife

The hub of Fort Lauderdale's gay nightlife is in Wilton Manors. Wilton Drive, aka "The Drive," has numerous bars, clubs, and lounges that cater to the LGBTQ+ community.

**Georgie's Alibi Monkey Bar**

**CAFÉS** | An anchor for the Wilton Manors LGBTQ+ community, this chill neighborhood drinking hole fills to capacity for cheap Long Island Iced Teas, darts, pool, and friendly people. ✉ *2266 Wilton Dr., Wilton Manors* ☎ *954/565–2526* 🌐 *www.alibiwiltonmanors.com.*

**Rosie's Bar & Grill**

**BARS** | Rosie's is very lively, pumping out pop tunes and award-winning burgers. It's the go-to gay-friendly place for affordable drinks and great times. Sunday brunch, with its cast of alternating DJs, is wildly popular. ✉ *2449 Wilton Dr., Wilton Manors* ☎ *954/563–0123* 🌐 *www.rosiesbarandgrill.com.*

# Western Suburbs and Beyond

West of Fort Lauderdale is an ever-evolving suburbia, where most of Broward's gated communities, golf courses, shopping outlets, casinos, and chain restaurants exist. As you reach the county's western side, the terrain takes on more characteristics of the Everglades, and you can see alligators sunning on canal banks with other exotic reptiles and birds.

## Sights

**Ah-Tah-Thi-Ki Museum**

**INDIGENOUS SIGHT | FAMILY** | Beyond the western suburbs of Broward County is Ah-Tah-Thi-Ki Museum, which means "a place to learn, a place to remember" in the Seminole language. This Smithsonian Affiliate documents the living history and culture of the Seminole Tribe of Florida through artifacts, exhibits, and experiential learning. There's a mile-long boardwalk above the swamplands (wheelchair-accessible) that leads you through the Big Cypress Seminole Reservation. At the midpoint of the boardwalk, you can take a break at the re-created ceremonial grounds. ✉ *30290 Josie Billie Hwy., Clewiston* ☎ *877/902–1113* 🌐 *www.ahtahthiki.com* 🎟 *$10* 🕒 *Closed holidays.*

★ **Butterfly World**

**ZOO | FAMILY** | More than 80 native and international butterfly species (more than 20,000 butterflies in total) live inside the first butterfly house in the United States and the largest in the world. The 3-acre site inside Coconut Creek's Tradewinds Park has aviaries, observation decks, waterfalls, ponds, and tunnels. There are lots of birds, too: kids love the lorikeet aviary, where birds alight on every limb. ✉ *Butterfly World, 3600 W. Sample Rd., Coconut Creek* ☎ *954/977–4400* 🌐 *www.butterflyworld.com* 🎟 *$32.50* ☞ *Tradewinds Park gate fee $1.50 per person on weekends and holidays.*

**Flamingo Gardens**

**WILDLIFE REFUGE | FAMILY** | Wander through the aviary, arboretum, and wildlife sanctuary at Flamingo Gardens, and don't miss the Everglades museum inside the historic Wray Home. A half-hour guided tram ride winds through tropical fruit groves and wetlands, where a large collection of Florida native wildlife lives (flamingos, alligators, bobcats, otters, panthers, and more). ✉ *Flamingo Gardens, 3750 S. Flamingo Rd., Davie* ☎ *954/473–2955* 🌐 *www.flamingogardens.org* 🎟 *$22.*

**Sawgrass Recreation Park**

**NATURE SIGHT | FAMILY** | Catch a good glimpse of plants and wildlife—from ospreys and alligators to turtles, snakes, and fish—on a 30-minute airboat ride through the Everglades. The fee covers admission to all nature exhibits as well as a visit to a model Seminole village.

**TIP→ Nature truly comes alive at night. Sawgrass Recreation Park offers longer nighttime airboat rides on Wednesday and Saturday at 8 pm, reservations required.** ✉ *1006 U.S. 27, Weston* ☎ *888/424–7262, 954/389–0202* 🌐 *www.evergladestours.com* 🎟 *$26.95; Gator Night tours $45.*

## Restaurants

**Georgia Pig BBQ & Restaurant**

**$ | AMERICAN | FAMILY** | When heading out to the area's western reaches, this postage-stamp–size outpost can add down-home zing to your day—if you can find it, that is. Breakfast, which includes sausage gravy and biscuits, is served 7–11 am, but the big attraction is barbecue beef, pork, or chicken, on platters or in sandwiches for lunch and dinner. **Known for:** North Georgia–style barbecue sauce; chopped pork sandwiches; open-pit cooking. [$] *Average main: $12* ✉ *1285 S. State Rd. 7, Fort Lauderdale* ✥ *U.S. 441, just south of Davie Blvd.* ☎ *954/587–4420* 🌐 *www.georgiapig.com* 💳 *No credit cards* 🕒 *Closed Sun.*

**Romeu's Cuban Restaurant**

**$ | CUBAN | FAMILY** | This family-owned Cuban spot serves popular Latin American dishes like oxtail, pork chunks, and lobster tail in creole sauce, all in hearty portions at affordable prices. Save room for dessert: the creamy guava cheesecake and *arroz con leche* are well worth

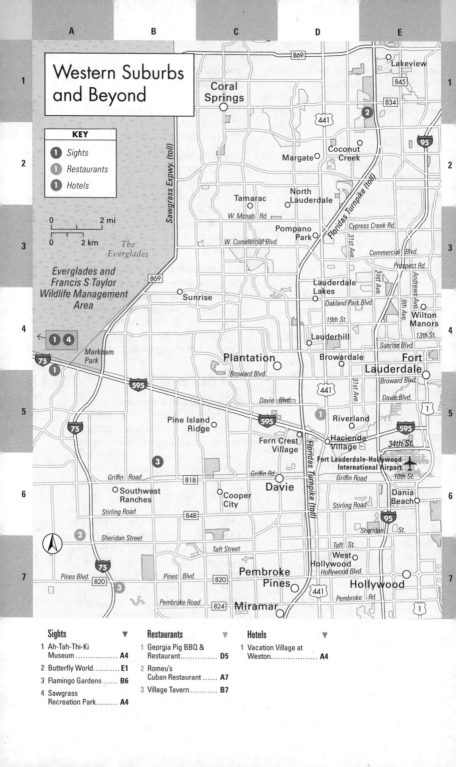

# Western Suburbs and Beyond

**KEY**

- ① Sights
- ① Restaurants
- ① Hotels

0 — 2 mi
0 — 2 km

*The Everglades*

*Everglades and Francis S Taylor Wildlife Management Area*

Lakeview
869
845
834
Coral Springs
441
2
I 95
Margate
Coconut Creek
Tamarac
North Lauderdale
W. Mcnab Rd.
Florida's Turnpike (toll)
Cypress Creek Rd.
31st Ave.
Pompano Park
W. Commercial Blvd.
Commercial Blvd.
Prospect Rd.
21st Ave.
Andrews Ave.
869
Sunrise
Lauderdale Lakes
Oakland Park Blvd.
9th Ave.
Wilton Manors
19th St.
13th St.
①④
75
Markham Park
Lauderhill
Browardale
Sunrise Blvd.
Fort Lauderdale
①
Plantation
Broward Blvd.
441
Broward Blvd.
595
Davie Blvd.
Davie Blvd.
75
Pine Island Ridge
595
① Riverland
595
Fern Crest Village
Hacienda Village
34th St.
③
Fort Lauderdale-Hollywood International Airport
Griffin Road
818
Griffin Rd.
Davie
Griffin Road
10th St.
Southwest Ranches
Cooper City
Dania Beach
Stirling Road
848
Stirling Road
95
②
Sheridan Street
Sheridan St.
Taft Street
Taft St.
West Hollywood
75
Pines Blvd.
820
Pines Blvd.
820
Pembroke Pines
Hollywood Blvd.
Hollywood
③
441
Pembroke Road
824
Miramar
Pembroke Rd.

the calories. **Known for:** brunch buffet on Sunday; classic Cuban favorites; consistently delicious dishes. [$] *Average main: $14* ✉ *Coquina Plaza, 6800 Dykes Rd., Weston* ☎ *954/252–9788* 🌐 *romeuscubanrestaurant.com.*

### ★ Village Tavern

**$$ | CONTEMPORARY | FAMILY** | Village Tavern is truly a neighborhood hub for those who love good food, good wine and cocktails, and great company. The bar scene is always fun, especially on Wine Wednesday, when all the wines (even the premium labels) are half-price by the glass. **Known for:** fresh ingredients; busy bar scene; outdoor dining. [$] *Average main: $19* ✉ *Shops at Pembroke Gardens, 14555 S.W. 2nd St.* ☎ *954/874–1001* 🌐 *www.villagetavern.com/location-pembroke-pines.*

## Hotels

### Vacation Village at Weston

**$ | RESORT | FAMILY** | Situated right between the Everglades and Fort Lauderdale, this family-friendly all-suite resort is located inside a golf community. **Pros:** washer/dryer in most rooms; fully stocked suites; free parking. **Cons:** car needed to get around; rooms need refresh; no pets allowed. [$] *Rooms from: $150* ✉ *16461 Racquet Club Rd., Weston* ☎ *800/760–7718* 🌐 *vacationvillageresorts.com/vacation_village_weston/index.html* 🛏 *1164 suites* 🍴 *No Meals.*

## Nightlife

Florida's cowboy country, around the town of Davie, offers country and western fun out in the 'burbs. In addition, South Florida's indigenous tribes have long offered gambling on territory near Broward's western suburbs. These casinos offer Vegas-style slot machines and even blackjack. Hollywood's Seminole Hard Rock Hotel & Casino offers the most elegant of Broward's casino experiences.

### Round Up Nightclub

**LIVE MUSIC** | Round Up is South Florida's hot country-music and nightclub venue in the heart of Broward's horse country. In addition to line dancing, the venue offers great libations, dance lessons, large-screen TVs, and theme nights coinciding with drink specials (Whiskey Wednesday, Friday Ladies Night, and the like). Open Wednesday through Sunday from 6 pm to 4 am; closed Monday and Tuesday.

**TIP→ Happy hour is a good bet, from 6 to 9.** ✉ *9020 W. State Rd. 84, Davie* ☎ *954/423–1990* 🌐 *www.roundupnightclub.com.*

## Shopping

### ★ Sawgrass Mills

**OUTLET | FAMILY** | This alligator-shaped megamall draws millions of shoppers a year to its collection of over 350 outlet stores, including more than 70 luxury brand outlets like Burberry, GUCCI, Jimmy Choo, Prada, Salvatore Ferragamo, The Company Store, Tory Burch, and Versace. According to the mall, it's the second-largest attraction in Florida—second only to Walt Disney World. Although this may sound like an exaggeration, prepare for crowds and to spend a full day here. ✉ *12801 W. Sunrise Blvd., Sunrise* ☎ *954/846–2350* 🌐 *www.simon.com/mall/sawgrass-mills.*

## Activities

### RODEOS

### Davie Pro Rodeo

**RODEO | FAMILY** | South Florida has a surprisingly established cowboy scene, concentrated in the western suburb of Davie. And for decades, the Davie Arena at the Bergeron Rodeo Grounds has hosted the area's riders and ropers. Throughout the year, the rodeo hosts national tours and festivals as well as the annual Southeastern Circuit Finals. Check the website for the exact dates of special events. ✉ *Bergeron Rodeo Grounds,*

*4201 S.W. 65th Way, Davie* ☎ *954/680–8005* ⊕ *davieprorodeo.com.*

# Lauderdale-by-the-Sea

*5 miles north of Fort Lauderdale.*

Just north of Fort Lauderdale proper, the low-rise family resort town of Lauderdale-by-the-Sea boasts shoreline access that's rapidly disappearing in neighboring beach towns. The closest and most convenient of the A1A cities to Fort Lauderdale proper embraces its quaint personality by welcoming guests to a different world, drawing cost-conscious families who are looking for fewer frills and longer stays.

## GETTING HERE AND AROUND

Lauderdale-by-the-Sea is just north of Fort Lauderdale. From Interstate 95, exit at Commercial Boulevard and head east past the Intracoastal Waterway. From U.S. 1 (Federal Highway), go east at Commercial Boulevard. If driving north on State Road A1A, simply continue from Fort Lauderdale Beach.

## ESSENTIALS

**VISITOR INFORMATION Lauderdale-by-the-Sea Chamber of Commerce.** ✉ *4201 N. Ocean Dr., Lauderdale-by-the-Sea* ☎ *954/776–1000* ⊕ *www.lbts.com.*

##  Beaches

### ★ Lauderdale-by-the-Sea Beach

**BEACH | FAMILY |** Preferred by divers and snorkelers, this laid-back beach is a gateway to magnificent coral reefs. When you're not underwater, look up and you'll likely see a pelican flying by. It's a super-relaxing retreat from the buzz of Fort Lauderdale's busier beaches. That said, the southern part of the beach is crowded near the restaurants at the intersection of A1A and Commercial Boulevard. The no-frills hotels and small inns for families and vacationers visiting

for a longer stay are typically filled with Europeans. Look for metered parking around Commercial Boulevard and A1A. **Amenities:** food and drink; lifeguards; parking (fee). **Best for:** family outings; snorkeling; swimming. ✉ *Commercial Blvd. at State Rd. A1A, Lauderdale-by-the-Sea* ⊕ *www.discoverlbts.com/beaches-parks/.*

##  Restaurants

### Aruba Beach Cafe

**$$$ | CARIBBEAN | FAMILY |** This casual beachfront eatery is arguably Lauderdale-by-the-Sea's most famous restaurant. Aruba Beach serves Caribbean-American cuisine, with standouts like conch chowder and conch fritters. **Known for:** Bimini bread with Aruba glaze; nightly live music; Sunday breakfast buffet. $ *Average main: $22* ✉ *1 Commercial Blvd., Lauderdale-by-the-Sea* ☎ *954/776–0001* ⊕ *www.arubabeachcafe.com.*

### ★ LaSpada's Original Hoagies

**$ | AMERICAN | FAMILY |** The crew at this seaside hole-in-the-wall puts on quite a show while assembling their sandwiches—locals rave that this indie chain has the best around. Fill up on the foot-long Monster (ham, turkey, roast beef, and cheese), Mama (turkey and Genoa salami), or hot meatballs marinara. **Known for:** the Monster, a foot-long sandwich with ham, turkey, roast beef, cheese; fresh bread; freshly sliced meats. $ *Average main: $12* ✉ *233 Commercial Blvd., Lauderdale-by-the-Sea* ☎ *954/776–7893* ⊕ *www.laspadashoagies.com* ☞ *There are 4 additional locations in Broward County.*

##  Hotels

### ★ Blue Seas Courtyard

**$$ | B&B/INN | FAMILY |** Husband-and-wife team Marc and Cristie Furth have run this whimsical Mexican-theme motel in Lauderdale-by-the-Sea since 1971. **Pros:** south-of-the-border vibe; friendly owners;

across the street from the beach. **Cons:** no ocean views; no on-site meal; limited number of rooms. $ *Rooms from: $240* ✉ *4525 El Mar Dr., Lauderdale-by-the-Sea* ☎ *954/772–3336* ⊕ *www.blueseascourtyard.com* ⇨ *12 rooms* ⓇⓄⓁ *No Meals.*

### High Noon Beach Resort
$$ | **B&B/INN** | **FAMILY** | This highly rated family-run hotel sits on 300 feet of beachy paradise with plenty of cozy spots, two heated pools, and an atmosphere that keeps visitors coming back for more. **Pros:** directly on the beach; free Wi-Fi; great staff. **Cons:** 45-day notice of cancellation; no maid service on Sunday; no guarantee for room type. $ *Rooms from: $250* ✉ *4424 El Mar Dr., Lauderdale-by-the-Sea* ☎ *954/776–1121* ⊕ *www.highnoonresort.com* ⇨ *41 rooms* ⓇⓄⓁ *No Meals.*

### ★ Plunge Beach Resort
$$ | **HOTEL** | **FAMILY** | Quietly tucked away on the beach, this seaside getaway has four buildings that offer standard rooms, studios, and bungalow suites with kitchenettes and dining areas. **Pros:** full beach service, including water activities; 24-hour fitness center; Wi-Fi throughout property. **Cons:** daily resort fee; limited balconies; main building requires crossing street for pool or beach. $ *Rooms from: $260* ✉ *4660 El Mar Dr., Lauderdale-by-the-Sea* ☎ *754/312–5775* ⊕ *www.plungebeachresort.com* ⇨ *163 rooms* ⓇⓄⓁ *No Meals.*

##  Activities

### Anglins Fishing Pier
**FISHING** | **FAMILY** | A longtime favorite for 24-hour fishing, it's a spot where you may catch snapper, snook, cobia, blue runner, and pompano. It's also the longest pier in South Florida. The on-site bait-and-tackle shop can advise newbies to advanced anglers. ✉ *2 Commercial Blvd., Lauderdale-by-the-Sea* ☎ *954/924–3613* ⊕ *www.boatlessfishing.com/anglins.htm* ▤ *$2 for sightseeing; $7 for adult fishing.*

# Pompano Beach

*3 miles north of Lauderdale-by-the-Sea.*

The high-rise scene resumes as soon as Route A1A enters this town directly north of Lauderdale-by-the-Sea. Sportfishing is big in Pompano Beach, as its name implies, but there's more to beachside attractions than the popular Fisherman's Wharf. Behind a low coral-rock wall, Alsdorf Park (also called the 14th Street boat ramp) extends north and south of the wharf along the road and beach.

### GETTING HERE AND AROUND
From Interstate 95, Pompano Beach exits include Sample Road, Copans Road, and Atlantic Boulevard.

### ESSENTIALS
**VISITOR INFORMATION Greater Pompano Beach Chamber of Commerce.** ✉ *2335 E. Atlantic Blvd., Pompano Beach* ☎ *954/941–2940* ⊕ *www.pompanobeachchamber.com.*

##  Sights

Pompano Beach is undergoing a huge growth spurt thanks to the multimillion-dollar development of the Pompano Beach Fishing Village, home to new hotels, tons of restaurants and shops, and more. To the north, Route A1A traverses the so-called Hillsboro Mile (actually more than 2 miles), a millionaire's row featuring some of Broward's most beautiful and expensive homes. The road runs along a narrow strip of land between the Intracoastal Waterway and the Atlantic Ocean, with bougainvillea and oleander edging the way and yachts docked along the banks. Traffic often moves at a snail's pace, especially in winter, as onlookers gawk at the beauty.

### Hillsboro Inlet Lighthouse
**LIGHTHOUSE** | **FAMILY** | About 2 miles north of Pompano Beach, you'll find a beautiful view across Hillsboro Inlet to a lighthouse, which is often called the

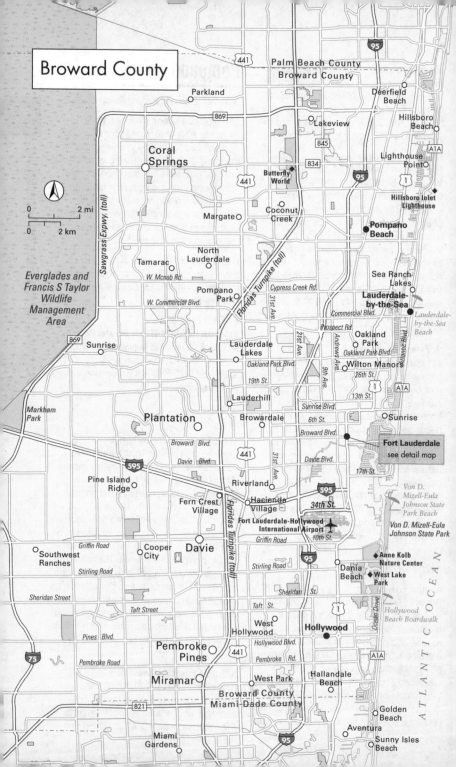

brightest lighthouse in the Southeast and has been used by mariners as a landmark for decades. When at sea you can see its light from almost halfway to the Bahamas. Although the octagonal-pyramid, iron-skeletal tower lighthouse is on private property (inaccessible to the public), it's well worth a peek, even from afar. The Hillsboro Lighthouse Preservation Society offers tours about eight times a year (sometimes on holiday weekends), and these include a boat ride to and from the lighthouse. Visit the society's website for the current schedule and tips on viewing vantage points. Tours cost around $35 per person. ✉ *2801, 907 Hillsboro Mile, Hillsboro Beach* ☎ *954/942–2102* 🌐 *www.hillsborolighthouse.org.*

## 🍴 Restaurants

**★ Beach House Pompano**

**$$$ | AMERICAN | FAMILY** | At this 12,000-square-foot oceanfront restaurant, second-floor stadium seating ensures all diners have ocean views while feasting on dishes from the scratch-made kitchen and wood-fired grill. You can't go wrong with the shucked-to-order oysters, the chef's choice fresh catch, or the cilantro key-lime chicken. **Known for:** amazing ocean views; wood-burning grill; great cocktails. [$] *Average main: $22* ✉ *270 N. Pompano Beach Blvd., Pompano Beach* ☎ *954/607–6530* 🌐 *beachhousepompano.com.*

## 🛏 Hotels

**Cottages by the Ocean**

**$$ | HOTEL | FAMILY** | For families favoring home-style comforts over resort-style amenities, Cottages by the Ocean is one of five beach-area properties run by Beach Vacation Rentals. **Pros:** shops within walking distance; no resort fees (though there are cleaning fees); complimentary Wi-Fi. **Cons:** not directly on beach; no pool; slightly dated decor. [$] *Rooms from: $214* ✉ *3309 S.E. 3rd St., Pompano Beach* ☎ *954/283–1111* 🌐 *4rentbythebeach.com/properties/cottages-by-the-ocean* 🛏 *6 rooms* 🍽 *No Meals.*

**Tru by Hilton Pompano Beach Pier**

**$ | HOTEL | FAMILY** | Just across the street from the Pompano Beach Pier, Tru by Hilton has spacious and clean rooms decorated in bright colors with comfortable Serta mattresses and plenty of natural sunlight (though the blackout curtains in every room come in handy, too). **Pros:** rooftop bar; heated pool and hot tub; near tons of restaurants and the pier. **Cons:** must request housekeeping; not directly on the water; off-site self-parking is $16 per day. [$] *Rooms from: $185* ✉ *200 N. Ocean Blvd., Pompano Beach* ☎ *954/943–4711* 🌐 *www.hilton.com* 🛏 *60 rooms* 🍽 *Free Breakfast.*

## 🏃 Activities

**SS *Copenhagen* Shipwreck**

**SCUBA DIVING** | The wreck of the SS *Copenhagen* lies in 15- to 30-foot depths just outside the second reef on the Pompano Ledge, 3.6 miles south of Hillsboro Inlet. The 325-foot-long steamer's final voyage, from Philadelphia to Havana, began May 20, 1900, ending six days later when the captain—attempting to avoid Gulf currents—crashed into a reef. In 2000, the missing bow section was identified a half mile to the south. The wreck, a haven for colorful fish and corals and a magnet for skin and scuba divers, became Florida's fifth Underwater Archaeological Preserve in 1994 and was listed on the National Register of Historic Places in 2001. Outfitters offer regular trips to the wreck site officially known as the SS *Copenhagen* State Underwater Archaeological Preserve. ✉ *Pompano Beach* 🌐 *museumsinthesea.com/copenhagen/index.htm.*

### FISHING

**Fisher Family Pier**

**FISHING | FAMILY** | After an $11.5 million rebuild, the 900-foot-long pier (formerly

Pompano Beach Pier) boasts shade structures, plenty of seating, Wi-Fi, and an underwater camera that allows for fish watching. The end of the pier is appropriately built into the shape of a Pompano fish. Anglers brag about catching barracuda, jack, and snapper here in the same sitting, along with bluefish, cobia, and, yes, even pompano. ⊠ *222 N. Pompano Beach Blvd., Pompano Beach* ☎ *954/786–4073* ⊕ *parks.pompanobeach-fl.gov/facilities/fisher-family-pier* ☞ *$6 daily fishing rate; 3 rod maximum.*

# Hollywood

*18 miles south of Pompano Beach.*

Hollywood has had several face-lifts to shed its old-school image, but there's still something delightfully retro about the city. New shops, restaurants, and art galleries open at a persistent clip, and the city has continually spiffed up its boardwalk—a wide pedestrian walkway along the beach—where local joggers are as commonplace as sun-seeking snowbirds from the North.

**GETTING HERE AND AROUND**
From Interstate 95, exit east on Sheridan Street or Hollywood Boulevard for Hollywood, or Hallandale Beach Boulevard for either Hollywood or Hallandale.

**ESSENTIALS**
**VISITOR INFORMATION** Hollywood Community Redevelopment Agency. ⊠ *1948 Harrison St., Hollywood* ☎ *954/924–2980* ⊕ *www.hollywoodcra.org.*

 **Sights**

★ **Art and Culture Center/Hollywood**
ARTS CENTER | FAMILY | The Art and Culture Center, which is southeast of Young Circle, has a great reputation for presenting ubercool contemporary art exhibitions and providing the community with educational programming for adults and children. Check online for the latest exhibition schedule. ⊠ *1650 Harrison St., Hollywood* ☎ *954/921–3274* ⊕ *www.artandculturecenter.org* ☜ *$7.*

**ArtsPark at Young Circle**
CITY PARK | FAMILY | In the center of downtown Hollywood, this 10-acre urban park has promenades and green spaces, public art, a huge playground for kids, a state-of-the-art amphitheater, and spaces for educational workshops like weekly glassblowing and jewelry making. There are food trucks and movie nights as well. ⊠ *1 N. Young Cir., Hollywood* ☎ *954/921–3500* ⊕ *www.hollywoodfl. org/65/ArtsPark-at-Young-Circle.*

**West Lake Park and Anne Kolb Nature Center**
NATURE SIGHT | FAMILY | Grab a canoe or kayak, or take a 40-minute guided boat tour at this lakeside park on the Intracoastal Waterway. At more than 1,500 acres, it's one of Florida's largest urban nature facilities. Extensive boardwalks traverse mangrove wetlands that shelter endangered and threatened species. At the Anne Kolb Nature Center, there's a 3,500-gallon aquarium, and a 65-foot observation tower showcases the entire park. The center's exhibit hall also has interactive displays explaining the park's delicate ecosystem. ⊠ *751 Sheridan St., Hollywood* ☎ *954/357–5163* ⊕ *www. visitlauderdale.com/listing/anne-kolb-nature-center/1214/* ☜ *Park: weekdays free, weekends and holidays $1.50.*

 **Beaches**

★ **Dr. Von D. Mizell–Eula Johnson State Park**
BEACH | FAMILY | Formerly known as John U. Lloyd Beach State Park, this 310-acre park was renamed in the 1970s in honor of the duo who led efforts to desegregate the area's beaches. Native sea grapes, gumbo-limbo trees, and other native plants offer shade. Nature trails and a marina are large draws; canoeing on Whiskey Creek is also popular. The

beaches are excellent, but beware of mosquitoes in summer. **Amenities:** ample trails; parking (fee); toilets. **Best for:** solitude; sunrise; water sports. ⊠ 6503 N. Ocean Dr., Dania Beach ☎ 954/923–2833 ⊕ www.floridastateparks.org/mizell ☞ $6 per vehicle.

★ **Hollywood Beach Broadwalk**

BEACH | FAMILY | The name might be Hollywood, but there's nothing hip or chic about Hollywood North Beach Park, which sits at the north end of Hollywood before the 2½-mile pedestrian Broadwalk begins. And this is a good thing. It's an easygoing place to enjoy the sun, sand, and sea. The year-round Dog Beach of Hollywood, between Pershing and Custer Streets, allows canine companions to join the fun a few days a week. Walk along the Broadwalk for a throwback to the 1950s, with mom-and-pop stores and ice cream parlors, where couples go for long strolls and families build sandcastles. The popular stretch has spiffy features like a pristine pedestrian walkway, a concrete bike path, a crushed-shell jogging path, an 18-inch decorative wall separating the Broadwalk from the sand, and places to shower off after a dip. **Amenities:** food and drink; lifeguards; parking (fee); showers; toilets. **Best for:** sunrise; swimming; walking. ⊠ 101 S. Broadwalk, Hollywood ⊕ www.broward.org/Parks/Pages/park.aspx?park=19 ☞ Parking in public lots: $3/hr weekdays and $4/hr weekends.

🍴 **Restaurants**

★ **Jaxson's Ice Cream Parlour & Restaurant**

$$ | AMERICAN | FAMILY | This mid-century landmark whips up malts, shakes, and jumbo sundaes from ice cream that is made on site daily. Founder Monroe Udell's trademarked Kitchen Sink—a small sink full of ice cream, topped by sparklers—is a real hoot for parties. **Known for:** license-plate decor; homemade ice cream; salads and sandwiches. Ⓢ Average main: $15 ⊠ 128 S. Federal Hwy., Dania Beach ☎ 954/923–4445 ⊕ www.jaxsonsicecream.com.

**The Le Tub Saloon**

$$ | AMERICAN | Despite molasses-slow service and an abundance of insects at sundown, this eatery is beloved by locals, and management seemed genuinely appalled when hordes of trend-seeking city slickers started jamming bar stools and tables after GQ and Oprah declared its thick, juicy Angus burgers the best around. Once a Sunoco gas station, this quirky waterside saloon has an enduring affection for claw-foot bathtubs; lunch will run you around $18 (burger $13.50; small fries $5). **Known for:** late-night service; vintage setting; great burgers and key lime pie. Ⓢ Average main: $16 ⊠ 1100 N. Ocean Dr., Hollywood ☎ 954/921–9425 ⊕ www.theletub.com.

**Taverna Opa**

$$$ | GREEK | FAMILY | It's a Greek throwdown every night at this Hollywood institution. Expect a lively night of great eats (including authentic hot and cold mezes and wood-fire-grilled meats and seafood), tabletop dancing, and lots of wine. **Known for:** near Water Taxi stop; celebratory atmosphere; menu of Greek favorites. Ⓢ Average main: $29 ⊠ 410 N. Ocean Dr., Hollywood ☎ 954/929–4010 ⊕ tavernaopa.com/hollywood.

**Villa Romana**

$$$ | ITALIAN | FAMILY | Located in downtown Hollywood, this isn't your typical white-table-cloth Italian restaurant. Sure, there's penne alla vodka, carbonara, and Bolognese (all delicious), but the fun twist is a Romanian menu that features dishes like goulash or sarmalute in foi de varza (minced pork and rice in cabbage leaves served with polenta and sour cream). **Known for:** great braised pork; unexpected Mediterranean and Eastern European flavors; extra-friendly staff. Ⓢ Average main: $22 ⊠ 1909 Hollywood Blvd., Hollywood ☎ 954/251–3698 ⊕ villaromanarestaurant.com.

**Hotels**

### ★ The Diplomat Beach Resort

$$$ | RESORT | FAMILY | This colossal 39-story, contemporary, multitower resort property sits on a 50,000-square-foot swath of Hollywood Beach and has become a destination for fun in the sun and culinary intrigue. **Pros:** coastal chic vibe; excellent dining; incredible ocean views. **Cons:** large complex; numerous conventioneers; expensive rates. ⓢ *Rooms from: $350* ⊠ *3555 S. Ocean Dr., Hollywood* ☎ *954/602–6000* ⊕ *www.diplomatresort. com* ⊋ *1000 rooms* ⦿ *No Meals.*

### ★ The Guitar Hotel at Seminole Hard Rock Hollywood

$$$ | HOTEL | Beaming with LED light shows that can be seen from miles away, this prominent 450-foot guitar-shaped hotel is a magnet for folks looking for Las Vegas–style entertainment (i.e., casinos that never close, clubbing, and hedonism). **Pros:** limitless entertainment; solid bars and restaurants; 24/7 gaming action. **Cons:** in an unsavory neighborhood; extra busy on the weekends; rental car necessary. ⓢ *Rooms from: $379* ⊠ *1 Seminole Way, Hollywood* ☎ *866/502–7529* ⊕ *www.seminolehardrockhollywood. com/hotel/the-guitar-hotel* ⊋ *638 rooms* ⦿ *No Meals.*

### Margaritaville Beach Resort

$$$ | RESORT | FAMILY | Inspired by legendary singer Jimmy Buffett's lifelong search for paradise, this tropical resort is at once accessible and upscale, with an attention to detail that sets it apart from many of its neighbors. **Pros:** oceanfront location; fun water activities; daily live entertainment. **Cons:** the surrounding area isn't very upscale; touristy vibe; must be a Jimmy Buffett fan. ⓢ *Rooms from: $340* ⊠ *1111 N. Ocean Dr., Hollywood* ☎ *954/874–4444* ⊕ *www.margaritaville-hollywoodbeachresort.com* ⊋ *349 rooms* ⦿ *No Meals.*

 **Nightlife**

### ★ Seminole Hard Rock Hotel & Casino Hollywood

CAFÉS | Seminole Hard Rock Hotel & Casino Hollywood is a Vegas-inspired gaming and entertainment complex in a fairly forlorn area of town. Once inside the Hard Rock fortress, you'll feel the excitement immediately. In addition to the AAA Four Diamond hotel, there's a monster casino, and a 7,000-seat performance venue (Hard Rock Live), plus dozens of restaurants, bars, and nightclubs. **■ TIP→ The Seminole Hard Rock Hotel & Casino is not to be confused with its neighbor, the Seminole Classic Casino.** ⊠ *1 Seminole Way, Hollywood* ☎ *866/502–7529* ⊕ *www. seminolehardrockhollywood.com.*

 **Shopping**

### ★ The Shops at Pembroke Gardens

SHOPPING CENTER | FAMILY | The Shops at Pembroke Gardens is an outdoor oasis with a variety of shops, restaurants, salons, and spas. From shops like White House Black Market and Sephora to local dining options like RA Sushi and Village Tavern, it's a popular hangout among locals and tourists. ⊠ *527 S.W. 145th Terr., Pembroke Pines* ☎ *954/450–1580* ⊕ *www.pembrokegardens.com.*

### 🏃 **Activities**

#### FISHING

**Chasin Finz Sport Fishing Charters**

FISHING | Go deep-sea fishing right out of Hollywood on Chasin Finz's 53-foot Hatteras sport fishing yacht, heading through the Intracoastal and through Port Everglades. On a half-day or full-day trip, you can expect to reel in kingfish, tuna, wahoo, and marlin while being guided by Captain Josh. Charters start at $200 per half-day per person or $100 per hour for private parties. ⊠ *1318 N. Ocean Dr., Hollywood* ☎ *754/800–9732* ⊕ *www. chasin-finz.com.*

# Chapter 7

# PALM BEACH AND THE TREASURE COAST

7

Updated by
Sara Liss

| ◉ Sights | 🍴 Restaurants | 🛏 Hotels | 🛍 Shopping | 🍸 Nightlife |
|---|---|---|---|---|
| ★★★★☆ | ★★★★☆ | ★★★★★ | ★★★★☆ | ★★☆☆☆ |

# WELCOME TO PALM BEACH AND THE TREASURE COAST

## TOP REASONS TO GO

★ **Exquisite resorts:** Two grandes dames, The Breakers and The Boca Raton, perpetually draw the rich, the famous, and anyone else who can afford the luxury. Eau Palm Beach and Four Seasons sparkle with service fit for royalty.

★ **Beautiful beaches:** From Jupiter, where dogs run free, to Stuart's tubular waves, to the broad stretches of sand in Delray Beach and Boca Raton, swimmers, surfers, sunbathers—and sea turtles looking for a place to hatch their eggs—all find happiness.

★ **Top-notch golf:** The Champion and re-envisioned The Fazio courses at PGA National Resort are world-renowned; pros sharpen up at PGA Village.

★ **Horse around:** Wellington, with its popular polo season, is often called the winter equestrian capital of the world.

★ **Excellent fishing:** The Atlantic Ocean, teeming with kingfish, sailfish, and wahoo, is a treasure chest for anglers.

1 **Palm Beach.** Tony beach town with luxury resorts and beautiful mansions.

2 **West Palm Beach.** It's not actually on the beach but has great arts and shopping scenes.

3 **Lake Worth.** Stop for its charming, artsy center.

4 **Delray Beach.** Its lively downtown is blocks from the ocean.

5 **Boca Raton.** Modernity mixes with historic buildings.

6 **Palm Beach Gardens.** Golfers love PGA National Resort and Spa.

7 **Singer Island.** Easy access to snorkeling at Peanut Island.

8 **Juno Beach.** Famous for its sea turtles.

9 **Jupiter and Vicinity.** Calm respite with a rugged coastline.

10 **Stuart and Jensen Beach.** Charming historic district and beach.

11 **Fort Pierce and Port St. Lucie.** Ample fishing and surfing.

12 **Vero Beach.** Cosmopolitan yet understated beach town.

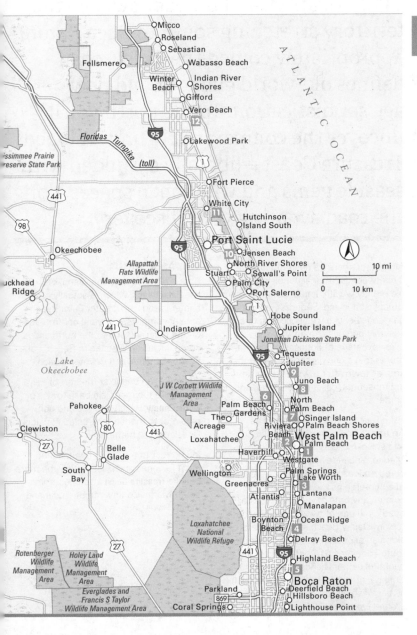

A golden stretch of the Atlantic shore, the Palm Beach area resists categorization, and for good reason: the territory stretching south to Boca Raton, appropriately coined the Gold Coast, defines old-world glamour and new-age sophistication. To the north you'll uncover the comparatively undeveloped Treasure Coast—liberally sprinkled with seaside gems and wide-open spaces along the road awaiting your discovery.

Altogether, there's a delightful disparity between Palm Beach, pulsing with old-money wealth, and under-the-radar Hutchinson Island. Seductive as the gorgeous beaches, eclectic dining, and leisurely pursuits can be, you should also take advantage of flourishing commitments to historic preservation and the arts, as town after town yields intriguing museums, galleries, theaters, and gardens.

Palm Beach, proud of its status as America's first luxe resort destination and still glimmering with its trademark Mediterranean-revival mansions, manicured hedges, and highbrow shops, can rule supreme as the focal point for your sojourn any time of year. From there, head off in one of two directions: south toward Delray Beach and Boca Raton along an especially scenic estate-dotted route known as A1A or back north to the beautiful barrier islands of the Treasure Coast. For rustic inland activities, such as bass fishing and biking atop the dike around Lake Okeechobee, head west.

## MAJOR REGIONS

About 70 miles north of Miami, off I–95, lies **Palm Beach,** which is actually on a barrier island. The greater Palm Beach area encompasses several communities on the mainland and to the north and south, including West Palm Beach, Lake Worth, Lantana, and Boynton Beach.

Just over the bridge at the Port of Palm Beach are the more laid-back towns of **North County,** which families and golf pros, not to mention the celebs on Jupiter Island, call home.

In contrast to the glitzy, uberplanned Palm Beaches and Boca Raton, the more bucolic **Treasure Coast** stretches from south Martin County into St. Lucie and Indian River Counties.

# Planning

## When to Go

The weather is optimal from November through May, but the trade-off is that roads, hotels, and restaurants are more crowded and prices higher. If the scene is what you're after, try the early weeks of December when the "season" isn't yet in full swing. But be warned that after Easter, the crowd relocates to the Hamptons, and Palm Beach feels like another universe. For some that's a blessing—and a great time to take advantage of lower summer lodging rates and dining deals—but you'll need to bring your tolerance for heat, humidity, and afternoon downpours.

## Getting Here and Around

### AIR

Palm Beach International Airport (PBI) is in West Palm, but it's possible (and sometimes cheaper) to fly to Fort Lauderdale (FLL), Miami (MIA), or Orlando (MCO). Do rent a car if you plan on exploring. Scenic Route A1A, also called Ocean Boulevard or Ocean Drive, depending on where you are, ventures out onto the barrier islands. Interstate 95 runs parallel to U.S. 1, a main north–south thoroughfare in the region (also known as Federal Highway), but a few miles inland.

**AIRPORT Palm Beach International Airport.** (PBI) ⊠ 1000 Turnage Blvd., West Palm Beach ⊹ From I-95, use airport flyover exit; from Florida's Tpke., use Southern Blvd. exit and drive east to airport exit ☎ 561/471–7420 ⊕ www.pbia.org.

### BUS

The county's bus service, Palm Tran, runs two routes (Nos. 44 and 40) that offer daily service connecting the airport, the Tri-Rail stop near it, and locations in central West Palm Beach. A network of 34 routes joins towns all across the area; it's $5 for a day pass. The free Downtown Trolley connects the West Palm Beach Amtrak station and the Tri-Rail stop in West Palm on its Green Line. Its Yellow Line makes continuous loops down Clematis Street, the city's main stretch of restaurants and watering holes interspersed with stores, and through The Square (formerly CityPlace), a shopping-dining-theater district, and to the Kravis Center. Hop on and off at any of the stops. The trolley's Yellow Line runs Sunday to Wednesday 11–9 and Thursday to Saturday 11–11. The trolley's Green Line, which stretches farther east, west, and south, and connects to Tri-Rail and Amtrak, runs weekdays 7–7, Saturday 9–7, and Sunday 11–7. A Blue Line, operating year-round, runs from downtown West Palm Beach to Northwood Village and the Palm Beach Outlets mall. Times are Thursday–Saturday, 11–10.

**CONTACTS Downtown Trolley.** ☎ 561/833–8873 ⊕ www.downtownwpb.com/trolley/. **Palm Tran.** ☎ 561/841–4287 ⊕ www.pbcgov.com/palmtran.

### TAXI

Several taxi companies and limousine services serve the area. The ride-sharing services Uber and Lyft are accessible as apps from your phone.

**CONTACTS Limos of Palm Beach.** ⊠ West Palm Beach ☎ 561/459–7128 ⊕ limosofpalmbeach.com.

### TRAIN

Amtrak stops daily in West Palm Beach. The station is at the same location as the Tri-Rail stop, so the same free shuttle, the Downtown Trolley, is available (via the trolley's Green Line).

Tri-Rail Commuter Service is a rail system with 18 stops altogether between West Palm Beach and Miami; tickets can be purchased at each stop, and a one-way trip from the first to the last point is $6.90 weekdays, $5 weekends. Three stations—West Palm Beach, Lake Worth, and Boca—have free shuttles to their downtowns, and taxis are on call at others.

A high-speed train line, the Brightline, connects downtown Miami to Fort Lauderdale and West Palm Beach in 30 and 60 minutes respectively.

**CONTACTS Amtrak.** ☎ 800/872–7245 ⊕ www.amtrak.com. **Brightline.** ⊠ Miami Central Station, 600 NW 1st Ave., Downtown ☎ 888/448–8491 ⊕ www.gobrightline.com. **Tri-Rail.** ☎ 800/874–7245 ⊕ www.tri-rail.com.

# Hotels

Palm Beach has a number of smaller hotels in addition to the famous Breakers. Lower-priced hotels and bed-and-breakfasts can be found in West Palm Beach, Palm Beach Gardens, and Lake Worth. Heading south, the ocean-side town of Manalapan has Eau Palm Beach Resort & Spa. The Seagate Hotel & Spa sparkles in Delray Beach, and the posh The Boca Raton lines the superlative swath of shoreline in Boca Raton. In the opposite direction there's the PGA National Resort & Spa, and on the opposite side of town on the ocean is the Marriott on Singer Island, a well-kept secret for spacious, sleek suites. Even farther north, Vero Beach has a collection of luxury boutique hotels, as well as more modest options along the Treasure Coast. To the west, towns close to Lake Okeechobee offer country-inn accommodations geared to bass-fishing pros.

# Restaurants

Numerous elegant establishments offer upscale American and international cuisine, but the area also is chock-full of casual waterfront spots serving affordable burgers and fresh seafood feasts. Snapper and grouper are especially popular here, along with the ubiquitous shrimp.

Happy hours and early-bird menus, Florida hallmarks, are great for budget-minded travelers, with several dinner entrées at reduced prices offered during certain hours, usually before 5 or 6.

*Restaurant prices are the average cost of a main course at dinner or, if dinner is not served, at lunch. Hotel prices are the lowest cost of a standard double room in high season. Hotel and restaurant reviews have been shortened. For full information, visit Fodors.com.*

| What It Costs in U.S. Dollars | | | |
|---|---|---|---|
| $ | $$ | $$$ | $$$$ |
| **RESTAURANTS** | | | |
| under $26 | $26–$30 | $31–$35 | over $35 |
| **HOTELS** | | | |
| under $200 | $200–$300 | $301–$400 | over $400 |

# Visitor Information

**CONTACTS Discover the Palm Beaches.** ⊠ 1555 Palm Beach Lakes Blvd., Suite 800, West Palm Beach ☎ 800/554–7256 ⊕ www.thepalmbeaches.com.

# Palm Beach

*70 miles north of Miami, off I–95.*

Long reigning as the place where the crème de la crème go to shake off winter's chill, Palm Beach continues to be a seasonal hotbed of platinum-grade consumption. It's been the winter address for heirs of the iconic Rockefeller, Vanderbilt, Colgate, Post, Kellogg, and Kennedy families. Strict laws govern everything from building to landscaping, and not so much as a pool awning gets added without a town council nod. Only three bridges allow entry, and huge tour buses are a no-no.

All this fabled atmosphere started with Henry Morrison Flagler, Florida's premier developer, and cofounder, along with John D. Rockefeller, of Standard Oil. No sooner did Flagler bring the railroad to Florida in the 1890s than he erected the famed Royal Poinciana and Breakers hotels. Rail access sent real-estate prices soaring, and ever since, princely sums have been forked over for personal stationery engraved with 33480, the zip code of Palm Beach (which didn't actually get its status as an independent municipality until 1911). Setting the tone in this town of unparalleled Florida opulence is the ornate architectural work of Addison Mizner, who began designing homes and public buildings here in the 1920s and whose Moorish-Gothic Mediterranean-revival style has influenced virtually all landmarks.

But the greater Palm Beach area is much larger and encompasses several communities on the mainland and to the north and south. To provide Palm Beach with servants and other workers, Flagler created an off-island community across the Intracoastal Waterway (also referred to as Lake Worth in these parts). West Palm Beach, now cosmopolitan and noteworthy in its own right, evolved into an economically vibrant business hub and a sprawling playground with some of the best nightlife and cultural attractions around, including the glittering Kravis Center for the Performing Arts, the region's principal entertainment venue. The mammoth Palm Beach County Judicial Center and Courthouse and the State Administrative Building underscore the breadth of the city's governmental and corporate activity.

The burgeoning equestrian development of Wellington, with its horse shows and polo matches, lies a little more than 10 miles west of downtown and is the site of much of the county's growth.

Spreading southward from the Palm Beach/West Palm Beach nucleus set between the two bridges that flow from Royal Poinciana Way and Royal Palm Way into Flagler Drive on the mainland are small cities like Lake Worth, with its charming artsy center, Lantana, and Manalapan (home to the fabulous Eau Palm Beach resort, formerly the Ritz-Carlton Palm Beach). All three have turf that's technically on the same island as Palm Beach, and at its bottom edge across the inlet is Boynton Beach, a 20-minute drive from Worth Avenue.

West Palm Beach itself doesn't have any beaches, so locals and guests hop over to Palm Beach or any of the communities just mentioned—or they head north, where there are also some great beaches.

### GETTING HERE AND AROUND

Palm Beach is 70 miles north of Miami (a 90-minute trip with traffic). To access Palm Beach off Interstate 95, exit east at Southern Boulevard, Belvedere Road, or Okeechobee Boulevard. To drive from Palm Beach to Lake Worth, Lantana, Manalapan, and Boynton Beach, head south on Ocean Boulevard/Route A1A; Lake Worth is roughly 6 miles south, and Boynton is another 6. Similarly, to reach them from West Palm Beach, take U.S. 1 or Interstate 95. To travel between Palm Beach and Singer Island, you must cross over to West Palm before returning to the beach. Once there, go north on U.S. 1 and then cut over on Blue Heron Boulevard/Route 708. If coming straight from the airport or somewhere farther west, take Interstate 95 up to the same exit and proceed east. The main drag in Palm Beach Gardens is PGA Boulevard/Route 786, which is 4 miles north on U.S. 1 and Interstate 95; A1A merges with it as it exits the top part of Singer Island. Continue on A1A to reach Juno Beach and Jupiter.

## ◉ Sights

Most streets around major attractions and commercial zones have free parking as well as metered spaces. If you can

Draped in European elegance, The Breakers in Palm Beach sits on 140 acres along the oceanfront.

stake out a place between a Rolls-Royce and a Bentley, do so, but beware of the "Parking by Permit Only" signs, as a $50 ticket might take the shine off your spot. Better yet, if you plan to spend an entire afternoon strolling Worth Avenue, park in the Apollo lot behind Tiffany's, midway off Worth on Hibiscus; some stores will validate your parking ticket.

### Bethesda-by-the-Sea

**CHURCH** | This Gothic-style Episcopal church had a claim to fame upon its creation in 1926: it was built by the first Protestant congregation in southeast Florida. Church lecture tours, covering Bethesda's history, architecture, and more, are offered at 12:05 on the second and fourth Sunday each month from September to mid-May (excluding December) and at 11:15 on the fourth Sunday each month from the end of May to August. Also notable are the annual Boar's Head and Yule Log festivals in January. Adjacent is the formal, ornamental Cluett Memorial Garden. ⊠ *141 S. County Rd., Palm Beach* ☎ *561/655–4554* ⊕ *www.bbts.org* ✉ *Free.*

### ★ The Breakers

**HOTEL** | Built by Henry Flagler in 1896 and rebuilt by his descendants after a 1925 fire, this magnificent Italian Renaissance–style resort helped launch Florida tourism with its Gilded Age opulence, attracting influential wealthy Northerners to the state. The hotel, still owned by Flagler's heirs, is a must-see even if you aren't staying here. Walk through the 200-foot-long lobby, which has soaring arched ceilings painted by 72 Italian artisans and hung with crystal chandeliers. Meet for a drink and a round of eclectic small plates at the HMF, one of the most beautiful bars in the state.

■ TIP→ **Book a pampering spa treatment or dine at the popular oceanfront Seafood Bar. The $35 parking fee is waived if you spend at least $35 anywhere in the hotel (just have your ticket validated).** ⊠ *1 S. County Rd., Palm Beach* ☎ *561/655–6611* ⊕ *www. thebreakers.com.*

# The Mansions of Palm Beach

Whether you have expensive taste or you just like to see how the other half lives, no trip to the island is complete without gawking at the megamansions lining its perfectly manicured streets.

No one is more associated with how the island took shape than Addison Mizner, architect extraordinaire and society darling of the 1920s. At the height of his career, Mizner designed more than 50 Palm Beach villas and Florida mansions for the nation's leading social families. However, Mizner did not do it alone. A "fab four" was really the force behind the residential streets as they appear today: Mizner, Maurice Fatio, Marion Sims Wyeth, and John Volk.

The four architects dabbled in different genres, some more so than others, but the unmissable style is Mediterranean revival, a Palm Beach hallmark mix of stucco walls, Spanish red-tile roofs, Italianate towers, Moorish-Gothic carvings, and the uniquely Floridian use of coquina, a grayish porous limestone made of coral rock with fossil-like imprints of shells. Mizner had quite the repertoire of signature elements, including using differently sized and shaped windows on one facade, blue tile work inside and out, and tiered roof lines (instead of one straight-sloping panel across, having several sections overlap like scales on a fish).

In 1979 the Landmark Preservation Commission was formed to combat the loss of the Town of Palm Beach's historic resources, and over the years its list has grown to include about 350 landmarked properties, sites, and vistas (look for small, oval-shape bronze plaques beside house numbers.) Additional properties have been designated as historically significant, to preserve homes that contribute to the charm and character of their neighborhoods.

The majority of preserved estates are clustered in three sections: along Worth Avenue, the few blocks of South County Road after crossing Worth and the streets shooting off it, and the 5-mile stretch of South Ocean Boulevard from Barton Avenue to near Phipps Ocean Park, where the condos begin cropping up.

If 10 miles of riding on a bike while cars zip around you isn't intimidating, a two-wheeled trip may be the best way to fully take in the beauty of the mansions and surrounding scenery. Otherwise, driving is a good alternative. Just be mindful that Ocean Boulevard is a one-lane road, so you can't go too slowly, especially at peak travel times. If gossip is more your speed, book Leslie Diver's Island Living Tours (☎ 561/309–5790); she's one of the town's leading experts on architecture *and* dish, both past and present.

**Top Self-Guided Stops:** (1) Casa de Leoni (450 Worth Ave., Addison Mizner); (2) Villa des Cygnes (456 Worth Ave., Addison Mizner and Marion Sims Wyeth); (3) Horgacito (17 Golfview Rd., Marion Sims Wyeth); (4) (220 and 252 El Bravo Way, John Volk); (5) (126 S. Ocean Blvd., Marion Sims Wyeth); (6) El Solano (720 S. Ocean Blvd., Addison Mizner); (7) Casa Nana (780 S. Ocean Blvd., Addison Mizner); (8) 920 and 930 S. Ocean Blvd., Maurice Fatio); (9) Il Palmetto (1500 S. Ocean Blvd., Maurice Fatio).

## El Solano

**HISTORIC HOME** | No Palm Beach mansion better represents the town's luminous legacy than the Spanish-style home built by Addison Mizner as his own residence in 1925. Mizner later sold El Solano to Harold Vanderbilt, and the property was long a favorite among socialites for parties and photo shoots. Vanderbilt held many a gala fundraiser here. Beatle John Lennon and his wife, Yoko Ono, bought it less than a year before Lennon's death. It's still privately owned and not open to the public, but it's well worth a drive-by on any self-guided Palm Beach mansion tour. ⊠ *720 S. Ocean Blvd., Palm Beach.*

## ★ Henry Morrison Flagler Museum

**HISTORIC HOME** | The worldly sophistication of Florida's Gilded Age lives on at Whitehall, the plush 55-room "marble palace" Henry Flagler commissioned in 1901 for his third wife, Mary Lily Kenan. Architects John Carrère and Thomas Hastings were instructed to create the finest home imaginable—and they outdid themselves. Whitehall rivals the grandeur of European palaces and has an entrance hall with a baroque ceiling similar to Louis XIV's Versailles. Here you'll see original furnishings; a hidden staircase Flagler used to sneak from his bedroom to the billiards room; an art collection; a 1,200-pipe organ; and Florida East Coast Railway exhibits, along with Flagler's personal railcar, No. 91, showcased in an 8,000-square-foot Beaux Arts–style pavilion behind the mansion. Docent-led tours and audio tours are included with admission. The museum's Café des Beaux-Arts, open from Thanksgiving through mid-April, offers a Gilded Age–style early afternoon tea for $60 (11:30 am–2:30 pm); the price includes museum admission. ⊠ *1 Whitehall Way, Palm Beach* ☎ *561/655–2833* ⊕ *www.flaglermuseum.us* 🗺 *$26.*

## Society of the Four Arts

**ARTS CENTER | FAMILY** | Despite widespread misconceptions of its members-only exclusivity, this privately endowed institution—founded in 1936 to encourage appreciation of art, music, drama, and literature—is funded for public enjoyment. The Esther B. O'Keeffe gallery building artfully melds an exhibition hall that houses traveling exhibits with a 700-seat theater. A library designed by prominent Mizner-peer Maurice Fatio, a children's library, a botanical garden, and the Philip Hulitar Sculpture Garden round out the facilities and are open daily. ⊠ *2 Four Arts Plaza, Palm Beach* ☎ *561/655–7227* ⊕ *www.fourarts.org* 🗺 *$5 gallery; special program costs vary.*

## ★ Worth Avenue

**PEDESTRIAN MALL** | Called "The Avenue" by Palm Beachers, this half-mile-long street is synonymous with exclusive shopping. Nostalgia lovers recall an era when faces or names served as charge cards, purchases were delivered home before customers returned from lunch, and bills were sent directly to private accountants. Times have changed, but a stroll amid the Spanish-accented buildings, many designed by Addison Mizner, offers a tantalizing taste of the island's ongoing commitment to elegant consumerism. Explore the labyrinth of nine pedestrian "vias" off each side that wind past boutiques, tiny plazas, bubbling fountains, and bougainvillea-festooned balconies; this is where the smaller, unique shops are. The Worth Avenue Association holds historic walking tours on Wednesday at 10:30 am during "the season" (December through April). The $25 fee benefits local nonprofit organizations. ⊠ *Worth Ave., Palm Beach* ✛ *Between Cocoanut Row and S. Ocean Blvd.* ☎ *561/659–6909* ⊕ *www.worth-avenue.com.*

##  Beaches

## Phipps Ocean Park

**BEACH** | About 2 miles south of "Billionaire's Row" on Ocean Boulevard sits this public oceanside park, with two metered parking lots separated by a fire station. There are four entry points to the beach, but the north side is better for beach-goers. At the southern entrance, there is a six-court tennis facility. The beach is narrow and has natural rock formations dotting the shoreline, making it ideal for snorkelers. There are picnic tables and grills on site, as well as the Little Red Schoolhouse, an 1886 landmark that hosts educational workshops for local kids. If a long walk floats your boat, venture north to see the megamansions, but don't go too far inland, because private property starts at the high-tide line. Parking is metered and time limits strictly enforced. There's a two-hour time limit for free parking—but read the meter carefully: it's valid only during certain hours at some spots. **Amenities:** lifeguards; parking (no fee); showers; toilets. **Best for:** solitude; walking. ⊠ *2201 S. Ocean Blvd., Palm Beach* ☎ *561/227–6450, 561/227–6450 tennis reservations* ⊕ *wpbparks.com* 🎫 *Free.*

**Town of Palm Beach Municipal Beach**

BEACH | You know you're here if you see Palm Beach's younger generation frolicking on the sands and locals setting up chairs as the sun reflects off their gleaming white veneers. The Worth Avenue clock tower is within sight, but the gateways to the sand are actually on Chilean Avenue, Brazilian Avenue, and Gulfstream Road. It's definitely the most central and longest lifeguarded strip open to everyone and a popular choice for hotel guests from the Colony, Chester-field, and Brazilian Court. Lifeguards are present from Brazilian Avenue down to Chilean Avenue. It's also BYOC (bring your own chair). You'll find no water-sports or food vendors here; however, casual eateries are a quick walk away. Metered spots line A1A. **Amenities:** life-guards; showers. **Best for:** sunset; swim-ming. ⊠ *S. Ocean Blvd., Palm Beach* ✛ *From Brazilian Ave. to Gulfstream Rd.* ☎ *561/838–5483 beach patrol* ⊕ *www. thepalmbeaches.com.*

## 🍴 Restaurants

**Almond**

$$ | AMERICAN | With an original location in Bridgehampton, New York, this Palm Beach outpost has garnered a loyal local following for its artisanal, market-driv-en menu featuring updated takes on classic French cuisine and international street food. Chef Jason Weiner sources produce locally from friends and grow-ers, such as Kai-Kai Farm and Swank Specialty Produce, to create dishes that are flavorful and memorable. **Known for:** brunch; nightly specials; outdoor seating on Royal Poinciana Way. Ⓢ *Average main: $29* ⊠ *207 Royal Poinciana Way, Palm Beach* ☎ *561/355-5080* ⊕ *almondrestau-rant.com/lens_galleries/palmbeach.*

★ **bûccan**

$$$ | ECLECTIC | An antidote to the some-times stuffy and "jackets-encouraged" atmosphere of most restaurants on the island, chef-owner Clay Conley's ode to eclectic American cuisine neatly straddles the line between fine dining and exciting gastropub. The restaurant attracts both old money and the younger set, with a buzzing bar-and-lounge scene and an open kitchen showcasing the culinary acrobatics on display. **Known for:** small sharing plates; hamachi tiradito; short-rib empanadas. Ⓢ *Average main: $32* ⊠ *350 S. County Rd., Palm Beach* ☎ *561/833–3450* ⊕ *www.buccanpalm-beach.com* ☾ *No lunch.*

★ **Café Boulud**

$$$$ | FRENCH | Palm Beach socialites just can't get enough of this prized restaurant by celebrated chef Daniel Boulud. This posh, French-American venue in the Brazilian Court hotel is casual yet elegant with a large and inviting bar that hosts a daily happy hour and a plush dining room that features a seashell-clad ceiling. **Known for:** house-cured charcuterie; Dover sole; an extensive wine list. Ⓢ *Av-erage main: $38* ⊠ *The Brazilian Court Hotel & Beach Club, 301 Australian Ave.,*

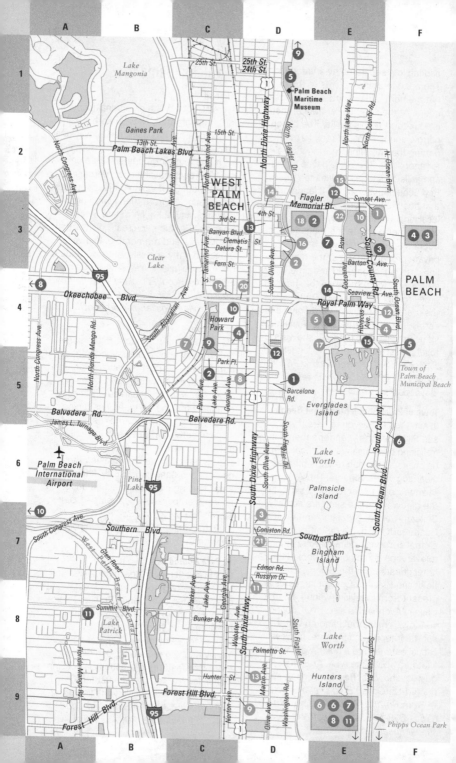

# Palm Beach and West Palm Beach

ATLANTIC OCEAN

**KEY**

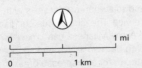

① Sights
① Restaurants
① Hotels

0 |———————| 1 mi
0 |———————| 1 km

*Palm Beach* ☎ *561/655–6060* 🌐 *www.cafeboulud.com.*

★ **Florie's**

**$$$$ | MEDITERRANEAN** | Led by decorated chef Mauro Colagreco of France's famed Mirazur, Florie's offers Mediterranean cuisine along with a wine program focused on sustainable winegrowing practices. The seasonally changing menu emphasizes dishes baked in the wood-fired oven along with lighter dishes like locally made *burrata* served with citrus salad, basil, coriander, raisins, and Sicilian pistachio, followed by desserts like white chocolate mousse with Florida passion fruit sorbet and coulis. **Known for:** seared snapper; outdoor patio with pool and beach views; seasonal ingredients. [$] *Average main: $39* ✉ *2800 S Ocean Blvd., Palm Beach* ☎ *561/533-3750* 🌐 *www.floriespb.com.*

★ **Henry's Palm Beach**

**$$ | AMERICAN** | Named after Florida visionary and resort founder Henry M. Flagler, this swanky spot is part of the culinary collection of The Breakers Palm Beach and features elevated comfort food like lobster rolls, chicken pot pie, and a daily homemade pasta, along with sophisticated cocktails. Located just a few minutes from the resort on Royal Poinciana Way, it is situated at Via Flagler by The Breakers and features a handsome bar with a colored mosaic limestone base and plum and gold leather bar stools. **Known for:** luxe vintage feel; weekend brunch; double-patty burger and strong cocktails. [$] *Average main: $28* ✉ *229 Royal Poinciana Way, Palm Beach* ☎ *561/206–1896* 🌐 *www.thebreakers.com/dining/henryspalmbeach* ⏲ *Closed Tues.*

★ **La Goulue**

**$$$$ | FRENCH** | The Palm Beach outpost of the famed New York City French restaurant, this shiny brasserie gets busy (and loud) on the weekends, when locals in blazers dine on bistro classics like onion soup gratiné and steak tartare. The dining room looks and feels like its Gallic sibling, with Majorelle chandeliers, a pewter bar, oak paneling, and brown banquettes. **Known for:** attentive service; cheese soufflé; prime rib special on Wednesday and Sunday. [$] *Average main: $39* ✉ *288 S County Rd., Palm Beach* ☎ *561/284-6292* 🌐 *www.lagouluepalmbeach.com.*

**PB Catch**

**$$$ | SEAFOOD** | As the name implies, it's all about fins and shells here, including the live ones that entertain diners in their tanks in the modern dining room. The menu includes a raw bar with a good selection of raw (or grilled) oysters and clams and the chef's "seacuterie" platter, a build-your-own sampler of such choices as salmon pastrami, citrus-cured fluke, cured sea bass, or octopus torchon. **Known for:** in-house cured fish; shellfish tower from the raw bar; craft cocktails. [$] *Average main: $35* ✉ *251 Sunrise Blvd., Palm Beach* ☎ *561/655–5558* 🌐 *www.pbcatch.com.*

**Pizza Al Fresco**

**$ | PIZZA** | The hidden-garden setting is the secret to the success of this European-style pizzeria, where you can dine under a canopy of century-old banyans in an intimate courtyard. Specialties are 12-inch hand-tossed brick-oven pizzas with toppings such as prosciutto, arugula, and caviar. **Known for:** caviar-and-smoked-salmon pizza; fresh salads; pet-friendly garden setting. [$] *Average main: $19* ✉ *14 Via Mizner, at Worth Ave., Palm Beach* ✣ *Tucked in a courtyard off Worth Ave.* ☎ *561/832–0032* 🌐 *www.pizzaalfresco.com.*

★ **Sant Ambroeus**

**$ | ITALIAN** | An outpost of the famed New York Italian spot, this chic café churns out crispy pizzas, delicate pasta dishes, and to-swoon-for desserts with polished service. The vibe is '60s era glam meets dreamy Milanese café, making it a hit with both socialites and shoppers, who stop in for an espresso break in between jaunts to the boutiques at Royal Poinciana Plaza. **Known for:** heavenly cacio e pepe; opulent decor; gelato. ⓢ *Average main: $24 ⊠ 340 Royal Poinciana Way, Palm Beach ☎ 561/285–7990 ⊕ www. santambroeus.com.*

 **Hotels**

### ★ The Brazilian Court Hotel

**$$$$ | HOTEL |** This posh boutique hotel, stomping ground of Florida's well-heeled, is full of historic touches and creature comforts—from its yellow facade with dramatic white-draped entry to modern draws like the renowned spa and Daniel Boulud restaurant. **Pros:** stylish and hip local crowd; charming courtyard; free beach shuttle. **Cons:** small fitness center; nondescript pool; 10-minute ride to ocean and suggested 24-hour advance reservation for shuttle. ⓢ *Rooms from: $609 ⊠ 301 Australian Ave., Palm Beach ☎ 561/655–7740 ⊕ www.thebrazilian-court.com ⇌ 80 rooms ⦿l No Meals.*

### ★ The Breakers Palm Beach

**$$$$ | RESORT | FAMILY |** More than an opulent hotel, The Breakers is a legendary 140-acre self-contained jewel of a resort built in a Mediterranean style and loaded with amenities, from a 20,000-square-foot luxury spa and grandiose beach club with four pools and a half-mile private beach to 10 tennis courts, croquet courts, and two 18-hole golf courses. **Pros:** impeccable attention to detail; beautiful room views; extensive activities for families. **Cons:** big price tag; short drive to reach off-property attractions; pools can get crowded. ⓢ *Rooms from: $699 ⊠ 1 S. County Rd., Palm Beach ☎ 561/655–6611, 888/273–2537 ⊕ www. thebreakers.com ⇌ 538 rooms ⦿l No Meals.*

### ★ The Colony

**$$$$ | HOTEL |** This exuberant and undeniably charming British-colonial-style hotel has spacious suites and chic decor and sits in a particularly convenient location, just one block from Worth Avenue and one block from a pretty beach on the Atlantic Ocean. **Pros:** unbeatable location; gorgeous decor; luxe touches like pillow-top mattresses and beach butler service. **Cons:** lobby is small; elevators are tight; beach is a stroll away. ⓢ *Rooms from: $600 ⊠ 155 Hammon Ave. ☎ 561/655–5430, 800/521–5525 ⊕ www. thecolonypalmbeach.com ⇌ 90 rooms ⦿l No Meals.*

### ★ Eau Palm Beach

**$$$$ | RESORT | FAMILY |** In the coastal town of Manalapan (just south of Palm Beach), this sublime, glamorous destination resort (formerly the Ritz-Carlton) showcases a newer, younger face of luxury, including a 3,000-square-foot oceanfront terrace, two sleek pools, a huge fitness center, and a deluxe spa. **Pros:** magnificent aesthetic details throughout; indulgent pampering services; excellent on-site dining. **Cons:** golf course is off property; 15-minute drive to Palm Beach; hefty parking fee per night. ⓢ *Rooms from: $560 ⊠ 100 S. Ocean Blvd., Manalapan ☎ 561/533–6000, 800/241–3333 ⊕ www.thecolonypalmbeach.com ⇌ 309 rooms ⦿l No Meals.*

### Fairfield Inn & Suites Palm Beach

**$$ | HOTEL |** The Fairfield is a good value for travelers who don't require room service or a fancy spa. **Pros:** great location on the Intracoastal Waterway; close to the beach; free self-parking. **Cons:** not a lot of closet space; nondescript rooms; parking lot uncovered. ⓢ *Rooms from: $209 ⊠ 2870 S. Ocean Blvd., Palm Beach ☎ 561/582–2585, 800/347–5434 ⊕ www. marriott.com ⇌ 98 rooms ⦿l Free Breakfast.*

### ★ Four Seasons Resort Palm Beach

**$$$$ | RESORT | FAMILY |** Couples and families seeking relaxed seaside elegance in a luxe yet understated setting will love this manicured 6-acre oceanfront escape at the south end of Palm Beach, with serene, bright, airy rooms in a cream-colored palette and spacious marble-lined baths. **Pros:** Cabana Terrace Rooms have direct access to

The Colony Palm Beach, known for its iconic pink exterior, is centrally located off Worth Avenue.

pool deck; all rooms have balconies; Michelin-starred chef heads Florie's restaurant; outstanding complimentary kids' program. **Cons:** 10-minute drive to downtown Palm Beach (but can walk to Lake Worth); hefty resort fee; pricey. $ *Rooms from: $739* ⊠ *2800 S. Ocean Blvd.* ☎ *561/582–2800, 800/432–2335* ⊕ *www.fourseasons.com/palmbeach* 🛏 *210 rooms* |◯| *No Meals.*

### The Tideline Resort & Spa

$$$ | **RESORT** | This Zen-like boutique hotel has a loyal following of young, cool travelers, who appreciate the updated rooms and the full-service spa. **Pros:** most rooms have beautiful views of the private beach; ultracontemporary vibe; luxury setting. **Cons:** a hike from shopping and nightlife; the infinity pool is across the driveway; hefty resort fee. $ *Rooms from: $340* ⊠ *2842 S. Ocean Blvd.* ☎ *561/540–6440, 888/344–4321* ⊕ *www. tidelineresort.com* 🛏 *134 rooms* |◯| *No Meals.*

### ★ White Elephant Palm Beach

$$$$ | **HOTEL** | The sister property to Nantucket's fabled White Elephant Resort, this black and white stunner is a total transformation of the former Bradley Park Hotel, which was one of the first hotels in the area in the 1920s. **Pros:** renovated, stylish rooms with private outdoor space; top-notch restaurant; luxe amenities include complimentary use of BMW and exclusive yacht access. **Cons:** beach is a five-minute drive (but there's a courtesy shuttle); no on-site spa; pricey. $ *Rooms from: $475* ⊠ *280 Sunset Ave.* ☎ *844/462–9483* ⊕ *www.whiteelephant-palmbeach.com* 🛏 *32 rooms* |◯| *No Meals.*

## ▽ Nightlife

Palm Beach is teeming with restaurants that turn into late-night hot spots, plus hotel lobby bars perfect for tête-à-têtes.

### ★ bûccan

**COCKTAIL LOUNGES** | At this hip Hamptons-esque scene, society darlings crowd the lounge, sipping killer cocktails like the French Pearl (gin, Pernod, lemon juice, mint) and Buccan T (vodka, black tea, cranberry, citrus, basil, and agave nectar). ⊠ *350 S. County Rd.* ☎ *561/833-3450* ⊕ *www.buccanpalmbeach.com.*

### Café Boulud
**BARS** | A sleek, redesigned dining room bar with bar bites from a special menu plus an extended happy hour draws locals and visitors alike. ■**TIP→ Dress to impress.** ⊠ *301 Australian Ave.* ☎ *561/655-6060* ⊕ *www.cafeboulud. com/palmbeach.*

### Cucina Palm Beach
**BARS** | Though this spot is popular for lunch and dinner, it's even more popular later at night. The younger, trendier set comes late to party, mingle, and dance into the wee hours. ⊠ *257 Royal Poinciana Way* ☎ *561/655-0770* ⊕ *www. cucinapalmbeach.com/nightlife.*

## 🛍 Shopping

As is the case throughout South Florida, many of the smaller boutiques in Palm Beach close during the summer, and most stores are closed on Sunday. Consignment stores in Palm Beach are definitely worth a look; you'll often find high-end designer clothing in impeccable condition.

### The Church Mouse
**OUTLET** | Many high-end resale boutique owners grab their merchandise at this thrift store run by the Episcopal Church of Bethesda-by-the-Sea, in business since 1970. The Mouse accepts cheese from October to June, Monday–Saturday, 10–4. The store's end-of-season sale draws crowds that line the block. You can feel good about your purchases here: proceeds go to regional nonprofits. ⊠ *378 S. County Rd., Palm Beach* ☎ *561/659-2154* ⊕ *www.bbts.org/about-us/church-mouse/* ⊙ *Closed Sun.*

### ★ Worth Avenue
**NEIGHBORHOODS** | One of the world's premier showcases for high-quality shopping runs half a mile from east to west across Palm Beach, from the beach to Lake Worth. The street has over 200 shops (more than 40 of them sell jewelry), and many upscale chain stores (Gucci, Hermès, Saks Fifth Avenue, Neiman Marcus, Louis Vuitton, Chanel, Cartier, Tiffany & Co., and Tourneau) are represented—their merchandise appealing to the discerning tastes of the Palm Beach clientele. Don't miss walking around the vias, little courtyards lined with smaller boutiques; historic tours are available each month during "the season" from the Worth Avenue Association.

■**TIP→ For those looking to go a little lighter on the pocketbook, just north of Worth Avenue, the six blocks of South County Road have interesting and somewhat less expensive stores.** ⊠ *Worth Ave., Palm Beach* ✛ *Between Cocoanut Row and S. Ocean Blvd.* ⊕ *www.worth-avenue.com.*

## 🏃 Activities

Palm Beach Island has two good golf courses—The Breakers and the Palm Beach Par 3 Golf Course—but only the latter is open to the public. Not to worry, there are more on the mainland, as well as myriad other outdoor sports and spectator opportunities, including a spring-training baseball stadium.

### The Breakers Golf Courses
**GOLF** | The Breakers' historic par-70 Ocean Course, the oldest 18 holes in all of Florida, as well as its contemporary Breakers Rees Jones Course, are open exclusively to members and hotel guests. The Ocean Course, redesigned to bring back its "vintage" feel, is located on site, on the grounds of the sprawling Breakers Palm Beach. The resort's sister course, designed by Rees Jones, is 10 miles west in West Palm Beach and replaces the former Breakers West course. A $250

greens fee for each includes range balls, cart, and bag storage; the John Webster Golf Academy at The Breakers offers private and group lessons. Discounts are given at the Ocean Course for afternoon starts and for adults accompanied by kids, who play for free. ⊠ *The Breakers Palm Beach, 1 S. County Rd., Palm Beach* ☎ *561/655–6611* ⊕ *www.thebreakers. com/activities/golf/courses* ⊠ *$250 for 18 holes, cart included* ⚑ *Ocean Course: 18 holes, 6177 yards, par 72; Breakers Rees Jones Course: 18 holes, 7100 yards, par 72.*

### Island Living Tours

GUIDED TOURS | Book a private mansion-viewing excursion around Palm Beach and hear the storied past of the island's upper crust. Owner Leslie Diver also hosts an Antique Row Tour and a Worth Avenue Shopping Tour. Vehicle tours are 90 minutes for the Best of Palm Beach and 2½ hours for a more extensive architecture and history tour. Costs are from $60 to $150 per person, depending on the vehicle used. Leslie also runs 90-minute bicycle tours through Palm Beach ($45, not including bike rental). One bicycle tour explores the Estate Section and historic Worth Avenue; another explores the island's lesser known North End. Call in advance for location and to reserve. ☎ *561/309–5790* ⊕ *www.islandlivingpb.com.*

### Lake Trail

BIKING | FAMILY | This palm-fringed trail, about 4 miles long, skirts the backyards of mansions and the edge of Lake Worth. The start ("south trail" section) is just up from Royal Palm Way behind the Society of the Four Arts; follow the signs and you can't miss it. As you head north, the trail gets a little choppy around the Flagler Museum, so most people just enter where the "north trail" section begins at the very west end of Sunset Avenue. The path stops just short of the tip of the island, but people follow the quiet residential streets until they hit North Ocean

Boulevard and the dock there, with lovely views of Peanut Island and Singer Island, and then follow North Ocean Boulevard the 4 miles back for a change of scenery. ⊠ *Parallel to Lake Way, Palm Beach* ✛ *Behind Society of the Four Arts.*

### ★ Palm Beach Bicycle Trail Shop

BIKING | Open daily year-round, the shop rents bikes by the hour or day, and it's about a block from the north Lake Trail entrance. The shop has maps to help you navigate your way around the island, or you can download the main map from the shop's website. They are experts on the nearby, palm-fringed, 4-mile Lake Trail. ⊠ *50 Cocoanut Row, Suite 117, Palm Beach* ☎ *561/659–4583* ⊕ *palmbeachbicycle.com.*

### ★ Palm Beach Par 3 Golf Course

GOLF | This course has been named the best par-3 golf course in the United States by *Golf Digest* magazine. The 18-hole course—originally designed by Dick Wilson and Joe Lee in 1961—was redesigned in 2009 by Hall of Famer Raymond Floyd. The par-3 course includes six holes directly on the Atlantic Ocean, with some holes over 200 yards. The grounds are exquisitely landscaped, as one would expect in Palm Beach. A lavish clubhouse houses Al Fresco, an Italian restaurant. A cart is an extra $15, but walking is encouraged. Summer rates are greatly discounted. ⊠ *2345 S. Ocean Blvd., Palm Beach* ☎ *561/547–0598* ⊕ *www. golfontheocean.com* ⊠ *$50 for 18 holes* ⚑ *18 holes, 2458 yards, par 58.*

# West Palm Beach

Once in the shadow of neighboring Palm Beach, West Palm Beach has come into its own. Its $30 million Centennial Square waterfront complex at the eastern end of Clematis Street, with piers, a pavilion, and an amphitheater, has transformed West Palm into an attractive, easy-to-walk downtown area—not to mention there's the Downtown Trolley that connects the shopping-and-entertainment mecca The Square (formerly known as CityPlace) with restaurant-and-lounge-lined Clematis Street. The Palm Beach Outlet Mall gives options to those looking for tony bargains. West Palm is especially well regarded for its arts scene, with unique museums and performance venues; a number of public art projects have appeared around the city.

The city's outskirts, vast flat stretches with strip malls and car dealerships, may not inspire but are worth driving through to reach attractions scattered around the southern and western reaches. Several sites are especially rewarding for children and other animal and nature lovers.

#  Sights

### Ann Norton Sculpture Gardens
**GARDEN** | This landmarked complex is a testament to the creative genius of the late American sculptor Ann Weaver Norton (1905–82), who was the second wife of Norton Museum founder, the industrialist Ralph H. Norton. A set of art galleries in the studio and main house where she lived is surrounded by 2 acres of gardens with 300 species of rare palm trees, eight brick megaliths, a monumental figure in Norwegian granite, and plantings designed to attract native birds. ⊠ *253 Barcelona Rd., West Palm Beach* ☎ *561/832–5328* ⊕ *www.ansg.org* ✆ *$15* ☾ *Closed Mon. and Tues. Closed July through October.*

### Armory Art Center
**ARTS CENTER** | Built by the Works Progress Administration (WPA) in 1939, this art deco facility is now a nonprofit art school hosting rotating exhibitions and art classes throughout the year. The Armory Art Center became an institution for art instruction when the Norton Museum Gallery and School of Art dropped the latter part of its name in 1986 and discontinued art-instruction classes. ⊠ *1700 Parker*

*Ave., West Palm Beach* ☎ *561/832–1776* ⊕ *www.armoryart.org* ✆ *Free.*

### Currie Park
**CITY PARK | FAMILY** | Frequent weekend festivals, including an annual celebration of seafood, take place at this scenic city park next to the Intracoastal Waterway. Sit on one of the piers and watch the yachts and fishing boats pass by. Put on your jogging shoes—the park is at the north end of a 6.3-mile waterfront biking-jogging-skating path. Tennis courts, a boat ramp, and a playground are here, along with the Maritime Museum. Diva-Duck tours launch from this park. ⊠ *N. Flagler Dr. at 23rd St., West Palm Beach* ☎ *561/804–4900* ⊕ *wpbparks.com.*

### Lion Country Safari
**ZOO | FAMILY** | Drive your own vehicle along 4 miles of paved roads through a cageless zoo with free-roaming animals (chances are you'll have an ostrich tapping at your window), and then let loose in a 55-acre fun-land with bird feedings, games, and rides. Audio included with admission narrates the winding trek past white rhinos, zebras, and ostriches grouped into exhibits like Gir Forest, which is modeled after a sanctuary in India and has native twisted-horned blackbuck antelope and water buffalo. (For obvious reasons, lions are fenced off, and no convertibles or pets are allowed.) Aside from dozens more up-close critter encounters after debarking, including a petting zoo, kids can go paddleboating, play a round of minigolf, climb aboard carnival rides, or have a splash in a 4,000-square-foot aquatic playground (some extra fees apply). ⊠ *2003 Lion Country Safari Rd., at Southern Blvd. W, West Palm Beach* ☎ *561/793–1084* ⊕ *www.lioncountrysafari.com* ✆ *$41, $8 parking.*

### ★ Manatee Lagoon
**WILDLIFE REFUGE | FAMILY** | Once a casual spot next to the local electric plant's discharge waters, this center celebrating the manatee—South Florida's popular

winter visitors—opened at a spot where the peaceful creatures naturally congregate. The airy, two-story facility is surrounded by wraparound decks to accommodate sea-cow spotters from fall to spring. Educational, interactive displays tell the story of this once-endangered species. A long deck along the seawall leads to picnic pavilions from where you can watch the action at nearby Peanut Island and the Port of Palm Beach. Free admission makes it group-friendly; a live "manatee cam" shows manatee counts before you go. The center offers various community events but requires advance registration; check their calendar for details. ⊠ *6000 N. Flagler Dr., West Palm Beach* ✛ *Entrance is on Flagler Dr., via 58th St. east of U.S. 1 and south of Port of Palm Beach flyover* ☎ *561/626–2833* ⊕ *www.visitmanateelagoon.com* 🖃 *Free* ☉ *Closed Mon.*

## Mounts Botanical Garden

**GARDEN** | The oldest public green space in the county is, unbelievably, across the road from the West Palm Beach airport; but the planes are the last thing you notice while walking around and relaxing amid the nearly 14 acres of tropical trees, rain-forest flora, and butterfly and water gardens. The gift shop contains a selection of rare gardening books on tropical climes. Frequent plant sales are held here, and numerous plant societies with international ties hold meetings open to the public in the auditorium. Experts in tropical edible and ornamental plants are on staff. ⊠ *531 N. Military Trail, West Palm Beach* ☎ *561/233–1757* ⊕ *www.mounts.org* 🖃 *$12* ☉ *Closed Mon.*

## National Croquet Center

**SPORTS VENUE** | The world's largest croquet complex, the 10-acre center is also the headquarters for the U.S. Croquet Association. Vast expanses of orderly lawns are the stage for fierce competitions. There's also a clubhouse with a pro shop and the Croquet Grille, with verandas for dining and viewing (armchair enthusiasts can enjoy the games for no charge). You don't have to be a member to try your hand out on the lawns, and on Saturday morning at 10 am, there's a free group lesson with an introduction to the game and open play; call in advance to reserve a spot. ⊠ *700 Florida Mango Rd., at Summit Blvd., West Palm Beach* ☎ *561/478–2300* ⊕ *www.croquetnational.com* 🖃 *Center free; full day of croquet $30.*

## ★ Norton Museum of Art

**ART MUSEUM** | **FAMILY** | The museum (constructed in 1941 by steel magnate Ralph H. Norton and his wife, Elizabeth) has grown to become one of the most impressive in South Florida, with an extensive collection of 19th- and 20th-century American and European paintings—including works by Picasso, Monet, Matisse, Pollock, Cassatt, and O'Keeffe—plus Chinese art, earlier European art, and photography. To accommodate the growing collection, the museum expanded to include 12,000 additional square feet of gallery space in a new west wing, event spaces, a garden, and a great hall.

■TIP→ **The popular Art After Dark, Thursday from 5 to 10 pm, is a gathering spot for art lovers, with wine and music in the galleries.** ⊠ *1451 S. Olive Ave., West Palm Beach* ☎ *561/832–5196* ⊕ *www.norton.org* 🖃 *$18* ☉ *Closed Wed.*

## Richard and Pat Johnson Palm Beach County History Museum

**HISTORY MUSEUM** | A beautifully restored 1916 courthouse in downtown is the permanent home of the Historical Society of Palm Beach County's collection of artifacts and records dating back before the town's start—a highlight is furniture and decorative objects from Mizner Industries (a real treat since many of his mansions are not open to the public). ⊠ *300 N. Dixie Hwy., West Palm Beach* ☎ *561/832–4164* ⊕ *www.historicalsocietypbc.org* 🖃 *Free* ☉ *Closed Sun. and Mon.*

## 🍴 Restaurants

**Avocado Grill**

$ | **ECLECTIC** | In downtown West Palm Beach's waterfront district, this hot spot is an alternative to the bar food, tacos, and burgers more common in the area. "Green" cuisine—seasonal salads, vegetarian dishes, and sustainably produced meats and seafood—is making waves at the avocado-theme restaurant. Small plates of stuffed zucchini blossoms, octopus with chorizo and fingerling potatoes, or a mushroom fricassee with grits and truffle oil are examples of plates designed for sharing. **Known for:** everything avocado, including wonderful guacamole; mushroom fricassee with cheddar grits; mixed seafood ceviche. [$] *Average main: $19* ✉ *125 Datura St., West Palm Beach* ☎ *561/623–0822* 🌐 *www.avocadogrillwpb.com.*

**Belle and Maxwell's**

$ | **AMERICAN** | Palm Beach ladies who lunch leave the island for an afternoon at Belle and Maxwell's, while young professionals loosen up after work at the wine bar, part of the bistro's expanded dining area. Tucked along Antique Row, it looks like a storybook tea party at lunch, with eclectic furnishings and decor and a charming garden. **Known for:** classic chicken marsala; extensive list of lunch salads; homemade desserts. [$] *Average main: $18* ✉ *3700 S. Dixie Hwy., West Palm Beach* ☎ *561/832–4449* 🌐 *www.belleandmaxwells.com* 🕒 *Closed Sun. No dinner Mon.*

★ **Grandview Public Market**

$ | **ECLECTIC** | **FAMILY** | This laid-back food hall and community-centric market complete with colorful murals is a crowd pleaser. There's plenty to taste, with 12 vendors selling everything from tacos to fried chicken to rolled ice cream. **Known for:** coffee; live music; tacos. [$] *Average main: $12* ✉ *1401 Clare Ave., West Palm Beach* 🌐 *www.grandviewpublic.com.*

★ **Grato**

$ | **TUSCAN** | **FAMILY** | A sprawling cavern of wood-fired pizzas, pastas, and cocktails, this sibling to popular bûccan is a hit. Soaring ceilings, concrete floors, dark wood, and an open kitchen provide a buzzy backdrop to dishes of nicely charred pies (made with organic flour) and homemade pastas. **Known for:** wood-fired pizzas; fresh pastas; busy bar scene. [$] *Average main: $24* ✉ *1901 Dixie Hwy., West Palm Beach* ☎ *561/404–1334* 🌐 *www.gratowpb.com.*

**Havana**

$ | **CUBAN** | **FAMILY** | Decorated with vintage travel posters of its namesake city, this two-level restaurant serves authentic Cuban specialties on the cheap, including great Cubanos (pressed roast pork sandwiches), arroz con pollo, and *ropa vieja.* The friendly place attracts a late-night crowd at its popular walk-up window. Get strong Cuban coffee (often awarded the best in Palm Beach County), sugary fried churros, and fruit juices in exotic flavors like mamey, mango, papaya, guava, and guanabana. **Known for:** late-night food service; Cuban sandwiches; picadillo Cubano. [$] *Average main: $15* ✉ *6801 S. Dixie Hwy., West Palm Beach* ☎ *561/547–9799* 🌐 *www.havanacubanfood.com.*

**Howley's**

$ | **AMERICAN** | Since 1950, this diner's eat-in counter and "cooked in sight, it must be right" motto have made it a congenial setting for meeting old friends and making new ones. Nowadays, Howley's prides itself on its kitsch factor and old-school eats like turkey pot pie and a traditional Thanksgiving feast, as well as its retro-redux dishes like a potato-and-brisket burrito. **Known for:** kitschy setting; retro diner specialties; late-night dining. [$] *Average main: $13* ✉ *4700 S. Dixie Hwy., West Palm Beach* ☎ *561/833–5691* 🌐 *www.sub-culture.org/howleys/.*

## Marcello's La Sirena

$$$ | **ITALIAN** | A longtime favorite of locals, this sophisticated Italian restaurant is in an unexpected, nondescript location on Dixie Highway away from downtown and central hubs. But warm hospitality from a husband-and-wife team, along with smart service and delectable traditional dishes, awaits. **Known for:** fresh pasta dishes; award-winning wine list; great desserts. $ *Average main: $31* ⊠ *6316 S. Dixie Hwy., West Palm Beach* ☎ *561/585–3128* ⊕ *www.lasirenaonline.com* ⊙ *Closed Sun.*

## ★ Mediterranean Market & Deli

$ | **MIDDLE EASTERN** | This hole-in-the-wall Middle Eastern bakery, deli, and market is packed at lunchtime with regulars who are on a first-name basis with the staff behind the counter. From the nondescript parking lot the place doesn't look like much, but inside, delicious hot and cold Mediterranean treats await the takeout crowd. **Known for:** lamb salad; gyros; freshly baked pita bread. $ *Average main: $10* ⊠ *327 5th St., West Palm Beach* ☎ *561/659–7322* ⊕ *www.mediterraneanmarketanddeli.com* ⊙ *Closed Sun.*

## Pistache French Bistro

$$ | **FRENCH** | Although "the island" is no doubt a bastion of French cuisine, this cozy bistro across the bridge on the Clematis Street waterfront entices a lively crowd looking for an unpretentious good meal. The outdoor terrace can't be beat, and the fabulous modern French menu with twists such as roasted sliced duck with truffled polenta is a delight. **Known for:** fresh seafood; cheese and charcuterie; great desserts. $ *Average main: $27* ⊠ *101 N. Clematis St., West Palm Beach* ☎ *561/833–5090* ⊕ *www.pistachewpb.com.*

## ★ Proper Grit

$$ | **AMERICAN** | This handsome chophouse situated on the ground floor of the buzzy Ben hotel serves Florida-inspired seafood and steaks with an emphasis on locally sourced ingredients. The indoor dining room is decked out in dark woods and floor-to-ceiling windows that open to outside seats offering views of the city's marina. **Known for:** craft cocktails; patio seating; aged steaks. $ *Average main: $30* ⊠ *The Ben, 251 N. Narcissus Ave., West Palm Beach* ☎ *561/655–4001* ⊕ *propergrit.com.*

## ★ The Regional Kitchen & Public House

$$ | **SOUTHERN** | *Top Chef* finalist and James Beard Award nominee Lindsay Autry debuted her own Southern-inspired American cuisine in The Square to the acclaim of local critics. The menu of updated comfort food includes fried green tomatoes, creamy tomato pie, pimento cheese done table-side, and shrimp and grits. **Known for:** reinvented Southern classics; table-side pimento cheese; warm tomato pie. $ *Average main: $29* ⊠ *The Square, 651 Okeechobee Blvd., West Palm Beach* ✛ *Directly across from Convention Center* ☎ *561/557–6460* ⊕ *www.eatregional.com* ⊙ *Closed Sun.*

## ★ RH Rooftop Restaurant

$ | **AMERICAN** | **FAMILY** | Atop the glossy Restoration Hardware store adjacent to The Square is this regal, glass-enclosed atrium outfitted with white couches, crystal chandeliers, lush greenery, and a tinkling fountain. It's proven a hit with all walks of life; everyone basks in the sun-filled room and tucks into seasonal comfort food (prime rib French dip, truffled grilled cheese) and lingers on exceptionally comfortable couches. **Known for:** lobster roll; beautiful atrium; brunch. $ *Average main: $20* ⊠ *560 Okeechobee Blvd., West Palm Beach* ☎ *561/804–6826* ⊕ *www.restorationhardware.com.*

## Rhythm Cafe

$ | **AMERICAN** | West Palm Beach's Rhythm Cafe is anything but Palm Beach formal (the decor includes a feathered pink flamingo perched on the terrazzo floor). Fun, funky, cheesy, campy, and cool all at once, the former 1950s-era drugstore-cum-restaurant on West

Palm Beach's Antique Row features an ever-changing creative menu of homemade items with Italian, Greek, American, and Creole influences. **Known for:** "tapas-tizer" small plates; fresh fish; graham-cracker-crusted key lime chicken. $ *Average main: $24* ✉ *3800 S. Dixie Hwy., West Palm Beach* ☎ *561/833-3406* 🌐 *www.rhythmcafe.com* ⏲ *No lunch.*

## Hotels

### ★ The Ben West Palm

$$$ | **HOTEL** | The glossy, handsome hotel which sits across the Intracoastal Waterway and is a block from Clematis Street radiates swagger, and, this being an Autograph Collection hotel, has numerous posh perks. **Pros:** excellent location and design; top-notch dining; the only rooftop waterfront drinking and dining outlet in downtown West Palm Beach. **Cons:** rooftop pool can get crowded; rooms on lower floors lack views; pricey parking fee. $ *Rooms from: $399* ✉ *251 N. Narcissus Ave., West Palm Beach* ☎ *561/655-4001* 🌐 *www.thebenwestpalm.com* 🛏 *208 rooms* 🍴 *No Meals.*

### Casa Grandview West Palm Beach

$$ | **B&B/INN** | In West Palm's charming Grandview Heights historic district—and just minutes away from both downtown and the beach—this warm and personalized B&B offers a wonderful respite from South Florida's big-hotel norm. **Pros:** daily dry-cleaning of all linens; complimentary soft drinks, coffee, and snacks (and lots of them) in lobby; simple keyless entry (number code lock system). **Cons:** cottages and suites have seven-day minimum; free breakfast in B&B rooms only; art deco suites don't have air-conditioning. $ *Rooms from: $289* ✉ *1410 Georgia Ave., West Palm Beach* ☎ *561/655-8932* 🌐 *www.casagrandview.com* 🛏 *17 rooms* 🍴 *Free Breakfast.*

### Grandview Gardens Bed & Breakfast

$$ | **B&B/INN** | Defining the Florida B&B experience, this 1925 Mediterranean-revival home overlooks a serene courtyard pool and has loads of charm and personality, while the fabulous owners provide heavy doses of bespoke service. **Pros:** innkeepers offer historic city tours; outside private entrances to rooms; free bicycle use. **Cons:** not close to the beach; in a residential area; rental car needed. $ *Rooms from: $225* ✉ *1608 Lake Ave., West Palm Beach* ☎ *561/833-9023* 🌐 *www.grandview-gardens.com* 🛏 *5 rooms, 2 cottages* 🍴 *Free Breakfast.*

### Hilton West Palm Beach

$$ | **HOTEL** | **FAMILY** | In downtown, the contemporary business hotel situated next door to the county convention center has a pool with cabanas many resorts would envy. **Pros:** walking distance to convention center, The Square, Kravis Center; resort-style pool; amenities geared toward business travelers. **Cons:** long ride to the beach; noise from downtown construction and trains; none of the charm of local B&Bs. $ *Rooms from: $279* ✉ *600 Okeechobee Blvd., West Palm Beach* ✣ *Adjacent to Palm Beach County Convention Center* ☎ *561/231-6000* 🌐 *www3.hilton.com* 🛏 *400 rooms* 🍴 *No Meals.*

## Nightlife

West Palm is known for its exuberant nightlife—Clematis Street and The Square are the prime party destinations. Downtown rocks every Thursday from 6 pm on with Clematis by Night, a celebration of music, dance, art, and food at Centennial Square.

### ★ Rocco's Tacos and Tequila Bar

**BARS** | In the last few years, Rocco's has taken root in numerous South Florida downtowns and become synonymous with wild nights of chips and guac, margaritas, and intoxicating fun. This is more of a scene than just a restaurant, and when Rocco's in the house and pouring shots, get ready to party hearty.

With pitchers of margaritas continuously flowing, the middle-age crowd is boisterous and fun, recounting (and reliving) the days of spring break debauchery from their preprofessional years. Get your party started here with more than 220 choices of tequila. There's another branch at 5250 Town Center Circle in Boca Raton, at 110 Atlantic Avenue in Delray Beach, and in Palm Beach Gardens in PGA Commons at 5090 PGA Boulevard. ✉ *224 Clematis St., West Palm Beach* ☎ *561/650–1001* ⊕ *www.roccostacos.com.*

##  Performing Arts

### Palm Beach Dramaworks (*pbd*)
**THEATER** | Housed in an intimate venue with only 218 seats in downtown West Palm Beach, the modus operandi is "theater to think about," with plays by Pulitzer Prize winners on rotation. ✉ *201 Clematis St., West Palm Beach* ☎ *561/514–4042* ⊕ *www.palmbeach-dramaworks.org.*

### Palm Beach Opera
**OPERA** | Still going strong after more than 60 years, three main-stage productions are offered during the season from January through April at the Kravis Center, with English-language supertitles. There's an annual Children's Performance when all tickets are $5, plus a free outdoor concert at the Meyer Amphitheatre in downtown West Palm Beach. Tickets start at $25. ✉ *1800 S. Australian Ave., Suite 301, administrative office, West Palm Beach* ☎ *561/833–7888* ⊕ *www.pbopera.org.*

### ★ Raymond F. Kravis Center for the Performing Arts
**ARTS CENTERS** | This is the crown jewel amid a treasury of local arts attractions, and its marquee star is the 2,195-seat Dreyfoos Hall, a glass, copper, and marble showcase just steps from the restaurants and shops of The Square. The center also boasts the 289-seat Rinker Playhouse, 170-seat Persson Hall, and

the Gosman Amphitheatre, which holds 1,400 total in seats and on the lawn. A packed year-round schedule features a blockbuster lineup of Broadway's biggest touring productions, concerts, dance shows, dramas, and musicals; the Miami City Ballet, Palm Beach Opera, and the Palm Beach Pops perform here. ✉ *701 Okeechobee Blvd., West Palm Beach* ☎ *561/832–7469 box office* ⊕ *www.kravis.org.*

##  Shopping

### ★ Antique Row
**NEIGHBORHOODS** | West Palm's U.S. 1, "South Dixie Highway," is the destination for those who love interesting home decor. From thrift shops to the most exclusive stores, it is all here within 40 stores—museum-quality furniture, lighting, art, junk, fabric, frames, tile, and rugs. So if you're looking for an art deco, French-provincial, or Mizner pièce de résistance, big or small, schedule a few hours for an Antique Row stroll. You'll find bargains during the off-season (May to November). Antique Row runs north–south from Belvedere Road to Forest Hill Boulevard, although most stores are bunched between Belvedere Road and Southern Boulevard. ✉ *U.S. 1, between Belvedere Rd. and Forest Hill Blvd., West Palm Beach* ⊕ *www.westpalmbeachantiques.com.*

### Clematis Street
**NEIGHBORHOODS | FAMILY** | If lunching is just as important as window-shopping, the renewed downtown West Palm around Clematis Street that runs west to east from South Rosemary Avenue to Flagler Drive is the spot for you. Centennial Park by the waterfront has an attractive design—and fountains where kids can cool off—which adds to the pleasure of browsing and resting at one of the many outdoor cafés. Hip national retailers such as Design Within Reach mix with local boutiques like third-generation Pioneer Linens, and both blend

in with restaurants and bars. ⊠ *Clematis St., West Palm Beach* ✥ *Between S. Rosemary Ave. and Flagler Dr.* ⊕ *www. westpalmbeach.com/clematis.*

★ **The Square**
NEIGHBORHOODS | FAMILY | The 72-acre, four-block-by-four-block commercial and residential complex centered on Rosemary Avenue has been revamped from CityPlace into The Square, with $550 million in upgrades to the pedestrian walkways, plus new retail, dining and public art installations. The mixed-use neighborhood attracts people of all ages to restaurants, a 20-screen AMC theater, live music at Copper Blues, the Harriet Himmel Theater, and the Improv Comedy Club. In the courtyard, Berlin-based artist Jeppe Hein has created a whimsical water pavilion, and live bands perform on weekends. The dining, shopping, and entertainment are all family-friendly; at night, however, a lively crowd likes to hit the outdoor bars. Among The Square's stores are such popular national retailers as H&M, Tommy Bahama, and Restoration Hardware. ⊠ *700 S. Rosemary Ave., West Palm Beach* ☎ *561/366–1000* ⊕ *www.thesquarewestpalm.com.*

⚙ **Activities**

**Fitteam Ballpark of the Palm Beaches**
BASEBALL & SOFTBALL | FAMILY | There's a lot to root for at this state-of-the-art baseball stadium. It plays host to spring training for the Houston Astros and the Washington Nationals, along with farm team play and numerous tournaments in the summer on its many fields. Seating includes lawn, bleacher, field boxes, and suites, with full food service in the latter two. A full bar overlooks left field. With free (and plenty of) parking—as well as reasonably priced tickets—it's a value day out. Check the website to see the other teams coming to play in Florida's "Grapefruit League" against the home teams. The stadium complements Roger Dean Stadium in Jupiter, which hosts the

spring games for the Miami Marlins and St. Louis Cardinals. Fields for lacrosse, football, and soccer are part of the massive complex and expected to draw those games; other community events are staged here. ⊠ *5444 Haverhill Rd., West Palm Beach* ✥ *Best exit off I–95 is 45th St.; off Florida's Tpke. is Okeechobee Blvd.* ☎ *561/500–4487* ⊕ *www. ballparkpalmbeaches.com* ⊠ *From $17.*

★ **International Polo Club Palm Beach**
POLO | Attend matches and rub elbows with celebrities who make the pilgrimage out to Palm Beach polo country (the western suburb of Wellington) during the January–April season. The competition is not just among polo players. High society dresses in their best polo couture week after week, each outfit more fabulous than the next; they tailgate out of their Bentleys and Rollses. An annual highlight at the polo club is the U.S. Open Polo Championship at the end of the season.

■ TIP→ **One of the best ways to experience the polo scene is by enjoying a gourmet brunch on the veranda of the International Polo Club Pavilion; it'll cost you from $100 to $120 per person depending on the month, but it's well worth it.** ⊠ *3667 120th Ave. S, Palm Beach* ☎ *561/204–5687* ⊕ *www. internationalpoloclub.com.*

# Lake Worth

*8 miles south of West Palm Beach.*

For years, tourists looked here mainly for inexpensive lodging and easy access to Palm Beach, since a bridge leads from the mainland to a barrier island with Lake Worth's beach. Now Lake Worth has grown into an arts community, with several blocks of restaurants, nightclubs, shops, and galleries, making this a worthy destination on its own.

The posh Palm Beach area has its share of luxury villas on the water; many are Mediterranean in style.

##  Sights

### Museum of Polo and Hall of Fame

**OTHER MUSEUM** | The history of the sport of kings is displayed in a time line here, with other exhibits focusing on polo ponies, star players, trophies, and a look at how mallets are made. It provides a great introduction to the surprisingly exciting, hoof-pounding sport that is played live on Sunday from January to April in nearby Wellington. ✉ *9011 Lake Worth Rd., Lake Worth* ☎ *561/969–3210* ⊕ *www.polomuseum.com* ✉ *Free (donations accepted)* ⊗ *Closed Sun. Closed Sat. May–Dec.*

## Beaches

### Lake Worth Beach

**BEACH | FAMILY** | This public beach bustles with beachgoers of all ages thanks to the prolific family offerings. The waterfront retail promenade—the old-fashioned nongambling Lake Worth "casino"—has a Mulligan's Beach House Bar & Grill, a T-shirt store, a pizzeria, and a Kilwin's ice cream shop. The beach also has a municipal Olympic-size public swimming pool, a playground, and a fishing pier— not to mention the pier's wildly popular daytime eatery, Benny's on the Beach (open for dinner weekends in season). Tideline Ocean Resort and Four Seasons guests are steps away from the action; Eau Palm Beach guests are a short bike ride away. **Amenities:** food and drink; lifeguards; parking (fee); showers; toilets; water sports. **Best for:** sunset; swimming. ✉ *10 S. Ocean Blvd., at A1A and Lake Ave., Lake Worth* ⊕ *www.lakeworth.org* ✉ *From $1, $2 per hr for parking.*

## Restaurants

### ★ Benny's on the Beach

**$** | **AMERICAN** | Perched on the Lake Worth Pier, Benny's has a walk-up bar, a takeout window, and a full-service beach-themed restaurant serving casual fare at bargain prices. "Beach Bread" is a take on a waffle sandwich; the fresh seafood is from Florida waters. Eat-in diners come here for long afternoons of beer and cocktails, enjoying prolific alfresco seating and a spectacular view of the sun glistening on the water and the waves crashing directly below. **Known for:** Florida seafood; beach brunch; afternoon drinks. $ *Average main: $15 ⊠ Lake Worth Beach, 10 S. Ocean Blvd., Lake Worth ⊹ On Lake Worth Pier ☎ 561/582–9001 ⊕ www. bennysonthebeach.com.*

### Paradiso

**$$$$ | ITALIAN** | Arguably downtown Lake Worth's fanciest restaurant, with sophisticated modern Northern Italian cuisine, this is a go-to place for a romantic evening. Waiters are on point and anticipate needs. **Known for:** whole branzino baked in a salt crust; extensive wine list; lighter lounge menu. $ *Average main: $42 ⊠ 625 Lucerne Ave., Lake Worth ☎ 561/547–2500 ⊕ www.paradisolake-worth.com.*

##  Hotels

### Mango Inn Bed and Breakfast

**$ | B&B/INN** | It's a 15-minute walk to the beach from this B&B dating from 1915, set in a lushly landscaped, mango tree–dotted property. **Pros:** close to shops and restaurants; breakfasts served poolside; some suites have whirlpool tubs. **Cons:** some rooms are quite small; beach is a walk away; decor is dated. $ *Rooms from: $190 ⊠ 128 N. Lakeside Dr., Lake Worth ☎ 561/533–6900, 888/626–4619 ⊕ www.mangoinn.com ↻ 11 rooms ⊙ Free Breakfast.*

### ★ Sabal Palm House

**$ | B&B/INN** | Built in 1936, this romantic, two-story B&B is a short walk from Lake Worth's downtown shops, eateries, and the Intracoastal Waterway, and each room is decorated with antiques and inspired by a different artist, including Renoir, Dalí, Norman Rockwell, and Chagall. **Pros:** on quiet street; hands-on owners; chairs and totes with towels provided for use at nearby beach. **Cons:** no pool; peak times require a two-night minimum stay; no parking lot. $ *Rooms from: $159 ⊠ 109 N. Golfview Rd., Lake Worth ☎ 561/582–1090, 888/722–2572 ⊕ www.sabalpalmhouse.com ↻ 7 rooms ⊙ Free Breakfast.*

##  Activities

### Palm Beach National Golf and Country Club

**GOLF** | Despite the name, this classic 18-hole course resides in Lake Worth, not in Palm Beach. It is, however, in Palm Beach County and prides itself on being "the most fun and friendly golf course" in Palm Beach County. The championship layout was designed by Joe Lee in the 1970s and is famous for its 3rd and 18th holes (the 3rd: a par-3 island hole with a sand bunker; the 18th: a short par 4 of 358 yards sandwiched between a wildlife preserve and water). Due to the challenging nature of the course, it's more popular with seasoned golfers. The Steve Haggerty Golf Academy is also based here. Summer rates are significantly discounted. ⊠ *7500 St. Andrews Rd., Lake Worth ☎ 561/965–3381 ⊕ www. palmbeachnational.com ⊠ $94 for 18 holes ⅄ 18 holes, 6734 yards, par 72.*

# Delray Beach

*15 miles south of West Palm Beach.*

Between Boca Raton and Boynton Beach, this popular beach town packs in art, a happening main street, tons of unique history, and miles of beach to soak up the sun—all completely walkable. Known for culturally rich attractions such as Morikami Museum and Japanese Gardens, Delray also has a few hotspot pedestrian areas. Atlantic Avenue, a mile-plus-long stretch of palm-dotted sidewalks lined with stores, art galleries, and restaurants, runs east–west and ends at the beach, and it's a lively place for a stroll, day or night. Another active pedestrian area, the Pineapple Grove Arts District, begins at Atlantic and stretches northward on Northeast 2nd Avenue about half a mile, and yet another active pedestrian way begins at the eastern edge of Atlantic Avenue and runs along the big, broad swimming beach that extends north to George Bush Boulevard and south to Casuarina Road.

## GETTING HERE AND AROUND

To reach Delray Beach from Boynton Beach, drive 2 miles south on Interstate 95, U.S. 1, or Route A1A.

#  Sights

### Cason Cottage Museum

**HISTORIC HOME** | This restored home that dates from about 1924 is a small museum run by the Delray Beach Historical Society. It's furnished as though the original inhabitants still lived there and filled with period relics, including a pump organ donated by descendants of a Delray Beach pioneer family. There's a garden of native plants out front and two small bungalow-style buildings on the property that have displays on the town's architectural evolution and history. The cottage is a block north of Atlantic Avenue and right across from the Delray Beach Center for the Arts at Old School Square. ⊠ 5 N.E. 1st St., Delray Beach ☎ 561/274–9578 ⊕ delraybeachhistory. org ☞ $4 ☉ Closed Sun.–Wed.

### Colony Hotel

**HOTEL** | The chief landmark along Atlantic Avenue since 1926 is this sunny Mediterranean-revival-style building, which is a member of the National Trust's Historic Hotels of America. Stay a night here or simply walk through the lobby to the parking lot where original garages still stand—relics of the days when hotel guests would arrive via chauffeured cars and stay there the whole season. The bar is a locals' gathering spot. ⊠ 525 E. Atlantic Ave., Delray Beach ☎ 561/276–4123 ⊕ colonyflorida.com.

### Delray Beach Center for the Arts at Old School Square

**NOTABLE BUILDING** | **FAMILY** | Instrumental in the revitalization of Delray Beach circa 1995, this cluster of galleries and event spaces was established in restored school buildings dating from 1913 and 1925. The **Cornell Museum of Art & American Culture** offers ever-changing exhibits on fine arts, crafts, and pop culture, plus a hands-on children's gallery. From November to April, the 323-seat **Crest Theatre** showcases national-touring Broadway musicals, cabaret concerts, dance performances, and lectures. ⊠ 51 N. Swinton Ave., Delray Beach ☎ 561/243–7922 ⊕ oldschoolsquare.org ☞ $8 for museum ☉ Closed Sun. and Mon.

### ★ Morikami Museum and Japanese Gardens

**GARDEN** | **FAMILY** | The boonies west of Delray Beach seem an odd place to encounter one of the region's most important cultural centers, but this is exactly where you can find a 200-acre cultural and recreational facility heralding the Yamato Colony of Japanese farmers that settled here in the early 20th century. A permanent exhibit details their history, and all together the museum's collection has more than 7,000 artifacts and works of art on rotating display. Traditional tea ceremonies are conducted monthly from October to June, along with educational classes on topics like calligraphy and sushi making (these require advance registration and come with a fee). The six main gardens are inspired by famous historic periods in Japanese garden design and have South Florida accents (think tropical bonsai), and the on-site Cornell Café serves light Asian fare at affordable prices. ⊠ 4000 Morikami Park Rd., Delray Beach ☎ 561/495–0233 ⊕ www.morikami.org ☞ $15 ☉ Closed Mon.

## Beaches

**★ Delray Municipal Beach**

**BEACH** | If you're looking for a place to see and be seen, head for this wide expanse of sand, the heart of which is where Atlantic Avenue meets A1A, close to restaurants, bars, and quick-serve eateries. Lounge chairs and umbrellas can be rented every day, and lifeguards man stations half a mile out in each direction. The most popular section of beach is south of Atlantic Avenue on A1A, where the street parking is found. There are also two metered lots with restrooms across from A1A at Sandoway Park and Anchor Park (bring quarters if parking here). On the beach by Anchor Park, north of Casuarina Road, are six volleyball nets and a kiosk that offers Hobie Wave rentals, surfing lessons, and snorkeling excursions to the 1903 SS *Inchulva* shipwreck half a mile offshore. The beach itself is open 24 hours, if you're at a nearby hotel and fancy a moonlight stroll. **Amenities:** food and drink; lifeguards; parking (fee); showers; toilets; water sports. **Best for:** partiers; swimming; windsurfing. ✉ *Rte. A1A and E. Atlantic Ave., Delray Beach* 🌐 *www.delraybeachfl.gov* 🎫 *$2 per 1 hr parking.*

## Restaurants

**★ Akira Back**

**$$** | **ASIAN** | Celebrity Chef Akira Back (whose restaurant in Seoul earned a Michelin star) brings his signature fusion showmanship to this buzzy eatery located in the trendy The Ray hotel. His modern Japanese fare incorporates Korean and global influences for a menu that offers everything from sushi tacos to robata-grilled lamb chops. Japanese A5 Wagyu is available, as are pricey cuts of sashimi like toro tuna, while the AB Tuna Pizza, laced with umami aioli, micro *shiso*, and white truffle oil is a must-order. **Known for:** bustling atmosphere; large sake selection; creative sushi rolls. [$] *Average main: $29* ✉ *233 NE 2nd Ave, Delray Beach* ☎ *561/739-1708* 🌐 *akirabackdelray.com.*

**Blue Anchor**

**$** | **BRITISH** | Yes, this pub was actually shipped from England, where it had stood for 150 years in London's historic Chancery Lane. There it was a watering hole for famed English residents, including Winston Churchill; here you may hear stories of lingering ghosts told over some suds. **Known for:** fish-and-chips; beer selection; late-night food spot. [$] *Average main: $18* ✉ *804 E. Atlantic Ave., Delray Beach* ☎ *561/272–7272.*

**City Oyster & Sushi Bar**

**$$** | **SEAFOOD** | This trendy restaurant mingles the personalities and flavors of a New England oyster bar, a modern sushi eatery, an eclectic seafood grill, and an award-winning dessert bakery to create a can't-miss foodie haven in the heart of Delray's bustling Atlantic Avenue. Dishes like the oyster bisque, New Orleans–style shrimp and crab gumbo, tuna crudo, and lobster fried rice are simply sublime. **Known for:** large selection of oysters; excellent desserts; loud and busy, especially in high season. [$] *Average main: $26* ✉ *213 E. Atlantic Ave., Delray Beach* ☎ *561/272–0220* 🌐 *www.cityoysterdelray.com.*

**★ Delray Beach Market**

**$** | **AMERICAN** | **FAMILY** | Known as Florida's largest food hall, this multistory venue features 25 local and regional eateries offering everything from casual bites and coffee to craft cocktails and composed meals. The high-energy atmosphere includes DJ-fueled brunches, kids' activities on the weekends, and holiday theme nights. **Known for:** craft cocktails; lively atmosphere; lots of choices. [$] *Average main: $19* ✉ *33 SE 3rd Ave, Delray Beach* ☎ *561/562-7000* 🌐 *www.delraybeachmarket.com.*

### ★ Lionfish Modern Coastal Cuisine

$$ | **AMERICAN** | Sustainable seafood is the focus at this airy "sea-to-table" spot that dabbles in sushi rolls, grilled fish, and creative American cuisine. The namesake lionfish (an invasive species that wreaks havoc on the local marine ecosystem) shows up in a ceviche bathed in avocado, key lime, and coconut or can be ordered whole and grilled with lemons, capers, and charred greens. **Known for:** lionfish ceviche; sushi rolls; creative cocktails. $ *Average main: $29* ⊠ *307 E. Atlantic Ave., Delray Beach* ☎ *561/639–8700* ⊕ *lionfishdelray.com.*

### ★ Taru

$$ | **AMERICAN** | The historic Sundy House, a 1902-built Victorian home with meandering gardens, ponds, and charming gazebo seating, is home to chef James Strine's "New Florida cuisine," which essentially comprises Caribbean-, Cuban-, and Latin-inspired dishes. The cocktails are refreshing, the lush outdoor setting is downright magical, and the gourmet comfort food has a creative streak. **Known for:** garden seating; creative small plates; legendary Sunday brunch. $ *Average main: $27* ⊠ *106 S. Swinton Ave., Delray Beach* ☎ *877/439–9601* ⊕ *www.sundyhouse.com.*

## 🛌 Hotels

### Colony Hotel & Cabaña Club

$ | **HOTEL** | Not to be confused with the luxurious Colony in Palm Beach, this charming hotel in the heart of downtown Delray dates back to 1926, and although it's landlocked, it does have a cabana club 2 miles away for hotel guests only. **Pros:** pet-friendly; full breakfast buffet included with rooms; free use of cabanas, umbrellas, and hammocks. **Cons:** no pool at main hotel building; must walk to public beach for water-sports rentals; AC can be loud in some rooms. $ *Rooms from: $195* ⊠ *525 E. Atlantic Ave., Delray Beach* ☎ *561/276–4123, 800/552–2363* ⊕ *www.thecolonyhotel.com* ⇗ *70 rooms* ❦ *Free Breakfast.*

### ★ Crane's Beach House Boutique Hotel & Luxury Villas

$$ | **HOTEL** | **FAMILY** | A tropical oasis, this boutique hotel is a hidden jungle of lush tropical plants, only a block from the beach. **Pros:** private location within the city setting; short walk to the beach; free parking. **Cons:** no water views; no restaurants on site; no fitness or spa facilities. $ *Rooms from: $249* ⊠ *82 Gleason St., Delray Beach* ☎ *866/372–7263, 561/278–1700* ⊕ *www.cranesbeachhouse.com* ⇗ *28 rooms, 4 villas* ❦ *No Meals.*

### Opal Grand Resort

$$$ | **HOTEL** | **FAMILY** | By far the largest hotel in Delray Beach, this resort, formerly a Marriott, has two towers on a stellar plot of land at the east end of Atlantic Avenue—it's the only hotel that directly overlooks the water, yet it is still within walking distance of restaurants, shopping, and nightlife. **Pros:** fantastic ocean views; pampering spa; two pools. **Cons:** chain-hotel feel; charge for parking; must rent beach chairs. $ *Rooms from: $349* ⊠ *10 N. Ocean Blvd., Delray Beach* ☎ *866/240–6316* ⊕ *www.opalgrand.com* ⇗ *277 rooms* ❦ *No Meals.*

### ★ The Ray

$$ | **HOTEL** | With sleek architecture and contemporary interior design, this newcomer's "tropical modern" aesthetic adds a refreshing urbane feel in Delray's Pineapple Grove Arts District. **Pros:** interesting modern art collection; trendy decor; excellent restaurants and rooftop pool on property. **Cons:** no spa; not situated on the beach, though there's a shuttle; resort fee. $ *Rooms from: $299* ⊠ *233 NE 2nd Ave, Delray Beach* ☎ *561/739-1700* ⊕ *www.therayhotel.com* ⇗ *141 rooms* ❦ *No Meals.*

### ★ The Seagate Hotel & Spa

$$$$ | **RESORT** | **FAMILY** | Those who crave luxury in its full glory (rooms with ultraswank tilework and fixtures, marble

vanities, seamless shower doors plus access to a spa, pools, and beach club) will love this LEED-certified hotel with a subtle Zen-coastal motif. **Pros:** two swimming pools; fabulous beach club; exceptionally knowledgeable concierge team. **Cons:** main building not directly on beach; daily resort fee; separate charge for parking. $ *Rooms from: $489* ✉ *1000 E. Atlantic Ave., Delray Beach* ☎ *561/665–4800, 877/577–3242* ⊕ *www. theseagatehotel.com* ⟿ *154 rooms* ⦿ *No Meals.*

##  Nightlife

### ★ Dada

**LIVE MUSIC** | Bands play in the living room of this historic house, though much of the action is outdoors on the lawn in fair weather, where huge trees and lanterns make it a fun stop for drinks or a group night out. It's a place where those who don't drink will also feel comfortable, however, and excellent gourmet nibbles are a huge bonus (a full dinner menu is available, too). A bohemian, young-er crowd gathers later, into the night. ✉ *52 N. Swinton Ave., Delray Beach* ☎ *561/330-3232* ⊕ *www.sub-culture.org/dada.*

### Jellies Bar at the Atlantic Grille

**BARS** | Within the Seagate Hotel, the fun and fabulous bar at the Atlantic Grille is known locally as Jellies Bar. The over-thirty set consistently floats over to this stunning bar to shimmy to live music Tuesday to Saturday; the namesake jelly-fish tank never fails to entertain as well. ✉ *The Seagate Hotel & Spa, 1000 E. Atlantic Ave., Delray Beach* ☎ *561/665–4900* ⊕ *www.theatlanticgrille.com.*

##  Activities

### Delray Beach Tennis Center

**TENNIS** | Each year this complex hosts simultaneous professional tournaments where current stars and legends duke it out. Florida's own Chris Evert hosts the Pro-Celebrity Tennis Classic charity event here. The rest of the time, you can practice or learn on 14 clay courts and seven hard courts; private lessons and clinics are available, and it's open from 7:30 am to 9 pm weekdays and until 6 pm weekends. Since most hotels in the area do not have courts, tennis players visiting Delray Beach often come here to play. ✉ *201 W. Atlantic Ave., Delray Beach* ☎ *561/243–7360* ⊕ *www.delraytennis. com.*

### Richwagen's Bike & Sport

**BIKING** | Rent bikes by the hour, day, or week (they come with locks, baskets, and helmets); Richwagen's also has copies of city maps on hand. A seven-speed cruiser rents for $60 per week, or $30 a day. They also rent bike trailers, child seats, and electric carts. ✉ *298 N.E. 6th Ave., Delray Beach* ☎ *561/276-4234* ⊕ *www.delraybeachbicycles.com* ⊘ *Closed Sun. and Mon.*

# Boca Raton

*6 miles south of Delray Beach.*

Less than an hour south of Palm Beach and anchoring the county's south end, upscale Boca Raton has much in common with its fabled cousin. Both reflect the unmistakable architectural influence of Addison Mizner, their principal developer in the mid-1920s. The meaning of the name Boca Raton (pronounced bo-ca rah- *tone*) often arouses curiosity, with many folks mistakenly assuming it means "rat's mouth." Historians say the probable origin is *boca ratones*, an ancient Spanish geographical term for an inlet filled with jagged rocks or coral. Miami's Biscayne Bay had such an inlet, and in 1823 a mapmaker copying Miami terrain confused the more northern inlet, thus mistakenly labeling this area Boca Ratones.

No matter what, you'll know you've arrived in the heart of downtown when

The Boca Raton Museum of Art has two sculpture gardens with more than 30 pieces of art.

you spot the historic town hall's gold dome on the main street, Federal Highway. Much of the Boca landscape was heavily planned, and many of the bigger sights are clustered in the area around town hall and Lake Boca, a wide stretch of the Intracoastal Waterway between Palmetto Park Road and Camino Real (two main east–west streets at the southern end of town).

### GETTING HERE AND AROUND

To get to Boca Raton from Delray Beach, drive south 6 miles on Interstate 95, Federal Highway (U.S. 1), or Route A1A.

##  Sights

### Boca Raton Museum of Art

**ART MUSEUM | FAMILY |** Changing-exhibition galleries on the first floor showcase internationally known artists—both past and present—at this museum in a spectacular building that's part of the Mizner Park shopping center; the permanent collection upstairs includes works by Picasso, Degas, Matisse, Klee, Modigliani, and Warhol, as well as notable African and pre-Columbian art. Daily tours are included with admission. In addition to the treasure hunts and sketchbooks you can pick up from the front desk, there's a roster of special programs that cater to kids, including studio workshops and gallery walks. ⊠ *501 Plaza Real, Mizner Park* ☎ *561/392–2500* ⊕ *www.bocamuseum. org* 🖃 *$12* 🕙 *Closed Mon. and Tues.*

### Gumbo Limbo Nature Center

**NATURE PRESERVE | FAMILY |** A big draw for kids, this stellar spot has four huge saltwater tanks brimming with sea life, from coral to stingrays to spiny lobsters, and touch tanks, plus a sea turtle rehabilitation center. Nocturnal walks in spring and early summer, when staffers lead a quest to find nesting female turtles coming ashore to lay eggs, are popular; so are the hatchling releases in August and September. (Call to purchase tickets in advance, as there are very limited spaces.) This is one of only a handful of centers that offer this. There is also a nature trail and butterfly garden, a ¼-mile boardwalk, and a 40-foot observation tower, where you're likely to see brown pelicans and osprey. ⊠ *1801 N. Ocean Blvd., Boca Raton* ☎ *561/544–8605* ⊕ *www.gumbolimbo.org* ✆ *Free ($5 suggested donation); turtle walks $15.*

### Old Floresta
**NEIGHBORHOOD** | This residential area was developed by Addison Mizner starting in 1925 and is beautifully landscaped with palms and cycads. Its houses are mainly Mediterranean in style, many with balconies supported by exposed wooden columns. Explore by driving northward on Paloma Avenue (Northwest 8th Avenue) from Palmetto Park Road, then weave in and out of the side streets. ⊠ *Paloma Ave., Boca Raton* ⊹ *North of W. Palmetto Park Rd.*

 Beaches

Boca's three city beaches (South Beach, Red Reef Park, and Spanish River Park, south to north, respectively) are beautiful and hugely popular, but unless you're a resident or enter via bicycle, parking can be very expensive. Save your receipt if you care to go in and out or to park hop—most guards at the front gate will honor a same-day ticket from another location if you ask nicely. Another option is the county-run South Inlet Park that's walking distance from the Waterstone Resort (formerly the Boca Raton Bridge Hotel) at the southern end of Lake Boca; it has a metered lot for a fraction of the cost but not quite the same charm as the others.

### Red Reef Park
**BEACH | FAMILY** | The ocean with its namesake reef that you can wade up to is just one draw: a fishing zone on the Intracoastal Waterway across the street, a 9-hole golf course next door, and the Gumbo Limbo Environmental Education Center at the northern end of the park can easily make a day at the beach into so much more. But if pure old-fashioned fun in the sun is your focus, there are

tons of picnic tables and grills and two separate playgrounds. Pack snorkels and explore the reef at high tide, when fish are most abundant. Swimmers, be warned: once lifeguards leave at 5, anglers flock to the shores and stay well past dark. **Amenities:** lifeguards; parking (fee); showers; toilets. **Best for:** snorkeling; swimming; walking. ⊠ *1400 N. Rte. A1A, Boca Raton* ☎ *561/393–7974, 561/393–7989 for beach conditions* ⊕ *www.myboca.us* ✆ *$16 parking (weekdays), $18 parking (weekends).*

### South Beach Park
**BEACH** | Perched high up on a dune, a large open-air pavilion at the east end of Palmetto Park Road offers a panoramic view of what's in store below on the sand that stretches up the coast. Serious beachgoers need to pull into the main lot a quarter mile north on the east side of A1A, but if a short-but-sweet visit is what you're after, the 15 or so one-hour spots with meters in the circle driveway will do (and not cost you the normal $15 parking fee). During the day, pretty young things blanket the shore and windsurfers practice tricks in the waves. Quiet quarters are farther north. **Amenities:** lifeguards; parking (fee); showers; toilets. **Best for:** sunset; swimming; walking; windsurfing. ⊠ *400 N. Rte A1A, Boca Raton* ⊕ *www.myboca.us* ✆ *$15 parking (weekdays), $17 parking (weekends).*

### Spanish River Park
**BEACH** | At 76 acres and including extensive nature trails, this is by far one of the largest ocean parks in the southern half of Palm Beach County and a great pick for people who want more space and fewer crowds. Big groups, including family reunions, favor it because of the number of covered picnic areas for rent, but anyone can snag a free table (there are plenty) under the thick canopy of banyan trees. Even though the vast majority of the park is separated from the surf, you never actually have to cross A1A to reach the beach because tunnels run under it

at several locations. **Amenities:** lifeguards; parking (fee); showers; toilets. **Best for:** solitude; swimming; walking. ✉ *3001 N. Rte. A1A, Boca Raton* ☎ *561/393–7815* 🌐 *www.myboca.us* 🎫 *$16 parking (weekdays), $18 parking (weekends).*

## 🍴 Restaurants

**★ Casa D'Angelo Ristorante**
**$$$$** | **ITALIAN** | The lines are deservedly long at this upscale Tuscan restaurant in Boca Raton. The outpost of the renowned Casa D'Angelo in Broward impresses with an outstanding selection of antipasti, carpaccios, pastas, and specialties from the wood-burning oven. **Known for:** wide range of antipasti; veal osso buco and scaloppine; extensive wine list. [$] *Average main: $38* ✉ *171 E. Palmetto Park Rd., Boca Raton* ☎ *561/996–1234* 🌐 *www.casa-d-angelo.com* ⏲ *No lunch.*

**Farmer's Table**
**$** | **AMERICAN** | Taking up the local-food mantle, the menu here includes inventive dishes following the seasons using locally sourced meats, seafood, and vegetables. Whenever possible, the foods are organic or sustainable. **Known for:** Buddha bowl with stir-fried vegetables and udon; good wine, cocktails, and beer; some vegan options. [$] *Average main: $22* ✉ *Wyndham Boca Raton, 1901 N. Military Trail, Boca Raton* ☎ *561/417–5836* 🌐 *www.farmerstableboca.com.*

## 🛏 Hotels

**★ The Boca Raton**
**$$$$** | **RESORT** | **FAMILY** | Addison Mizner built this Mediterranean-style hotel in 1926, and additions over time have created a sprawling, sparkling resort, one of the most luxurious in all South Florida and a destination unto itself. **Pros:** superexclusive—grounds are closed to the public; decor strikes the right balance between historic roots and modern comforts; plenty of activities. **Cons:** daily resort charge; pricey; conventions often crowd common areas. [$] *Rooms from: $509* ✉ *501 E. Camino Real, Boca Raton* ☎ *561/447–3000, 888/543–1277* 🌐 *www.bocaresort.com* 🛏 *635 rooms* 🍽 *No Meals.*

**★ The Boca Raton Beach Club**
**$$$$** | **RESORT** | **FAMILY** | Dotted with turquoise lounge chairs, ruffled umbrellas, and white-sand beaches, this contemporary resort looks as if it were carefully replicated from a retro-chic postcard. **Pros:** great location on the beach; kids' activity center; on-site pool and dining. **Cons:** pricey; the main resort's restaurants are a shuttle ride away; resort fee. [$] *Rooms from: $542* ✉ *900 S. Ocean Blvd., Boca Raton* ☎ *888/564–1312* 🌐 *www.thebocaraton.com/suites-rooms/beach-club* 🛏 *212 rooms* 🍽 *No Meals.*

**Waterstone Resort & Marina**
**$$** | **HOTEL** | The sleek, modern resort is home to the only waterfront dining in Boca Raton as well as light and airy rooms with views of the Intracoastal Waterway and the ocean. **Pros:** short walk to beach; pet-friendly; waterfront views throughout. **Cons:** parking fee; no quiet common space; some rooms noisy from nearby bridge traffic. [$] *Rooms from: $289* ✉ *999 E. Camino Real, Boca Raton* ☎ *561/368–9500* 🌐 *www.waterstoneboca.com* 🛏 *139 rooms* 🍽 *No Meals.*

## 🏃 Activities

**The Boca Raton Golf Course**
**GOLF** | The Resort Course at The Boca Raton is dedicated to both of the resort's former golf pros, Tommy Armour and Sam Snead. Legendary Sam Snead was the head pro in the 1960s, Tommy Armour from the mid-1920s to the mid-1950s. The par-71 course is popular due to its many elevation changes and its Hugh Hughes–designed water feature. Nowadays there's also a second course located off site, the Country Club Course, with a Dave Pelz Scoring Game School

that *is* open to the public. Resort Course play is just for guests and members. ✉ *501 E. Camino Real* ☎ *561/447–3078* ⊕ *www.bocaresort.com* ✉ *Resort Course: 18 holes for $225, 9 holes for $164; Country Club Course: 18 holes for $97, 9 holes for $65* 🏌 *Resort Course: 18 holes, 6253 yards, par 71; Country Club Course: 18 holes, 6714 yards, par 71.*

### Force-E
**SCUBA DIVING** | This company, in business since the late 1970s, rents, sells, and repairs scuba and snorkeling equipment—and organizes about 80 dive trips a week from the Palm Beach Inlet to Port Everglades in Broward County. The PADI–affiliated five-star center has instruction for all levels and offers private charters, too. They have two other outposts besides this Boca Raton location—one to the north in Riviera Beach and one to the south in Pompano Beach. ✉ *2621 N. Federal Hwy., Boca Raton* ☎ *561/368–0555, 561/368–0555* ⊕ *www.force-e.com.*

# Palm Beach Gardens

*13½ miles north of West Palm Beach.*

This relaxed, upscale residential community is known for its high-profile golf complex, the **PGA National Resort & Spa.** Although not on the beach, the town is less than a 15-minute drive from the ocean. Malls and dining are centered on the main street, PGA Boulevard, running east from the resort to U.S. 1.

## 🍴 Restaurants

### ★ The Butcher's Club
**$$$$** | **STEAKHOUSE** | Located in the PGA National Resort & Spa, this eatery draws guests, locals, and tourists alike eager for a taste of its upscale cuts of steak and Macallan cocktails. Opened in 2022 as part of a resort-wide renovation, the swanky 1950's style chophouse is headed up by *Top Chef* winner Jeremy Ford.

**Known for:** wide range of steaks; raw bar; extensive wine list. $ *Average main: $38* ✉ *PGA National Resort & Spa, 400 Ave. of the Champions, Palm Beach Gardens* ☎ *561/627–4852* ⊕ *www.pgaresort.com/ dine/the-butchers-club.*

### Café Chardonnay
**$$$** | **AMERICAN** | A longtime local favorite, Café Chardonnay is charming and romantic and has some of the most refined food in the suburban town of Palm Beach Gardens. Soft lighting, warm woods, white tablecloths, and cozy banquettes set the scene for a quiet lunch or romantic dinner. **Known for:** outstanding wine list; innovative specials; many locally sourced ingredients. $ *Average main: $34* ✉ *The Gardens Square Shoppes, 4533 PGA Blvd., Palm Beach Gardens* ☎ *561/627–2662* ⊕ *www.cafechardonnay.com* ⊘ *No lunch weekends.*

### ★ Coolinary Cafe
**$** | **AMERICAN** | It's tucked away in a strip mall and has only 50 seats inside (counting the bar) and a handful out on the sidewalk, but everything down to the condiments is made in house here. Rabbit sausage and noodles or lamb meatball risotto are examples on the seasonal one-page menus the chef puts together daily. **Known for:** small, focused regular menu; fresh fish specials; long waits for dinner in season. $ *Average main: $22* ✉ *Donald Ross Village Plaza, 4650 Donald Ross Rd., Suite 110, Palm Beach Gardens* ☎ *561/249–6760* ⊕ *www.thecoolpig.com* ⊘ *Closed Sun.*

### The Cooper
**$** | **AMERICAN** | **FAMILY** | With a contemporary farm-to-table menu and spacious dining rooms and bars, this spot in PGA Commons has plenty of local fans. Happy-hour crowds fill the patio bar–lounge area to sip the craft cocktails and nibble from a cheese or *salumi* board. **Known for:** wide-ranging American menu; extensive wine list; gluten-free options. $ *Average main: $23* ✉ *PGA Commons, 4610 PGA Blvd., Palm Beach Gardens*

☎ 561/622–0032 ⊕ www.thecooperres-
taurant.com.

### Spoto's Oyster Bar
**$$ | SEAFOOD |** If you love oysters and
other raw bar nibbles, head here, where
black-and-white photographs of oyster
fisherman adorn the walls. The polished
tables give the eatery a clubby look.
**Known for:** wide range of oysters and
clams; fresh seafood; live music in the
Blue Point Lounge. Ⓢ *Average main:
$26* ⊠ *PGA Commons, 4560 PGA Blvd.,
Palm Beach Gardens* ☎ *561/776–9448*
⊕ *spotos.com.*

##  Hotels

### Hilton Garden Inn Palm Beach Gardens
**$$ | HOTEL |** A hidden find in Palm Beach
Gardens, this hotel sits on a small lake
next to a residential area but near two
shopping malls and close to PGA golf
courses. **Pros:** 24-hour free business
center; walk to two different malls with
shops, restaurants, and movie theaters;
rooms were recently renovated. **Cons:**
15 minutes from the beach; outdoor self
parking; pool closes at dusk. Ⓢ *Rooms
from: $209* ⊠ *3505 Kyoto Gardens Dr.,
Palm Beach Gardens* ☎ *561/694–5833,
561/694–5829* ⊕ *hiltongardeninn3.hilton.
com* ⇱ *180 rooms* ❁ *No Meals.*

### ★ PGA National Resort & Spa
**$$$ | RESORT |** This golfer's paradise,
home to five championship courses
and the site of the yearly Honda Classic
pro-tour tournament, is a sleek modern
playground with a gorgeous zero-entry
lagoon pool, seven different places to
eat, and a full-service spa with unique
mineral-salt therapy pools. **Pros:** dream
golf facilities; affordable rates for top-
notch amenities; close to shopping malls.
**Cons:** no beach shuttle; difficult to get
around if you don't have a car; long drive
to Palm Beach proper. Ⓢ *Rooms from:
$348* ⊠ *400 Ave. of the Champions,
Palm Beach Gardens* ☎ *561/627–2000,*

*800/633–9150* ⊕ *www.pgaresort.com*
⇱ *339 rooms* ❁ *No Meals.*

##  Shopping

### ★ The Gardens Mall
**MALL | FAMILY |** One of the most refined
big shopping malls in America, the
160-store Gardens Mall in northern Palm
Beach County has stores like Chanel,
Tory Burch, Louis Vuitton, and David
Yurman, along with Saks Fifth Avenue
and Nordstrom. There are also plenty of
reasonably priced national retailers like
H&M and Abercrombie & Fitch, Bloom-
ingdale's, and Macy's. This beautiful mall
has prolific seating pavilions, making it
a great place to spend a humid summer
afternoon. ⊠ *3101 PGA Blvd., Palm
Beach Gardens* ☎ *561/775–7750* ⊕ *www.
thegardensmall.com.*

## Activities

Spring-training fans travel to the area to
see the Cardinals and Marlins tune up for
their seasons at Roger Dean Stadium in
Palm Beach Gardens and to watch their
AAA feeder teams in summer. Port St.
Lucie and Vero Beach stadiums and more
teams are only a short drive up Interstate
95.

### ★ PGA National Resort & Spa
**GOLF |** If you're the kind of traveler who
takes along a set of clubs, you'll achieve
nirvana on the greens of PGA National
Resort & Spa. The five championship
courses are open only to hotel guests
and club members, which means you'll
have to stay to play, but packages that
include a room and a round of golf are
reasonably priced. The Champion Course,
redesigned by Jack Nicklaus and famous
for its Bear Trap holes, is the site of the
yearly Honda Classic pro tournament. The
four other challenging courses are also
legends in the golfing world: the Palmer,
named for its architect, the legendary
Arnold Palmer; the Fazio (formerly the
Haig) and the Squire, both from Tom

and George Fazio; and the Karl Litten–designed Estates, the sole course not on the property (it is located 5 miles west of the PGA resort). ⊠ *PGA National Resort & Spa, 1000 Ave. of the Champions, Palm Beach Gardens* ☎ *561/627–1800* ⊕ *www.pgaresort.com/golf/pga-national-golf* ⌨ *$409 for 18 holes for Champion Course, Fazio Course, and Squire Course; $250 for 18 holes for Palmer Course and Estates Course* ⚑*. Champion Course: 18 holes, 7048 yards, par 72; Palmer Course: 18 holes, 7079 yards, par 72; Fazio Course: 18 holes, 6806 yards, par 72; Squire Course: 18 holes, 6465 yards, par 72; Estates Course: 18 holes, 6694 yards, par 72.*

# Singer Island

*6 miles north of West Palm Beach.*

Across the inlet from the northern end of Palm Beach is Singer Island, which is actually a peninsula that's big enough to pass for a barrier island, rimmed with mom-and-pop motels and high-rises. Palm Beach Shores occupies its southern tip (where tiny Peanut Island is a stone's throw away); farther north are Riviera Beach and North Palm Beach, which also straddle the inlet and continue on the mainland.

 Beaches

★ **John D. MacArthur Beach State Park**
BEACH | FAMILY | If getting far from rowdy crowds is your goal, this spot on the north end of Singer Island is a good choice. Encompassing 2 miles of beach and a lush subtropical coastal habitat, inside you'll find a great place for kayaking, snorkeling at natural reefs, bird-watching, fishing, and hiking. You might even get to see a few manatees. A 4,000-square-foot nature center has aquariums and displays on local flora and fauna, and there's a long roster of monthly activities, such as surfing clinics, art lessons, and live bluegrass music. ■TIP→ **Check the website for times and costs of activities. Amenities:** parking (fee); showers; toilets; water sports. **Best for:** solitude; surfing; swimming; walking. ⊠ *10900 Jack Nicklaus Dr., North Palm Beach* ☎ *561/624–6950* ⊕ *www.macarthurbeach.org* ⌨ *Parking $5, bicyclists and pedestrians $2.*

**Peanut Island Park**
BEACH | Partiers, families, and overnight campers all have a place to go on the 79 acres here. The island, in a wide section of the Intracoastal between Palm Beach Island and Singer Island, with an open channel to the sea, is accessible only by private boat or water taxi, two of which set sail regularly from the Riviera Beach Municipal Marina and the Sailfish Marina. Fun-loving seafarers looking for an afternoon of Jimmy Buffett with picnics aboard pull up to the day docks or the huge sandbar to the north—float around in an inner tube, and it's spring break déjà vu. Walk along the 20-foot-wide paver-lined path encircling the island, and you'll hit a 170-foot fishing pier, a campground, and the lifeguarded section to the south that is particularly popular with families because of its artificial reef. There are picnic tables and grills, but no concessions. A new ordinance means alcohol possession and consumption is restricted to permit areas. **Amenities:** lifeguards (summer only); showers; toilets. **Best for:** partiers; sunrise; swimming; walking. ⊠ *6500 Peanut Island Rd., Riviera Beach* ☎ *561/845–4445* ⊕ *discover. pbcgov.org/parks* ⌨ *Beach free; water taxi $12; park stay $17.*

 Hotels

**Palm Beach Marriott Singer Island Beach Resort & Spa**
$$$$ | RESORT | FAMILY | Travelers with a desire for the cosmopolitan but requiring the square footage and comforts of home revel in these one- and two-bedroom suites with spacious, marble-tiled,

granite-topped kitchens. **Pros:** wide beach; genuinely warm service; sleek spa. **Cons:** no upscale dining nearby; unspectacular room views for an oceanside hotel; hefty resort fee. [$] *Rooms from: $509* ✉ *3800 N. Ocean Dr., Singer Island, Riviera Beach* ☎ *561/340–1700, 877/239–5610* 🌐 *www.marriott.com* 🛏 *202 suites* 🍴 *No Meals.*

**Sailfish Marina Resort**

$ | **HOTEL** | A marina with deepwater slips—and a prime location at the mouth to the Atlantic Ocean on the Intracoastal Waterway across from Peanut Island—lures boaters and anglers here to these rather basic rooms, studios, and efficiencies. **Pros:** great waterfront restaurant; inexpensive rates; pretty grounds. **Cons:** not directly on beach; area attracts a party crowd and can be noisy; dated decor. [$] *Rooms from: $150* ✉ *98 Lake Dr., Palm Beach Shores* ☎ *561/844–1724* 🌐 *www.sailfishmarina.com* 🛏 *30 units* 🍴 *No Meals.*

## Activities

**Sailfish Marina**

**FISHING** | **FAMILY** | Book a full or half day of deep-sea fishing for up to six people with the seasoned captains and large fleet of 28- to 65-foot boats. A ship's store and restaurant are also on site. ✉ *Sailfish Marina Resort, 98 Lake Dr., Palm Beach Shores* ☎ *561/844–1724* 🌐 *www.sailfishmarina.com.*

# Juno Beach

*12 miles north of West Palm Beach.*

This small town east of Palm Beach Gardens has 2 miles of shoreline that becomes home to thousands of sea turtle hatchlings each year, making it one of the world's densest nesting sites. A 990-foot-long pier lures fishermen and beachgoers seeking a spectacular sunrise.

## Sights

★ **Loggerhead Park Marine Life Center of Juno Beach**

**WILDLIFE REFUGE** | **FAMILY** | Located in a certified green building in Loggerhead Park—and established by Eleanor N. Fletcher, the "turtle lady of Juno Beach"—the center focuses on the conservation of sea turtles, using education, research, and rehabilitation. The education center houses displays of coastal natural history, detailing Florida's marine ecosystems and the life and plight of the various species of sea turtles found on Florida's shores. You can visit recovering turtles in their outdoor hospital tanks; volunteers are happy to tell you the turtles' heroic tales of survival. The center has regularly scheduled activities, such as Kids' Story Time and Junior Vet Lab, and most are free of charge. During peak nesting season, the center hosts night walks to experience turtle nesting in action. Given that the adjacent beach is part of the second-biggest nesting ground for loggerhead turtles in the world, your chances of seeing this natural phenomenon are pretty high (over 15,000 loggerheads nested here during one recent season). ✉ *14200 U.S. 1, Juno Beach* ☎ *561/627–8280* 🌐 *www.marinelife.org* 🎟 *Free.*

## Beaches

**Juno Beach Ocean Park**

**BEACH** | **FAMILY** | An angler's dream, this beach has a 990-foot pier that's open daily, like the beach, from sunrise to sunset—but from November through February, the pier gates open at 6 am and don't close until 10 pm on weeknights and midnight on weekends, making it an awesome place to catch a full sunrise and sunset (that is, if you don't mind paying the small admission fee). A concession stand on the pier sells fish food as well as such human favorites as burgers, sandwiches, and ice cream.

Away from developed shorelines, Jupiter's Blowing Rocks Preserve is rugged and otherworldly.

Rods and tackle are rented here. Families adore this shoreline because of the amenities and vibrant atmosphere. There are plenty of kids building sandcastles but also plenty of teens gathering and hanging out along the beach. Pets are not allowed here, but they are allowed on Jupiter Beach. **Amenities:** food and drink; lifeguards; parking (no fee); showers; toilets. **Best for:** sunrise; sunset; swimming. ⊠ *14775 U.S. 1, Juno Beach* ☎ *561/799–0185 for pier* ⊕ *discover.pbcgov.org/parks* 🖃 *$4 to fish, $1 to enter pier; beach free.*

# Jupiter and Vicinity

*12 miles north of West Palm Beach.*

Jupiter is one of the few towns in the region not fronted by an island but still quite close to the fantastic hotels, shopping, and dining of the Palm Beach area. The beaches here are on the mainland, and Route A1A runs for almost 4 miles along the beachfront dunes and beautiful homes.

Northeast across the Jupiter Inlet from Jupiter is the southern tip of Jupiter Island, which stretches about 15 miles to the St. Lucie Inlet. Here expansive and expensive estates often retreat from the road behind screens of vegetation, and the population dwindles the farther north you go. At the very north end, which adjoins tiny Hobe Sound in Martin County on the mainland, sea turtles come to nest.

## GETTING HERE AND AROUND

If you're coming from the airport in West Palm Beach, take Interstate 95 to Route 706. Otherwise, Federal Highway (U.S. 1) and Route A1A are usually more convenient.

##  Sights

### ★ Blowing Rocks Preserve

BEACH | FAMILY | Managed by the Nature Conservancy, this protected area on Jupiter Island is headlined by an almost otherworldly looking limestone shelf that fringes South Florida's most turquoise waters. Also protected within its 73 acres are plants native to beachfront dunes, coastal strands (the landward side of the dunes), mangrove swamps, and tropical hardwood forests. There are two short walking trails on the Intracoastal side of the preserve, as well as an education center and a butterfly garden. The best time to come and see the "blowing rocks" is when a storm is brewing: if high tides and strong offshore winds coincide, the sea blows spectacularly through the holes in the eroded outcropping. During a calm summer day, you can swim in crystal clear waters on the mile-long beach and climb around the rock formations at low tide. Park in one of the two lots, because police ticket cars on the road. ⊠ *574 S. Beach Rd., CR 707, Hobe Sound* ☎ *561/744–6668* ⊕ *www. nature.org/blowingrocks* ⊠ *$2.*

## Dubois Home

**HISTORIC HOME** | Take a look at how life once was at this modest pioneer outpost dating from 1898. Renovated to repair hurricane damage to its structure, it's a picture of life before South Florida became a resort area. Sitting atop an ancient Jeaga mound 20 feet high and looking onto the Jupiter Inlet, it has Cape Cod as well as Old Florida design. It's in Dubois Park, worth a visit for its lovely beaches and swimming lagoons. Docents lead tours Tuesday and Thursday, 10–1. The park is open dawn to dusk. ⊠ *19075 Dubois Rd., Jupiter* ☎ *561/966-6600* ⊕ *discover.pbcgov.org/parks/Locations/DuBoisPioneer.aspx* ⊠ *$2.*

## ★ Hobe Sound Nature Center

**NATURE PRESERVE** | **FAMILY** | Though located in the Hobe Sound National Wildlife Refuge, this nature center is an independent organization. The exhibit hall houses live baby alligators, crocodiles, a scary-looking tarantula, and more—and is a child's delight. Just off the center's entrance is a mile-long nature trail loop that snakes through three different kinds of habitats: coastal hammock, estuary beach, and

sand pine scrub, which is one of Florida's most unusual and endangered plant communities and what composes much of the refuge's nearly 250 acres.

■ TIP→ **Among the center's more popular events are the annual nighttime sea turtle walks, held between May and June; reservations are accepted as early as April 1.** ⊠ *13640 S.E. U.S. 1, Hobe Sound* ☎ *772/546–2067* ⊕ *www.hobesoundnaturecenter.com* ⊠ *Donations accepted* ⊘ *Closed Sun.*

## ★ Jonathan Dickinson State Park

**STATE/PROVINCIAL PARK** | **FAMILY** | This serene state park provides a glimpse of predevelopment "real" Florida. A beautiful showcase of Florida inland habitat, the park teems with endangered gopher tortoises and manatees. From Hobe Mountain, an ancient dune topped with a tower, you are treated to a panoramic view of this park's more than 11,000 acres of varied terrain and the Intracoastal Waterway. The Loxahatchee River, named a National Wild and Scenic River, cuts through the park and is home to plenty of charismatic manatees in winter and alligators year-round. Two-hour boat tours of the river depart daily. Kayak rentals are available, as is horseback riding (it was reintroduced after a 30-year absence). Among the amenities are a dozen newly redone cabins for rent, tent sites, bicycle and hiking trails, two established campgrounds and some primitive campgrounds, and a new food-and-beverage garden with wine, beer, and local foods. The park is also a fantastic birding location, with about 150 species to spot. ⊠ *16450 S.E. U.S. 1, Hobe Sound* ☎ *772/546-2771* ⊕ *www. floridastateparks.org* ⊠ *Vehicles $6, bicyclists and pedestrians $2.*

## ★ Jupiter Inlet Lighthouse & Museum

**LIGHTHOUSE** | **FAMILY** | Designed by Civil War hero lieutenant George Gordon Meade, this working brick lighthouse has been under the Coast Guard's purview since 1860. Tours of the 108-foot-tall landmark are held approximately every half hour and are included with admission. (Children must be at least 4 feet tall to go to the top.) The museum tells about efforts to restore this graceful spire to the way it looked from 1860 to 1918; its galleries and outdoor structures, including a pioneer home, also showcase local history dating back 5,000 years. ✉ *Lighthouse Park, 500 Capt. Armour's Way, Jupiter* ☎ *561/747–8380* 🌐 *www.jupiterlighthouse.org* 🎟 *$12* 🕒 *Closed Mon. and Tues.*

## Beaches

**Carlin Park**

**BEACH** | About ½ mile south of the Jupiter Beach Resort, the quiet beach here is just one draw; the manicured park, which straddles A1A, is chock-full of activities and amenities, and it has the most free parking of any beach park in the area. Several picnic pavilions (including a few beachside), two bocce ball courts, six lighted tennis courts, a baseball diamond, a wood-chip-lined running path, and an amphitheater that hosts free concerts and Shakespeare productions are just some of the highlights. **Amenities:** food and drink; lifeguards; parking (no fee); showers; toilets. **Best for:** swimming; walking. ✉ *400 S. Rte. A1A, Jupiter* 🌐 *discover.pbcgov.org/parks/Locations/Carlin.aspx.*

**Hobe Sound National Wildlife Refuge**

**BEACH** | Nature lovers seeking to get as far as possible from the madding crowds will feel at peace at this refuge managed by the U.S. Fish & Wildlife Service. It's a haven for people who want some quiet while they walk around and photograph the gorgeous coastal sand dunes, where turtles nest and shells often wash ashore. You can't actually venture within most of the 735 protected acres, so if hiking piques your interest, head to nearby Jonathan Dickinson State Park. **Amenities:** parking (fee); toilets. **Best for:** solitude; surfing; walking. ✉ *198 N. Beach Rd., Jupiter Island* ✥ *At end of N. Beach Rd.* ☎ *772/546–6141* 🌐 *www.fws.gov/hobesound* 🎟 *$5.*

★ **Jupiter Beach**

**BEACH** | Famous throughout all Florida for a unique pooch-loving stance, the town of Jupiter's beach welcomes Yorkies, Labs, pugs—you name it—along its 2½-mile oceanfront. Dogs can frolic unleashed (once they're on the beach) or join you for a dip. Free parking spots line A1A in front of the sandy stretch, and there are multiple access points and continuously refilled scooper-bag boxes. The dog beach starts on Marcinski Road (Beach Marker No. 25) and continues north until Beach Marker No. 59. Before going, read through the guidelines posted on the Friends of Jupiter Beach website; the biggest things to note are be sure to clean up after your dog and to steer clear of lifeguarded areas to the north and south. ■ **TIP→ Dogs fare best early morning and late afternoon, when the sand isn't too hot for their paws.** **Amenities:** showers; toilets. **Best for:** walking. ✉ *2188 Marcinski Rd., Jupiter* ✥ *Across street from parking lot* ☎ *561/748–8140* 🌐 *www.friendsofjupiterbeach.org.*

## Restaurants

**Guanabanas**

$ | **SEAFOOD** | Expect a wait for dinner, which is not necessarily a bad thing at this island paradise of a waterfront restaurant and bar. Take the wait time to explore the bridges and trails of the open-air tropical oasis, or grab a chair by the river to watch the sunset, listen to the live band, or nibble on some conch fritters at the large tiki bar until your table is ready. **Known for:** water views from the outdoor dining area; live music; weekend breakfast. [$] *Average main: $18* ✉ *960 N. Rte. A1A, Jupiter* ☎ *561/747–8878* 🌐 *www.guanabanas.com.*

## Florida's Sea Turtles: Nesting Season

From May to October, turtles nest all along the Florida coast. Female loggerhead, Kemp's ridley, and other species living in the Atlantic Ocean or Gulf of Mexico swim as much as 2,000 miles to the Florida shore. By night they drag their 100- to 400-pound bodies onto the beach to the dune line. Then each digs a hole with her flippers, drops in 100 or so eggs, covers them up, and returns to sea.

The babies hatch about 60 days later. Once they burst out of the sand, the hatchlings must get to sea rapidly or risk becoming dehydrated from the sun or being caught by crabs, birds, and other predators.

Instinctively, baby turtles head toward bright light, probably because for millions of years starlight or moonlight reflected on the waves was the brightest light around, serving to guide hatchlings to water. Many coastal towns enforce light restrictions during nesting months. Florida homeowners are asked to dim their lights on behalf of baby sea turtles.

At night, volunteers walk the beaches, searching for signs of turtle nests. Upon finding telltale scratches in the sand, they cordon off the sites, so beachgoers will leave the spots undisturbed. (It is illegal to disturb turtle nests.) Volunteers also keep watch over nests when babies are about to hatch and assist disoriented hatchlings.

Several local organizations offer nightly turtle walks during nesting season. Most are in June and July, starting around 8 pm and sometimes lasting until midnight. Expect a $10 to $15 fee. Call in advance to confirm times and to reserve a spot—places usually take reservations as early as April. If you're in southern Palm Beach County, contact Boca Raton's **Gumbo Limbo Nature Center** (☎ *561/338–1473*). The **John D. MacArthur Beach State Park** (☎ *561/624–6952*) is convenient for Palm Beach–area visitors at the northern end of Singer Island. **Hobe Sound Nature Center** (☎ *772/546–2067*) is farther up. Treasure Coasters in or near Vero Beach can go to **Sebastian Inlet State Park** (☎ *321/984–4852* 🌐 *www.floridastateparks.org*).

**Little Moir's Food Shack**

$ | **SEAFOOD** | This local favorite is not much to look at and a bit tricky to find, but well worth the search. The fried-food standards you might expect at such a casual, small place that uses plastic utensils are not found on the menu; instead there are fried tuna rolls with basil and panko-crusted fried oysters with spicy fruit salad. **Known for:** fresh fish; good beer selection; long lines during the season. [$] *Average main: $17* ✉ *103 S. U.S. 1, Jupiter* ☎ *561/741–3626* 🌐 *www.littlemoirs.com/food-shack* 🕓 *Closed Sun.*

**Sinclair's Ocean Grill**

$$$ | **SEAFOOD** | This upscale restaurant at the Jupiter Beach Resort & Spa has a slick, contemporary look and is a favorite of locals in the know. The menu has a daily selection of fresh fish, such as Atlantic black grouper over lemon crab salad, sesame-seared tuna, and mahimahi with fruit salsa. **Known for:** fresh fish; weekend brunch; drinks in Sinclair's Lounge. [$] *Average main: $31* ✉ *Jupiter Beach Resort, 5 N. Rte. A1A, Jupiter* ☎ *561/746–2511* 🌐 *www.jupiterbeachresort.com.*

## Hotels

**★ Jupiter Beach Resort & Spa**
**$$$ | RESORT | FAMILY** | Families love this nine-story hotel filled with rich Caribbean-style rooms containing mahogany sleigh beds and armoires; all rooms have balconies, and many have stunning views of the ocean and local landmarks like the Jupiter Lighthouse and Juno Pier. **Pros:** fantastic beachside pool area with hammocks and a firepit; marble showers; great restaurant. **Cons:** $35 nightly resort fee; no covered parking; bathtubs in suites only. [$] *Rooms from: $360* ✉ *5 N. Rte. A1A, Jupiter* ☎ *561/746–2511, 800/228–8810* 🌐 *www.jupiterbeachresort.com* 🛏 *168 rooms* 🍴 *No Meals.*

**Wyndham Grand Jupiter at Harbourside Place**
**$$$ | HOTEL** | This luxury waterfront hotel is in an upscale complex of business and retail development just minutes from the beach. **Pros:** convenient to plaza shops and restaurants; only minutes from the beach; boat docks and fitness center available. **Cons:** no covered walkway to restaurant; no green spaces; pricey. [$] *Rooms from: $309* ✉ *Harbourside Place, 122 Soundings Ave., Jupiter* ☎ *561/273–6600* 🌐 *www.wyndhamgrandjupiter.com* 🛏 *179 rooms* 🍴 *No Meals.*

## Activities

**Abacoa Golf Club**
**GOLF** | Built in 1999, the tagline for this Joe Lee–designed 18-hole course in Jupiter is "public golf at its finest." Most of the courses in this golfing community are private, but the range at Abacoa is on par with them and membership *isn't* required (nor are deep pockets). Since 2013, $1 million has been spent to renovate the facilities throughout the course and clubhouse. One of the course's more interesting features is the several elevation changes throughout, which is a rarity in flat Florida. The course caters to golfers at all skill levels. The greens fee ranges from $45 to $110 (including cart), depending on time of year, time of day, and weekday versus weekend. ✉ *105 Barbados Dr., Jupiter* ☎ *561/622–0036* 🌐 *www.abacoagolfclub.com* 🎟 *$100 for 18 holes* ⛳ *18 holes, 7200 yards, par 72.*

**Golf Club of Jupiter**
**GOLF** | Locally owned and operated since 1981, this Lamar Smith–designed golf club features a public championship golf course—the "Jupiter" course—with 18 holes of varying difficulty. It has a course rating of 69.9 and a slope rating of 117 on Bermuda grass. There's a full-time golf pro on staff and an on-site bar and restaurant. ✉ *1800 S. Central Blvd., Jupiter* ☎ *561/747–6262* 🌐 *www.golfclubofjupiter.com* 🎟 *$59 for 18 holes* ⛳ *18 holes, 6275 yards, par 70.*

**★ Jonathan Dickinson State Park River Tours**
**BOATING | FAMILY** | Boat tours of the Loxahatchee River and guided horseback rides, along with canoe, kayak, bicycle, and boat rentals, are offered daily. The popular Wilderness Guided Boat Tour leaves four times daily at 9 and 11 am and 1 and 3 pm (for best wildlife photos take the 11 or 1 tour). The pontoon cruises for 90 minutes up the Loxahatchee in search of manatees, herons, osprey, alligators, and more. The skipper details the region's natural and cultural history. From Thursday to Monday, the boat also stops at the Trapper Nelson Interpretive Site for a tour of the home of a local legend, the so-called Wildman of the Loxahatchee. ✉ *Jonathan Dickinson State Park, 16450 S.E. U.S. 1, Jupiter* ☎ *561/746–1466* 🌐 *https://www.jdstatepark.com/boat-tours/* 🎟 *$6 park admission; boat tours $23.*

**★ Jupiter Outdoor Center**
**CANOEING & ROWING** | See animals, from otters to eagles, along 8 miles of the Loxahatchee River in Riverbend County Park daily except Tuesday and Wednesday. Canoes and two-person kayaks are

available for rent. Bike rentals are available, too. ⊠ *Riverbend County Park, 9060 W. Indiantown Rd., Jupiter* ☎ *561/944-2841* ⊕ *www.jupiteroutdoorcenter.com* ☜ *From $35 for 4 hrs for kayak rentals.*

### Roger Dean Chevrolet Stadium

**BASEBALL & SOFTBALL** | It's a spring-training doubleheader: both the St. Louis Cardinals and the Miami Marlins call this 6,600-seat facility home base from February to April. The rest of the year, two minor-league teams (Jupiter Hammerheads and Palm Beach Cardinals) share its turf. In the Abacoa area of Jupiter, the grounds are surrounded by a mix of restaurants and sports bars for pre- and postgame action. ⊠ *4751 Main St., Jupiter* ☎ *561/775–1818* ⊕ *rogerdeanchevroletstadium.com* ☜ *From $12.*

# Stuart and Jensen Beach

*22 miles north of Jupiter.*

The compact town of Stuart lies on a peninsula that juts out into the St. Lucie River off the Indian River and has a remarkable amount of shoreline for its size. It scores huge points for its charming historic district and is the self-described "Sailfish Capital of the World." On the southern end, you'll find Port Salerno and its waterfront area, the Manatee Pocket, which are a skip away from the St. Lucie Inlet.

Immediately north of Stuart is down-to-earth Jensen Beach. Both Stuart and Jensen Beach straddle the Indian River and occupy Hutchinson Island, the barrier island that continues into the town of Fort Pierce. Between late April and August, hundreds, even thousands, of turtles come here to nest along the Atlantic beaches. Residents have taken pains to curb the runaway development that has created commercial crowding to the north and south, although some high-rises have popped up along the shore.

## GETTING HERE AND AROUND

To get to Stuart and Jensen Beach from Jupiter and Hobe Sound, drive north on Federal Highway (U.S. 1). Route A1A crosses through downtown Stuart and is the sole main road throughout Hutchinson Island. Route 707 runs parallel on the mainland directly across the tidal lagoon.

## ESSENTIALS

**VISITOR INFORMATION Martin County Convention & Visitors Bureau.** ⊠ *2410 S.E. Monterey Rd., Stuart* ☎ *772/288–5451, 877/585–0085* ⊕ *www.discovermartin. com.*

 **Sights**

Strict architectural and zoning standards guide civic-renewal projects in the heart of Stuart. Antiques stores, restaurants, and more than 50 specialty shops are rooted within the two-block area of Flagler Avenue and Osceola Street north of where A1A cuts across the peninsula (visit ⊕ *www.stuartmainstreet.org* for more information). A self-guided walking-tour pamphlet is available at assorted locations to clue you in on this once-small fishing village's early days.

### Elliott Museum

**HISTORY MUSEUM | FAMILY** | The museum's glittering, green-certified 48,000-square-foot facility houses a permanent collection along with traveling exhibits. The museum was founded in 1961 in honor of Sterling Elliott, an inventor of an early automated-addressing machine, the egg crate, and a four-wheel bicycle, and it celebrates history, art, and technology, much of it viewed through the lens of the automobile's effect on American society. There's an impressive array of antique cars, plus paintings, historic artifacts, and nostalgic goods like vintage baseball cards and toys. ⊠ *825 N.E. Ocean Blvd., Jensen Beach* ☎ *772/225–1961* ⊕ *elliott-museum.org* ☜ *$16.*

# Lake Okeechobee

Forty miles west of West Palm Beach, amid the farms and cattle pastures rimming the western edges of Palm Beach and Martin Counties, is **Lake Okeechobee,** the second-largest freshwater lake completely within the United States. It's girdled by 120 miles of road, yet remains shielded from sight for almost its entire circumference. (The best place to view it is in Port Mayaca on the north side—where you can get great sunset shots—and the Okeechobee docks on the northwest.) Lake Okeechobee—the Seminole's "Big Water" and the gateway of the great Everglades watershed—measures 730 square miles, at its longest roughly 33 miles north–south and 30 miles east–west, with an average natural depth of only 10 feet (flood control brings the figure up to 12 feet and deeper). Six major lock systems and 32 separate water-control structures manage the water and allow boaters to cross the state through its channels from the Atlantic Ocean to the Gulf of Mexico.

Encircling the lake is a 34-foot-high grassy levee, and atop it is the Lake Okeechobee Scenic Trail, a segment of the Florida National Scenic Trail that's an easy, flat ride for bikers. Anglers have a field day here as well, with great bass and perch catches.

**■ TIP →** There's no shade, so wear a hat, sunscreen, and bug repellent (a must). Be sure to bring lots of bottled water, too, because restaurants and stores are few and far between.

**Florida Oceanographic Coastal Center**
**NATURE SIGHT | FAMILY |** This hydroland is the place to go for an interactive marine experience and to live the center's mission "to inspire environmental stewardship of Florida's coastal ecosystems through education and research." Petting and feeding stingrays can be done at various times; in the morning, a sea turtle program introduces you to three full-time residents. Make sure to catch the "feeding frenzy," when keepers toss food into the 750,000-gallon lagoon tank and sharks, tarpon, and snook swarm the surface. Join a 1-mile guided walk through the coastal hardwood hammock and mangrove swamp habitats, or explore the trails on your own—you may see a dolphin or manatee swim by. ⊠ *890 N.E. Ocean Blvd., Stuart* ☎ *772/225–0505* ⊕ *www.floridaocean.org* ☑ *$16* ⊘ *Closed Mon. and Tues.*

**Gilbert's Bar House of Refuge Museum**
**HISTORY MUSEUM |** Built in 1875 on Hutchinson Island, this is the only remaining example of 10 such structures that were erected by the U.S. Life-Saving Service (a predecessor of the Coast Guard) to aid stranded sailors. The displays here include antique lifesaving equipment, maps, artifacts from nearby wrecks, and boatbuilding tools. The museum is affiliated with the nearby Elliott Museum; package tickets are available. ⊠ *301 S.E. MacArthur Blvd., Jensen Beach* ☎ *772/225–1875* ☑ *$8.*

## 🏖 Beaches

**Bathtub Reef Beach**
**BEACH | FAMILY |** Rough tides are often the norm in this stretch of the Atlantic Ocean and frequently take away the beach, but a charming enclave at the southern end of Hutchinson Island—after the Marriott's beach and right by the Indian River Plantation luxury development—provides a perfect escape for families with young children and anyone who likes to snorkel. The waters are shallow and usually calm,

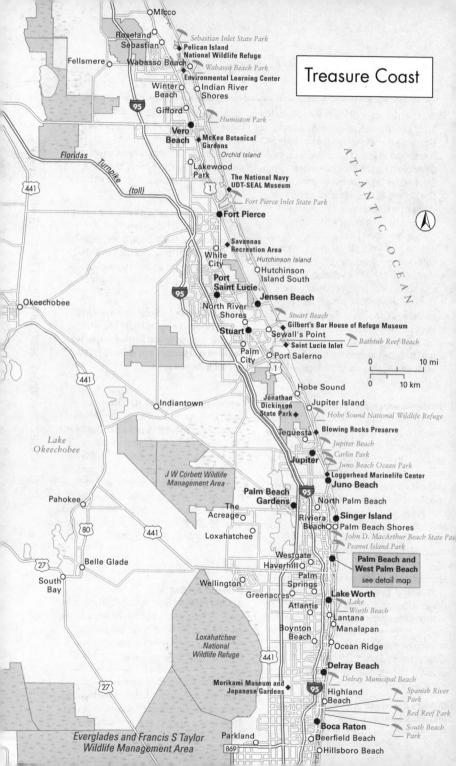

and kids can walk up to the reef and see a dazzling assortment of fish. The parking lot is small, so get there early. **Amenities:** parking (no fee); lifeguards; toilets. **Best for:** snorkeling; swimming. ✉ *1585 S.E. MacArthur Blvd., Stuart* ☎ *772/320–3112* 🌐 *www.martin.fl.us/BathtubReefBeach.*

**Stuart Beach**

**BEACH** | **FAMILY** | When the waves robustly roll in, the surfers are rolling in, too. Beginning surfers are especially keen on Stuart Beach because of its ever-vigilant lifeguards, and pros to the sport like the challenges that the choppy waters here bring. But the beach is equally popular with surf fishers. Families enjoy the snack bar known for its chicken fingers, the basketball courts, the large canopy-covered playground, and the three walkways interspersed throughout the area for easy ocean access. **Amenities:** food and drink; lifeguards; parking (no fee); showers; toilets. **Best for:** surfing; swimming. ✉ *889 N.E. Ocean Blvd., Stuart* 🌐 *cityofstuart.us.*

## 🍴 Restaurants

**Conchy Joe's**

**$$** | **SEAFOOD** | Like a hermit crab sliding into a new shell, Conchy Joe's moved up from West Palm Beach to its current home, a 1920s rustic stilt house on the Indian River. It's full of antique fish mounts, gator hides, and snakeskins and is a popular tourist spot—but the waterfront location, very casual vibe, and delicious seafood lure locals, too. **Known for:** conch chowder; grouper marsala; live reggae Thursday–Sunday. [$] *Average main: $27* ✉ *3945 N.E. Indian River Dr., Jensen Beach* ☎ *772/334–1130* 🌐 *www.conchyjoes.com.*

**District Table and Bar**

**$** | **AMERICAN** | Farm-fresh foods with a Southern accent are served at this chef-owned restaurant with a theater kitchen, where comfort foods are taken to new levels. (Slow Food, a group that celebrates local foods and artisans, has given the restaurant a "Snail of Approval.") The vibe is both hipster and rustic melded into an open (and often noisy) space; the chefs provide entertainment, and the bar is lively. On an ever-changing menu (check the website for the current list), find homemade condiments and jams served with crab hush puppies, sweet-tea fried chicken, or blackened Gulf shrimp. **Known for:** farm-to-table menu; lively bar scene; everything homemade, including condiments and jams. [$] *Average main: $23* ✉ *900 S.E. Indian St., Stuart* ☎ *772/324–8357* 🌐 *www.districttableandbar.com* 🕓 *Closed Mon.*

**11 Maple Street**

**$$$$** | **ECLECTIC** | This cozy spot is as good as it gets on the Treasure Coast. Soft music and a friendly staff set the mood in the antiques-filled dining room of this old house, which holds only 21 tables. **Known for:** nice selection of wines; good desserts; Old Florida setting in vintage house. [$] *Average main: $42* ✉ *3224 N.E. Maple Ave., Jensen Beach* ☎ *772/334–7714* 🌐 *www.elevenmaple.com* 🕓 *Closed Sun. and Mon. No lunch.*

★ **Talk House**

**$** | **FRENCH** | French and American influences are clear in the Swiss chef's dishes, from rack of lamb with Dijon mustard to grilled filet mignon stuffed with Roquefort and fresh spinach. The formal dining room has subtle, elegant touches, such as votive candlelight and white tablecloths. **Known for:** refined Continental cuisine; elegant atmosphere; more casual bar menu. [$] *Average main: $25* ✉ *514 N. Dixie Hwy., Stuart* ☎ *772/692–3662* 🌐 *stuartstalkhouse.com* 🕓 *Closed Mon. No lunch.*

## 🛏 Hotels

**Marriott Hutchinson Island Beach Resort, Golf & Marina**

**$$** | **RESORT** | **FAMILY** | With a 77-slip marina, a full water-sports program, a golf course, two pools, tons of tennis courts, and children's activities, this self-contained resort is excellent for families, most of whom prefer to stay in the tower directly on the ocean. **Pros:** attentive, warm staff; rooms are comfortable and casually chic; all rooms have balconies. **Cons:** common areas are a bit dated; no spa; daily resort fee. [$] *Rooms from: $230* ✉ *555 N.E. Ocean Blvd., Stuart* ☎ *772/225–3700, 800/775–5936* 🌐 *www.marriott.com* 🛏 *274 rooms* 🍴 *No Meals.*

**Pirate's Cove Resort & Marina**

$ | **RESORT** | This cozy enclave on the banks of the Manatee Pocket with ocean access at the southern end of Stuart is the perfect place to set forth on a day at sea or wind down after one—it's relaxing and casual and has amenities like a swimming-pool courtyard, restaurant, and fitness center. **Pros:** spacious tropical-theme rooms; great for boaters, with a 50-slip, full-service, deepwater marina; each room has a balcony overlooking the water. **Cons:** lounge gets noisy at night; decor and furnishings are pretty but not luxurious; pool is on the small side. [$] *Rooms from: $190* ✉ *4307 S.E. Bayview St., Port Salerno* ☎ *772/287–2500* 🌐 *www.piratescoveresort.com* 🛏 *50 rooms* 🍴 *No Meals.*

## Shopping

More than 60 restaurants and shops with antiques, art, and fashion draw visitors downtown along Osceola Street.

**B&A Flea Market**

**MARKET** | A short drive from downtown and operating for more than two decades, the oldest and largest weekend-only flea market on the Treasure Coast has a street-bazaar feel, with shoppers happily scouting the 500 vendors for the practical and unusual. A produce market carries local tropical fruits and vegetables. If you have an open mind and love to shop garage sales, you'll do just fine here. ✉ *2885 S.E. U.S. 1, Stuart* ☎ *772/288–4915* 🌐 *www.bafleamarket.com.*

## Activities

★ ***Island Princess* Cruises**

**ENTERTAINMENT CRUISE** | Cruise the Indian River and St. Lucie River as well as Jupiter Sound aboard the *Island Princess,* an 82-footer that docks at the Sailfish Marina in Stuart. In season, there are nature cruises and cruises that go through the St. Lucie River locks. Have lunch during their Jupiter Island cruise, embarking Tuesday and weekends year-round. The schedule, which changes often, is posted on the company's website. All ages are welcome, and advance reservations are required. ✉ *Sailfish Marina, 3585 S.E. St. Lucie Blvd., Stuart* ☎ *772/225–2100* 🌐 *www.islandprincesscruises.com* 🎟 *Cruises from $40.*

**Sailfish Marina of Stuart**

**FISHING** | Nab a deep-sea charter here to land a sailfish, a popular sport fish that is prolific off the St. Lucie Inlet. This is the closest public marina to the St. Lucie Inlet. Recently expanded, it is home to *Island Princess* Cruises, which takes visitors to Vero Beach or Jupiter via the Intracoastal Waterway. ✉ *3565 S.E. St. Lucie Blvd., Stuart* ☎ *772/283–1122* 🌐 *www.sailfishmarinastuart.com.*

# Fort Pierce and Port St. Lucie

*11 miles north of Jensen Beach.*

About an hour north of Palm Beach, Fort Pierce has a distinctive rural feel—but it has a surprising number of worthwhile attractions for a town of its size, including those easily seen while following Route 707 on the mainland (A1A on Hutchinson Island). The downtown is expanding and sports new theater revivals, restaurants, and shops. A big draw is an inlet that offers fabulous fishing and excellent surfing. Nearby Port St. Lucie is largely landlocked southwest of Fort Pierce and is almost equidistant from there and Jensen Beach. It's not a big tourist area except for two sports facilities near Interstate 95: the St. Lucie Mets' training grounds, Tradition Field, and PGA Village. If you want a hotel directly on the sand or crave more than simple, motel-like accommodations, stay elsewhere and drive up for the day.

### GETTING HERE AND AROUND

You can reach Fort Pierce from Jensen Beach by driving 11 miles north on Federal Highway (U.S. 1), Route 707, or Route A1A. To get to Port St. Lucie, continue north on U.S. 1 and take Prima Vista Boulevard west. From Fort Pierce, Route 709 goes diagonally southwest to Port St. Lucie, and Interstate 95 is another choice.

##  Sights

### National Navy UDT-SEAL Museum

**OTHER MUSEUM | FAMILY |** Commemorating the more than 3,000 troops who trained on these shores during World War II, when this elite military unit got its start, there are weapons, vehicles, and equipment on view. Exhibits honor all frogmen and underwater demolition teams and depict their history. The museum houses the lifeboat from which SEALs saved the *Maersk Alabama* captain from Somali pirates in 2009. Kids get a thrill out of the helicopters and aircraft on the grounds. ⊠ *3300 N. Rte. A1A, Fort Pierce* ☎ *772/595–5845* ⊕ *www.navysealmuseum.com* ⊠ *$15* ⊙ *Closed Mon.*

### Savannas Recreation Area

**NATURE PRESERVE | FAMILY |** Once a reservoir, the 550 acres have been returned to their natural wetlands state. Today the wilderness area has campgrounds, interpretive trails, and a boat ramp, and the recreation area is open year-round. Canoe and kayak rentals are available

Thursday through Monday. A dog park (open daily) is also on site. Amenities include showers, toilets, and free Wi-Fi for campers. ⊠ *1400 E. Midway Rd., Fort Pierce* ☎ *772/464–7855* ⊕ *www.stlucie-co.gov/parks/savannas.htm* ⊠ *Free; $26 for campers (full service).*

##  Beaches

### Fort Pierce Inlet State Park

**BEACH |** Across the inlet at the northern side of Hutchinson Island, a fishing oasis lures beachgoers who can't wait to reel in snook, flounder, and bluefish, among others. The park is also known as a prime wave-riding locale, thanks to a reef that lies just outside the jetty. Summer is the busiest season by a long shot, but don't be fooled: it's a laid-back place to sun and surf. There are covered picnic tables but no concessions; however, from where anglers perch, a bunch of casual restaurants can be spotted on the other side of the inlet that are a quick drive away. Note that the area of Jack Island Preserve has been closed indefinitely. **Amenities:** lifeguards (summer only); parking (fee); showers; toilets. **Best for:** solitude; surfing; walking. ⊠ *905 Shorewinds Dr., Fort Pierce* ☎ *772/468–3985* ⊕ *www.floridastateparks.org* ⊠ *Vehicle $6, bicyclists and pedestrians $2.*

##  Activities

The region's premier dive site is on the National Register of Historic Places. The *Urca de Lima* was part of the storied treasure fleet bound for Spain that was destroyed by a hurricane in 1715. It's now part of an underwater archaeological preserve about 200 yards from shore, just north of the National Navy UDT-SEAL Museum and under 10 to 15 feet of water. The remains contain a flat-bottom, round-bellied ship and cannons that can be visited on an organized dive trip.

## Clover Park

**BASEBALL & SOFTBALL** | Out west by Interstate 95, this Port St. Lucie baseball stadium, formerly known as Tradition Field, is where the New York Mets train; it's also the home of the St. Lucie Mets minor-league team. ⊠ *525 N.W. Peacock Blvd., Port St. Lucie* ☎ *772/871–2115* ⊕ *www.milb.com/st-lucie.*

## Dive Odyssea

**SCUBA DIVING** | This full-service dive shop offers kayak rentals, tank rentals, and scuba lessons. The shop can arrange a scuba charter in Jupiter or Palm Beach (two-tank dive trips typically start at $65), but Dive Odyssea no longer offers dive trips of its own. ⊠ *Fort Pierce Inlet, 621 N. 2nd St., Fort Pierce* ☎ *772/460–1771* ⊕ *www.diveodyssea.com.*

## PGA Village

**GOLF** | Owned and operated by the PGA of America, the national association of teaching pros, PGA Village is the winter home to many Northern instructors, along with permanent staff. The facility is a little off the beaten path and the clubhouse is basic, but serious golfers will appreciate the three championship courses by Pete Dye and Tom Fazio and the chance to sharpen their skills at the 35-acre PGA Center for Golf Learning and Performance, which has nine practice bunkers mimicking sands and slopes from around the globe. Between the Fazio-designed Wanamaker Course, the Ryder Course, and the Dye-designed Dye Course, there are 54 holes of championship golf at PGA Village. Also affiliated is the nearby St. Lucie Trail Golf Club, another Fazio design. Beginners can start out on the lesser known (and easier) 6-hole PGA Short Course. Holes are 35 to 60 yards each, and course play is free. ⊠ *1916 Perfect Dr., Port St. Lucie* ☎ *772/467–1300, 800/800–4653* ⊕ *www.pgavillage.com* 🖃 *Wanamaker Course $131; Ryder Course $131; Dye Course $131; St. Lucie Trail Golf Club $89* 🏌 *Wanamaker Course: 18 holes, 7123 yards, par 72; Ryder Course: 18 holes, 7037 yards, par 72; Dye Course: 18 holes, 7279 yards, par 72; St. Lucie Golf Club Trail Course: 18 holes, 6901 yards, par 72.*

# Vero Beach

*12 miles north of Fort Pierce.*

Tranquil and picturesque, this upscale Indian River County town has a strong commitment to the environment and culture, and it's also home to eclectic galleries and trendy restaurants. Downtown Vero is centered on the historic district on 14th Avenue, but much of the fun takes place across the Indian River (aka the Intracoastal Waterway) around Orchid Island's beaches. It was once home to the Dodgers Spring Training base, and there's still a strong affinity for baseball here. It's a kid-friendly place, with the former Dodgertown Stadium hosting Little League tournaments and plenty of parks around. Its western edges are still home to cattlemen and citrus growers.

### GETTING HERE AND AROUND

To get here, you have two basic options: Route A1A along the coast (not to be confused with Ocean Drive, an offshoot on Orchid Island) or either U.S. 1 or Route 605 (also called Old Dixie Highway) on the mainland. As you approach Vero on the latter, you pass through an ungussied-up landscape of small farms and residential areas. On the beach route, part of the drive bisects an unusually undeveloped section of the Florida coast. If flying in, consider Orlando International Airport, which is larger and a smidge closer than Palm Beach International Airport.

 **Sights**

### Environmental Learning Center

**NATURE SIGHT** | Off Wabasso Beach Road, the 64 acres here are almost completely surrounded by water. In addition to a 600-foot boardwalk through the mangrove shoreline and a 1-mile canoe trail, there are aquariums filled with Indian River creatures. Boat and kayak trips to see the historic Pelican Island rookery are on offer along with guided nature walks and touch-tank encounters. Call or check the center's website for times. ⊠ *255 Live Oak Dr., Vero Beach* ☎ *772/589–5050* ⊕ *www.discoverelc.org* ⊠ *$5* ⊗ *Closed Mon.*

### ★ McKee Botanical Garden

**GARDEN** | On the National Register of Historic Places, the 18-acre plot is a tropical jungle garden—one of the most lush and serene around. This is *the* place to see spectacular water lilies, and the property's original 1932 Hall of Giants, a rustic wooden structure that has stained-glass and bronze bells, contains what is claimed to be the world's largest single-plank mahogany table at 35 feet long. There's a bamboo pavilion, a gift shop, and a café (open for lunch Tuesday through Saturday and Sunday in season), which serves especially tasty snacks and sandwiches. ⊠ *350 U.S. 1, Vero Beach* ☎ *772/794–0601* ⊕ *www.mckeegarden. org* ⊠ *$15* ⊗ *Closed Mon.*

### Pelican Island National Wildlife Refuge

**WILDLIFE REFUGE** | Founded in 1903 by then-president Theodore Roosevelt as the country's first national wildlife refuge, the park encompasses the historic Pelican Island rookery itself—a small island in the Indian River lagoon and important nesting place for 16 species of birds such as endangered wood storks and, of course, brown pelicans—and the land surrounding it overlooking Sebastian. The rookery is a closed wilderness area, so there's no roaming alongside animal kingdom friends; however, there is an 18-foot observation tower across from it with direct views and more than 6 miles of nature trails in the refuge. Another way to explore is via guided kayak tours from the Florida Outdoor Center. Make

sure to bring a camera—it's a photographer's dream. ⊠ *Rte. A1A, Vero Beach* ✤ *1 mile north of Treasure Shores Park. Take A1A and turn on Historic Jungle Trail* ☎ *772/581–5557* ⊕ *www.fws.gov/pelicanisland* ⊠ *Free.*

## 🌊 Beaches

Most of the beaches in the Vero Beach area are clustered around South Beach Park or line Ocean Drive around Beachland Boulevard just north of Humiston Park. Humiston Park is smack-dab in the main commercial zone, with restaurants galore, including the lauded Citrus Grillhouse at its southern tip.

### Humiston Park

**BEACH** | Just south of the Driftwood Resort on Ocean Drive sits Humiston Park, one of the best beaches in town. Parking is free and plentiful, as there's a large lot on Easter Lily Lane and spots all over the surrounding business district. The shore is somewhat narrow, and there isn't much shade, but the vibrant scene and other amenities make it a great choice for people who crave lots of activity. With lifeguards on duty daily, there's a children's playground, plus a ton of hotels, restaurants, bars, and shops within walking distance. **Amenities:** food and drink; lifeguards; showers; toilets. **Best for:** partiers; sunsets; swimming; walking. ⊠ *3000 Ocean Dr., at Easter Lily La., Vero Beach* ☎ *772/231–5790.*

### ★ Sebastian Inlet State Park

**BEACH** | **FAMILY** | The 1,000-acre park, which runs from the tip of Orchid Island across the passage to the barrier island just north, is one of the Florida park system's biggest draws, especially because of the inlet's highly productive fishing waters. Views from either side of the tall bridge are spectacular, and a unique hallmark is that the gates never close— an amazing feature for die-hard anglers who know snook bite better at night. Two jetties are usually packed with fishers

## Did You Know?

McKee Botanical Garden's 18 acres are home to more than 10,000 native tropical plants and one of Florida's best collections of water lilies.

and spectators alike. The park has two entrances, the entrance in Vero Beach and the main entrance in Melbourne (✉ 9700 Rte. A1A).

Within the park's grounds, you'll discover a wonderful two-story restaurant that overlooks the ocean, a fish and surfing shop, two museums, guided sea turtle walks in season, 51 campsites with water and electricity, and a marina with powerboat, kayak, and canoe rentals. **Amenities:** food and drink; parking (fee); showers; toilets; water sports. **Best for:** sunrise; sunset; surfing; walking. ✉ 14251 N. Rte. A1A, Vero Beach ☎ 321/984–4852 ⊕ www.floridastateparks.org ⌲ $8.

### Wabasso Beach Park
**BEACH | FAMILY |** A favorite for local surfboarding teens and the families at the nearby Disney's Vero Beach Resort, the park is nestled in a residential area at the end of Wabasso Road, about 8 miles up from the action on Ocean Drive and 8 miles below the Sebastian Inlet. Aside from regular amenities like picnic tables, restrooms, and a dedicated parking lot (which really is the "park" here—there's not much green space—and it's quite small, so arrive early), the Disney crowd walks there for its lifeguards (the strip directly in front of the hotel is unguarded), and the local crowd appreciates its conveniences, like a pizzeria and a store that sells sundries, snacks, and beach supplies. **Amenities:** food and drink; lifeguards; parking (no fee); showers; toilets. **Best for:** surfing; swimming. ✉ 1820 Wabasso Rd., Vero Beach.

## 🍴 Restaurants

### The Lemon Tree
**$ | AMERICAN | FAMILY |** If Italy had old-school luncheonettes, this is what they'd look like: a storefront of yellow walls, dark-green booths, white linoleum tables, and cascading sconces of faux ivy leaves and hand-painted Tuscan serving pieces for artwork. It's self-described by the husband-and-wife owners (who are always at the front) as an "upscale diner," and locals swear by it for breakfast (served all day) and lunch. **Known for:** shrimp scampi; treats on the house; waits during the high season. $ Average main: $11 ✉ 3125 Ocean Dr., Vero Beach ☎ 772/231–0858 ⊘ No dinner.

### Ocean Grill
**$$ | SEAFOOD |** Opened in 1941, this family-owned Old Florida–style restaurant combines its ocean view with Tiffany-style lamps, wrought-iron chandeliers, and paintings of pirates. Count on at least three kinds of seafood any day on the menu, along with steaks, pork chops, soups, and salads. **Known for:** just OK food; great drinks; the Pusser's Painkiller. $ Average main: $28 ✉ 1050 Beachland Blvd., Vero Beach ☎ 772/231–5409 ⊕ www.ocean-grill.com ⊘ Closed 2 wks around Labor Day. No lunch Sun.

### ★ The Tides
**$$$ | ECLECTIC |** A charming cottage restaurant west of Ocean Drive prepares some of the best food around—not just in Vero Beach, but all of South Florida. The chefs, classically trained, give a nod to international fare with disparate dishes such as tuna *tataki*, Asian-inspired carpaccio with satay, penne *quattro formaggi*, and classic lobster bisque. **Known for:** fresh Florida fish; jumbo crab cakes with corn-and-pepper sauce; chef's table with wine pairings. $ Average main: $32 ✉ 3103 Cardinal Dr., Vero Beach ☎ 772/234–3966 ⊕ www.tidesofvero.com ⊘ No lunch.

## 🛏 Hotels

### ★ Costa d'Este Beach Resort
**$ | RESORT |** This stylish, contemporary boutique hotel in the heart of Vero's bustling Ocean Drive area has a gorgeous infinity pool overlooking the ocean and a distinctly Miami Beach vibe—just like its famous owners, singer Gloria Estefan and producer Emilio Estefan. **Pros:** all

rooms have balconies or secluded patios; huge Italian marble showers; complimentary signature mojitos on arrival. **Cons:** spa is on the small side; rooms have only blackout shades; daily resort fee. [$] *Rooms from: $189* ✉ *3244 Ocean Dr., Vero Beach* ☎ *772/562–9919* 🌐 *www.costadeste.com* 🛏 *94 rooms* 🍴 *No Meals.*

**The Driftwood Resort**

**$ | RESORT | FAMILY** | On the National Register of Historic Places, the two original buildings of this 1935 inn were built entirely from ocean-washed timbers with no blueprints; over time more buildings were added, and all are now decorated with such artifacts as ship's bells, Spanish tiles, a cannon from a 16th-century Spanish galleon, and plenty of wrought iron, which create a quirky, utterly charming landscape. **Pros:** central location right on the beach; laundry facilities; weekly treasure hunt is a blast. **Cons:** older property; rooms can be musty; no-frills furnishings. [$] *Rooms from: $150* ✉ *3150 Ocean Dr., Vero Beach* ☎ *772/231–0550* 🌐 *www.verobeachdriftwood.com* 🛏 *100 rooms* 🍴 *No Meals.*

★ **Kimpton Vero Beach Hotel & Spa**

**$$$ | RESORT | FAMILY** | With a sophisticated, relaxed West Indies feel, this luxurious five-story beachfront hotel at the north end of Ocean Drive is an inviting getaway and, arguably, the best on the Treasure Coast. **Pros:** beautiful pool; complimentary daily wine hour with hors d'oeuvres; pet-friendly. **Cons:** can get pricey; some rooms overlook parking lot; resort fee. [$] *Rooms from: $399* ✉ *3500 Ocean Dr., Vero Beach* ☎ *772/231–5666* 🌐 *www.verobeachhotelandspa.com* 🛏 *102 rooms* 🍴 *No Meals.*

## Shopping

Crossing over to Orchid Island from the mainland, the Merrill P. Barber Bridge turns into Beachland Boulevard; its intersection with **Ocean Drive** is the heart of a commercial zone with a lively mix of shops, restaurants, and art galleries.

Just under 3 miles north of that roughly eight-block stretch on A1A is a charming outdoor plaza, the **Village Shops.** It's a delight to stroll between the brightly painted cottages that have more unique, high-end offerings.

Back on the mainland, take 21st Street westward and you'll come across a small, modern shopping plaza with some independent shops and national chains. Keep going west on 21st Street, and then park around 14th Avenue to explore a collection of art galleries and eateries in the historic downtown.

## Activities

**Sandridge Golf Club**

**GOLF** | The Sandridge Golf Club features two public 18-hole courses designed by Ron Garl: the Dunes course, with 6 holes located on a sand ridge, and the Lakes course, named for—you guessed it—the ubiquitous lakes around the course. The Dunes course, opened in 1987, follows a history-steeped pathway once used during mining operations. The Lakes course, opened in 1992, is renowned for the very challenging, par-4 14th hole with an island green. There's a pro shop on site offering lessons and clinics. ✉ *5300 73rd St., Vero Beach* ☎ *772/770–5000* 🌐 *www.sandridgegc.com* 🎟 *$50 for 18 holes with cart* ⛳ *Dunes Course: 18 holes, 6817 yards, par 72; Lakes Course: 18 holes, 6181 yards, par 72.*

# Index

# Photo Credits

**Front Cover:** Lumiere / eStock Photo [Description: Florida, Palm Beach, Worth Avenue, Clock Tower, beach, palm tree]. **Back cover, from left to right:** Irina Wilhauk/Shutterstock. Sean Pavone/Shutterstock. Seastock/iStock-673784050. **Spine:** Michael Phillips/iStockphoto. **Interior, from left to right:** JHPhtography/Shutterstock (1). Romrodphoto/Shutterstock (2-3). FloridaStock/Shutterstock (5). **Chapter 1: Experience South Florida:** Fotomak/shutterstock (6-7). Sean Pavone/Shutterstock (8-9). Courtesy of Art Deco Tours (9). Vito Palmisano/iStockphoto (9). William Rodrigues Dos Santos/Dreamstime (10). Pola Damonte/Shutterstock (10). Juneisy Q. Hawkins/Shutterstock (11). Courtesy Miami Design District (12). Michael Marko/Ball & Chain (12). Romrodphoto/Shutterstock (12). Courtesy of Hemingway Home (12). Courtesy of Miami Dolphins (13). Sean Pavone/Shutterstock (13). Eric Laignel/1 Hotel South Beach (14). Galina Savina/Shutterstock (14). David Sutta/Fairchild Tropical Botanic Garden (15). Comeirrez/Shutterstock (18). Hunt Consulting/Shutterstock (18). Olyina/Shutterstock (18). Voloshin311/Shutterstock (18). Andrew Meade (19). Neosiam/Dreamstime (19). Bonchan/Shutterstock (19). Norikko/Shutterstock (19). Alexander Demyanenko/Shutterstock (20). Kamira/Shutterstock (20). Luke Popwell/Dreamstime (20). Simon Dannhauer/Shutterstock (21). Dmitry Vinogradov/Dreamstime (21). Scott Rudd/Courtesy of Art Basel (22). Wangkun Jia/Shutterstock (22). Richard Goldberg/Shutterstock (22). Zachary Balber/Courtesy of The Bass, Miami Beach (22). Courtesy of Oriol Tarridas Photography (23). Comayagua99/WikimediaCommons (23). Felix Mizioznikov/Dreamstime (23). Daniel Bock/Courtesy of Museum of Contemporary Art North Miami (MOCA) (23). **Chapter 3: Miami and Miami Beach:** Coraline M/Shutterstock (41). Roxana Gonzalez/ Shutterstock (44). Jupiter Images/Brand X/Alamy (45). Alena Haurylik/Shutterstock (45). Ltishankov/Dreamstime (55). Nicholas Pitt/Alamy (57). DK/Alamy (57). Nicholas Pitt/Alamy (58). Phillip Pessar/Flicker (58). Ian Patrick/Alamy (58). Laura Paresky (58). Sdf_qwe/Shutterstock (58). Pressebildagentur/Alamy (60). Ian Patrick/Alamy (60). culliganphoto/Alamy (60). John Tunney/Dreamstime (68). Garth Aikens/Miami Beach Convention Center (93). SpVVK/Vlad Kryhin/iStockphoto (107). **Chapter 4: The Everglades:** Jo Crebbin/Shutterstock (117). tbkmedia.de/Alamy (122-123). inga spence/Alamy (126). FloridaStock/Shutterstock (126). Louise Wolff/wikimedia (126). Andrewtappert/wikimedia (126). David R. Frazier Photolibrary, Inc./Alamy (126). Larsek/Shutterstock (127). umar faruq/Shutterstock (127). Caleb Foster/Shutterstock (127). mlorenz/Shutterstock (127). Peter Arnold, Inc./Alamy (127). John A. Anderson/Shutterstock (128). FloridaStock/Shutterstock (128). Norman Bateman/Shutterstock (128). FloridaStock/Shutterstock (128). Speyside snaps/Shutterstock (129). Jerry Zitterman/Shutterstock (129). Krzysztof Slusarczyk/Shutterstock (129). Norman Bateman/Shutterstock (129). Steven Widoff/Alamy (135). Jimfeng/iStockphoto (139). Marc Muench/Alamy (143). Visit Florida/YoungGator (153). **Chapter 5: The Florida Keys:** Ventdusud/Shutterstock (155). Gregory Wrona/Alamy (158). Fotoluminate LLC/shutterstock (159). Michael Ventura/Alamy (159). Stephen Frink/Florida Keys News Bureau (166). Korzeniewski/Dreamstime (178). PBorowka/Shutterstock (180). Melissa Schalke/iStockphoto (184). Marilyn Scavo/iStockphoto (190). CedarBendDrive/Flickr (202). Starwood Hotels & Resorts (211). Daniel Korzeniewski/Shutterstock (213). Varina C/Shutterstock (221). **Chapter 6: Fort Lauderdale and Broward County:** Sepavo/Dreamstime (223). Eric Gevaert/Shutterstock (237). Lago Mar Resort & Club - Fort Lauderdale (240). Serenethos/Dreamstime (242). **Chapter 7: Palm Beach and the Treasure Coast:** Sean Pavone/shutterstock (257). Sargent Photography/South Florida (264). The Colony at Palm Beach (272). FloridaStock/Shutterstock (282). Bowiet44/WikimiediaCommons (288). Lisa DeGroot/Visit Florida (295). Berniephil/Dreamstime (308). **About Our Writers:** All photos are courtesy of the writers except for the following: Sara Liss, courtesy of Michael Pisarri.

*Every effort has been made to trace the copyright holders, and we apologize in advance for any accidental errors. We would be happy to apply the corrections in the following edition of this publication.*

# Fodor's SOUTH FLORIDA

**Publisher:** Stephen Horowitz, *General Manager*

**Editorial:** Douglas Stallings, *Editorial Director;* Jill Fergus, Amanda Sadlowski, *Senior Editors;* Brian Eschrich, Alexis Kelly, *Editors;* Angelique Kennedy-Chavannes, *Assistant Editor*

**Design:** Tina Malaney, *Director of Design and Production;* Jessica Gonzalez, *Senior Designer;* Erin Caceres, *Graphic Design Associate*

**Production:** Jennifer DePrima, *Editorial Production Manager;* Elyse Rozelle, *Senior Production Editor;* Monica White, *Production Editor*

**Maps:** Rebecca Baer, *Senior Map Editor;* David Lindroth, Mark Stroud (Moon Street Cartography), *Cartographers*

**Photography:** Viviane Teles, *Senior Photo Editor;* Namrata Aggarwal, Neha Gupta, Payal Gupta, Ashok Kumar, *Photo Editors;* Eddie Aldrete, *Photo Production Intern;* Kadeem McPherson, *Photo Production Associate Intern*

**Business and Operations:** Chuck Hoover, *Chief Marketing Officer;* Robert Ames, *Group General Manager*

**Public Relations and Marketing:** Joe Ewaskiw, *Senior Director of Communications and Public Relations*

**Fodors.com:** Jeremy Tarr, *Editorial Director;* Rachael Levitt, *Managing Editor*

**Technology:** Jon Atkinson, *Director of Technology;* Rudresh Teotia, *Associate Director of Technology;* Alison Lieu, *Project Manager*

**Writers:** Amber Love Bond, Sara Liss

**Editors:** Kayla Becker, Jacinta O'Halloran

**Production Editor:** Elyse Rozelle

17th Edition

ISBN 978-1-64097-579-8

ISSN 1526-2219

**SPECIAL SALES**
This book is available at special discounts for bulk purchases for sales promotions or premiums. For more information, e-mail SpecialMarkets@fodors.com.

PRINTED IN CANADA

10 9 8 7 6 5 4 3 2 1

# About Our Writers

**Amber Love Bond** is a Miami-based freelance food and travel writer. In addition to updating the Fort Lauderdale, Everglades, and Miami and Miami Beach chapters for Fodor's, Amber also contributes to *American Way*, *Eater*, and more. She also has a position on the Board of Directors for the United States Bartenders' Guild's Miami Chapter. You can find her at the opening of every restaurant, sipping cocktails at Miami's coolest bars, or hanging on the beach with her laptop in tow.

**Sara Liss** has been a freelancer for lifestyle publications for more than ten years. She served as founding editor of UrbanDaddy Miami is now the Senior Food Writer at Miami.com. Her main beat is food but she dabbles in travel and design writing and has started Saffron Supper Club, a roving Middle-Eastern culinary experience and Friday Beach, a neighborhood celebration that happens in her town of Surfside. Her current outlets include Modern Luxury publications, *Condé Nast Traveler*, the *Miami Herald* and *WHERE* magazine. She is the author of *Miami Cooks: Recipes from the City's Favorite Restaurants*. She updated the Florida Keys and Palm Beach and Treasure Coast chapters this edition.